The BJP and the Com[...]
Politics in Ind[...]

University of Plymouth Library

Subject to status this item may be renewed
via your Voyager account

http://voyager.plymouth.ac.uk

Exeter tel: (01392) 475049
Exmouth tel: (01395) 255331
Plymouth tel: (01752) 232323

The BJP

and the

Compulsions of Politics
in India

Second Edition

edited by

Thomas Blom Hansen
Christophe Jaffrelot

OXFORD

UNIVERSITY PRESS

OXFORD
UNIVERSITY PRESS

YMCA Library Building, Jai Singh Road, New Delhi 110 001

Oxford University Press is a department of the University of Oxford. It furthers the
University's objective of excellence in research, scholarship, and education .
by publishing worldwide in

Oxford   New York

Athens   Auckland   Bangkok   Bogota   Buenos Aires   Cape Town
Chennai   Dar es Salaam   Delhi   Florence   Hong Kong   Istanbul   Karachi
Kolkata   Kuala Lumpur   Madrid   Melbourne   Mexico City   Mumbai
Nairobi   Paris   São Paolo   Shanghai   Singapore   Taipei   Tokyo   Toronto   Warsaw

with associated companies in   Berlin   Ibadan

Oxford is a registered trade mark of Oxford University Press
in the UK and in certain other countries

Published in India
By Oxford University Press, New Delhi

First published 1998
Oxford India Paperbacks 1999
Second Edition 2001

ISBN 019 565 6148

Typeset by Excellent Laser Typesetters, Pitampura, Delhi
Printed in India at Pauls Press, New Delhi 110 020
Published by Manzar Khan, Oxford University Press
YMCA Library Building, Jai Singh Road, New Delhi 110 001

Contents

III DIVIDED THEY STAND

Contributors

JAMES CHIRIYANKANDATH is Lecturer in Third World politics and international relations at London Guildhall University since 1993. He has published widely on Indian politics and commented on South Asian affairs for British newspapers and BBC World Service radio and television.

THOMAS BLOM HANSEN is Associate Professor, International Development Studies, Roskilde University, Denmark. He has written numerous articles in Indian and Scandinavian journals. He has recently published *The Saffron Wave*.

CHRISTOPHE JAFFRELOT is Deputy Director of the Centre d'Etudes et de Recherches Internationales (CERI) in Paris. Chief editor of *Critique Internationale*, he has recently published *The Hindu Nationalist Movement and Indian Politics, 1925 to 1990s* (Viking, 1999).

ROB JENKINS is Lecturer in Politics at Birkbeck College, University of London. He is the author of the forthcoming, *Democracy and the Politics of Economic Reform in India*.

JAMES MANOR is a Professorial Fellow of the Institute of Development Studies, University of Sussex. His most recent books include (as co-author with Richard Crook) *Democracy and Decentralization in South Asia and West Africa. Participation, Accountability and Performance* (Cambridge, 1999) and (as editor), *Nehru to the Nineties: The Changing Office of Prime Minister in India* (Viking, 1995).

GHANSHYAM SHAH is Professor in Social Sciences at Centre of Social Medicine & Community Health, Jawaharlal Nehru University, Delhi. He is the author of several books including *Caste Association and Political Process in Gujarat, Protest Movements in Two Indian States, Social Movements,* and *Public Health and Urban Development*.

GURHARPAL SINGH teaches at Hull University. He has published *Communism in Punjab*, *Punjabi Identity* (ed. with Ian Talbot), and until 1997, was the editor of the *International Journal of Punjab Studies*.

JASMINE ZÉRININI-BROTEL is a Ph.D student from Paris Panthéon-Sorbonne University specializing in UP politics. She spent two years researching the topic under the auspices of the French Centre for Human Sciences, New Delhi.

Introduction:
The Rise to Power of the BJP

THOMAS BLOM HANSEN
CHRISTOPHE JAFFRELOT

The Eleventh General Election in India (1996) catapulted the BJP to a position of the largest political party in India. The election performance was not linked directly to militant propagation of *Hindutva* as in the case of the 1991 elections. The Jana Sangh, and later the Bharatiya Janata Party have always oscillated between a militant and a moderate approach to politics.[1] So far, the Hindu nationalist parties could make progress only on the basis of a militant strategy or of a nation-wide seat adjustments. For the first time in 1996, the BJP increased its share of representatives in the Lok Sabha through a rather moderate campaign and limited alliances with regional parties.

In the 1990s, the BJP gradually shifted from the ethno-religious mobilization of the Ramjanmabhoomi movement towards a softer policy. This change occured partly because the party leaders feared that the Vishva Hindu Parishad would overshadow their organization and that they would lose control of the Hindu nationalist political agenda to these more extremist forces, and partly as a reaction to the BJP's defeat in several states of the Hindi belt in the 1993 state elections. BJP's continued ambivalence between the militant strategy and the moderate one reflected a deeper tension between ideological purity and pragmatism in the Hindu nationalist movement.

---

[1] This is one of the key arguments in Jaffrelot, C., *The Hindu Nationalist Movement and Indian Politics* (New Delhi: Penguin India, 1996).

THE 1996 ELECTIONS AND NEW POLITICAL COMPULSIONS

When releasing the party's election manifesto to the press prior to the 1996 election campaign, Advani devoted a lot of time to the Hindutva issues and Ayodhya. But Vajpayee became the party's main campaigner, partly by default since Advani had given up the idea of contesting elections because of his alleged implication in the infamous Hawala case. In any case, the party as well as the RSS were willing to project its most acceptable and liberal face to fit in its moderate strategy.

Besides the rejection of a militant line and the selection of a 'moderate leader', the third, related element of the moderate electoral strategy consisted in the making of new alliances. In addition to its traditional seat adjustment with the Shiv Sena, the BJP entered into new alliances with parties which had no ideological affinities with Hindu nationalism, the Samta Party in Bihar and the Haryana Vikas Party of Bansi Lal in Haryana.

Through protracted efforts to 'normalize' itself the party had ostensibly moved closer than ever before to the desired position where it could replace the Congress as a nation-wide political structure. However, when in May 1996 Atal Bihari Vajpayee was given two weeks to construct a parliamentary majority for a BJP-government, it soon became amply clear that the BJP had won elections but certainly not the political power. The tactical unity of centrist and left-of-centre forces which the surge of Hindutva had made imperative in the 1990s presented the more immediate obstacle for a dominant BJP-led political formation at the centre. But more importantly, the overall logic of electoral politics in India had over the last decade been transformed in such a way that the *locus classicus* of political power in India—the one-party dominance at the centre which remains the tantalizing object of BJP's strategies—seemed to have become a thing of the past.

The segmentation and protracted collapse of the edifice of the once mighty Congress party since the mid-1980s have in many ways been interwoven with a broader diversification of political actors and political stances in the states, along with proliferation of distinct regional political dynamics which have circumscribed the potential space and authority of dominant political parties at the national level. Clearly, the terms of political dominance have changed both at the level of the individual states and at the national level, away from centralized power-broking and cooptation, and towards a more complex mechanism of negotiation, alliance and coalition-building. In this emerging environment of coalition politics, the Sangh Parivar's traditions of ideological homogeneity and purity, of discipline and centralized devising of strategies, and of commitment to the building of a strong, incorporative national culture, polity and state, may well prove to be a liability rather than an asset for the BJP.

Seen in retrospect, the Indian political scene has in the last decade and a half, or more, been structured by three overall transformations. The first transformation is the emergence of still more distinct regional polities in each state, with distinct political cultures, distinct political vernaculars and distinct configurations of caste-mobilization and alliances. Regionalization of Indian politics seems to be a long-term tendency inextricably linked to the differential regional histories and local dynamics of Congress in various states, and reinforced by the emergence of distinct vernacular public spheres since the linguistic reorganization of states in the 1950s. Indira Gandhi's centralization of the Congress party was an attempt to curtail and stem this process, but it had the reverse effect as it actually stimulated regional sentiments. Outside the Hindi belt, the entrance of a large number of representatives of lower-caste groups and minorities within the Congress, striving to construct and consolidate these groups as stable constituencies for the party, did in several ways prepare the ground for the subsequent articulations of a more autonomous lower-caste/OBC-politics in the 1980s.

Indeed the second transformation has been the emergence of Other Backward Classes (OBCs) and the Scheduled Castes as more distinct and self-conscious political constituencies. The subversion of upper-caste political dominance and assertion of non-Brahmin and popular identities in the political field has a long history in south India and Maharashtra, where it provided central underpinnings for the assertion of regional identities. The ascendancy of large peasant communities to political prominence in north India from the 1970s onwards was intimately connected with transformations in the structure of agrarian production and rural power in the wake of the green revolution.

The so-called 'Mandalization' of the political scene in north India after V. P. Singh's decision to implement the recommendations of the Mandal Commission in 1990 was undoubtedly a supraregional phenomenon—but it was built upon patterns of caste mobilization with distinct characteristics from state to state. The configurations of caste mobilization and consolidation of caste constituencies in Bihar, for instance differs in substantial ways from neighbouring Uttar Pradesh. These increasing efforts aiming at mobilizing the OBC-groups and Scheduled Castes as self-conscious groups with corporate interests, a shared discourse and a permanent structure of political representation has also produced new political vernaculars and new symbolic strategies on part of the leaders appealing to lower-caste groups.

These articulations of self-consciously 'plebeian' political identities and the concomitant crisis of the conventional modality of paternalistic and clientelistic mobilization of the masses by élite groups may plausibly be seen as signs of a certain democratization of Indian democracy. This is a broad and complex process driven by the uneven dissemination, through democratic politics and competitive mass mobilization, of notions of equality between social and cultural groups in terms of certain entitlements to be claimed from the state: education, social mobility, government jobs, official recognition of certain community practices, etc. It is obvious, however, that it is the élite among the OBC-groups, the so-called 'creamy layer', who have so far been the prime beneficiaries in terms of actually getting education, positions and recognition. But it is doubtful whether these groups over time can retain their monopoly on expressing and representing the drive for social mobility and recognition which this process gives rise to.

Historically, the first victim of this confluence of lower-caste mobilization and regional assertion has been the dominance of Congress at the state level. This was true of Tamil Nadu in the 1960s, Andhra Pradesh and Karnataka in the 1980s, and of the most of north India from the late 1980s onwards. The interesting feature of especially northern and western India is that the protracted demise of the Congress here has been executed interchangeably by the Janata Party, Samajwadi Party and other parties appealing to the upwardly mobile OBCs and peasant communities, and by the BJP campaigning explicitly on a nationalist and communal platform.

This points to the third major transformation in Indian politics, namely the growing constituency for Hindu nationalist politics among upper-caste Hindus, urban middle classes and upwardly mobile groups in northern and western India. Initially, the spectacular growth of the BJP in the political field since 1989 could be accounted for as transient protests against the corruption and intransigence of the established parties, as an expression of protest and defiance vis-à-vis 'Mandalization' and 'plebeianization' of political life, as well as an emotional wave energized by the Sangh Parivar's systematic reactivation of anti-Muslim stereotypes and memories of communal clashes and violence.

However, as the BJP has become more consolidated in the political field as a large and stable political formation, it has also become increasingly clear that its trajectory, its electoral strategies and its future prospects are crucially dependent on its manoeuvring skills and popular appeals under the two-fold constraints mentioned above: regionalization and the rise of lower-caste mobilization.

The Sangh Parivar and the BJP have for years resolved to restructure the political culture of Indian state, to introduce higher moral standards for the conduct of elected representatives, to reduce corruption and to strengthen the authority and quality of governance. This has in no small measure been objectives flowing from a general 'anti-political' discomfort within the Sangh Parivar with the ambiguities inherent in the practice of democratic and negotiated compromises and a preference for a virtuous government by a strong, though not necessarily centralized state. As the BJP has grown and diversified, as the party has won, lost and regained power in various states, and as the party's strategists and elected representatives have acquired skills and rationalities prevailing in the political field, along with a good deal of its vices such as corruption and unbridled nepotism, the imperatives of competitive politics, etc. What the BJP activists in a telling phrase call the 'compulsions of politics', have taken on a new urgency.

This volume ventures to analyse from a variety of angles how the BJP deals with these constraints and compulsions in different states, and which tensions and contradictions this *de facto* diversification of BJP's strategies has given rise to within the Hindu nationalist movement. The various contributions also attempt to map out the specific dynamics of how caste groups and other communities are approached and re-configured through the process of political mobilization for or against Hindutva and for or against dominant élites and dominant political problematics and idioms in the respective states. Lastly, this volume tries to shed some light on some of the tensions within the Sangh Parivar in terms of contentions over authority, factionalism as well as ideological differences regarding, for instance the attitude to the current policies of economic liberalization.

INDIRECT MANDALIZATION: THE SOCIAL RATIONALE OF REGIONAL SEAT ADJUSTMENTS

Ever since V. P. Singh announced the implementation of the recommendations of the Mandal commission and L. K. Advani subsequently commenced his *Rath yatra* from Somnath to Ayodhya, the mobilization around lower-caste identities and Hindutva, have emerged as two crucial poles in the political field in India. The BJP's agitation for the Ram temple and against the Mandal issues fed effectively into its rallying of upper-caste communities in the Hindi belt.

In Gujarat and Maharashtra, the BJP has with some success made itself a rallying point for the OBC-votes, though the BJP in Maharashtra remains deeply dependent on Shiv Sena's ability to appeal to lower-caste voters and make inroads into the historical support to Congress from the large Maratha-caste cluster. As shown by Ghanshyam Shah in his contribution, the split of the BJP in Gujarat in 1996 was intimately connected to the continuing battles between a leadership with conventional upper-caste's condescending attitude to the lower castes and the ambitious OBC-entrants and leaders trying to 'make it' in the party as well as in the larger Hindu nationalist movement. The events in Gujarat dealt a lethal blow to the BJP's protracted efforts to portray itself as the champion of Dalits and lower-caste Hindus in that state.

While lower-caste mobilization has appeared as one of the most persistent countervailing forces which the expansion of the Sangh Parivar have generated, the BJP has consistently tried to work out a formula that could incorporate the growing tendency towards lower-caste insubordination within the organicist conception of Hindu society which has been a cornerstone in the ideological constructions of the RSS since its inception. While dwelling on the need for social harmony, the BJP tries to defuse the mobilization power of the low-caste movements, the Janata Dal, Samajwadi Party and Bahujan Samaj Party, and even to comply with some of their prominent stands. Its 1996 manifesto even says that 'the BJP will continue with the existing policy on reservations till social and economic equity is achieved'.[2]

The BJP leaders were, in other words, well aware of the need to capture a fraction of the low-castes' votes but remained averse to the adoption of any kind of 'Mandalization', through the nomination of a large number of OBC candidates and especially the promotion of a large number of the OBC leaders within the party apparatus. A promising alternative consisted in making alliances with regional parties with a strong base among low and intermediate castes. This kind of arrangement was already prevalent in Maharashtra where the RSS and then its political offshoots, the Jana Sangh and the BJP, tended to be associated with the Brahmins, while the Shiv Sena recruited many supporters among the intermediate and low castes.[3] The seat adjustment made between the Samta Party and the BJP in Bihar gave birth to a similar sociological combine. The Samta Party was born in 1995 when fourteen MPs—mostly from Bihar—led by former socialist George Fernandes and Nitish Kumar broke away from the Janata Dal. The alliance with the Samta Party enabled the party to make inroads among Kurmis and Koeris and the party was able to win 18 seats and get 20.5 per cent of the valid votes in 1996 (as against, respectively, 5 and 12.9 per cent in 1991). Though it was a surprising move for the old socialists to enter into alliance with the BJP, it can be explained. First, the BJP had been an active ally of all non-Congress alliances in Bihar, which always claimed to be somewhat anti-establishment. Secondly, the alliance was rather consistent from the perspective of the economic agendas of both parties, where especially the defense of owner cultivators was a shared concern.[4]

In Haryana, the BJP, whose influence has traditionally been confined to the urban dwellers, and especially the Punjabi

[2] Bharatiya Janata Party, *For a Strong and Prosperous India—Election Manifesto 1996*, p. 60. See f/n 2.

[3] See Hansen, T. Blom, 'The Vernacularization of Hindutva: Shiv Sena and BJP in Rural Maharashtra', *Contributions to Indian Sociology*, vol. 30, no. 2 (1996), pp 177–214.

[4] We are grateful to Anand Kumar for these insights.

refugees,[5] aligned itself with Haryana Vikas Party whose leader Bansi Lal has a strong base among Jats. This alliance enabled the BJP to win four seats in a state where it had not won any in 1991.

Apparently, the BJP admitted the need to become more rural and even to 'Mandalize' itself though indirectly. This compromise seems to be an outcome of the inner debate between the advocates of 'social engineering' and those who did not want to indulge in this kind of tactic but stuck to the logic of sanskritization, as Christophe Jaffrelot argues in this volume.

The fact that these three states where the BJP made party alliances in 1996 were the only ones—along with Assam and Orissa—where it could register a significant advance, bears witness to its sociological and geographical limitations.

HINDU NATIONALISM AND REGIONALIZATION OF POLITICS

In 1996, the BJP won 161 seats, as against 136 of the Congress–I, but in terms of valid votes its progress was negligible: it received the support of 20.3 per cent of the electors, while the Congress–I retained 29.7 per cent of the valid votes. The BJP also remained a predominantly urban party since 32 per cent of the urban electorate voted for it as against 19 per cent of the rural electorate as a whole. If one considers the upper-caste graduates living in towns and cities, 52 per cent of this category opted for the BJP in 1996.[6] The social profile of the BJP's electorate is an asset in as much the élite plays an important part in the shaping of the public opinion, but it is also a drawback in a country where 74 per cent of the population lives in villages, where the OBCs represent 52 per cent of the society and where the literacy rate is little over 50 per cent. Most of the new seats it won came from the states where it was already strong, such as Madhya Pradesh. In terms of seats, the real breakthroughs were in Bihar, Maharashtra, and Haryana, but they were largely due to alliances with regional parties. In traditional or recent strongholds such

[5] Wallace, P., 'The Regionalization of Indian Electoral Politics 1989–90: Punjab and Haryana', in H. Gould and S. Ganguly (eds), *India Votes* (Boulder: Westview Press, 1993), p. 150.

[6] See Yadav, Y., 'How India Voted', *India Today*, 31 May 1996, the main source of information in this section.

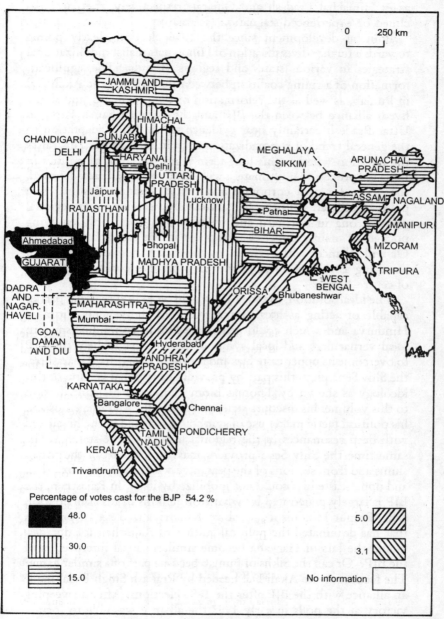

0   250 km

JAMMU AND KASHMIR

HIMACHAL

CHANDIGARH
DELHI
PUNJAB

HARYANA
Delhi
UTTAR
PRADESH

MEGHALAYA
SIKKIM
ARUNACHAL
PRADESH

Jaipur
RAJASTHAN

Lucknow

ASSAM
NAGALAND

Patna
MANIPUR

BIHAR
MIZORAM

Bhopal

MADHYA PRADESH

TRIPURA

GUJARAT
Ahmedabad

WEST
BENGAL

ORISSA
Bhubaneshwar

DADRA
AND
NAGAR.
HAVELI

MAHARASHTRA
Mumbai

GOA,
DAMAN
AND DIU

Hyderabad
ANDHRA
PRADESH

KARNATAKA

Bangalore
Chennai

TAMIL
NADU
PONDICHERRY

KERALA

Trivandrum

Percentage of votes cast for the BJP 54.2 %

48.0

30.0

15.0

5.0

3.1

No information

Votes Won by the BJP during the 1996 Lok Sabha Elections (State-wise)

as in Himachal Pradesh and Gujarat, respectively, the party declined or experienced stagnation (see map).

Political development since the 1996 election clearly points towards a further diversification of Hindu nationalist mobilizational strategies in various states and regions of India. The significant formation of a ruling coalition between the BJP and the Akali Dal in Punjab, as well as the reformation of the pragmatic (and short-lived) alliance between the BJP and the Bahujan Samaj Party in Uttar Pradesh certainly bear evidence to the BJP's adaptation to the general trend of regionalization of politics in India. This raises the question whether this long-term regionalization of politics in India is a process that ultimately will defeat, or has already defeated, the very idea of a corporate and unified 'Hindu Rashtra' as a political project. Will the BJP ultimately become a metaregional party strong in northern and western India, and only enjoying pockets of mainly upper-caste support in the east and the south? Or will alliances with regional parties make the party capable of emerging as the centre of gravity in a broader coalition of right-of-centre forces?

The ideal solution, for the BJP, would be to find regional parties capable of acting as local 'interpreters' of the general idiom of Hindutva and which could generalize Hindu communalism into local vernaculars and local symbolic inventories to help the BJP to overcome its upper-caste bias and northern image. In Maharashtra, the Shiv Sena plays this part by providing a regional version of this ideology as shown by Thomas Blom Hansen in his contribution to this volume: his discourse tries to capture the Maratha ethos and his political tactic makes use of symbols associated with Shivaji and with deep resonances in the regional history of the state. At the same time the Shiv Sena provides mass support from the urban slums and from sections of the peasantry which BJP, with its urban and upper-caste bias could not mobilize by itself. In Rajasthan, the BJP is largely penetrated by what Rob Jenkins in his contribution calls 'Rajput Hinduism', a robust Kshatriya'ized set of practices that has dominated the political culture of Rajasthan for decades. Could the Jats of Haryana become similarly local interpreters of the BJP? Or can the Sikhs of Punjab become part of a similar game? The faction of the Akali Dal headed by Prakash Singh Badal made an alliance with the BJP after the 1996 elections. After a sweeping victory at the polls in early 1997 the alliance was able to form a cabinet in the state of Punjab. From the Hindu nationalist point of view, Sikhism is no more than a current of Hinduism, and although many Sikhs may accuse Badal of compromising their ethno-religious identity because of the tie between Akali Dal and BJP, the resentment against Congress' heavy-handed policies in Punjab was so strong that it overrode these worries and led to the landslide victory for the alliance. These are the questions explored by Gurharpal Singh in his contribution.

The BJP has probably reached its saturation point in the northern and western states in the late 1990s and to expand further in geographical terms, the party needs to make more alliances. However, such a configuration may be difficult to set up in south India where the BJP remains very weak. James Manor shows below that even in Karnataka, the only southern state where the party won seats, its support remains confined in a few pockets. In a similar vein James Chiriyankandath clearly indicates below that Kerala's regional culture so far has not proved very conducive to the BJP—neither to the appeal of Hindutva among Hindu communities, nor to any regional formations keen on aligning themselves with a powerful national party as the BJP.

IDEOLOGICAL PURITY OR POLITICAL PRAGMATISM?

The third cluster of issues, besides caste politics and regionalization, dealt with in this volume has to do with the difficulties the Sangh Parivar as a whole encounters in coming to terms with the specificities and compulsions of the political field and the concomitant diversification and specialization of strategies within the Hindu nationalist movement.

An increasing source of embarrassment and confusion in the BJP is the issue of corruption. The BJP had placed corruption high on the agenda during the election campaign in 1996 and used the slogan 'To change the culture of governance, Vote BJP' intensively. Being out of power the members of the BJP were spared the opprobrium the Congressmen had to suffer for they were also blamed for using their black money more likely for their personal needs and not for the party's benefit. In addition, the BJP benefited from the image of integrity and even asceticism cultivated by some of its cadres and inherited from the RSS. However, this asset may be dwindling because of the coming in of new members and the party's tendency to fall in line with the general trend of more leaders and candidates with criminal records: in 1993–5, out of the 126 MLAs of Uttar Pradesh charged of a criminal case (pending in the court), 49 belonged to the BJP (which had 177 MLAs) as against 41 (out of 105) that belonged to the Samajwadi Party.[7]

So far as ideology *per se* is concerned, the nature of the relationship between the RSS and the BJP seems less self-evident than before. The VHP and its cohort of belligerent *sadhus* and *sants* still aspire to renew the communal campaign around the shrines in Kashi and Mathura. Reacting to the apparent moderation of the BJP, the VHP's *Dharma Sansad* in November 1996 called for the 'liberation of the Krishna Janmabhoomi' in Mathura. However, further agitations were postponed, probably after pressure from the RSS and the BJP leadership who feared that such an agitation would undermine the image of moderation which the party has been working on since 1993.

On the issue of the management of the economy and the party's stand on the liberalization policy, the obvious contradiction between the rhetoric of *Swadeshi* and the rather pragmatic governance of the economy by the Hindu nationalist cabinets in western India had generated conflicts between the BJP and RSS and its recent offshoot, the Swadeshi Jagaran Manch (SJM), as Thomas Blom Hansen explores in Chapter 10 in this volume.

In addition, the BJP has been increasingly affected by factionalism which has hit the party in Madhya Pradesh, Gujarat, and also in Rajasthan where the authority of Shekhawat has been challenged on several occasions. It has been most conspicuously in Gujarat where the protracted struggle between the BJP leadership and Sankarsinh Waghela has resulted in a vertical split in the party and Waghela's emergence as the chief minister of the state, as Ghanshyam Shah discusses below. In Madhya Pradesh rampant factionalism has prevented party elections from being held according to the schedule but, as Christophe Jaffrelot shows, the party structure seems to be resilient enough to endure it. In many other states the BJP, once known for its discipline, has suffered severe setbacks on this account.

The main contention of the volume is that the strength and tenacity of BJP and Hindu nationalist politics in India will be

---

[7] *Sunday*, 8 May 1994, p. 67.

determined by the party's and the Hindu nationalist movement's ability to adapt to the characteristics of regional politics, of specific configurations of caste politics and the peculiar compulsions and idioms of the different political fields it engages with. If that does not happen, the BJP is likely to shrink to a party of northern and western India. If the BJP, on the other hand, succeeds in this endeavour some of its monolithic and authoritarian features will probably be challenged and the party may be 'normalized' into an amorphous mechanism of bargaining like most other political parties in India. But this requires an emancipation from the RSS, which given the symbiotic relation between the two organizations seems rather unlikely in the short-term perspective. Free from the RSS's influence the BJP may be set for a more independent course, but may in the same move also lose the widespread organizational infrastructure of the entire Hindu nationalist movement which for years has given it an edge over most contenders in the field of political mobilization. However, the attraction of power is so strong that differences may recede in the background.

SHORT CUTS TO POWER: FROM LUCKNOW TO DELHI

The BJP seized power in Uttar Pradesh in October 1997 by splitting the BSP and the Congress, reportedly offering the breakaway groups portfolios and large amounts of money. The new chief minister, Kalyan Singh, even gave cabinet positions to allegedly corrupt and criminal elements and in the process formed a jumbo cabinet of 91 ministers. Subsequently, the BJP list for the Legislative Council also included known criminals. At the state level this 'horse-trading' and promise of ministerships were justi-fied in the name of *apadharma*, the Brahmin's dharma of survival. In other words, the end justifies the means.

The party's success in Uttar Pradesh emboldened it to repeat the Lucknow tactics in Delhi. It tried to engineer defections first in Gujarat and then in the centre. The bid to form a Vajpayee-led government by accepting anyone's support was part of a concerted effort to break the barrier of unacceptability. The shift suggested the BJP's readiness to compromise the principles which it pre-tended to be the very embodiment of and to look for short cuts to power.

From 1997 onwards, the party focused all its attention on setting up an alternative coalition by wooing regional forces. Its most significant achievement was its alliance with the AIADMK which gave the party a foothold in Tamil Nadu. It gradually succeeded in forging alliances with a dozen parties, most of which were factions and breakaway groups, such as Mamata Banerjee's Trinamool Congress in West Bengal, Naresh Agarwal's Loktantrik Congress in Uttar Pradesh, Lakshmi Parvati's splinter of the Telugu Desam Party in Andhra Pradesh (an alliance which did not last for a long time), and Bhigu Phukan's breakaway faction of the Asom Gana Parishad. In contrast when the BJP failed to prove its majority in 1996, it had three allies—the Samta Party, the Shiv Sena, and the Haryana Vikas Party. The logic of these alliances was dictated by expediency and there was little by way of ideological justification. As the leader of the AIADMK, Jayalalitha put it, the alliance was only for seat sharing and had nothing to do with ideology. These deals and alliances, beginning with Kalyan Singh's decimation of the Congress in Uttar Pradesh, have undeniably helped the BJP gain national spread, overcome its isolation and establish, symbolically, a pan-Indian presence.

The results from the 12th Lok Sabha election in 1998 confirmed the overall tendency towards regionalization of Indian politics and the protracted construction of Atal Bihari Vajpayee's thirteen-party coalition government in late March 1998 demonstrated that Indian prime ministers would henceforth be made and unmade in state capitals rather than in Delhi. Probably the most remarkable thing about this second round of General Elections in 18 months was how little it changed the overall balance of power between the main forces in Indian politics. On their own, the two main parties either maintained their share of seats, as did the Congress inspite of a reduced share of the overall vote, or won moderately, as the BJP did. The major novelty of the 1998 election was undoubtedly that most political parties recognized the importance of electoral alliances and that these pragmatic alliances subsequently strength-ened a range of regional political formations.

What can be observed is the crisis and possible demise of an entire political culture based on the production of a 'majoritarian consensus' around a single political party, led by a paramount political chief, to whom charismatic and mythical qualities are attributed as s/he assumes a powerful position. This majoritarian political culture certainly lives on and thrives at the level of the states, notably in states where powerful regional formations rule or where so-called 'mercurial personalities' such as Jayalalitha, Thackeray and Laloo Prasad Yadav are consistently able to reproduce a massive following around their whimsical political leadership. But even at the state level, this does not work wonders any more. Small parties or splinter groups with a standing in a few regions or communities in a single state are no longer struck with awe when approached by a national political party. They either put up a tough bargain, or run for the Lok Sabha in their own right. In the contemporary scenarios of Indian electoral politics, small parties, or even independents, enjoy unprecedented possibilities of bringing themselves into strategically significant positions in the parliamentary game. This mobilization of hitherto marginal regional votes, in combination with the heightened level of political mobilization among Dalits and OBC groups, have undoubtedly contributed to the increased turnout at the elections from 57 per cent in 1996 to 62 per cent in 1998.

The majoritarian political culture which is so deeply ingrained in the minds of most political leaders and activists and which the electoral system of single mandate constituencies reproduces and favours, seems to be losing its relevance at the national level. In its place a new mode of political conduct, based on 'negotiated consensus' among aligned partners and shifting patterns of alliance and accommodation within the ruling coalition, is growing. In some ways, the former Prime Minister Inder Kumar Gujral almost personified the new 'weak' style of leadership which coalition politics and negotiated consensus demands: a leadership capable of mediation, coordination and public upmanship rather than the tactics of heavy-handed leadership, manipulation, and destruction of opposition which was always part of the Congress-style majoritarian political culture. Whether out of compulsion or conviction, Gujral tried this out in various ways but it did not earn him much respect or approval, not even from his own cabinet ministers who tried their best to isolate him during the January–February 1998 election campaign.

It was a decision of the Congress to withdraw support to the UF cabinet, on the basis of the Jain Commission's indications of the DMK's knowledge of the conspiracy to assassinate Rajiv Gandhi, which was the immediate cause of the elections. In retrospect, it seems likely that the Congress strategy of mobilizing

Votes won by major parties and alliances as a proportion of total valid votes, Lok Sabha elections, 1998 (*in per cent*)

| State/Territory | BJP | BJP allies | Parties and alliances | | United Front | Other parties and independents |
			Congress (I)	Congress (I) allies		
Andhra Pradesh	18.30	1.20	37.55	—	38.37	4.58
Arunachal Pradesh	21.75	—	23.90	—	1.89	52.47
Assam	24.47	—	38.97	—	18.16	18.40
Bihar	22.03	15.46	6.94	24.75	15.50	15.31
Goa	30.18	—	31.53	—	13.15	25.14
Gujarat	47.72	—	37.95	—	3.47	10.87
Haryana	18.89	11.60	26.02	—	1.07	42.42
Himachal Pradesh	48.60	—	43.57	—	2.02	5.81
Jammu and Kashmir	23.31	—	22.54	—	36.66	17.49
Karnataka	26.96	11.50	36.23	—	21.82	3.49
Kerala	8.02	—	36.55	7.13	42.40	5.90
Madhya Pradesh	45.86	—	38.46	—	2.65	13.04
Maharashtra	23.11	19.26	43.48	2.61	3.81	7.72
Manipur	12.61	—	18.60	—	20.47	48.32
Meghalaya	9.01	—	47.62	—	1.99	41.38
Mizoram	2.94	—	34.86	—	—	62.20
Nagaland	—	—	86.70	—	—	13.30
Orissa	21.43	27.80	40.27	—	6.45	4.05

(*Cont.*)

State/Territory	Parties and alliances					
	BJP	BJP allies	Congress (I)	Congress (II) allies	United Front	Other parites and independents
Punjab	14.90	32.87	25.87	9.44	8.64	8.28
Rajasthan	41.65	—	44.45	—	6.57	7.32
Sikkim	—	—	33.11	65.72	—	1.17
Tamil Nadu	6.86	41.75	5.43	—	43.42	2.53
Tripura	8.19	—	42.12	—	48.80	0.90
Uttar Pradesh	36.44	1.49	5.99	1.16	29.48	25.44
West Bengal	10.00	24.14	14.98	2.03	46.65	2.19
Andaman and Nicobar	35.53	—	35.91	—	5.67	22.89
Chandigarh	42.39	—	38.72	—	1.61	17.28
Dadra & Nagar Haveli	52.29	—	4.02	—	—	43.69
Daman and Diu	41.96	—	1.98	—	—	56.06
Delhi	53.51	—	42.64	—	2.76	1.08
Lakshadweep	—	—	51.55	—	48.45	—
Pondicherry	—	25.09	32.13	—	41.11	1.67
India	25.46	11.59	25.68	3.59	22.42	11.26

Notes: 1. Total number of constituencies considered 537.
2. Results were not available for Ladakh and Udhampur (Jammu and Kashmir), Patna (Bihar), and Mandi (Himachal Pradesh).
3. Data for Purulia (West Bengal) and Sitamarthi (Bihar) were omitted because of errors in the data on the Election Commission.

the legacy of the Nehru dynasty and fielding Sonia Gandhi as the star campaigner following an emotionally highly charged 'memory-trail' of her deceased husband's previous campaign routes, was charted well before the elections. As Sonia Gandhi entered the election campaign with full force in January 1998 and began drawing large crowds in many parts of the country, the confrontation between the BJP and the Congress became the central axis of the themes and rhetoric of the election campaign. BJP's initial self-confident assertion of itself as a moderate, centrist party, its projection of Vajpayee as the elder statesman and capable leader, and its projection in opinion polls as the winning party, was shaken. The BJP was forced into the defensive, especially in states where the Congress has retained a sizable local infrastructure enabling the party to link Sonia Gandhi's campaign to local issues and grievances.

Sonia Gandhi's entry into the election campaign stopped the ongoing disintegration of the Congress, for a time at least, and enabled the party to hold on to its tally from the 1996 elections.

However, Congress efforts neither revitalized the party, nor produced any new viable leadership or vision. There was, on the contrary, a strangely travestic quality to Sonia Gandhi's campaign. The cardboard cutouts of herself and Priyanka, the public gestures, the minute details of dress and decoration, the venues and even the style of oratory adopted by Sonia Gandhi, cited, copied or drew on the style developed by Indira Gandhi in the 1970s. The party seemed trapped in a genre of public performance and electoral campaigning that it could neither escape nor renew. Also in terms of building electoral alliances, the Congress seemed inept and ineffective and unable to abandon the older heavy-handed habits of the party.

The rise of the BJP during the 1998 general elections was modest. In terms of seats, its tally reached 178, as against 161 in 1996. While its share of valid votes registered a more significant increase, from 20.3 per cent to about 25.6 per cent, it was on the same footing as the Congress. Interestingly, the BJP did not make much progress in its northern and western strongholds where it has more or less reached its saturation point. In the Hindi belt (Uttar Pradesh, Madhya Pradesh, Himachal Pradesh, Rajasthan, Bihar,

Haryana, and Delhi) it won 122 seats, as against 119 in 1996. In its more recent (1998) western conquests, Gujarat and Maharashtra, its tally was 23, as against 34 in 1996. The party lost in most of the states where it was in power for some time, Rajasthan, Haryana, and Maharashtra. In the former it could retain only 5 of its 12 seats, while the Congress party staged a comeback. In Maharashtra, the BJP kept 4 of its 18 seats and the Shiv Sena 6 of its 15 seats, but both parties maintained their share of votes. The anti-incumbency feelings of the Indian citizens, did not spare the Hindu nationalist parties.

The BJP's gains came from east and south India where it used to be almost non-existent. The four southern states gave the BJP 20 seats as against 6 (all in Karnataka) in 1996 and in Orissa and West Bengal, it jumped from zero to 8. In terms of valid votes, the BJP remained below 10 per cent in West Bengal, Kerala, and Tamil Nadu but made remarkable progress in Andhra Pradesh (from 5.1 per cent to 18.3 per cent), Orissa (from 13.3 per cent to 21.43 per cent), and, Assam (from 16.6 per cent to 24.47 per cent) where it did not yield seats yet. It also consolidated its position in Karnataka.

This breakthrough, however was possible only because of the new alliances that the BJP had made with the regional parties in these states. In each of them, the BJP was associated with regional parties which did surprisingly well by cashing in on the anti-incumbency reflex. The AIADMK and its local allies enabled the BJP-led coalition to win 30 seats out of 39. The Biju Janata Dal, the product of a scission of the Janata Dal in Orissa, founded three months before the elections, won 28 per cent of the votes and 9 seats. The same thing was repeated as the Trinamool Congress, of the West Bengal Congress dissident, Mamata Banerjee, wrested 7 seats. Even though it won only 3 seats, the Lok Shakti of R. K. Hegde earned 11 per cent of the votes and helped the BJP enormously during the election campaign. Older allies were also unexpectedly successful except the Haryana Vikas Party which did not escape the anti-incumbency reflex and lost 3 of its 4 seats. The Akali Dal, even though it was in power for more than one year, won as many seats as it did in 1996–8. The Samta Party expanded its base towards UP and won 10 of its 12 seats in Bihar. While the BJP's achievement must not be underestimated, the party relied heavily on surprisingly successful regional allies this time and herein lies the main explanation for its progress and, more importantly, for its capacity to form the government.

Even though the BJP-led alliance represented only 250 seats in the Lok Sabha, the President asked Atal Bihari Vajpayee to form the government in March 1998. For the first time the BJP was in a pivotal position, at the centre of a large coalition of 12 parties. Can we reasonably look at the Vajpayee government as a milestone towards a new realignment, a consummation of the emergence of the BJP as a mainstream party?

Most political parties, when they are about to capture power or when they control the reins of government, naturally tend to adopt moderate policies on critical issues. That the BJP is quite capable of altering its strategy is evident after 1992 when it shifted from the ethno-religious mobilization of the Ramjanmabhoomi movement towards a more pragmatic policy. However, even as the party moderated its public stance by toning down the anti-Muslim attitude, the competing pressure to sustain its commitment to Hindutva was unmistakable. This is apparent if we shift the focus from the formal pronouncements and public speeches in New Delhi designed for the middle-class and English-language media in metropolitan centres, to the extremist rhetoric in the 1998 election campaign at the state- and constituency-level or the actions of a BJP government when it occupies office at the state level. In Maharashtra, the Shiv Sena–BJP government has abolished the Minorities Commission, tried its best to sabotage the Srikrishna Commission of Inquiry into the Bombay riots, cut the grants-in-aid to the Urdu Academy, displaced Muslims in the name of slum clearance and denied them rehabilitation, and withdrawn criminal cases related to riots against Bal Thackeray and other Shiv Sena leaders. Similarly, the Kalyan Singh government, while making Sanskrit compulsory from Class III, ignored the claims of Urdu in Uttar Pradesh.

Shifting its ideological stance is central to the BJP's strategy. But as long as the party remains under the influence of the RSS,[8] it may not be able to adapt itself to moderating requirements of

---

[8] The election of Kushabhau Thakre as party chief in 1998 suggests that, inspite of Vajpayee's preference for Shekhawat who would have helped the BJP to emancipate itself from the RSS.

governance or dilute its Hindutva ideology. The third part of
the present volume will focus on the tensions within the Sangh
Parivar. The first two ones are dealing with the strategies of the BJP
for expanding beyond its north Indian electoral strongholds and
beyond its upper-caste social basis. Therefore the book shows that
the making of alliances with other parties and the wooing of new
groups are the main compulsions of politics the BJP had to face in
the late 1990s.

PART I

BJP AND THE CASTE BARRIER: BEYOND THE 'TWICE-BORN'?

Ψ

1

The Sangh Parivar Between Sanskritization and Social Engineering

CHRISTOPHE JAFFRELOT

The Hindu nationalist movement has always been known for its upper-caste, even brahminical character. While this feature was also typical of the early Congress, it was especially pronounced in the case of the Rashtriya Swayamsevak Sangh (RSS—Association of national volunteers) and its affiliates. This specificity stemmed from the content of the Hindutva ideology itself which was shaped by Maharashtrian Brahmins and relied on an organic view of society. In this perspective, the sanskritization path remained the main avenue for social mobility.

However, this élitist orientation has become a liability, especially for the political offshoot of the so-called *Sangh Parivar* which needed to broaden its base for contesting elections. In the 1990s, after the 'Mandal affair', leaders of the Bharatiya Janata Party have been inclined to make room for non-upper-castes people within the party. This policy, which is often described as 'social engineering', is gradually gaining momentum, but meets oppositions within the Hindu nationalist movement from those, often with an RSS background, who remain faithful to the traditional world-view of the movement, as well as from those who object that the BJP may lose its traditional base if it runs after low-caste voters. A tension has, therefore, developed between advocates of 'social engineering' and leaders who still regard sanskritization as the main instrument for social change and the spread of the Hindu nationalist ideology, as I shall try to show in the first half of this essay.

In the second half, I shall focus on the state of Madhya Pradesh to assess the BJP's social profile at the local level. In this area, where the leftist parties and the Janata Dal play a marginal role and where the Congress has been dominated by upper-caste leaders till recently, the BJP seems to have a long way to make before changing its upper-caste image, not only because its apparatus is still dominated by élite groups, but also because its OBC and Scheduled Castes leaders often comply with the traditional ethos of sanskritization. However things are changing, largely under two kinds of pressure, the rise of the BSP and Digvijay Singh's strategy of coopting non-upper-castes leaders.

THE UPPER-CASTE TRADITION OF THE RSS

As in any form of ethnic nationalism, Hindu nationalism, in its formative phase at least, looked at the society as an organic, harmonious whole.[1] In the case of the Rashtriya Swayamsevak Sangh the emphasis on social organicism reflected an upper-caste— and more especially a brahminical—view of society. While the RSS was conceived primarily as an egalitarian vanguard of the 'Hindu Rashtra' (Hindu nation), its leaders' conception of the ideal society continued to be based on the *varna* system. M. S. Golwalkar, in 1938, wrote: 'It is none of the so-called drawbacks of the Hindu social order, which prevents us from regaining our ancient glory.'[2] In a later speech that opened with an eulogy to the 'scientific' nature of the varna system he elaborates this point:

If a developed society realizes that the existing differences are due to the scientific social structure and that they indicate the different limbs of the body social, the diversity would not be constructed as a blemish.[3]

[1] I have developed this argument in the first chapter of *The Hindu Nationalist Movement and Indian Politics, 1925–90s* (New Delhi: Viking, 1996).
[2] Golwalkar, M. S., *We, or Our Nationhood Defined* (Nagpur: Bharat Publications, 1939), p. 63.
[3] *Organiser*, 1 Dec. 1952, p. 7.

Following in the footsteps of Golwalkar, Deendayal Upadhyaya, another Brahmin trained in the RSS and the chief ideologue of the Jana Sangh in the 1950s and 1960s, rejected the theory of a social contract and explained that society is 'self-born' as an 'organic' entity:

In our concept of four castes [varna], they are thought of as analogous to the different limbs of Virat-Purusha [the primeval man] [...]. These limbs are not only complementary to one another, but even further, there is individuality, unity. There is complete identity of interest, identity of belonging [...]. If this idea is not kept alive, the castes, instead of being complementary, can produce conflict. But then this is distortion [...]. This is indeed the present condition of our society.[4]

The stress Golwalkar and Upadhyaya put on social unity in an organicist perspective echoed the classical world-view of the Brahmins who dominate the varna hierarchy. This kind of élitism was even obvious in the anti-Muslim prejudice which Hindu nationalists displayed and which was nourished by the sentiment of the upper-caste superiority. For instance, S. P. Mookerjee, the founder of the Jana Sangh used revealing arguments while resigning himself to the Partition of Bengal in 1946:

If Bengal is converted into Pakistan [...] Bengal Hindus are placed under a permanent tutelage of Muslims. Judging from the manner in which attacks on Hindu religion and society have been made, [this] means an end of Bengali Hindu culture. In order to placate *a set of converts from low caste Hindus to Islam*, very ancient Hindu culture will be sacrificed.[5]

J. Chatterji convincingly considers that these sentences reflect 'the bhadralok concern with "Hindu culture"' (in the sense, we could add, of the upper castes' high tradition). For this author, these views showed 'that at least for Shyam Prasad, caste attitudes continued to remain ingrained despite the caste consolidation campaign and new "Hindu togetherness" it claimed to engender.'

The Hindu culture which the RSS championed was that of the high tradition and even its techniques bore the mark of brahminical culture. Anxious to refashion the Hindu character to make it nationalist, Hedgewar believed that work to this end carried on in

[4] Upadhyaya, D., *Integral Humanism* (New Delhi: Bharatiya Jana Sangh, 1965), p. 43.
[5] Cited in Chatterji, J., *Bengal Divided—Hindu Communalism and Partition, 1932–47* (Cambridge: Cambridge University Press, 1994), p. 231. Emphasis added.

the *shakha*s should be inspired by the notion of *samskars*. In this context, the term designates all the 'good influences' which can be exerted in the formation of character, especially of young people. At the elementary level, to recommend a healthy lifestyle, for instance, is a way of bestowing the benefits of samskars. Such a discipline was of course observed particularly among Brahmins, whose status in itself implied respect for these values. The emphasis on samskars, which is still prevalent within the Sangh Parivar, is in accordance with its upper-caste bias. The RSS was intended to grow by attracting in the shakhas those Hindus who valued this ethos, either because they belonged to the upper castes or because they wanted to emulate them. Therefore, the technique of 'conversion' of low-caste people to Hindutva relied on the same logic as the imitation of the Brahmins which M. N. Srinivas has analysed as a process of 'sanskritization'.[6]

The traditional Hindu nationalist view of society partly explains the way the RSS criticized the announcement by V. P. Singh on 7 August 1990 that the recommendations of the Mandal Commission report would be implemented. Reacting to the 'Rajah's castewar', the *Organiser* (the RSS's mouthpiece) attacked not only the politics of quotas in favour of the OBCs, denounced as the pampering of vote-banks, but also the policy of positive discrimination in itself from its traditional organicist angle:

The havoc the politics of reservation is playing with the social fabric is unimaginable. It provides a premium for mediocrity, encourages brain-drain and sharpens caste-divide.[7]

On the implicit assumption that it was virtually harmonious, the 'social fabric' is regarded here as in need of preservation from state intervention.

In addition to the implementation of the Mandal Commission report, the electoral success of the Samajwadi Party and the Bahujan Samaj Party in Uttar Pradesh in 1993 acted as a catalyst within the RSS. The *Organiser* then came to embrace publicly the cause of the upper castes. M. V. Kamath, a regular columnist, wrote an article reflecting the same apprehensions as the ones expressed by the Maharashtrian Brahmins who joined the RSS in the 1920s

[6] Srinivas, M. N., *Social Change in Modern India* (New Delhi: Orient Longman, 1995 [1966]), p. 7.
[7] *Organiser*, 26 August 1990, p. 15.

and 1930s in reaction to the Ambedkar movement:

[A]lready one smells violence in the air. Tensions are rising [...]. There is today an urgent need to build up moral and spiritual forces to counter any fall-out from an expected Shudra revolution.[8]

Interestingly, Kamath used the word Shudra (instead of OBCs for instance), that is the term which designates the fourth order in the varma system. However, Kamath had nothing new to offer as is testified by a subsequent article, significantly entitled 'The Demonization of Upper Castes', whose opening and concluding paragraphs are highly revealing:

A massive effort is being made by the likes of Mulayam Singh Yadav, Laloo Prasad Yadav, Kanshi Ram and his consort Mayawati to damn the so-called upper castes as the ones that kept the so-called Backward Castes suppressed all these centuries. A giant guilt complex is being sought to be thrust on the upper caste [sic] and many of them, unfortunately, are succumbing to it. It is time the truth is told. [...]

The Mulayam Singh Yadavs and others of his ilk are ignorant of history and sociology. The so-called upper castes are not responsible for 'oppressing' the OBCs. On the contrary they would like to help but can hardly do if a caste war is waged against them by the likes of Kanshi Ram. Reservations and other mechanisms will not improve the lot of the OBCs, nor can they help in establishing a casteless society. A casteless society can only be established by the exertions of the upper castes and not by the hate-mongering of the likes of Kanshi Ram. SCs, OBCs and others need the upper castes. Putting the latter down in an act of vengeance will only retard the process of eliminating caste from our society and the country. We need cooperation, not confrontation for India to grow rich once again.[9]

This kind of discourse echoes the unitarian, almost 'oecumenical' overtone of Hindu nationalism since its ideological crystallization in the 1920s. While the victory of the SP–BSP alliance acted as a catalyst, its policy in Uttarakhand further radicalized the reaction of the RSS. This hill area of north-west Uttar Pradesh was the setting for an agitation against the 27 per cent scheme implemented by Mulayam Singh Yadav's government, the demonstrators arguing that OBCs constituted only 2 per cent of the local population whereas the upper castes represented 60 per cent. The RSS-backed Uttaranchal Pradesh Sangharsh Samiti revived the latent movement

[8] Kamath, M. V., 'Is Shudra Revolution in the Offing?', ibid., 1 May 1994, p. 6.
[9] Kamath, M. V., 'The Demonization of Upper Castes', *Organiser*, Depavali Special, 30 Oct. 1994, pp 23–4.

for a separate state of Uttarakhand and the *Organiser*, while
supporting it, seized this opportunity to make more general points.
In a longish editorial V. P. Bhatia explained that upper castes were
so numerous in Uttarakhand because when they conquered this
area 'Panwar rulers who came from the plains strengthened the
varna system' and 'many local tribes were also accepted as Brahmin
castes': 'Thus the Uttarakhandis are being punished for wiping out
the hereditary caste system, whereas they ought to be emulated
everywhere else.'[10] The Uttarakhandis appear as role models because their upper-caste leaders, while strengthening the varna
system, have assimilated the local backward castes and tribes. From
Bhatia's point of view there is no contradiction between the fact
that Uttarakhandis have stengthened the varna system *and* yet have
wiped out the caste system: they have applied the logic of
sanskritization (inherent in the varna system) to such an extent that
low castes have almost vanished. This reasoning is in accordance
with Hedgewar's notion of samskars and the typically nationalist
Hindu view that, in the end, all the castes could be pure provided
they follow the brahminical high tradition. But in contrast with the
oecumenical implications of this vision, Bhatia arraigns 'the-thick-
ening creamy layers of self-centred fat cats of the OBC and Dalit
fraternities.'[11] Simultaneously, the *Organiser* vindicated brahminism.
In a long article, Ram Swarup, one of the pillars of the Deendayal
Research Institute (an offshoot of the RSS), argued that Brahmins
were at the forefront of the anti-colonial movement and that anti-
brahminism was a construct of the British and the missionaries:

Brahmins began to be described as exploiters and authors of the iniquitous
caste system. Much scholarship and intellectual labour was put into the thesis
before it acquired its present momentum. [...] Anti-brahminism originated in
anti-Hindu circles and prospered in the same. When they attacked Brahmins,
their target was unmistakenly Hinduism.[12]

The equation established by Ram Swaroop between Hinduism
and brahminism is significant of an upper caste and sanskritized
view of society.

[10] Bhatia, V. P., 'What Will They Do When They Reach 100 Per Cent
Reservations?', *Organiser*, 27 Nov. 1994, p. 11.
[11] Ibid.
[12] Swarup, Ram, 'Colonial Genesis of Anti-brahminism', *Organiser*, 19 May
1996, p. 11.

The RSS high command followed more or less the same line as the *Organiser*. The General Secretary of the RSS, H.V. Seshadri, reacted to the victory of the SP–BSP alliance in terms which showed that the organization was not prepared to let the BJP follow a similar strategy relying on caste identities:

Social justice can be rendered to the weaker sections of society only when the entire society is imbued with the spirit of oneness and internal harmony. Society is like a living body and its weak limbs get strengthened by the entire body coming to its aid in every possible manner. And this becomes possible when the life-force of the body remains active and powerful. The life-force in the case of society is its vibrant awareness of its abiding oneness. That alone will result in a spirit of harmony among all its sections and ensuring of equality, dignity, security and justice, especially to its weaker parts. And this precisely is the path the Sangh has been pursuing through its shakha technique of social reorganisation for the past 68 years.[13]

Such a discourse echoed the organicist conceptions expounded by Golwalkar or Upadhyaya. Accordingly, Rajendra Singh, the new *sarsanghchalak* of the RSS criticized caste-based reservations on several occasions in late 1994 and early 1995, during his first tour in his new position. He even declared that 'in no other country of the world there is such a provision of reservation, even when there are backward people.'[14] According to him, 'There should be a gradual reduction in the job quotas,'[15] even for the Scheduled

---

[13] *Organiser*, 19 Dec. 1993, p. 17. Seshadri had criticized the SP and the BSP in a similar way in a previous issue of *Organiser*: '...in any confrontation with the rest of the society, the weaker sections always stand to lose. It is only with the goodwill and cooperation of the entire society that they can get the necessary opportunities to raise themselves up. The very concept of social justice implies recognition of equality, dignity and opportunity in every sphere of national life by the entire society. And this is possible only when the society becomes imbued with the spirit of oneness and harmony among all sections just as a weak limb can get strengthened only when the entire bodily life-force is quite active and ensures that the entire body goes out to continuously nurture that limb. This is exactly how the Hindutva life-force works in the case of our society' (Ibid., 5 Dec. 1993, p. 7).

[14] *National Mail*, 1 March 1995. In December 1994, Rajendra Singh had already concluded a two day RSS training camp by saying, 'Providing any form of reservation or privileges to the people of any particular caste or community on the basis of reservation would not be beneficial...' (Ibid., 21 Dec. 1994). He repeated the same thing in Jabalpur (Ibid., 21 Dec. 1994).

[15] *Organiser*, 18 Dec. 1994, p. 20.

Castes. Referring to the notion of 'social engineering', he objected that 'the term is not clear' and added:

The prevailing real-politic [sic] has been creating bitterness and hatred between various sections of society. It can be removed only with the help of service projects inspired by compassion, fellow-feeling and social harmony. We therefore propose to lay greater stress on this aspect of our work.[16]

In this perspective, the RSS launched in January 1996 a new programme called *samarasya sangama* (confluence for harmony), which provided that the RSS workers should adopt one village in order to contribute to its development in order, in the words of Rajendra Singh, to promote 'social harmony between various sections of the society and social assimilation.'[17]

The notion of samarasya sangama has eclipsed that of 'Hindu Sangathan' in the RSS discourse: while the priority remains to organize Hindus, unity is not intended to be achieved *against* 'the other' any more but through the integration of the low castes. 'Social harmony' and 'social assimilation' have become the key words in the RSS to designate this effort to defuse caste contradictions. In addition to these two expressions, 'compassion' is also often used, even though the Dalits reject this word for its patronizing overtones.

Yet, the RSS discourse is not merely paternalist and reactionary. In late 1996, Rajendra Singh in the ritual address delivered by the RSS sarsanghchalak on the day of Vijaydashami, always an important occasion, declared that the reservations should not exceed 50 per cent of the posts because 'it is also necessary that integrity, ability and meritorious qualities find the highest place in administration.'[18] The RSS therefore backed up its defence of social status quo by invoking individual merit, a modern notion to which the upper-caste middle class refers to assiduously when they oppose positive discrimination. The use of modern notions such as individual merit by the RSS leaders, however, can fit in their worldview (which is still largely imbued with non-individualistic values) because it can be seen as a translation of the upper-caste notion of the refined self: Brahmins are supposed to sustain a fully evolved personality more than anybody else. High education and

[16] *Organiser*, 27 March 1994, p. 17.
[17] *Organiser*, 14 Jan. 1996, p. 7.
[18] *Organiser*, 10 Nov. 1996, p. 10.

good jobs have also become elements of status to such an extent that 'sanskritization' and 'westernization' are not antinomic. And merit is often referred to for preventing low-caste people from achieving any social mobility and preserving the status quo. In this respect, two paradigms, 'meritocracy' and 'social organicism', which belong to different *weltanschauungs*, can converge and serve the same purpose. Thus, the RSS tends to stick to its classical denying of social conflicts and to reassert its apprehensions towards positive discrimination by relying on 'traditional' as well as 'modern' arguments.

THE BJP IN QUEST OF A COMPROMISE

The upper-caste character of Hindu nationalism has become a greater handicap for the BJP in the 1990s because of the growing political consciousness of the low castes in the wake of the 'Mandal affair'. The party could not ignore the OBCs which account for 52 per cent of the population and which were especially mobilized in its strongholds of north India. However to *endorse* their grievances would have compromised its traditional support among the upper castes and would have implied acceptance of internal divisions in the 'Hindu nation' against which the RSS had laboured for more than seventy years.

The Hindu Nationalist Dilemma in the Post-Mandal Context

The 1993 election results, when the BJP lost both Uttar Pradesh and Madhya Pradesh partly because of the OBC and Dalit voters, led the party leaders to promote a larger number of low-caste people in the party apparatus. In January 1994, Hukumdev Narain Yadav, an Ahir, was appointed as special invitee to the party's national executive and Uma Bharti, a Lodhi, became chief of the Bharatiya Janata Yuva Morcha (the youth wing of the BJP). Uma Bharti looked at herself as representing 'the poors'—especially the low castes and the women, within the BJP.[19] In 1997, she took part in the debate on the Women Reservation Bill to contradict the high command's line by declaring that 'if social justice has to be done,

[19] 'If you would like to call me a leader, then I am a leader of the poor people [...] But I have a sympathy for women. Especially, I don't like seeing women at work. When I see their hands, they become so rough' (Interview with Uma Bharti, New Delhi, 12 February 1994). Such a discourse can also be interpreted as reflecting

The Sangh Parivar 31

there should be quotas for women belonging to backward classes and Dalits.'[20] Just before becoming chief of the BJYM, she had said:

We should change the image of the party as a party of those who sit and smoke in air-conditioned rooms. This may hurt some but we should go ahead with it. We have to go to the grassroots, to the Dalits. The party has become complacent after the Ram Janmabhoomi movement. Kanshi Ram has woken us up.[21]

The main advocate of the inclusion of an increasing number of low-caste members at all the levels of the party apparatus was K. N. Govindacharya, himself a Brahmin and one of the BJP General Secretaries.[22] He called this policy 'social engineering'. However, such a strategy was opposed by some of his colleagues and the RSS leaders who objected in principle to any artificial transformation of the so-called social equilibrium and who did not want to give new importance to castes as a result of pressures from the 'Mandal affair'. Murli Manohar Joshi, a former president of the BJP, opposed this move and even implicitly questioned the notion of affirmative action by asking 'What social justice has been brought in the name of social engineering? Rural poverty has increased and most of the rural poor continue to be Dalits.'[23]

In a way the BJP fell in line with the mother organization, the RSS, during the all-party meeting on reservations that was held in 1995 under the auspices of the then Union Welfare Minister, Sitaram Kesri since its representative, Atal Bihari Vajpayee, alone opposed the extension of reservations in promotion for the

---

sanskritization values: one can resort to such arguments to reiterate the conventional upper-caste practice of maintaining women in seclusion (a point I owe to Thomas Hansen).

[20] Cited in the *Times of India*, 21 June 1997.

[21] Cited in the *Times of India*, 26 Dec. 1993.

[22] An RSS *pracharak* by training, Govindacharya had joined politics through the protest movement of Jaya Prakash Narayan, in which he had taken part while he was based at Bihar. (Interview with K. N. Govindacharya, New Delhi, 19 Nov. 1990.)

[23] Interview in *Sunday*, 26 Jan. 1997, p. 13. M. M. Joshi was not alone in expressing reservations vis-à-vis Govindacharya's programme. Sunder Singh Bhandari, one of the BJP Vice-Presidents declared for instance: 'We will keep social equilibrium in mind. It is an expansion programme and there is no question of being lopsided.' (Cited in the *Times of India*, 26 Dec. 1993.)

Scheduled Castes and Scheduled Tribes and refused to express a willingness to increase the ceiling of 50 per cent reservation for these two categories and the OBCs.[24]

However, as the eleventh general elections approached, the BJP amended its earlier position on the reservation issue. Before the 1991 elections the BJP had expressed very general views: 'Reservation should [...] be made for other backward classes broadly on the basis of the Mandal Commission Report, with preference to be given to the poor amongst these very classes and [...] [a]s poverty is an important contributory factor for backwardness, reservation should also be provided for members of the other castes on the basis of their economic condition.'[25] In 1996, it retained the discourse of the RSS but made more precise promises. The party's manifesto put a stress on social harmony[26] and the section entitled 'Our Social Philosophy' implicitly drew its inspiration from the notion of 'integral humanism' evolved by Deendayal Upadhyaya:

The Bharatiya Janata Party's social philosophy, which is the bedrock of its social agenda, is rooted in integral humanism. It rules out contradictions between society and its various components, as also between society and the individual, or, for that matter, between the family, the basic building brick of our social structure, and the individual.[27]

But the BJP admitted that the existing quotas in favour of the Scheduled Castes and the Other Backward Classes could not be put into question. However, this concession was conditional and

---

[24] S. Kesri consulted the political parties prior to bringing before the Parliament a constitution amendment bill designed to nullify the 50 per cent ceiling imposed by the Supreme Court on reservation and a bill seeking extension of reservation in promotions for the Scheduled Castes and Scheduled Tribes in government jobs beyond 1997. Adressing a convention of the Scheduled Castes and Scheduled Tribes MLAs, Ministers, Mayors, Deputy Mayors, corporators and panchayat office-bearers in Bhopal, he denounced the BJP as the biggest enemy of the SCs, STs and OBCs on the basis of Vajpayee's stand (*National Mail*, Bhopal, 19 May 1995).

[25] Bharatiya Janata Party, *Towards Ram Rajya—Mid-Term Poll to Lok Sabha, May 1991: Our Commitments*, New Delhi, 1991, p. 27.

[26] The manifesto also said: 'The task is nothing short of rekindling the lamp of our eternal *Dharma*, that *Sanatan* thought which our sages bequeathed to mankind—a social system based on compassion, cooperation, justice, freedom, equality and tolerance.' (Bharatiya Janata Party, *For a Strong and Prosperous India—Election Manifesto 1996*, New Delhi, 1996, p. 5).

[27] Ibid., p. 59.

associated with the creation of new quotas based on economic criteria:

The BJP is committed to providing both social and economic justice to the socially and educationally backward classes (Other Backward Classes) through the instrument of reservations. At the same time, we hold that the path to progress of all sections of our people lies not through social divisions brought by casteist politics but through social harmony. The BJP advocates:

1. Continuation of reservations for the Other Backward Classes till they are socially and educational [sic] integrated with the rest of society;

2. A uniform criteria [sic] for demarcating the 'creamy layer';

3. Flow of reservation benefits in an ascending order so that the most backward sections of the OBCs get them first;

4. Ten per cent reservation on the basis of economic criteria to all economically weaker sections of society, apart from the Scheduled Castes/ Scheduled Tribes and the Other Backward Classes.[28]

Thus, the BJP admits the inevitability of quotas for the OBCs but tries to combine the criterion of caste with socio-economic criteria. This compromise reflects the debate within the 'Sangh Parivar' between the advocates of 'social engineering' in favour of the low castes and those who want to abstain from acknowledging caste conflicts. While the former succeeded in making reservations part of the manifesto, the BJP did not substantially increase the number of the non-upper-caste members in the party apparatus and among the party candidates.

The Still Marginal Position of the BJP Non-Élite Groups

The non-élite groups have always been under represented among the Jana Sangh and then the BJP activists. In the study conducted in 1987 in Uttar Pradesh, Delhi, Rajasthan and Haryana, Y. K. Malik and J. F. Marquette show that the BJP has less number of activists working as agriculturalist than the other parties and more number of white-collar activists than the others.[29]

At the apex of the party structure, an indication of the élitist bias of the party is furnished by the over-representation of

[28] Ibid., p. 62. This programme recalls the Social Charter adopted by the 1993 plenary session of the BJP, where L. K. Advani succeeded M. M. Joshi as the party president (*India Today*, 15 July 199a3, p. 39).

[29] Malik, Y. K., and J.F. Marquette, *Political Mercenaries and Citizen Soldiers*, (Delhi: Chanakya, 1990), p. 113.

high-caste people among the Jana Sangh Working Committee and the BJP National Executive Committee. As shown in Table 1.1, between 1954–67 and 1972–5 a large number of the members of the former came from this background: 78 out of 105. The large numbers of Brahmins and Banias and the substantial representation of Khattris must also be underlined. The latter reflected the role of the Punjabis (often with an Arya Samaj background, such as in the case of B. Madhok or K. N. Sahni) in the making of the Jana Sangh. The presence of low-caste leaders in the Jana Sangh's top leadership is very limited, even if most of the nine unidentified members happened to belong *en bloc* to this category.

The composition of the BJP National Executive between 1980–91 seems to be slightly more balanced: the over-representation of the upper castes eroded, while the number of low-caste members marginally increased. In any case, Brahmins and Banias continued to make up about one-third of the total members.

TABLE 1.1:   Social Profile of the Jana Sangh Working Committee and BJP National Executive

Caste Groups and Communities	Jana Sangh Working Comittee (1954–67 & 1972–7)	BJP National Executive (1980–91)	BJP National Executive (1993–5)*
Upper Castes	78 (74.2)	57 (58.2)	57 (56.4)
Brahmin	35 (33.3)	23 (23.5)	26 (25.7)
Rajput	7 (7)	7 (7.1)	4 (3.9)
Bania/Jain	11 (10.5)	11 (11.2)	13 (12.8)
Khattri	14 (13.5)	8 (8.1)	8 (7.9)
Kayasth	9 (8.5)	5 (5.1)	4 (3.9)
Sindhi	2 (1.9)**	3 (3)**	2 (2)**
Intermediate Castes	10 (9.5)	9 (9.2)	6 (5.9)
Reddy	1 (0.9)	2 (2)	1 (1)
Lingayat	–	2 (2)	1 (1)
Kamma	–	1 (1)	1 (1)
Nair	4 (3.8)	1 (1)	1 (1)
Jat	2 (1.9)	–	–
Maratha	1 (0.9)	–	–
Patidar	2 (1.9)	2 (2)	2 (2)
Other	–	1 (1)	–

(Cont.)

Other Backward Classes	1 (0.9)	8 (8.1)	8 (7.9)
Yadav	1	2 (2)	1 (1)
Lodhi	–	1 (1)	2 (2)
Other	–	5 (5.1)	5 (4.9)
Scheduled Castes	3 (2.8)	5 (5.1)	5 (4.9)
Scheduled Tribes	1 (0.9)	2 (2)	2 (2)
Muslims	–	5 (5.1)	3 (2.9)
Sikhs	1 (0.9)	2 (2)	1 (1)
Unidentified	9 (8.5)	10 (10.2)	20 (19.8)
TOTAL	104 (100)	98 (100)	101 (100)

* The 'special invitees' to the National Executive have not been taken into account.
** Including two Amils.
Note: Percentages are given in parenthesis.

The over-representation of upper-caste leaders has become less pronounced among the Hindu nationalist parliamentary candidates. Obviously, the party tried to project a face more amenable to the OBC voters. However, it did not run after the OBC votes by fielding many more OBC candidates. In Uttar Pradesh, the figure remained the same in 1991 and 1996.

TABLE 1.2: Caste and Community Background of the Candidates in 1991 and 1996 General Elections in Uttar Pradesh (Party-wise)

	Brahmins		Rajputs		OBC		Muslims		SC	
	1996	1991	1996	1991	1996	1991	1996	1991	1996	1991
BJP	19	22	20	13	15	15	0	0	18	20
Con (I)	25	19	13	11	12	10	10	11	18	19
Con (T)	21	–	14	–	5	–	12	–	18	–
SP	2	10	7	10	21	18	14	17	16	18
BSP	2	0	5	0	30	13	23	12	22	37

Source: India Today, 15 May 1996, p. 32.

In Rajasthan, the BJP fielded three Rajputs, three Brahmins, two Banias and only one Jat (the ex-Maharani of Bharatpur).[30] (In addition, four seats were reserved for the Scheduled Castes and

[30] *Frontline*, 12 July 1996, p. 92.

three candidates for the Scheduled Tribes.) In Bihar, before the eleventh general elections, the BJP allotted 11 seats to the upper castes, including six to Brahmins, but it also gave a ticket to 10 OBCs, including, however, five Banias. By contrast, the Congress nominated 19 upper caste candidates, including seven Brahmins. However, it gave 15 seats to the OBCs, including six to Yadavs, and it allotted seven seats to Muslims. In Madhya Pradesh, the BJP fielded more OBC candidates than the Congress-I, 10 as against six. This was in sharp contrast with the situation prevailing in the 1980s, as we shall see below.

While the number of BJP candidates from the OBCs is steadily increasing, the entry of the BJP MPs from this milieu has remained at a lower level than that of the Congress' and Janata Dal's MPs, as Table 1.3 shows.

In 1989 and 1991, the BJP still had at least 50 per cent of its Hindi-belt MPs coming from the upper castes, a percentage significantly higher than that of the Congress and Janata Dal. Though the upper castes' share was substantially eroded in 1996, it still remained very high (41.3 per cent), whereas the OBCs represent only 17.3 per cent of the total. Their percentage is on the rise mainly because of Kurmi and Lodhi MPs.

The exit poll made by the Centre for the Study of Developing Societies for *India Today* after the 1996 general elections confirmed this trend: the upper-castes are still over-represented among the BJP electorate, while the Scheduled Castes and Scheduled Tribes are significantly under-represented. The OBC groups are also under-represented, but to a lesser extent (Table 1.4).

However, the forward-castes' votes polarize in favour of the BJP in Maharashtra, Uttar Pradesh and Bihar, where respectively 50, 64 and 67 per cent of the upper castes preferred this party. The BJP also remains a predominantly urban party since 32 per cent of the urban dwellers voted for it as against 19 per cent of the people from the rural constituencies. If one considers upper-caste graduates living in towns and cities, 52 per cent of this category opted for the BJP in 1996.

While the BJP leaders who favoured 'social engineering' to deal with the rise of the OBC and Dalit politics had little room for manoeuvring because of the conservative attitude of the RSS and even some of the party cadres, they succeeded in questioning the reservations of the Hindu nationalist movement regarding job

TABLE 1.3: Caste-wise Distribution of the Hindi-Belt MPs (Party-wise)

Castes and Communities	1989			1991			1996		
	BJP	Congress	JD	BJP	Congress	JD	BJP	Congress	JD
Upper Castes	33 (51.5)	13 (37.1)	32 (30.5)	47 (54.6)	18 (30)	10 (18.9)	53 (43.8)	10 (29.4)	3 (12)
Brahmin	13 (20.3)	6 (17.4)	8 (7.6)	25 (29)	7 (11.6)	2 (3.7)	24 (19.8)	6 (17.6)	1 (4)
Rajput	10 (15.6)	3 (8.6)	18 (17.14)	16 (18.6)	4 (6.6)	8 (15)	18 (14.9)	2 (5.8)	2 (8)
Bhumihar	0 –	1 (2.8)	2 (1.9)	0 –	2 (3.3)	0 –	1 (0.8)	0 –	0 –
Bania/Jain	4 (6.3)	2 (5.7)	1 (0.9)	2 (2.3)	2 (3.3)	0 –	6 (5)	2 (5.8)	0 –
Kayasth	2 (3.1)	0 –	3 (2.8)	2 (2.3)	2 (3.3)	0 –	2 (1.6)	0 –	0 –
Other*	4 (6)	1 (2.8)	1 (0.9)	2 (2.3)	1 (1.6)	0 –	2 (1.6)	0 –	0 –
Intermediate Castes	1 (1.5)	3** (8.6)	13 (12.4)	4 (4.65)	8 (13.3)	1 (1.9)	7 (5.8)	6 (17.6)	0 –
Jat	0 –	1 (2.8)	13 (12.4)	3 (3.5)	7 (11.6)	1 (1.9)	6 (5)	6 (17.6)	0 –

(Cont.)

	1989			1991			1996		
Castes and Communities	BJP	Congress	JD	BJP	Congress	JD	BJP	Congress	JD
Maratha	1 (1.5)	1 (2.8)	0 –	1 (1.15)	1 (1.6)	0 –	1 (0.8)	0 –	0 –
OBC	10 (15.6)	2 (5.71)	28 (26.5)	13 (15.1)	8 (13.3)	21 (39.6)	21 (17.3)	2 (5.8)	14 (56)
Yadav	1 (1.5)	1 (2.8)	17 (16.2)	0 –	1 (1.6)	12 (22.6)	2 (1.6)	0 –	11 (44)
Kurmi	5 (7.8)	1 (2.8)	6 (5.7)	8 (9.3)	3 (5)	7 (13.2)	9 (7.4)	0 –	2 (8)
Lodhi	2 (3.1)	0 –	1 (0.9)	3 (3.5)	0 –	0 –	4 (3.3)	0 –	0 –
Other	2 (3.1)	0 –	4 (3.6)	2 (2.3)	4 (6.5)	2 (3.6)	6 (4.9)	2 (5.8)	1 (4)
SC	11 (17.2)	7 (20)	20 (19)	15 (17.4)	10 (16.6)	13 (24.5)	27 (22.3)	5 (14.7)	4 (16)
ST	11 (9.4)	7 (20)	2 (1.9)	3 (3.5)	11 (18.3)	0 –	9 (7.4)	6 (17.6)	0 –
Muslim	1 (1.5)	2 (5.7)	8 (7.6)	0 –	3 (5)	7 (13.2)	0 –	2 (5.8)	3 12

(*Cont.*)

Sikh	1 (1.5)	0 –	0 –	1 (1.2)	0 –	0 –	1 (0.8)	0 –	0 –
Christian	0 –	1 (2.8)	0 –	0 –	0 –	1 (1.8)	0 –	0 –	1 (4)
Sadhu	0 –	0 –	0 –	2 (2.3)	0 –	0 –	0 –	0 –	0 –
Unidentified	1 (1.5)	0 –	1 (0.9)	1 (1.2)	2 (3.3)	0 –	3 (2.5)	2 (5.8)	1 (4)
TOTAL	64 (100)	35 (100)	105 (100)	86 (100)	60 (100)	53 (100)	121 (100)	34 (100)	25 (100)

Sources: Who's who in Lok Sabha for 1989, 1991 and 1996.

* Khattri, Amil, Tyagi.

** One Bishnoi must be added to Jats and Marathas.

Note: Percentages are given in parenthesis.

quotas for the OBCs and a slight increase in the number of the non-élite party candidates and MPs is noticeable.[31] However, one might wonder who these OBC figures of the BJP are and also what, besides these isolated figures, is the situation of the non-élite groups within the party. To find answers to these questions, our overview of the national scene needs to be supplemented by a regional study.

TABLE 1.4:   Caste Background of the Parties' Electorates

	Cong (I)	BJP	NF/LF	BSP	State Parties	Others
Forward	29	33	17	1	10	10
OBC	25	23	25	2	18	7
SC	31	11	21	16	14	7
ST	47	17	15	2	7	12

Source: India Today, 31 May 1996, p. 27.

THE BJP AND THE EMERGENCE OF NON-ÉLITE GROUPS IN MADHYA PRADESH POLITICS

In the late 1980s, a systematic survey edited by F. Frankel and M. S. A. Rao on 'the decline of a social order' (a phrase used as the sub-title of the book in reference to the caste system) almost eluded Madhya Pradesh—and rightly so because in this state the old 'social order' had shown a strong resilience. In particular, the OBCs had not emerged as a significant force in political terms. One of the appendixes of the first volume of this book showed that in 1984 Madhya Pradesh had the lowest proportion of MPs from this category, namely 5 per cent.[32] This figure reflected the low level of mobilization of this group.

[31] When Vajpayee formed his 13-day long government after the 1996 election, he made a point to include in it representatives of different social groups: one member of the Scheduled Castes, Suraj Bhan, one of the Scheduled Tribes, Karia Munda, one Muslim, Sikander Bakht, one Sikh, Sartaj Singh, one woman, Sushma Swaraj and one person from the south, Dhananjaya Kumar. Besides, the BJP nominated Suraj Bhan to the post of Deputy Speaker of the Lok Sabha, and he was duly elected. However, the OBCs were not represented.
[32] Frankel, F., and M. S. A. Rao (eds), Dominance and State Power in Modern India (Delhi: Oxford University Press, 1989), p. 422.

In contrast to the situation prevailing in the neighbouring states of Uttar Pradesh and Bihar, the OBCs of Madhya Pradesh have no tradition of political organization and mobilization. Undoubtedly, their fragmentation stunted feelings of caste solidarity. As is clear from Table 1.5, with the exception of the Ahirs (Yadavs), none of the OBCs represent more than 5 per cent of the state population.[33] The regional contrasts were also very significant, none of these castes being evenly spread over the whole state: while Ahirs accounted for more than 5 per cent of the population in Chhattisgarh and Vindhya Pradesh, they were weak in Madhya Bharat; while the Telis were the largest caste in Chhattisgarh, they accounted for less than 3 per cent of the population in other regions. A similar argument could be applied, although to a lesser extent, to the Kurmis in Vindhya Pradesh and to the Lodhis in Mahakoshal.[34]

The weakness of the OBCs also stems naturally from the weight of the upper castes: in Madhya Bharat and Vindhya Pradesh, the 'twice-borns' and Kayasths represent about one-fifth of the population. Their strength does not rely on this demographic advantage alone. In fact the domination of Rajputs was especially maintained to a greater extent in Madhya Pradesh because of the large number of former princely states: there were 35 in Vindhya Pradesh, 25 in Madhya Bharat and a dozen in Chhattisgarh. Rajahs and Maharajahs (sometimes with a Maratha background in the western part of the state) headed networks of Rajput *zamindars* and *jagirdars*. In Madhya Bharat and Vindhya Pradesh demographic weight and socio-political domination are concomitant: Rajputs represent, for instance the largest caste in Madhya Bharat with more than 9 per cent of the regional population. Besides, by contrast with Uttar Pradesh and Rajasthan where Jats can be recognized as the dominant caste in several places, in Madhya Pradesh the intermediate (or middle) castes who could have acted as the spearhead of anti-establishment movements are neither

[33] These figures draw from the 1931 census as castes have not been as meticulously enumerated, since then, except the Scheduled Castes.

[34] The fragmentation is also linguistic since Madhya Pradesh 'speaks' many dialects. That might not have been an obstacle for the educated élite but it certainly hindered the interactions between members of the few OBCs which are spread over the whole state.

TABLE 1.5: Caste Groups and Communities of Madhya Pradesh (based on the census of 1931)

Category	Madhya Bharat*	MB%	Vindhya	VP%	Mahakoshal	MK%	Chhattisgarh	Chhatt%	MP	MP%
Upper Castes	13,25,105	18.50	6,43,467	21.67	6,17,028	11.69	2,02,330	3.25	27,87,930	12.88
Brahmin	4,69,264	6.55	4,11,404	13.85	2,41,142	4.57	1,03,924	1.67	12,25,734	5.66
Rajput	6,48,197	9.05	1,39,837	4.71	2,97,663	5.64	58,553	0.94	11,44,250	5.29
Bania	1,58,994	2.22	68,301	2.30	52,982	1.00	30,704	0.49	3,10,981	1.44
Kayasth	48,650	0.68	23,925	0.81	25,241	0.48	9,149	0.15	1,06,965	0.49
Intermediary Castes	62,305	0.87	10,026	0.34	1,56,335	2.96	10,473	0.17	2,39,139	1.11
Maratha	30,116	0.42	32	–	30,160	0.57	6,846	0.11	67,154	0.31
Kunbi	32,189	0.45	9,994	0.34	1,26,175	2.39	3,627	0.06	1,71,985	0.80
OBCs	26,70,639	37.30	12,26,646	41.03	19,14,249	39.64	3,13,55,715	50.34	90,66,636	41.44
Jat	52,550	0.73	146	–	–	–	–	–	24,707	0.11
Ahir	1,88,712	2.63	1,80,082	6.06	2,52,944	4.79	5,23,012	8.40	11,44,750	5.29
Kurmi	1,14,245	1.60	1,41,147	4.75	1,36,384	2.58	1,79,284	2.88	5,71,070	2.64
Gujari	2,06,136	2.88	1,045	0.04	57,762	1.09	1,088	0.02	2,66,031	1.23
Lodhi	1,46,567	2.04	80,243	2.70	2,30,573	4.37	58,736	0.94	51,61,119	2.25
Kachhi	2,32,967	3.25	1,80,421	6.08	–	–	–	–	4,13,388	1.91
Kirar	1,08,623	1.52	2,601	0.09	–	–	–	–	1,11,224	0.51
Gadaria	1,33,674	1.87	63,004	2.12	–	–	–	–	1,96,678	0.91
Kumhar	1,12,765	1.57	51,606	1.74	46,582	0.88	46,475	0.75	2,57,428	1.19
Mali	73,391	1.02	3,547	0.12	1,19,694	2.27	1,78,070	2.88	3,74,702	1.73
Teli	1,11,911	1.56	85,790	2.90	1,22,740	2.30	5,82,098	9.35	9,02,539	4.02
Bairagi	49,171	0.69	1,154	0.04	7,883	0.15	27,706	0.44	2,33,290	0.93
Khati	1,12,810	1.58	0	0	–	–	–	–	1,12,810	0.52

(Cont.)

Lohar, Luhar	56,445	0.79	44,494	1.50	66,737	1.26	66,505	1.07	2,34,181	1.08
Nai	99,967	1.40	52,474	1.76	65,475	1.24	49,932	0.80	2,67,848	1.24
Bhoi, Dhimar,										
Kahar	81,337	1.14	86,846	2.92	1,39,601	2.64	49,304	0.79	3,57,088	1.65
Sondhya	78,840	1.10	3	0.00	–	–	–	–	78,843	0.36
Dangi	38,898	0.54	6,166	0.21	–	–	–	–	45,064	0.21
Deswali	21,001	0.30	3	0.00	–	–	–	–	21,004	0.10
Dhakad	65,228	0.91	27	0.00	–	–	–	–	65,255	0.30
Darzi	41,014	0.57	15,446	0.52	20,903	0.40	4,015	0.06	81,378	0.38
Sutar, Barhai	40,220	0.56	28,180	0.95	42,222	0.80	1,473	0.02	1,12,095	0.52
Sonar, Sunar	44,119	0.62	26,096	0.88	52,075	0.99	22,086	0.35	1,44,376	0.67
Dhobi	64,402	0.90	31,898	1.07	49,945	0.95	84,090	1.35	2,30,335	1.06
Mankad	22,109	0.31	0	0.00	–	–	–	–	22,109	0.10
Banjara	61,828	0.86	54	0.00	25,755	0.49	14,895	0.24	1,02,532	0.47
Barai, Tamboli	14,046	0.20	13,547	0.46	–	–	–	–	27,593	0.13
Kotwai	8,289	0.12	20,282	0.68	–	–	–	–	28,571	0.13
Kalal	33,461	0.47	29,721	1.00	–	–	–	–	63,182	0.29
Khangar	20,202	0.28	16,378	0.55	11,695	0.22	–	–	48,275	0.22
Kalar	–	–	–	–	56,362	1.07	94,472	1.52	1,50,834	0.70
Panka	–	–	–	–	–	–	1,99,838	30.21	1,99,838	0.91
Kewat	–	–	–	–	–	–	1,81,806	2.92	1,81,806	0.84
Others	2,35,711	3.29	64,235	2.16	4,08,917	11.15	7,70,830	12.37	14,79,693	6.84
SCs	11,94,296	16.68	4,36,498	14.70	6,28,313	11.90	7,81,117	12.54	30,40,224	14.05
Chamar	6,44,731	9.00	3,13,160	10.55	6,28,313	11.90	7,81,117	4.93	15,10,577	6.98
Koli, Koshti*	1,11,541	1.56	66,313	2.23	–	–	57,805	0.93	2,35,659	1.09
Balai	2,89,022	4.04	74	0.00	–	–	–	–	2,89,096	1.34
Bhangi	29,328	0.41	9,199	0.31	–	–	–	–	38,527	0.18

(Cont.)

Category	Madhya Bharat*	MB%	Vindhya	VP%	Mahakoshal	MK%	Chhattisgarh	Chhatt%	MP	MP%
Satnami	–	–	–	–	–	–	3,51,165	5.64	3,51,165	1.62
Others	1,19,674	1.67	47,752	1.61	–	–	65,097	1.05	2,32,523	1.07
STs	9,06,659	13.10	4,29,841	14.48	13,23,000	25.06	19,77,000	31.74	46,36,500	21.62
Bhil	4,52,346	6.32	1,639	0.06	–	–	–	–	4,53,985	2.10
Bhilala	2,32,230	–	0	–	–	–	–	–	2,32,230	1.07
Mina	95,389	1.33	397	0.01	–	–	–	–	95,786	0.44
Sahariya	79,749	1.11	888	0.03	–	–	–	–	80,637	0.37
Gond	59,331	0.83	2,21,466	7.46	9,98,958	18.92	8,96,560	14.39	21,76,315	10.06
Patlia	19,408	0.27	–	–	–	–	10,80,440	17035	10,99,848	5.08
Jains**	83,082	1.16	11,062	0.37	44,526	0.84	5,145	0.08	1,43,815	0.66
Muslims	4,52,844	6.91	78,323	2.64	2,33,393	4.42	69,258	1.11	8,33,818	3.85
Pathan	1,16,367	1.62	25,051	0.84	–	–	–	–	–	–
Shaikh	1,36,298	1.90	26,164	0.88	–	–	–	–	–	–
Sikhs	1,214	0.02	200	–	2,128	0.04	–	–	3,542	0.02
Christians	9,576	0.13	631	0.02	–	–	1,138	0.02	11,345	0.05
Others	–	0.57	–	–	–	–	4,67,383	0.75	46,783	0.22
TOTAL 1	65,58,117	94.67	27,58,371	95.52	49,18,972	96.55	62,28,959	100	2,04,64,419	91.10
Others	6,03,784	40.76	2,72,293	4.48	4,31,327	3.45	–	–	13,07,404	4.10
TOTAL 2	71,61,901	100	29,69,437	100	5,27,96,347	100	62,28,959	100	2,16,39,931	100

* Includes Datia state which belongs to the same region but was administered by the Central India Agency before Independence.

** Not included in the ground total since they appear elsewhere as Banias.

numerous nor large enough: the Marathas represent an almost negligible quantity and many of them belong to the élite of the princely states whose ruling families have come from the same milieu; they tend, therefore, to emulate the Rajputs.[35]

This sociological context partly explains the comparatively small number of the OBCs among the state deputies. In the state legislature, the OBCs did not represent more than 15 per cent of the MLAs before the 1980 elections, while the upper castes, for the first time, accounted for less than 50 per cent of the assembly (see Table 1.6). However, since the 1980s, and especially the early 1990s, the Congress and the BSP stimulated and exploited the growing mobilization of the OBCs, Dalits and Scheduled Tribes.

The OBCs' Growing Mobilization and the Congress' Tactics Before the 1993 Elections

In 1981, Arjun Singh, the then Chief Minister, appointed a Commission named after its Chairman, Ramji Mahajan, a former state minister, to identify the needs of the OBCs in the state. Madhya Pradesh was then the only big state, along with West Bengal, 'which ha[d] never prepared a list of the OBCs or taken any separate action for their upliftment.'[36] The Mahajan Commission report was submitted in late 1983. It identified 80 OBCs (out of which 24 were Muslim) which represented 48.08 per cent of the state's population. The report recommended the reservation of 35 per cent of the posts in the state administration for the OBCs.[37] The Arjun Singh government implemented one recommendation regarding the quotas for the OBCs in the technical colleges and the granting of scholarships from fifth class to the higher classes, but the former point was challenged before the courts which issued a stay order.[38]

---

[35] This kshatriyaization process was well illustrated by several marital alliances, such as the wedding of Jivaji Rao Scindia with Vijaya Raje Scindia.

[36] Mandal, B. P., *Report of the Backward Classes Commission* (New Delhi: Government of India, 1980), First Part, p. 11.

[37] See *Madhya Pradesh Rajya Picchra Varg Ayog—Antim Prativedan*, Bhopal, 1983.

[38] Interview with Ramji Mahajan, 19 Feb. 1994, Bhopal.

TABLE 1.6: Social Profile of the Madhya Pradesh Vidhan Sabha (1952–80)

Caste Groups and Communities	In the State Population	1952*	1957	1962	1967	1972	1977	1980
Forward Castes	9.9 M (18.69)	216 (63.6)	167 (57.9)	149 (51.7)	163 (54.6)	159 (53.8)	166 (51.6)	144 (44.9)
Backward Castes	25.7 M (48.08)	21 (6.1)	17 (6)	26 (9)	22 (7.4)	30 (10.1)	43 (13.4)	51 (16)
Scheduled Castes	6.9 M (13.09)	51 (15)	45 (15.6)	46 (16)	43 (15)	38 (11.8)	45 (14.4)	46 (14.4)
Scheduled Tribes	10.7 M (20.14)	52 (15.3)	59 (20.5)	67 (23.3)	68 (23)	69 (23.3)	66 (20.6)	79 (24.7)
TOTAL	53.2 M (100)	340 (100)	288 (100)	288 (100)	296 (100)	296 (100)	320 (100)	320 (100)

Source: Ramji Mahajan, *Madhya Pradesh Rajya Pichra Varg Ayog–Antim Prativedan*, Bhopal, December 1983, p. 193.

* The figures of this column are probably based on the Assemblies of the old Madhya Pradesh, Madhya Bharat, Vindhya Pradesh and Bhopal state.

Note: Percentages are given in parenthesis.

The Sangh Parivar 47

In late 1992, R. Mahajan challenged Sunderlal Patwa, the BJP Chief Minister, to call for a discussion of his report.[39] During the election campaign of 1993, Madhavrao Scindia and Arjun Singh demanded its implementation and the Congress-I took full credit for implementing the Mandal recommendations. The Congress-I stimulated this emerging consciousness as well as drew electoral dividends from it. In late 1991, the Sahu Samaj (an association of Telis) of Bhopal district held a convention where the Union Minister of State for Finance, S. Potolukhe, declared that the association was in favour of complete implementation of the Mandal Commission Report.[40] In early 1992, the ninth annual conference of the Sahu Sangh of Raipur district was inaugurated by the Minister of State for Cooperation, Kriparam Sahu, who stressed 'the need for tightening the grip of the Sahu community on politics' and declared that the number of MPs and MLAs from the community should be increased.[41] Besides, Telis and Kurmis also mobilized increasingly in the early 1990s, especially during the election campaigns. In November 1993, the Kurmis of Hoshangabad division held a large convention and then made it known that candidates from their section should be given due weight in the allocation of electoral tickets.[42]

In the 1993 elections the Congress-I nominated a large number of the OBCs: as many as 70 tickets—a record—were given to them. The Scheduled Tribes and Scheduled Castes were given their due share, respectively 74 and 45 tickets. Brahmins received 57, Rajputs 39, Banias 16 (if Jains are included in this category) and Kayasths four (see Table 1.7).[43] The Congress strategy towards the OBCs caused additional damage to the BJP. The party won only 117 of the 320 seats compared to the 219 which it had obtained in 1990.

[39] *Statesman* (Delhi), 1 Dec. 1992.
[40] Ibid., 23 Dec. 1991.
[41] Ibid., 5 Jan. 1992.
[42] Ibid., 19 Nov. 1993.
[43] I could only interview a small minority of these candidates. These figures are based on field work at the district and state headquarters of the Congress party. Those concerning the BJP were collected the same way but I have interviewed a much larger number of candidates.

48   CHRISTOPHE JAFFRELOT

TABLE 1.7:   Caste-wise Distribution of the Congress and BJP Candidates
in the 1993 Assembly Elections in Madhya Pradesh

Caste Groups and Communities	Congress		BJP	
Upper Castes	117	(36.8)	129	(40.3)
Brahmin	57		53	
Rajput	39		27	
Bania/Jain	16		44	
Kayasth	4		3	
Khattri	1		2	
Intermediated Castes	4	(1.2)	1	(0.3)
Other Backward Classes	70	(22)	67	(21)
Scheduled Castes	45	(14.1)	44	(13.8)
Scheduled Tribes	74	(23.2)	75	(23.4)
Muslims	6	(1.8)	1	(0.3)
Unidentified	2	(0.6)	3	(0.9)
TOTAL	318	(100)	320	(100)

Note: Percentages are given in parenthesis.

The BJP in Madhya Pradesh—Still an Upper-Caste Party

The BJP did not react very efficiently to the Congress' tactical use of the 'OBC card'. In October 1993, Patwa announced that if his party was returned to power it would ensure early implementation of the Mandal Commission Report but continued to reject the Mahajan Commission's recommendations for the state. However, the BJP nominated nearly as many OBC candidates as the Congress-I. Out of the 317 candidates whose caste or tribe could be identified, as well as 44 Scheduled Caste members and 75 Scheduled Tribe members, we find 53 Brahmins, 27 Rajputs, 33 Banias, 11 Jains, two Khattris, three Kayasths, one Maratha and 67 OBCs. Yet, the BJP candidates from the latter category did not attract much support from the voters belonging to the same milieu: only 21 and 16 candidates from the OBCs and the Scheduled Tribes were elected respectively in 1993, as against 42 from the upper castes (including 22 Brahmins) (see Table 1.8). According to press reports, of a total of 171 Congress MLAs whose social background has been identified, 125 belonged to the

TABLE 1.8 Caste Background of the MLA from the Jana Sangh and BJP in Madhya Pradesh (1952–93)

Castes and Communities	1952	1957	1962	1967	1972	1977	1980	1985	1990	1993
Upper castes	4 (80)	7 (70)	14 (37.8)	35 (47.9)	25 (49)	67 (56.8)	22 (40)	22 (39.9)	79 (36.2)	49 (43)
Brahmin	2 (40)	1 (10)	7 (18.9)	14 (19.1)	7 (13.7)	32 (27.1)	8 (14.5)	11 (20)	31 (14.2)	22 (19.2)
Rajput	–	1 (10)	3 (8.1)	7 (9.5)	10 (19.6)	8 (6.7)	3 (5.4)	4 (7.2)	17 (7.8)	10 (8.7)
Bania/Jain	2 (40)	5 (50)	4 (10.8)	9 (12.3)	4 (7.8)	20 (16.9)	8 (14.4)	7 (12.6)	24 (10.9)	14 (12.3)
Kayasth	–	–	–	4 (5.4)	4 (7.8)	4 (3.3)	1 (1.8)	–	3 (1.3)	1 (0.9)
Khattri	–	–	–	–	–	2 (1.7)	1 (1.8)	–	1 (0.4)	1 (0.9)
Sindhi	–	–	–	1 (1.3)	–	1 (0.8)	1 (1.8)	–	2 (0.9)	1 (0.9)
Middle castes	–	–	2 (5.4)	–	–	2 (1.7)	1 (1.8)	–	–	1 (0.8)
Maratha	–	–	2 (5.4)	–	–	2 (1.7)	1 (1.8)	–	–	1 (0.8)
Other Backward Classes	–	2 (20)	3 (8.1)	9 (12.3)	8 (15.6)	11 (9.1)	10 (16.2)	15 (27.2)	48 (21.7)	21 (18.4)
Jat	–	–	–	–	–	1 (0.8)	1 (1.8)	–	1 (0.4)	1 (0.9)
Yadav	–	–	–	–	1 (1.9)	1 (0.8)	1 (1.8)	1 (1.8)	5 (2.3)	3 (2.7)
Kurmi	–	1 (10)	–	2 (2.7)	1 (1.9)	3 (2.5)	2 (3.6)	3 (5.4)	8 (3.6)	3 (2.7)
Teli	–	–	–	2 (2.7)	1 (1.9)	–	1 (1.8)	3 (5.4)	5 (2.3)	1 (0.9)
Kirar	–	–	–	1 (1.3)	1 (1.9)	2 (1.7)	1 (1.8)	–	4 (1.8)	2 (1.8)
Panwar	–	–	–	–	1 (1.9)	1 (0.8)	3 (5.4)	–	5 (2.3)	2 (1.8)
Gujar	–	–	1 (2.7)	2 (2.7)	2 (3.9)	–	1 (1.8)	–	–	–

(Cont.)

Castes and Communities	1952	1957	1962	1967	1972	1977	1980	1985	1990	1993
Raghuwanshi	–	–	–	1 (1.3)	–	–	–	–	3 (1.3)	–
Pokhal	–	–	–	–	–	–	–	–	1 (0.4)	–
Others	–	–	2 (5.4)	1 (1.3)	1 (1.9)	3 (2.5)	–	8 (14.5)	16 (7.3)	9 (8.1)
Scheduled Castes	1 (20)	1 (10)	8 (21.6)	16 (21.9)	8 (15.6)	20 (16.9)	12 (21.8)	7 (12.7)	36 (16.5)	27 (23.6)
Scheduled Tribes	–	1 (10)	9 (24.3)	13 (17.8)	11 (21.5)	17 (14.4)	10 (18)	10 (18.1)	53 (24.3)	16 (14)
Muslims	–	–	–	–	–	–	–	1 (1.8)	2 (0.9)	–
Sikhs	–	–	–	–	–	1 (0.8)	–	–	1 (0.4)	–
TOTAL	5 (6) (100)	10 (10) (100)	37 (41) (100)	73 (78) (100)	51 (51*) (100)	118	55 (60) (100)	55 (58) (100)	218 (219) (100)	114 (117) (100)

* The Jana Sangh had won only 48 seats in 1972 but the party succeeded in winning three more seats in subsequent by-elections.
NB: I have not been able to identify the caste of some MLAs; the last line indicates the total number of those whose caste was known and the total of MLAs in parenthesis.
Note: Percentages are given in parenthesis.

Scheduled Castes, Scheduled Tribes and the OBCs, while 19 were
Rajputs, and 19 Brahmins.[44] The Tribals alone accounted for 53
and the Scheduled Castes for 16, which means that 56 of the 171
identified MLAs were from the OBCs and eight upper-castes MLAs
from the Bania or other élite groups. The comparison between the
MLAs from the BJP and the Congress therefore shows that, while
both parties fielded almost the same number of candidates from
the Scheduled Tribes and the OBCs, the Congress succeeded in
having many more MLAs returned from these categories. The large
number of BJP-MLAs from the Scheduled Castes (27) cannot be
easily interpreted because in contrast to the situation prevailing in
most of the constituencies reserved for the Scheduled Tribes, in
these constituencies the Scheduled Castes never represent the
majority of the voters, not even a substantial number of them. The
main question, therefore, concerns the difficulties of the BJP in its
efforts to attract voters from the Scheduled Tribes and the OBCs.

The inability of the BJP to retain the tribal votes[45] can be
explained. First, the BJP government interfered with the right, till
then granted to the tribals, to produce up to five litres of liquor
for their domestic consumption. According to the new rules the
traders alone were allowed to provide this alcohol. Secondly, the
policy of the BJP government towards the *tendu*-leaf gatherers—
mainly tribals—affected their wages. In 1990, the BJP government
handed over the post-harvest operations to private traders who had
strongly resented the cooperative scheme introduced by Arjun
Singh in the 1980s. Apparently, Patwa 'bowed to the tendu
lobby'[46] and especially to a cartel of about 20 trading families
among which L. Aggarwal, the State BJP President, was prominent. The fact that the gatherers were given up to about Rs 1000
per head in certain districts as bonus during the President's rule,
was even more damaging for the BJP since such a decision was
associated with the Congress-I administration. The difficulties the
BJP met in getting OBC MLAs returned is more difficult to
understand.

[44] *Times of India*, 8 Dec. 1993.

[45] In 1990, the BJP had won 54 of the 75 seats reserved for the Scheduled Tribes;
in 1993, it secured only 16 such seats. By contrast, according to the CSDS Data
unit, the Congress-I won in 60 constituencies where the tribals account for more
than 30 per cent of the population (out of 84 such constituencies). I am grateful
to Yogendra Yadav, from the CSDS, for these figures.

[46] Singh, N.K., 'A New Leaf', *India Today*, 15 Feb. 1991, p. 58.

While the proportion of the OBC candidates fielded by the BJP for the assembly elections increased, the proportion of the party's MLAs from these castes fell from 27.2 per cent in 1985 to 18.4 per cent in 1993. At the same time, the proportion of upper-caste MLAs in the BJP's assembly party slightly increased from 39.9 per cent to 43 per cent (see Table 1.8). This apparent contradiction reflects the fact that the BJP fielded more OBC candidates in constituencies where it was still weak. It is also a sign that the party remained identified with the upper castes although it had nominated more OBC candidates.

THE SANSKRITIZED ETHOS OF THE NON-UPPER CASTE BJP WORKERS

The OBC candidates from the BJP are not projected as Backward Caste leaders. This is largely due to the Hindu nationalist ideology: the RSS and its offshoots insist on the need to put the emphasis on the Hindu sense of belonging to an organic community, the 'Hindu nation' [rashtra], rather than to any particular castes. The RSS relied on the attractiveness of the Hindu 'high tradition' over members of the low castes, as shown by its use of the notion of samskars. And in fact many low caste swayamsevaks have joined the movement as part of a desire for sanskritization:[47] their aim was to emulate high-caste behaviour patterns and they continued to stick to this ethos rather than to show pride in their low extraction. According to Uma Bharti, herself a Lodhi from Vindhya Pradesh, the acceptance of such an outlook has given low-caste leaders of the BJP a 'Brahmin's mentality'. She even complains that 'BJP-OBC candidates have an upper-caste mentality. They do not show their caste.'[48]

This attitude was especially clear in the case of the few Scheduled Caste deputies from the BJP, with an RSS background, whom I

[47] This observation which was suggested by my field work in Madhya Pradesh probably applies to the whole Hindi belt. In their book, Andersen and Damle convincingly attribute the appeal of the RSS to the low castes of north India in part to the process of sanskritization (Andersen, W. and S. Damle, *The Brotherhood in Saffron* (New Delhi: Vistaar, 1987, pp 45, 102). See also, about the vote of some untouchables in favour of the Jana Sangh in Delhi, Andersen, W. and M. K. Saini, 'The Basti Julahan By-election', *Indian Journal of Political Science*, 30, July–Sept. 1969, pp 260–76.

[48] Interview with Uma Bharti, New Delhi, 12 Feb. 1994.

was able to interview. Satyanarayan Jatiya, who has been elected five times MP from Ujjain since 1980 and became Union Minister in 1998, joined the RSS in his childhood and became imbued with its ideology to a great extent. He stressed that he had been determined to learn Sanskrit and that he belonged to associations of sankritists.[49] In 1977 in the Vidhan Sabha he took the oath in Sanskrit. He fully subscribes to the Hindu nationalist reinterpretation of the varnas by ideologues such as D. Upadhyaya and M. S. Golwalkar. During an interview conducted soon after the 'Mandal affair' he argued that:

Varna vyavastha was the *vyavastha* in which there was no difference between men. It was the arrangement of the society in which some people will do this job and this group this job. But at a latter stage it became rigid. So this is the evil of the society that should be removed.[50]

Another prominent Scheduled Caste MP with an RSS background, Phool Chand Verma, returned four times from Shajapur, showed a similar sense of sankritization. When I met him in 1992 he had just lost his father and was strictly observing the ritual shaving and the period of seclusion, a typically upper caste observance. Undoubtedly, these Scheduled-Caste leaders owed their electoral success to the non-Dalit voters to a large extent.
. Many OBC leaders from the 'Sangh Parivar' displayed similar attitudes and downplayed their social origin, even after the 'Mandal affair'. Right from the pre-Independence period, the RSS *pracharaks* recruited swayamsevaks who were not from the high castes largely on the basis of the sanskritization process. A darzi, for instance, joined in 1943 because he was impressed by the pracharaks' austerity. He even compared them to *gurus* because of their determination to endure hunger and thirst for the benefit of their work. This man clearly sought a closer rapprochement with the high castes through the RSS as suggested by the fact that he became involved in a caste association designed to grant the status of kshatriyas to darzis.[51] Similar attitudes are visible today among the young generation of BJP leaders. Prahlad Singh Patel (elected in Seoni), a Lodhi who at 29 became the youngest MP of Madhya Pradesh in 1989, was especially well known for his quasi-brahminical

[49] He is the Secretary of the Sansadiya Sanskrit Parishad based in Delhi.
[50] Interview with Jatiya, 3 Dec. 1990, Ujjain.
[51] Interview with Govind Ram Tailor, 15 Oct. 1991, Mandsaur.

campaign in favour of temperance.[52] However, he went to jail in 1995, apparently because of his use of some muscle power.

As a rule, the BJP leaders from the OBC refrained from appearing as spokesmen for their social milieu. They were even reluctant to indicate their caste. Bherulal Patidar, a prominent minister in Patwa's government and the Deputy Speaker of the Vidhan Sabha since 1993, did not easily acknowledge that he was a Kurmi.[53] Similarly Babulal Gaur, another prominent minister in the BJP government between 1990 and 1992, said that he was an Ahir and not a Yadav (the term used by the most militant members of this caste in the Hindi belt), and he stressed the special relationship that this caste of herdsmen entertained with Krishna;[54] for him, the Krishna cult was obviously a means to integrate into the high tradition of Hinduism. A similar attitude was displayed by the head of the state Pichre Varg Morcha (the Backward Classes Front of the BJP in Madhya Pradesh), Babulal Bhanpur. He emphasized the fact that his caste people, Kushwaha (or Kachhi), were descendants of Kush, one of Sita's sons. The emphasis he put on this aspect of the myth of Ram was also a reflection of his effort to be integrated into the high tradition of Hinduism.[55] Both men, Bhanpur and Gaur expressed reservations about the introduction of quotas in favour of the OBCs. The latter followed the line defined by the high command against caste-based reservations when he declared, soon after the Mandal agitation: 'Unconditional system is bad for our nation. We don't want to divide our society. We want to unite our society [...] If we divide our society, our nation will go to hell.' Bhanpur, whose organization was not terribly active, gave similar arguments.[56]

The Madhya Pradesh BJP certainly has a vocal OBC leader in Uma Bharti but she has never been fully accepted by the party chiefs in the state. She did not enter the Sangh Parivar through the Rashtrasevika Samiti, but was introduced into the Hindu nationalist movement by Vijaya Raje Scindia, via the Vishva Hindu Parishad. In addition, women have never played a prominent role

---

[52] Interview with P. S. Patel, 21 Aug. 1992, Bhopal.
[53] Interview with B. Patidar, 17 Feb. 1994, Bhopal.
[54] Interview with Babulal Gaur, 17 Nov. 1990, Bhopal.
[55] Interview with Babulal Bhanpur, 13 Nov. 1990, Bhopal.
[56] The obviously lucrative occupation of Bhanpur in the management of a prosperous marketing society suggests that he worked less with peasants and more with merchants.

within the overwhelmingly masculine party that is the BJP. Rajmata Scindia stands as an exception because of her princely status and also because she was largely introduced to Hindu nationalism by S. Angre, her private secretary. More importantly, Uma Bharti always showed an independent style, shaped in the VHP mould and based on a rhetoric of extremism. While the BJP seeks publicity, till recently it valued discipline more than anything else. As a result, the state-party leaders never gave big responsibilities to Uma Bharti, who merely became Vice President of the BJP Madhya Pradesh Kisan Morcha (the peasant front of the party in the state) whose president was R. K. Kusmariya a Kurmi and an RSS man, and an MP elected from Damoh in 1991.

In addition to the reluctance of the low-caste BJP leaders to appear as spokesmen for 'their' community, another reason for the party's difficulties in attracting the OBC voters lay in the continuing over-representation of upper-caste people among the BJP cadres.

AN UPPER-CASTE LEADERSHIP

The BJP remained largely identified with the upper castes also because the party apparatus was continuously in the hands of leaders belonging to this section of society, both at the local as well as the state level. As far as the top leaders are concerned, the composition of Patwa's government between 1990–2 is a good indication of the persisting domination of the upper castes. As shown in Table 1.9, out of 31 members, 17 belonged to the upper castes, seven to the OBCs, three to the Scheduled Tribes, two to the Scheduled Castes, and there was one Muslim. By contrast, the government of Digvijay Singh, who succeeded Patwa as the Chief Minister, while it gave a smaller share to the OBCs also reduced the share of the upper castes, and significantly increased that of the Scheduled Tribes. The latter trend was reinforced during the subsequent reshuffles after tribal leaders protested against the upper-caste domination and demanded the nomination of an Adivasi to the post of Chief Minister. In order to defuse these tensions Digvijay Singh inducted four more Tribal leaders in his government as ministers. Tribals were also appointed to the two key posts in the Madhya Pradesh Congress Committee in 1997, as the President and the Working President.

TABLE 1.9: Caste-wise and Community-wise Composition of the BJP Government (1990-2*) and the Congress Governments (1993-6) in Madhya Pradesh

Caste Groups and Communities	BJP 1990-2	Congress 1993-5	Congress 1995-6
Upper Castes	16 (51.6)	13 (36.1)	17 (38.6)
Brahmin	6	5	8
Rajput	2	6	8
Bania/Jain	6	2	1
Khattri	1	0	0
Kayasth	1	0	0
Other Backward Classes	7 (22.5)	7 (19.4)	10 (22.7)
Jat	1	0	–
Ahir	1	3	2
Kurmi	2	1	2
Kirar	1	0	0
Lodhi	1	0	0
Mali	0	1	1
Teli	1	1	1
Panwar	0	0	1
Others	0	1	3
Scheduled Castes	2 (6.4)	3 (8.3)	3 (6.8)
Scheduled Tribes	3 (9.7)	9 (25)	13 (29.5)
Muslim	1 (3)	1 (2.7)	0
Sikh	0	1 (2.7)	1 (2.3)
Christian	0	1 (2.7)	–
Unidentified	2 (6.4)	1 (2.7)	0
TOTAL	31 (100)	36 (100)	44 (100)

* While 23 members were originally sworn-in, their number gradually increased because of several ministerial reshuffles.

Note: Percentages are given in parenthesis.

So far as the party apparatus is concerned, in 1990, out of 41 presidents of the BJP district units, 63.4 per cent belonged to the upper castes and their share grew in 1994 to reach 67.8 per cent. Among them, only 21.9 per cent were OBCs in 1990, and the erosion of their representation left them with only 19.6 per cent of these posts in 1994. The proportion of the tribals increased (from 2.4 per cent to 8.9 per cent) but that of the Scheduled Castes fell from a meagre 2.4 per cent to zero. The Congress figures tended to be similar till recently, when the share of the OBCs, increased significantly at the expense of the upper castes (see Table 1.10). Thus, at the local level the BJP hierarchy was overwhelmingly dominated by upper-caste members, even in the 'Tribal districts'.

In 1990–4, except for Jhabua, in all the districts where the Scheduled Tribes were in a majority, such as Bastar, Mandla and Surguja, the presidents of the BJP district units were Brahmins and Banias. In addition, the tribal leaders of the party were not well integrated, as the tensions between Larang Sai and S. Patwa testified. The former, a senior leader from Surguja district (Chhattisgarh), had been active in the Hindu nationalist party since the 1960s (he won the Assembly seat of Samri in 1967 before becoming an MP in 1977 and in 1989). Sai, who had been the appointed Minister of State in Morarji Desai's government and appeared as the main Tribal leader of the BJP in Madhya Pradesh, accused Patwa's government of 'exploiting the Tribals' in 1992—an oblique reference to the new tendu-leaf policy. The Chief Minister replied vehemently and Sai was suspended from the primary membership of the party. This decision to demote a senior party leader caused many protests and was eventually reversed.[57] Another prominent Tribal leader from the BJP, Baliram Kashyap, an MLA from Bhanpuri since 1972 and Tribal Welfare Minister between 1990–2, often opposed Patwa. In 1993, his son Dineshkumar Kashyap, the outgoing MLA of Jagdalpur (Bastar district), was denied the party ticket; he contested as an Independent.

The atmosphere created by the 'Mandal affair' did not lead either to a substantial promotion of the OBC, ST or SC leaders in the party hierarchy as demonstrated in Table 1.11 which shows the caste-wise and community-wise distribution of the Madhya Pradesh BJP State Executive Committees elected in the 1990s: in 1991 two-thirds of the members belonged to the upper castes while only 14 per cent came from the OBCs, 8 per cent from the Scheduled Tribes and 6 per cent from the Scheduled Castes. Significantly, except one Tribal and one Scheduled Caste member,

---

[57] *National Mail*, 4, 5 and 20 April 1992. In the same vein, in September 1992, a Scheduled Caste MLA, Narayan Singh Keshri, regretted the anti-low-caste attitude of Patwa. He was dismissed from the chairmanship of the Slum Clearance Board.

TABLE 1.10: Presidents of the District units of the Congress and BJP in the 1990 (caste- and community-wise)

Castes and Communities	BJP 1990	BJP 1994*	Congress 1994	Congress 1996	Congress 1997
Upper castes	26 (63.4)	38 (67.8)	32 (61.5)	28 (53.8)	30 (50)
Brahmin	11 (27)	13 (23.2)	16 (30.7)	17 (32.6)	11 (18.3)
Rajput	3 (7.3)	11 (19.6)	7 (13.5)	5 (9.6)	9 (15)
Bania/Jain	8 (19.5)	11 (19.6)	9 (17.3)	6 (11.5)	8 (13.3)
Kayasth	1 (2.4)	3 (5.3)	–	–	–
Khattri	2 (4.8)	–	–	–	2 (3.3)
Sindhi	1 (2.4)	–	–	–	–
Intermediate Castes	–	–	3 (5.7)	3 (5.7)	2 (3.3)
Maratha	–	–	3 (5.7)	3 (5.7)	2 (3.3)
Other Backward Classes	9 (21.7)	11 (19.6)	9 (17.3)	8 (15.4)	16 (26.6)
Teli	1 (2.4)	5 (8.9)	1 (1.9)	1 (1.9)	–
Gujar	2 (4.8)	–	–	–	2 (3.3)
Yadav	1 (2.4)	1 (1.8)	2 (3.8)	1 (1.9)	1 (1.6)
Kirar	1 (2.4)	–	2 (3.8)	1 (1.9)	1 (1.6)
Kurmi	–	3 (5.6)	2 (3.8)	2 (3.8)	1 (1.6)
Panwar	–	–	–	1 (1.9)	2 (3.3)
Others	4 (9.7)	2 (3.6)	2 (3.8)	2 (3.8)	9 (15)
Scheduled Castes	1 (2.4)	–	–	1 (1.9)	2 (3.3)
Scheduled Tribes	1 (2.4)	5 (8.9)	3 (5.7)	4 (7.7)	3 (5)
Sikh	–	1 (1.8)	–	–	–
Muslims	–	–	4 (7.7)	4 (7.7)	6 (10)
Unidentified	4 (9.7)	1 (1.8)	1 (1.9)	4 (7.7)	1 (1.6)
TOTAL	41 (100)	56 (100)	52 (100)	52 (100)	60 (100)

* The figures of this column are based on the updated list that was available in the state BJP office in 1997.
Note: Percentages are given in parenthesis.

TABLE 1.11: Caste-wise and Community-wise Composition of Recent BJP State Executive Committees and Pradesh Congress Committees in Madhya Pradesh

Caste Groups and Communities	BJP 1991	BJP 1994	BJP 1996	Congress 1992	Congress 1995	Congress 1997
Upper Castes	66 (66)	70 (59.3)	57 (58.7)	32 (55.2)	105 (48.2)	24 (43.6)
Brahmin	31	33	20	16	52	10
Rajput	11	14	13	7	27	8
Banya/Jain	15	14	16	6	16	3
Kayasth	6	8	5	2	4	2
Khattri	–	–	1	1	4	1
Sindhi	3	1	1	0	2	–
Other	–	–	1	–	–	–
Intermediate Castes	1 (1)	2 (1.7)	3 (3)	1 (1.7)	–	1 (1.8)
Maratha	1	2	3	1	–	–
Other Backward Classes	14 (14)	23 (19.5)	18 (18.5)	9 (15.5)	30 (13.7)	8 (14.5)
Yadav	3	2	1	1	5	1
Kurmi	2	4	7	4	6	–
Teli	2	4	2	0	1	1
Others	7	13	8	4	18	6
Scheduled Castes	6 (6)	7 (5.9)	7 (7.2)	9 (15.5)	18 (8.2)	5 (9.1)
Scheduled Tribes	8 (8)	9 (7.6)	6 (6.1)	4 (6.9)	19 (8.7)	10 (18.2)
Muslims	4 (4)	2 (1.6)	2 (2)	2 (3.4)	13 (6)	3 (5.5)
Sikhs	1 (1)	1 (0.8)	1 (1)	–	2 (0.9)	1 (1.8)
Christians	–	2 (1.7)	1 (1)	–	1 (0.4)	2 (3.6)
Unidentified	–	2 (1.7)	2 (2)	1 (1.7)	30 (13.7)	1 (1.8)
TOTAL	100 (100)	118 (100)	97 (100)	58 (100)	218 (100)	55 (100)

Note: Percentages are given in parenthesis.

none of these 'subalterns' held one of the 15 posts of office-bearers
(President, Vice-presidents, General Secretaries, Secretaries or Treasurer); they were merely members of the State Executive. The
BJP's defeat in 1993 did not significantly affect the relative
proportions of the different castes and communities within the
State Executive Committee: the committee designated in 1994 was
still dominated by the élite groups (59.3 per cent), even though the
share of the OBCs rose to 19.5 per cent, while the Scheduled Tribes
had 7.6 per cent and the Scheduled Castes 5.9 per cent representation in the State Executive. Only one Kurmi and one Tribal held
posts of responsibility in a team of nine persons heading the State
Executive Committee. The proportions were almost the same in
the 1996 committee but this time there were four OBCs, one
Scheduled Caste member and one Scheduled Tribes member
among the 15 Office-bearers (Vice Presidents, General Secretaries,
Secretaries and Treasurer). By contrast, in the Pradesh Congress
Committee appointed in 1992, while the president, Digvijay Singh
was a Rajput, one Scheduled Caste member, one Scheduled Tribe
member and one Muslim were the three vice-presidents. More
importantly, the share of the Scheduled Tribes increased, from
6.9 per cent in 1992 to 18.2 per cent in 1997, when the Tribals were
given the charge of the President and the Working President of the
MPCC-I. Simultaneously, the share of the upper castes decreased
from 55.2 per cent in 1992 to 43.6 per cent in 1997. Otherwise,
once again, the social profile of the PCC was only slightly different
from that of the BJP State executive.

The over-representation of the upper castes among the BJP
cadres results from the conjunction of two phenomena. First, the
party apparatus comprises many former pracharaks, seconded by
the RSS to the BJP for organizational tasks; and most of the RSS
pracharaks, till recently, came from the upper castes, particularly
the Brahmin *jatis*, often with a Maharashtrian background. Second,
the traditional élitist profile continues because the party establishment has not undergone any significant renewal in the last decades,
which means that the traditional base of the Hindu nationalist
movement among the Brahmins and the Banias remain over-
represented.

Thus, while the BJP nominated an increasing number of OBC
and Tribal candidates at the time of elections, not only did the
latter not project themselves as low-caste leaders because of their
interest in sanskritization, but also the party apparatus remained

dominated by upper-caste leaders. As a result, the BJP could easily
be denounced as a 'Bania–Brahmin party'. Indeed, among the State
Executive Committee as it was constituted in 1997, Brahmins were
by far the largest group and if one adds the Jains, Sindhis and
Banias, the merchant communities outnumbered Rajputs who are
far more numerous in the general population. However, the
Congress' growing attention towards non-élite groups (especially
the Tribals) and the rise of the Bahujan Samaj Party posed a threat
to the BJP and the 1996 elections acted as a catalyst in this respect.

THE IMPACT OF THE 1996 ELECTION

The Congress, the BSP and the Coveted Vote of the 'Bahujans'

After its success in the 1993 elections, the Congress decided to
further cultivate the OBCs, Scheduled Castes and Scheduled
Tribes, three categories that are increasingly known as the 'bahujans'
in the Hindi belt, i.e. the masses, the bulk of the people. The first
decision of Digvijay Singh was to announce 14 per cent reservation
for the OBCs in employment in government departments, public
undertakings and local bodies.[58] This quota was extended to
27 per cent in September 1995. In the Madhya Pradesh Public
Service Reservation for the Scheduled Castes, Scheduled Tribes and
Other Backward Classes (Amendment) Bill, 1995, the reservation
for the STs and OBCs was increased from 18 and 14 per cent to
23 and 27 per cent for the two upper classes of the administration
and from 20 and 14 per cent to 23 and 27 per cent for class III and
IV. Thus the implementation of the 35 per cent of the Mahajan
Commission report was partly applied.[59] It was difficult to go
beyond 27 per cent for the OBCs, since the total amount of the
reservations had already reached 69 per cent for class I and II
(where 15 per cent of the posts are reserved for the SCs), and
70 per cent for class III and IV (where 16 per cent are reserved for
the SCs)—4 per cent of the posts have been reserved for the upper-
castes poors. The Act was passed with a unanimous voice vote.
During the Assembly debate the BJP leaders from the OBCs and
SCs could only approve of this move but regretted too that the
'general quota', intended to cater to the needs of the poor from

[58] Furthermore, his government relaxed the upper-age limit by five years for
the entry of the OBCs in government service (*National Mail*, 7 Dec. 1994).
[59] The claimant who had filed the case challenging the validity of the
recommendations was apparently convinced to withdraw it.

the upper castes was so small.[60] Few days later, Babulal Gaur, who was more and more projected by the BJP as its OBC leader in Madhya Pradesh, acted as the Chairman of the reception committee to a state level Yadavi Shankhnad programme, and in his speech he could only thank Digvijay Singh for sanctioning 5000 sq ft of land for the Yadav community.[61] It was very difficult, indeed, for the BJP to criticize the government's policy towards the OBCs.

So far as the Scheduled Castes and Scheduled Tribes were concerned, the students belonging to these categories were freed from the requirement of producing caste and income certificates every year and their scholarships have been raised and linked to the price index. More importantly, a special recruitment drive was launched in April 1995 to fill the backlog vacancies reserved for the SCs and STs—about one year later 11,894 such vacancies were filled.[62] One month after, the government formulated new rules under the Scheduled Castes and Scheduled Tribes (Prevention of Atrocities) Act, 1989: state and district level vigilance committes were constituted to prevent atrocities and monitor relief and rehabilitation of affected persons; financial compensations were increased in case of murder, rape or dacoity.[63] Soon before the 1996 elections, 504 sensitive areas of 32 districts were identified for effective enforcement of the Act and 19 police stations were opened for this purpose.[64] And the last official figures pertaining to atrocities show a slight decrease. The government also decided to renovate the Bhandarpuri temple, the birth place of Ghasidas, the guru-founder of the Satnami sect—among which the BSP had established pockets of influence in Chhattisgarh. Furthermore, it allowed the tribals to gather tendu leaves from sanctuaries and reserved forest areas and, finally, the state assembly passed a resolution in favour of the Sixth Schedule of the Constitution granting autonomy to tribals in their districts, something the centre has not accepted yet.[65]

In spite of these measures—which were publicized but not always implemented—Digvijay Singh was attacked by non-upper caste Congress leaders who demanded that the Chief Minister

[60] *National Mail*, 20 Sept. 1995.
[61] Ibid., 9 Oct. 1995.
[62] Ibid., 10 August 1996.
[63] Ibid., 8 May 1995.
[64] Ibid., 1 April 1996.
[65] *Times of India*, 18 April 1995 and 12 June 1995.

should come from their ranks, as promised by Arjun Singh before the 1993 elections. The Scheduled Tribes leaders (such as Dilip Singh Bhuria and Ajit Jogi) were especially vehement. Digvijay Singh tried to defuse these tensions by appointing an ever larger number of non-upper castes office-bearers in Congress and ministers in his government. Soon after he took over he appointed two deputy Chief Ministers, one Yadav (Subhash Yadav) and one from the Scheduled Tribes (Piyarelal Kanwar); Parasram Bharadwaj, a Scheduled Caste leader, was appointed as PCC-I chief in 1994. So far as the tribal leaders were concerned, their share in the governement increased substantially between 1993–7 as was noticed above.

The Congress could not derive many electoral advantages from these measures during the eleventh general elections, when it could retain only eight seats, largely because of their poor implementation and factionalism; but it was able to develop a pro-poor rhetoric based on caste identities which the BJP had to match.

In addition to the Congress party's tactical moves, the BJP is exposed in Madhya Pradesh to the rise of the Bahujan Samaj Party. In 1993, the BSP, with 11 seats and 7 per cent of the valid votes made inroads in districts adjacent to Uttar Pradesh, and more especially in constituencies which were already pockets of influence of the Janata Dal and, before that, of the Socialists. In 1993, the BSP snatched four seats from the Janata Dal and one from the CPI, all of them in Rewa and Morena districts. In 1996, the party won two seats as against one in 1991 and its nominees came second in other four constituencies, again located in districts bordering Uttar Pradesh and in Chhattisgarh. While the party received only 8.18 per cent of the valid votes in the state, in Vindhya Pradesh and in the region of Gwalior it polled about one-fifth of the valid votes. Here, the BSP has been able to cut into the Scheduled Caste base of the Congress but it has also made progress at the expense of the BJP by diverting many of its OBC votes. Even though the BJP won 27 out of 40 seats during the 1996 Lok Sabha elections, its share of valid votes registered a slight decrease, from 42 to 41.32 per cent and this downward trend has been especially clear in the district bordering Uttar Pradesh where the Bahujan Samaj Party has made progress. In addition to these gains, one year after the 1996 election the BSP succeeded in attracting Arvind Netam, an ex-Congress leader who exerts some influence in the Tribal belt of Madhya Pradesh.

The BJP's Reaction: Social Adaptation and Doctrinal Dilution

The number of OBCs who were given a BJP ticket had already doubled from four to nine between 1989–94, while those of upper-caste candidates remained the same (see Table 1.12). In 1996, the BJP appointed a still larger number of OBC candidates at the time of the parliamentary elections, so that the Congress could only lag behind. After the 1993 defeat, Vikram Verma (an MLA from Dhar), a farmer from the Jat community, had been appointed leader of the opposition in Bhopal Assembly, where Bherulal Patidar (an MLA from Mhow in Indore district) also a farmer, had become the Deputy Speaker; and Babulal Gaur (an MLA from Govindpura in Bhopal district), well known for his trade union background, had become the Chief Whip. But power remained within the hands of senior leaders such as S. Patwa (a Jain), L. N. Pandey (a Brahmin) and K. Thakre (a Kayasth). The real changes occurred after the 1996 elections.

The BJP felt so much concerned about the rise of the BSP that its leader appointed a Janadhar Badhao Samiti (Committee for broadening the base of the party). In its report, the committee explained the rise of the BSP from two points of view: first, 'the political understanding and awareness of this group (the Scheduled Castes, Scheduled Tribes and OBCs) has improved because they have realized that social status and economic prosperity can be acquired only through political power.'[66] Secondly, 'the Dalit, Adivasi and OBC leaders of the other parties have a much less collective political acceptance.'[67] The first recommendation of the committee to face the new challenge was 'to achieve integration and participation of these groups on the basis of social and economic engineering.'[68] The notion of integration harks back to the old sanskritization strategy—Gandhi and Upadhyaya are still referred to in this respect. But the idea of social engineering has introduced a new dimension, that the non-élite groups should be given their due share. The report dares to say: 'Many upper-castes members within the party do not like the idea of social equality. Our leaders from the high castes therefore should be influenced

---

[66] Bharatiya Janata Party, *Janadhar badhao samiti ka prativedan*, Bhopal, BJP, 1997, p. 2 (Hindi).

[67] Ibid., p. 3.

[68] Ibid., p. 4.

to welcome the feelings of equality.'[69] In concrete terms this means that the Dalit, Adivasi and OBC leaders should be shown respect and should be promoted in the political sphere. The report advocates that data concerning the social composition of each constituency be collected, computerized and taken into account before the distribution of tickets. Not only that but the party should also 'demand proportional representation in Parliament and State legislatures' for the OBCs,[70] something the Congress government has more or less granted to them at the local level in the framework of the new Panchayati Raj, but which is a completely new demand from the BJP.

TABLE 1.12: Social Profile of the Congress and BJP Candidates in Madhya Pradesh (from the 1984 to the 1996 general elections)

Party Caste Groups and Communities	BJP (1984)	BJP (1989)	BJP (1991)	BJP (1996)	Congress (1996)
Upper castes	14	13	13	13	17
Brahmin	7	4	6	5	7
Rajput	2	4	4	4	6
Bania/Jain	4	3	2	3	3
Kayasth	1	2	1	1	1
Other Backward Classes	5	4	9	10	6
Lodhi	1	2	2	2	–
Kurmi	2	2	3	3	3
Teli	–	–	2	2	1
Panwar	–	–	1	–	1
Kirar	–	–	–	1	–
Ranghuwanshi	1	–	1	–	–
Other	1	–	–	2	1
Scheduled Castes	6	5	6	6	4
Scheduled Tribes	9	8	9	9	11
Muslims	1	1	1	0	1
Sikhs	–	1	1	1	–
Unidentified	4	1	1	0	1
TOTAL	39	33	40	39	40

[69] Ibid., p. 5.
[70] Ibid., p. 6.

The eight-member committee which authored the report comprised only two persons from the upper castes and was headed by Babulal Gaur. In the mid-1990s Gaur increasingly projected himself as an OBC leader too; he took part in 1997 in the activities of the Pichre Varg Morcha whose new President, Kriparam Sahu was a Teli leader. In late April 1997 he advocated the need for reservations in favour of the OBCs while opening the Morcha's annual convention. Three months later he presided over the launch of an agitation by the Morcha for '27 per cent reservation'. In October he took part in the Valmiki Jayanti, the most important festival for the Bhangis, the scavengers who are one of the lowest among the Scheduled Castes. The BJP tried also to woo the tribals by organizing in September 1997 an 'awareness rally' as well as a three-day training camp for the Tribal MLAs and MPs in Bilaspur— Advani inaugurated it and Vajpayee was the chief guest.

The militancy showed by Babulal Gaur on behalf of the non-upper-caste groups stands in strong contrast to his earlier discourse. The words used by the Janadhar Badhao Samiti are significant in themselves: the Scheduled Castes are not designated as Harijans any more but as Dalits and the Scheduled Tribes are not presented as Vanavasis any more but as Adivasis.[71] This transition from sanskritization to 'social engineering', an expression used in the report, probably reflects personal ambitions: the party has promoted Gaur because it needed an OBC leader to respond to the rise of the BSP, but he has exploited this pivotal situation to play 'the OBC card' (another expression found in the report). Babulal Gaur explicitly cashes in on the dynamics created by the BSP to improve the representation of the non-upper-caste groups within the BJP apparatus:

In North India, all parties are dominated by Brahmins, Thakurs and Banias. After fifty years of Independence, we people could not get an equal share in politics. Therefore these people (who support the BSP) want to snatch the power from the upper castes. The Bahujan Samaj Party is not a party but a movement. It's a one man show and a one woman show. This party has no future but it promotes a good cause, it enhances the feelings of the people.

[71] While most of the tribals designate themselves as Adivasis (litt. 'those who were there first or before') because they claim to descend from the original inhabitants of India, the Hindu nationalists preferred to call them Vanavasis (litt. 'those of the forest') since the original population, in their view, constituted of the Aryans.

Some of our party members do not give their share to the Dalits, the Tribals and the OBCs. They should meet these people and give them an equal share in all spheres of life. These people should be given proper respect on the *manch* [platform]. Our OBC leaders are brave, they fight in the field. They say 'our leaders are *vyaparis* [merchants], where are we?.' This is the loud thinking among the OBCs: they want their share. Though the RSS and the BJP do not believe in the caste system, due to circumstances and to the other parties, they'll have to think over these issues. L. N. Pandey [then State BJP president] and Patwa are bound to change over this problem if they want the party to go ahead. We have been given posts, Vikram Verma is leader of the opposition, Bherulal Patidar is deputy speaker, I am one of the party general secretaries myself, but this is only the first step.[72]

Obviously, Babulal Gaur covets the post of State party president and his recent militancy can be largely explained by the fact that the Madhya Pradesh BJP organized inner elections in late 1997 after a gap of four years. The emergence of an alternative discourse to that of sanskritization in Madhya Pradesh unit of the BJP, to be more precise, the adaptation of the notion of 'social engineering' to this local context, can be explained by the rise of the BSP but also by the race for the top posts within the party. That factionalism contributes to change in the social profile of a party is not a new concept in itself. In several state units of the Congress faction, leaders have tried to compete with others by coopting low-caste and tribal leaders in order to broaden their base. This is what Digvijay Singh has been doing in Madhya Pradesh and this tactic, eventually, has given a greater influence to representatives of non-élite groups.

The president of the Madhya Pradesh BJP, who was eventually designated in early November 1997 was a Tribal, Nandkumar Sai, the MP of Raigarh and the chief of the Scheduled Tribes wing of the party in the state. For the first time in its history, the chief of the BJP in Madhya Pradesh is not from the upper castes. The BJP has obviously been led to emulate the Congress and the BSP to compete more efficiently with them. Such a development bears testimony to the party's capacity of adaptation, but this flexiblity may also imply a further dilution of its doctrine. Interestingly, Babulal Gaur claims that he drew his inspiration from Ram Manohar Lohia, whose portrait is hanged next to that of Golwalkar in his office. Other low-castes leaders coopted by the BJP in the

[72] Interview with Babulal Gaur, Bhopal, 4 November 1997.

recent years have not even heard of Golwalkar and Upadhyaya but they know their Ambedkar.

CONCLUSION

Admittedly, the main limitations of the BJP, the reasons why it is not yet in a position to gain power at the centre on its own, lie in its weak South-Indian base and its rather upper-caste profile. To overcome the latter obstacle, some party leaders have proposed a programme of 'social engineering' consisting in supporting positive discrimination and promoting a larger number of low-caste people within the party apparatus and among its election candidates. The RSS leaders disapproved of this policy because it conflicted with their organicist conception of society, which is typical of Hindu nationalism. The BJP leaders sharing these views showed reluctance too. The compromise which has been gradually evolved consisted in accepting caste-based reservations and fielding more non-upper-caste election candidates without really changing the party apparatus or its irenic discourse. As a result, the social composition of the BJP high command has remained almost unaffected but the share of the upper-caste members among the party's MPs has steadily declined in the Hindi belt, whereas that of the Scheduled Castes and OBCs has tended to increase.

However, as my survey of the BJP's candidate recruitment policy in Madhya Pradesh suggests it is necessary to take account of the political socialization which has accompanied the selection and training of the party's OBCs and Scheduled Castes leaders. Traditionally, their early experience of the RSS and its doctrines has often given them a sanskritized view of their social world, and induced them to value caste cooperation and interdependence rather than caste conflict, and to relate their notions of Hindu tradition to upper-caste ideas rather than to the local and popular ones and to the customs of their home village. They, therefore differed markedly from those leaders who represented demands for low-caste solidarity and for positive discrimination for their caste fellows.

However, the situation is changing as suggested by recent developments in Madhya Pradesh. The threat posed by the BSP—and other rivals to a lesser extent—have led the BJP to promote non-élite party leaders who now tend to project themselves as anti-establishment leaders. The new discourse of Babulal Gaur illustrates this evolution. It may not be easily dealt with by the BJP, especially because the new assertiveness of the OBCs, Dalits and even Tribals have made any clientelistic, vertical arrangement difficult to maintain. If the BJP happens to advocate the cause of these groups, it may lose parts of its base among the upper castes. This is probably one of the reasons—along with the fear to dilute its Hindu nationalist ideology—why the BJP high command embraced another tactic based on 'indirect mandalization' during the 1996 general election.

'Indirect mandalization' then consisted in making alliances with regional parties with a strong base among the low and intermediate castes rather than promoting such people within the party apparatus. The seat adjustment between the Samta Party and the BJP in Bihar is a case in point. In the 1995 state assembly elections, out of the 41 BJP winners, four were Brahmins, four were Rajputs, one was a Bhumihar, four were Kayasths and six Banias. There were only two Kurmis, two Yadavs and two Koeris among the party MLAs. On the contrary, the Samta Party, despite its bad performance, had three Kurmis, two Koeris and one Dusadh among its seven MLAs. While the BJP had polled only 16 per cent of the votes in 1991 largely because it remained identified with the upper castes and the tribal belt of the south, its alliance with the Samta Party enabled it to make inroads in northern and central districts thanks to their base among Kurmis and Koeris. In several constituencies, these low castes were allied to the forward castes (Brahmins, Rajputs, Bhumihars and Kayasths), which helped the BJP a great deal. The party won 18 seats (as against five in 1991). In Haryana, the BJP, whose influence has traditionally been confined to the urban dwellers, and especially the Punjabi refugees, did not make an alliance with the OBCs but with a party rooted in the countryside anyway. Indeed, the Haryana Vikas Party launched by an ex-Congressman, Bansi Lal, has a strong base among Jats. This alliance enabled the BJP to win four seats in a state where it had not won any in 1991.

Interestingly, Bihar and Haryana were among the states where the party registered its best results in terms of valid votes respectively +5 per cent and +11 per cent: these were the states where it had made new alliances with regional parties commanding a complementary base among intermediate and low castes. Apparently, the BJP admitted the need to become more rural and even to 'mandalize' itself but indirectly. This compromise may well be the outcome of the inner debate between the advocates of 'social engineering' and those of status quo who did not want to indulge in this kind of tactic.

Simultaneously, the BJP seemed to be heading for indirect 'dalitization', as suggested by its alliance with the BSP. By the end of June 1995 the BJP had agreed to support Mayawati as the new Chief Minister of Uttar Pradesh, to overthrow Mulayam Singh Yadav's government but also to improve the image of the BJP among the Scheduled Castes.[73] He reiterated this manoeuvre six months after the 1996 State Assembly elections. Indirect 'dalitization' seemed to be the only way for the BJP to circumscribe the Yadavs (whose interests are embodied in Mulayam Singh) and to overcome the contradictions which appeared in the 1996 assembly elections. Soon after the Lok Sabha elections, at the National Executive meeting which took place in June 1996, Kalyan Singh, had insisted that the party should endorse an unprecedented large number of non-upper-caste candidates for the coming Assembly election in the state. Indeed, the BJP nominated OBC candidates in 190 out of the 420 constituencies in the elections which took place in September 1996. However, this move seems 'to have alienated the upper-caste support base of the party and adversely affected its fortunes.'[74] It won only 174 seats, whereas it had secured a majority in 236 of the assembly segments in the Lok Sabha elections. The relative alienation of the upper-caste voters partly resulted from the distribution of 45 per cent of the tickets to the OBCs and also of the projection of Kalyan Singh as the party candidate for chief ministership. The BJP was in a dilemma in Uttar Pradesh since, when it tried to further enlarge its support base among these groups the party was not able to retain its upper-caste base. The BJP leaders probably thought that the BSP could have helped the party

---

[73] Commenting on the way M. S. Yadav's government had been toppled, the special representative of the *Organiser* wrote: 'The support extended to Mayawati was not only tactically sound (to end the *goondaraj* in the State) but also in tune with the party's philosophy of Hindutva which abhors untouchability. BJP has always believed in empowerment of the weaker sections. Its stance on UP developments has sent strong signals to the weaker sections....' (*Organiser*, 25 June 1995, p. 3).

[74] 'Uttar Pradesh—Calculations Gone Awry', *Economic and Political Weekly*, 12–19 October 1996, p. 2773.

to solve these contradictions but the alliance broke after six months in 1997.

It remains to be seen whether the alliances with other non-élite (OBC or Jat-based) parties will last and whether they will be sufficient to benefit—or not to suffer—from the growing political mobilization of the plebeian groups. If it is so, the BJP will be probably obliged to promote some of its leaders from these groups, which is the new trend in Madhya Pradesh. In both cases—whether the party follows indirect or direct mandalization—it may well face caste-based contradictions and dilute its doctrinal purity by questioning more and more the RSS's stand on the reservation issue, for instance.

Ψ

2

The BJP in Uttar Pradesh:
From Hindutva to Consensual Politics?

JASMINE ZÉRININI–BROTEL

In five years, the Bharatiya Janata Party (BJP) has assumed, in India's most populous state, a predominant position reaching beyond the limits of the Ayodhya mobilization. Though hardly expanding in terms of seats or percentage of vote since the 1991 Lok Sabha elections (see Table 2.1), the BJP has nevertheless confirmed its successful replacement of the Congress party (I) as the main figure of UP's political scene benefiting from the divisions of the two main opposition parties, the Samajwadi Party (SP) and the Bahujan Samaj Party (BSP).

TABLE 2.1:   Results for the General Elections of 1991 and 1996
Based on Seats and Percentage of Votes (Party-wise)

Party/Seats	1991	1996
Number of seats	84	85
BJP	51 (32.8)	52 (33.5)
INC	5 (18.3)	5 (8)
JD	22 (21.3)	2 (4.5)
SP	—	15 (20.4)
BSP	0 (8.7)	6 (19.9)
AIIC (T)	—	2 (2.9)

Source: David Butler, Ashok Lahiri and Prannoy Roy, *India Decides. Elections 1952–95*, Delhi, Books and Things, 1995; Centre for the Study of Developing Societies, New Delhi, 1996.

Note: Percentages are given in parenthesis.

The decline of the Congress and the growth of sectional politics openly based on caste and community have been factors of growth as well as barriers for the BJP (up to now). While the communalization of UP society made the 1991 victory possible, it has since then prevented the BJP from regaining power in the state. The fragmentation of Uttar Pradesh's Hindu electorate along castes lines also remains a major drawback in the BJP's unitarian approach, best expressed by Hindutva. This fragmentation has provoked a dead-end situation where no party on its own has been able to win elections and because of which the state has undergone three spells of President's Rule since 1993.

The image which the BJP tried to put across during the campaign for the 1996 general elections has come from an acknowledgement of the situation and the resulting isolation of the party. Facing the growth of sectional parties in the UP turf and of regional parties in most of the other states in the country, the BJP has chosen to distance itself from a political agenda favouring Hindus, too overtly and to reappropriate much of the Congress's former electoral platform of nationwide stability. Though Hindutva remains the party's central ideology, it is not expressed in the usual aggressive way. The agreement reached with the BSP in March 1997, and the breaking of this alliance barely seven months later illustrates both the BJP's new strategy and the tensions it provokes.[1] To understand how a party best known for exclusive reliance on its own network came to the conclusion that alliance was necessary, we shall first have to go into the causes of the BJP's expansion in UP since the beginning of the 1990s, then analyse the factors which have led it to reconsider its strategy. In the new context, the future of such an ideology as Hindutva is at stake. The path followed by the BJP since the last general and UP Assembly elections seems to imply a dilution of the BJP's Hindu nationalism and an attempt at reoccupying the middle-ground position left vacant by the Congress. We shall try to see whether this process has any chance of success and what it implies for UP society.

---

[1] The BJP and the BSP had agreed to share power on a six-month rotating basis, the BSP assuming power first. Less than a month after Kalyan Singh took over, the BSP withdrew its support accusing its former coalition partner of taking anti-Dalit measures. This enabled Kalyan Singh to engineer massive defections from the Congress, the Janata Dal and the BSP and form a new government.

FROM THE BHARATIYA JANA SANGH TO THE BHARATIYA JANATA PARTY: A STUDY IN 'SOCIAL ENGINEERING'

In its 30 years of existence, the Bharatiya Jana Sangh (BJS or JS) made little impact on the determinants of UP politics. Though right from Independence, there was scope in UP for the political articulation of Hindu orthodoxy,[2] up to 1991, the main issues at play were caste, class and community, and not Hindu Rashtra.[3] The failure of the Jana Sangh in UP can largely be ascribed to an inability to comprehend and adapt to the changing social criteria of vote, partly springing from the restricted social origin of its leaders. In fact, the growth of a middle peasantry benefiting from the land and agrarian reforms of the 1960s introduced an essential new dynamics into the politics of the state. In the face of these developments, the INC chose to consolidate around its Forward Caste, Muslims and Scheduled Caste base[4] and the appeal of a Hindu nationalist party withered. Indeed, as from the late 1960s onwards, extended political power tended to be conceived of as a necessary counterpart of increased economic strength caste allegiance, not the unity of the 'Hindu nation', was considered the most efficient means to this end.[5] In addition, the traditionalism of the dominant faction in the UP Congress, pressing for a ban on cow slaughtering and for the adoption of a minor status for Urdu, also drew voters away from the Jana Sangh.

Therefore, the scope of the Hindu nationalists' influence in UP remained limited to the urban centres where their ethics based on

---

[2] Through Congressmen like Sardar Patel, G. B. Pant and P. Tandon, for instance.

[3] See some of Zoya Hasan's articles on the subject, for instance 'Power and Mobilization: Patterns of Resilience and Change in UP Politics', in Francine R. Frankel and M. S. A. Rao (eds), *Dominance and State Power in Modern India. Decline of a Social Order*, vol. I (Delhi: Oxford University Press, 1993), pp 132–203; or 'Communal Mobilization and Changing Majority in Uttar Pradesh', in David Ludden (ed.), *Making India Hindu. Religion, Community and the Politics of Democracy in India* (Delhi: Oxford University Press, 1996), pp 81–97.

[4] While the upper castes found in the Congress their best representative—in terms of access to power, their presence in the INC is still unrivalled—the Scheduled Castes and the Muslims were drawn to it by the schemes of poverty alleviation and secularism.

[5] On the impact of peasant politics in UP from the mid-1960s, see Brass, Paul R., 'The Politicization of the Peasantry in a North Indian State', *Journal of Peasant Studies*, 7 (4), July 1980 and 8(1), October 1980.

'the principles of corporatism and of family solidarity'[6] was finding a concerned ear in the merchant Bania caste in particular, while the voting pattern showed a thinly spread presence over the whole of the state. From its inception until the late 1980s, the fate of the BJP, then under the leadership of Murli Manohar Joshi, himself a Brahmin from UP, popular with the RSS workers, was very much a replay of that of the unsuccessful Jana Sangh. In the 1984 and 1989 Vidhan Sabha elections, its percentage of vote was lower than the Jana Sangh's had ever been (see Table 2.3) and the party seemed at a loss to find a place of its own between the still predominant Congress-I and the new embodiment of peasant politics, the Janata Dal. In the mid-1980s, the emergence of anti-minority themes in the Congress-I's rhetoric, first under Indira Gandhi, then under Rajiv Gandhi, further fragilized the BJP's choice to stand as a political platform for India's religious majority.

However, the handling of the Shah Bano case and the lifting of the Babri Masjid locks gave the BJP leaders the opportunity to strategically reposition their party at a time when their adoption by the Congress had given these themes a wider appeal and, perhaps more importantly, a larger respectability. Community relations occupied the centre of the political scene in UP after 1986 and were only overshadowed by the implementation of the Mandal Commisssion report by V. P. Singh's government in 1990.

In a nutshell, until the general (see Table 2.2) and assembly elections of 1991 (see Table 2.3), the BJP, much like its predecessor the Jana Sangh, had no solid base to speak of in UP, and in electoral terms it stood as a marginal party.

TABLE 2.2: Vote Shares for the BJS/BJP in Lok Sabha
Elections Until 1991

	1952	1957	1962	1967	1971	1977	1980	1984	1989	1991
% of votes	7.3	14.8	17.6	22.6	12.3	—	—	6.4	7.6	32.8

Source: David Butler, Ashok Lahiri and Prannoy Roy, *India Decides. Elections 1952–95*, Delhi, Books and Things, 1995.

[6] Graham, Bruce D., *Hindu Nationalism and Indian Politics. The Origins and Development of the Bharatiya Jana Sangh* (Cambridge: Cambridge University Press, 1990), p. 159. See in particular pp 220–52 for an analysis of the electoral fortunes of the Jana Sangh in Uttar Pradesh.

TABLE 2.3:   Vote Shares for the BJS/BJP in Vidhan Sabha
Elections Until 1991

	1952	1957	1962	1967	1971	1974	1980	1985	1989	1991	1993
% of votes	6.5	9.8	16.5	21.7	17.9	17.1	10.8	9.9	11.6	31.5	33.4

Source: David Butler, Ashok Lahiri and Prannoy Roy, *India Decides. Elections 1952–95*, Delhi, Books and Things, 1995.

In the 1991 general elections, the BJP won a tally of 51 seats in UP, gathering nearly 33 per cent of the total vote, while the INC was washed out with only five seats and less than 20 per cent of the vote, behind even the Janata Dal.

The BJP's Ayodhya campaign spread in UP's villages and towns with great facility, in particular during the *rath yatra* of the party's new president, L. K. Advani in September and October 1990, which did not actually enter UP, but was stopped in Bihar by Laloo Prasad Yadav. It was helped by the fact that the Congress party was paralysed after the opening of the locks of the Babri Masjid and the *shilanyas* ceremony that took place during its rule in the state. The statements that N. D. Tiwari and many other state leaders now make that they were forced by Rajiv Gandhi to agree to it must be interpreted as a sign of the Congress's loss of political initiative and direction by the end of the rule of the Rajiv Gandhi government.[7] While the INC was faltering, the BJP had regained an aggressive president in the person of L. K. Advani, had proceeded to an extension of its organizational structure in the districts, supporting itself on the old RSS network, and had given its position in favour of the unity of the 'Hindu nation' a more assertive exposure. Meanwhile, the INC's support base had been eroded by its unability to either convince Muslims that it was a staunch defender of secularism or convince Hindus that it was their best ally.

[7] Interviews conducted with Muslims MPs elected on Congress tickets in the 1980s show that their resentment is not directed towards N. D. Tiwari but towards the central leadership—Rajiv Gandhi and his team of self-appointed advisors. To quote one of them, 'after 1986, the Congress became coward. It is responsible for the communalization of politics but it could not check it.' Interview, Varanasi, 10 April 1996.

The BJP's overwhelming victory in the 1991 Assembly elections relied on the insecurity of the upper castes, both towards the Muslims and the OBCs, given the latter's new assertiveness. The strength of the 'Ram wave' was evident even in regions where Muslims where hardly present at all, such as Garhwal and Kumaon, the religious fervour of the inhabitants having, it seems, supplemented the feeling of vulnerability. As put by a Congress MP from the region, who had been ousted during the wave: 'They—the inhabitants of Uttarkhand—are Brahmins and Rajputs, they are God-fearing, being the highest in the religious hierarchy. How could they not be deeply moved by the BJP's mobilization?'[8] What he meant was that the scope of the BJP's victory in 1991 was very special and essentially rested on the religious or, in other parts of UP, communal feelings of the voters. To this process, the decision to implement the Mandal report provided further fuel. The BJP's withdrawal of support to the V. P. Singh government gave it even more credential among the upper castes as well as among those of the Backward Castes evicted from the Mandal Commission's definition of the OBC category.

In addition, the BJP's victory was also helped by its superior organizational capacities,[9] the dismal record of the Janata Party in power at the centre as well as the slow degradation of economic conditions in UP since the beginning of the decade. In that sense, the outcome of the 1991 Assembly elections was the result of two movements: one fast drift towards the communalization of UP politics and another trend expressing rejection at the Congress's and the Janata Dal's record in ruling the state. After 1991, the consolidation of the party has to be seen in the new light of wider social mobilization and disappearance of the Congress from the centre of the political stage.

THE CONSOLIDATION OF THE BJP AFTER 1991

By the beginning of the 1990s, two features characterized the Congress party in UP. On the one hand, its organization, once present in every district and virtually every *tehsil* of the state with

[8] Interview, Almora, 30 June 1997.
[9] See Jayaprasad, K., 'Campaign Strategy of the BJP in 1991' and Kumar, V. P., 'Campaign Strategy of the INC (I) in 1991', *UP Journal of Political Science*, vol. 3, no. 1–2, 1991.

workers able to mobilize voters at short notice, had by then completely collapsed.[10] So-called party workers were still there but were not acting anymore as a link between the electorate and their political representatives. On the other, the security which the party had enjoyed in the state since it had assumed power after Independence had reduced it to a monumental body unable to react quickly to new challenges. This view is well expressed in the following description made by a Congressman from Uttarkhand: 'In 1991, it was a wave. A wave goes very fast, you cannot fight it. We had been given no time to fight it, we could not find the energy to prepare and mobilize against it.' 'Energy' and contact with the masses indeed appear to be what the Congress had slowly lost during the years in power. After the BJP's victory, it did not regain that 'energy', even when it dismissed the Kalyan Singh government after to the demolition of the Babri Masjid. The years 1993–5 actually saw the completion of the collapse of the Congress organization in UP and the shrinking of the party's capacity to determine the country's agenda.

Right from the 1960s, the importance of UP in terms of seats in the national Assembly had put the party organization in the state under the direct pressure of Indira Gandhi, worried by the danger to her leadership, should a popular politician emerge from UP. Congress Chief Ministers, as well as the various layers of party leaders, were characterized by their submission to the Prime Minister's Office in New Delhi and the frailty of their personal following in the state. N. D. Tiwari for instance seemed to have been such a hot favourite for the post of Chief Minister because in spite of his efforts, he had little impact on the political machinery of the party in the state and his own base was limited to the 19 assembly seats of Uttarkhand. This focus on internal political power widened the gap between the party's and the electorate's preoccupations. As a result, the pace of development has been considerably slower in UP than in most of the other states ruled by the Congress for a long spell of time.

The violence of the 1980s which escorted the decline of Congress rule (see Table 2.4) gave the BJP the opportunity to assert its image as a clean, organized and efficient party that would

---

[10] 'They say "there are no roads, so how can we go?"' complained to me a former MLA and MP of the apathy of the workers in his district.

revitalize the state. The Kalyan Singh government sealed the fate of the Congress system of patronage and utter dominance of the state apparatus by upper castes. That it can boast of precious little in those very fields were the Congress had failed did not check the BJP's progression, because from the early 1990 the politics of caste and community had taken a lead over the politics of development.

TABLE 2.4: Vote Shares and Number of Seats for the Congress-I in Vidhan Sabha Elections Since 1980

	1980	1985	1989	1991	1993	1996
% of votes	37.7	39.3	27.9	17.4	15	8.35
seats	309	269	94	46	29	33

Source: David Butler, Ashok Lahiri and Prannoy Roy, *India Decides. Elections 1952–95*, Delhi, Books and Things, 1995; Election Commission of India, New Delhi, *Statistical Report on the General Elections, 1996 to the Legislative Assembly of Uttar Pradesh*, New Delhi, 1997.

After 1990, the caste polarization around the Mandal issue played two different parts in BJP's evolution. For one, it kept the OBCs hoping to benefit from the Mandal reservations away from the party. But it also brought support from Brahmins, forsaking the Congress for the BJP, while recruitment of OBCs excluded from the benefits of Mandal or in conflict with the numerous and powerful Yadav caste, also played an important part in bringing the BJP to power as well as in broadening its social base.[11]

The caste origin of the BJP-MLAs of 1991 shows that greater attention was given to the constituencies' social composition. In the new context introduced by the Mandal controversy and the greater role the OBCs were demanding to play in politics, relying on the original Brahmin–Bania combine could have proved disastrous. The proportion of MLAs of the various caste-groups in 1985, 1989 and 1991 shows that the BJP gave particular attention to balance them and to integrate some of the smallest

[11] The gains in western UP have as much to do with the Jats' exclusion from Mandal and the Sainis' and Lodhs' enmity with Yadavs than with their religious conscienceness.

castes. While in 1985, out of 4 BJP-MLAs from the Backward Castes, 3 Lodhs and one Yadav could be found, the proportion of these castes had been reduced by 1989 (respectively 3 and 1 out of 11 MLAs) with the appearance of the Kurmi, Kewat and Jat legislators. By 1991, other smaller castes relevant locally such as the Mallah or Tyagi in Eastern UP and Saini and Gujjar in Western UP were to be found in numbers in their ranks and they remained among the candidates of the Assembly elections of 1996.[12] Another interesting trend was the appearance of Kurmi legislators in a vast proportion and the subsequent decrease in the number of Yadavs. In 1991, out of 40 OBC MLAs in the BJP, 12 were Kurmis and 11 Lodhis, while only 5 were Yadavs. This shift was to remain a characteristic of the BJP, forging an OBC support base around a Kurmi/Lodhis axis with smaller castes coming to reinforce it. In addition to this, the adequacy of the candidates with their socio-economic background was not overlooked, in spite of the significance of communal mobilization, and this enabled the BJP to secure a seat in more constituencies than the former sort of polarization may have allowed. In 1996 again, a similar process was repeated.

The years 1985–91 also saw the BJP's Scheduled Caste base expand following the same process of integration of different caste-groups. In 1985, out of the two BJP-MLAs, one was a Valmiki and the other a Chamar. In 1985, out of the two BJP-MLAs from the Scheduled Castes, one was a Valimiki and the other a Chamar. In 1989, the BJP had secured 13 reserved seats—more than for members of the Backward castes—and 4 Koris, 2 Dhobis, 1 Baiswar and 3 Chamars could be identified among them. In 1991, the success of the process was visible through the appearance in the BJP's ranks of Khatik, Gond, Darkhar, Pasi, Shilpkar and Dohare MLAs in addition to the already present Valmiki, Dhobi, Baiswar and Chamar. The 4 castes of Chamar, Pasi, Dhobi and Kori accounted for 36 out of 57 Scheduled Castes MLs, but most of the small castes were to remain among the party's MLAs elected in 1993 and 1996. Interestingly enough, the same held for the same held for the Chamar, Dhobi and Kori and Pasi castes for whose vote most parties are vying.

---

[12] These are the provisional findings of our analysis of the origin of the BJP-MLAs from 1985 onwards.

Candidates in reserved constituencies are not elected by a majority of Scheduled Castes voters. Therefore, it is not possible to say that the precise caste of the candidate is determinant. What seems important here is the deliberate choice made by the BJP to select a candidate from a smaller caste.

Some cases such as the Baiswar, Khatik and Dharkar are particularly interesting, insofar as they show the BJP's adeptness at 'studying the social conditions'.[13] These three castes belong to the higher levels of the SC hierarchy and Baiswar and Khatik have recently made some progress in education. In eastern UP, some members of the Khatik community have striven to draw their castemen into the political mainstream, in the 1980s through the Janata Dal then more recently through the BJP, while drawing their attention to the necessity of social reforms to improve their position in society. It did not seem antithetic to a former Khatik Janata Dal MP from the region, himself a founding-member of an association promoting the repudiation of Brahmin priests in Scheduled Castes ceremonies and advocating the adoption by the Scheduled Castes of names usually reserved for the Forward Castes, to have been displaced by his brother-in-law contesting on a BJP ticket. To him, the community's interests were not jeopardized.[14]

The diversification of MLAs' origins after 1989 was however not complemented to the same extent by that of the party's MPs from Uttar Pradesh.[15] In 1989, Brahmins, Kurmis and Scheduled Castes each accounted for two of the party's MPs, while one MP was a Kacchi and another a Rajput. In 1991, out of the party's 51 MPs, 28 belonged to the upper castes, 2 were Jats and only 9 came from the Other Backward Castes and 10 from the Scheduled Castes. Most presumably, this sudden rise in the proportion of upper caste MPs is due to the nature of the 1991 mobilization: both the anti-Mandal and the Ayodhya campaigns were led by upper and intermediary castes. In selecting candidates from these castes, the BJP was reflecting the involvement of the electorate and having a

[13] To account for the BJP's victory in a long-time CPI Kurmi-dominated stronghold, one respondent explained that after many years of 'studying', the BJP had decided to field a Kurmi as well.

[14] Interview Raj Nath Sonkar Shastri, Varanasi district, 11 March 1996.

[15] I am indebted to Christophe Jaffrelot for sharing these results with me.

higher chance of seeing its candidates elected. Indeed, by 1996, upper castes accounted for 20 of the party's 52 MPs—Brahmin and Rajput in equal proportion—while the number of the OBCs had risen to 8 and that of SCs to 14. Therefore, it seems that the type of social equation put together by the BJP has varied with the disappearance of religious mobilization and has to some extent followed the demands for wider representation coming from a section of the OBCs and the SCs.

Another relevant criterion of the BJP's expansion after 1991 is the party's regional progression, showing a diffusion of the party's support throughout UP (see Table 2.5).

TABLE 2.5:   Regional Breakdown of Votes in 1991, 1993 and 1996 Vidhan Sabha Elections

Regions	Number of Seats	1991	1993	1996
Uttarkhand	19	15 (79%)	10 (50%)	17 (89%)
Rohilkhand	50	27 (34%)	24 (48%)	22 (44%)
Oudh	109	51 (47%)	43 (39%)	35 (32%)
Poorvanchal	91	39 (43%)	26 (29%)	34 (37%)
Bundelkhand	22	10 (45%)	8 (36%)	7 (32%)
Lower Doab	64	26 (41%)	22 (34%)	21 (33%)
Upper Doab	70	38 (54%)	44 (63%)	37 (53%)

Considering that the results of 1991 have not been equalled since then, except in Uttarkhand and in the Upper Doab, Figure 2.1 enables us to see three kinds of patterns. Firstly, there is a clear stabilization in the Lower Doab, where the share of votes gained by the BJP remains virtually at the 1993 level. This is the only region where stability can be found. In the others recession or progression are evident.

In Oudh and Rohilkhand, two places where communalization had brought the BJP many seats in 1991, the regular decrease is related to the reaction of the Muslim electorate, which after 1991 contributed to the rise of the Samajwadi Party in this part of the state. In 1996, the relative downplaying of the Hindutva motto was also detrimental to the BJP in withdrawing that part of the electorate which voted in 1991 and 1993 on religious criteria but who were not hard-core supporters of Hindutva.

The most striking features of Figure 2.1 are the sharp progression of the party in the two agrarian zones of Poorvanchal and the Upper Doab where Backward and Other Backward Castes are economically dominant. In the Upper Doab in particular, the BJP remains in a predominant position with more than 50 per cent of

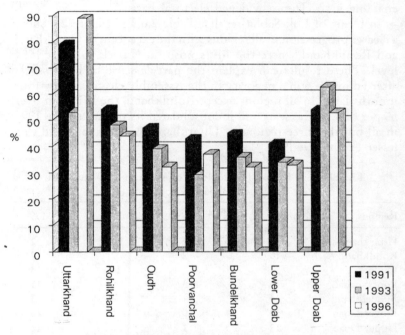

FIGURE 2.1: Percentage of Seats Gained by Region for 1991, 1993 and 1996 Vidhan Sabha Elections (Region-wise)

the seats, while in Poorvanchal also it has gained since 1993. In these two regions, the demise of the Janata Dal which attracted votes from the rural middle castes and middle classes has given the BJP a shot in the arm. The Samajwadi Party, essentially because of the central position of Yadavs in its structure, has not been able to claim the full heritage of the Janata Dal. Social tensions between Yadavs and Jats and Sainis in the West and Yadavs and Kurmis in the East have contributed to a split in the Janata Dal's following. Contrary to 1991, the BJP's progression in the Upper Doab is no longer linked to the religious feelings of the voters. It now benefits from the degradation of their economic position and a sense of betrayal after Ajit Singh's shift to the Congress.[16] Yet, to take the example of the Jats' support to the BJP in and after 1991, it appears that economic issues took a second position in their voting criteria, preceded by their staunch rejection of Mandal. Mandal indeed appears as the dominant moment in the BJP's expansion phase, enabling it to claim a widened electoral basis.[17]

In terms of Lok Sabha results, Table 2.6 and Figure 2.2 show a clearer progression in all regions with the exception of Uttarkhand and Rohilkhand where the BJP's position is back to a pre-1991 level. These results can explain the party's sense of helplessness after failing to win a majority in the Assembly elections only four months later. In all regions except Rohilkhand, the BJP won over 50 per cent of the seats and it consolidated its position since 1991 in all but the three regions of Uttarkhand, Bundelkhand and to a lesser extent, Oudh.[18]

TABLE 2.6:   Regional Breakdown of Votes in 1989 and 1991
Lok Sabha Elections

Regions	Number of Seats	1989	1991	1996
Uttarkhand	4	2	4	2
Rohilkhand	10	2	7	2
Oudh	21	1	14	13
Poorvanchal	19	3	9	11
Bundelkhand	4	1	4	3
Lower Doab	14	0	5	10
Upper Doab	13	1	8	11

[16] See the findings of Lieten, G. K., 'Inclusive View of Religion: A Rural Discourse in Uttar Pradesh', *Economic and Political Weekly*, 8 June 1996, for expression of economic discontent and support for the BJP in a village of Muzaffarnagar district.

[17] See Gupta, Dipankar, *Rivalry and Brotherhood* (Delhi: Oxford University Press, 1997).

[18] In Uttarkhand, what could appear to be a setback is only a momentary revival of N. D. Tiwari's influence in the region, benefiting from an anti-Congress and independent mood. In the Assembly elections, only four months later, the AIIC (T) was wiped out for linking with the SP under the United Front list. Under the SP–BSP government headed by Mulayam Singh, Uttarkhand demonstrators were violently assaulted and some of them killed by the police in Muzaffarnagar on 2 October 1994.

The results of the 1996 elections—both General and Assembly—are more balanced than those of 1991 and 1993. They seem to show that the BJP has reached

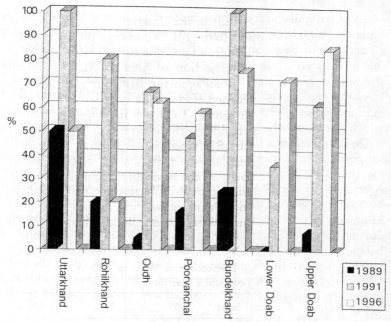

FIGURE 2.3:   Percentage of Seats Gained by the BJP in 1989, 1991 and 1996 Lok Sabha Elections (Region-wise)

LIMITS TO THE BJP'S EXPANSION IN UP

The dismissal of its government and the imposition of President's Rule following the destruction of the Babri Masjid, seem to have brought an important change in the BJP's conception of its priorities. The expansion of its social base appears to have been identified as the main challenge towards gaining power in the 1996 elections. In 1995, by deciding to support the BSP government, the party seemed to have made the portent conclusion of going the way the Congress party had done in the 1970s and 1980s: associate its own Forward Caste base with the Scheduled Castes. In terms of

---

a stage where consolidation has occured because of the dedramatized scene and decline of the Janata Dal and Congress. Yet, this is also disappointing from the point of view of the party's strategists since the BJP's growth has not matched the fall of the Congress, resulting in a vacuum where the SP as well as the BSP can fit.

external compulsions, the firm support given to Mulayam Singh
Yadav by his own caste—about 8 per cent of UP's population and
20 per cent of Backwards—and the emergence of Dalits as one of
the most politicized section of UP society gave sense to this
attempt at garnering their support. The alliance also seemed
workable due to the Dalits' unclear approach to Hindutva. The
indifference of Dalits to Hindutva is an interesting phenomenon
which paradoxically helps the BJP. To some of them, Hindutva
is not perceived as a threat and it seems that since 1995, the BJP's
support of the Mayawati government has led more Dalits to vote
for the BJP. A similar pattern was observed during the 1996
Assembly elections when the Dalits voted for Congress candidates
because of the alliance between the Congress and the BSP.
Mulayam Singh's refusal to accept Mayawati's Chief Ministership
during the talks that followed the 1996 Assembly elections is
balanced by the BJP's and even the Congress's 'progressive'
attitude towards her. To quote an influencial exponent of the Dalit
views, 'the threat of social fascism (power to the Backward Castes)
is greater than the threat of communal fascism (power to the
BJP).'[19]

In terms of internal dynamics, however this strategy meant
reducing the weight in the UP unit of BJP of the OBC lobby (led
by Kalyan Singh) which was staunchly opposed to this decision.
Quite significantly, this conflict revealed the difficulty for any
party to win the majority of seats in UP's increasingly fragmented
society, and it indicated that the problems which had led to the
INC's demise from the foreground of state politics now had to be
dealt with by the BJP.

Starting in the early 1980s under the influence of Sanjay Gandhi,
the Congress had tried to integrate other sections of society because
the traditional equation of support (Forward Castes, Scheduled
Castes and Muslims) came to be increasingly challenged both
externally, by the Lok Dal and later the Janata Dal and internally
by the party's own political vacillation. The rise in the number
of Backward leaders elected on a Congress ticket in the 1985 and
1989 Assembly elections proved that, although Forward Castes
were to remain dominant in the party other sections could
be sucessfully brought in. Indeed, while in 1985, Backwards

[19] Conference of Chandra Bhan Prasad from the *Dalit Shiska Andolan*
(New Delhi: Teen Murti Library, 12 August 1997).

represented only about 12 per cent of Congress MLAs against over 38 per cent for Forward Castes, by 1989 their proportion had risen to 18 per cent. Yet, the rise was not complemented by a fall in the percentage of upper-caste MLAs, who still accounted for over 36 per cent of MLAs, but by a decline in the Scheduled Castes legislators, falling from 28 to only 20 per cent.

However, the resistance of the Forward caste lobby in the Congress prevented the growth of any real Backward influence inside the party. One of the few influential Backward leaders in the 1980s in the UP Congress acknowledged the difficulty of selecting his candidates from a district were Backwards represented over 20 per cent of the population, being able to place only one of them—who incidentally won—in the 25 years he had spent in the party.[20] By 1993, BCs MLAs only accounted for 7 per cent of the 28 Congress MLAs, while FCs remained at 43 per cent.

The resilience of the old power structure in the Congress cannot adequately be transposed onto the BJP to account for the tensions within its leadership. As has been argued previously, the BJP has been careful, since 1985, to integrate UP's main castes, whether more numerous or more politically conscious, into the party. Though their chief political association is not with BJP but with the SP and the BSP respectively, Yadav and Chamar legislators have been elected on BJP tickets.

Instead of trying to break Chamar votes for the BSP or Pasi votes for the Janata Dal, the BJP has focused on empowerment of the other castes. This strategy has paid dividends electorally. In the Scheduled Castes categories, the smaller castes are often unhappy with the larger Chamar-dominated Dalit movements, in particular the BSP, and thus willing to associate with non-Scheduled Castes groups in order to enter the political mainstream. It seems that until the 1990s, the Khatiks of UP had preferred to side with the peasant parties rather than with the INC and the Chamars.[21] The search for a separate identity that crosses through the larger groups be it Backward Castes or Scheduled Castes, is being aptly used by the BJP as a way of further dividing SP and BSP votes. The choice of a Baiswar[22] candidate for the 1991, 1993 and 1996 Assembly

[20] Interview Shyam Lal Yadav, Varanasi, 5 April 1996.

[21] Interview Raj Nath Sonkar Shastri, Varanasi district, 11 March 1996.

[22] Baiswar are only about 16,000 but they are concentrated in Sonebhadra, Mirzapur and Varanasi districts.

elections in Robertsganj constituency (Sonebhadra district) is an example that the BJP is still trying to bring smaller Scheduled Castes into the party, in particular in the eastern part of UP where Chamars are not as socially dominant and politically aware as their Jatav subcaste in western UP.

The limits of the design are evident. However politically conscious other castes may become, Chamars will still represent 60 per cent of UP's Scheduled Castes. Kanshi Ram and Mayawati have managed to convince them of the necessity of being in charge of the Scheduled Caste movement, not merely ranking behind the Congress. Consequently, the BJP's possibility for expansion among Chamars seems determined by their dissatisfaction with the BSP.

With the Backward and Other Backward Castes, the situation is more complex because economic issues play an important part in their choice of political association. The economic situation of the rural middle classes has stagnated since the mid-1980s, contributing to their political volatility between the Janata Dal and the Bharatiya Janata Party. The reservation issue has been the main polarizing factor in the recent years, drawing some castes to the JD and others to the BJP. The last elections have shown the consistent support of former Chief Minister Kalyan Singh's caste, the Lodh, to his party as well as, locally, that of smaller OBCs such as Kewats, Muraos or Maurya, Mallahs and Gujjars. It seems that the very same process of matching going on within the Scheduled Caste group is also taking place inside the BC and OBC categories, namely an association of the various small castes against the larger ones such as the Yadav, or to some extent the Jat, which have been the leading and most dominant rural castes in terms of political representation. If the BJP has taken this demand into account through the selection of candidates belonging to these castes, they have also been careful not to jeopardize their position with the two large groups of Lodhs and Kurmis,[23] and these two castes still represented a very large share of BJP MLAs from the Backward Castes in the 1991 and 1996 Assemblies.

So far, the backbone of the BJP electorate remains the upper castes. During the electoral campaign, some commentators found evidence of a uniform pattern of votes in the villages, with

[23] According to the 1931 Census, Lodhs and Kurmis represented over 5 per cent of the state's population as against nearly 9 per cent for the Yadavs. The other main backward castes ranged between 0.7 and 2.8 per cent of the population.

Brahmins loudly voicing their support for the BJP[24] while other castes seemed more reserved or undecided. The SP and the BSP BJP-supported governments of 1993–5 have contributed to the weakening of upper-caste ascendancy in UP and intensified feelings of insecurity born of the economic rise of the Backward Castes and the new reservation programmes. These feelings are quite distinct in cities like Varanasi, Gorakhpur and Lucknow which are connected to a large rural hinterland. The sense of isolation, developing into an 'inferiority complex of the majority',[25] is a vital factor behind the massive Brahmin and Bania vote for the BJP as a reply to Muslim, Backward or Scheduled Caste political assertion. Though Christophe Jaffrelot has essentially used this concept in the context of Hindu–Muslim relations, it seems to us that, in some cases, it can also be applied to the upper-caste community and their relations with the other castes. We shall take here the example of the upper-caste Bengali community in Varanasi to illustrate the growth of this feeling in the recent years. Concentrated in a small segment of the city, located between the Ganges and a large Muslim settlement, they used to support the left parties until the mid-1970s, but have since then been increasingly responding to the Jana Sangh and later to the BJP's rhetoric. The INC candidate for the 1996 Assembly elections in the City South constituency, himself a Bengali Brahmin and a former socialist, explained this evolution as a consequence of their position as a 'minority' in Varanasi.[26] Bengalis are indeed a minority in Varanasi city (about 25,000 voters in City South) but as a part of the larger upper-caste group, they are a majority both in the city and the constituency. Therefore, the important fact is not their numerical superiority but their psychological inferiority feeling against other castes which they perceive as increasingly influential and well-organized.[27] The BJP has responded to this feeling of vulnerability by choosing upper-caste candidates in the urban constituencies, while they hardly are numerous among its candidates in the rural areas.

[24] Hasan, Mushir-ul & Saeed Naqvi, 'Caste is the Vote', *Outlook*, 8 May 1996.
[25] As Christophe Jaffrelot has named it. See his *Hindu Nationalist Movement and Indian Politics, 1925 to the 1990s*, Delhi: Viking Press, 1996.
[26] Interview, Dev Prat Majumdar, Varanasi, 9 April 1997.
[27] The Yadav community, visually very present in Varanasi, as they are supposed to own the myriad of stray cattle that throng the streets, have often been described to me as a 'mafia' by upper-caste members, stressing not so much their presumed illegal dealings as the sense of insecurity of the respondents.

Our hypothesis is that whereas, this choice in the 1980s reflected the party's reliance on urban upper-caste support, in particular, Brahmins and Banias today, considering the party's efforts at building a social base among other groups, it is much more a sign of the BJP's willingness to oblige upper castes in what they consider as restoring their legitimate dominance in a crumbling social order. Electorally, this strategy is very successful as Figure 2.3 shows. The rise of the BJP in cities since 1989 is remarkable. Since the last general elections, only two of UP's main cities, most remarkably, those with the highest Muslim population,[28] are not represented by BJP MPs. This quasi-monopoly over urban representation is reinforced by the domination of Municipal Legislative Councils in the KAVAL towns (Kanpur, Agra, Varanasi, Allahabad, Lucknow) and is likely to go on as more and more upper castes leave UP's countryside for its growing cities.

Therefore in the current situation, cities seem to provide the safest reservoir of votes for the BJP but this is at the price of an

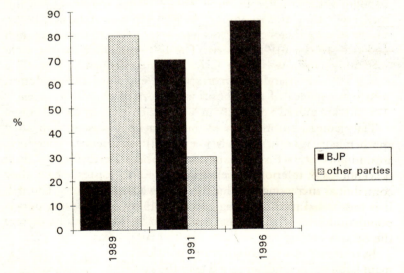

FIGURE 2.3:   Presence of the BJP in Lok Sabha Constituencies Comprising UP's Major Cities

[28] We have taken into account Kanpur, Lucknow, Varanasi, Agra, Allahabad, Meerut, Ghaziabad, Bareilly, Moradabad, Dehra Dun, Aligarh, Jhansi, Saharanpur, Gorakhpur and Shahjahanpur.

alienation of BC and SC voters. Though the BJP seems to be attempting to bring them behind the upper-castes,[29] the gains are not sufficient to bring the party to power, since the upper-castes do not represent more than 20 per cent of UP's population and with the decline of the Congress, the pattern of vote in UP has shown a remarkable volatility. In 1996, 15 of the 51 seats that the BJP had won in 1991 were returned to the opposition, i.e. 30 per cent of them. While some seats can still be considered as safe, in particular in the cities, the BJP's support is not unconditional, as can be seen in Table 2.5. Some MPs have not been renominated and some other have not been returned because of their complete idleness and in the worst cases, corruption, after their victory in 1991. In the last general elections, the Samajwadi Party progressed even more at the expense of the BJP than it regained former JD seats while the BSP got one-third of its seats from those same constituencies.

TABLE 2.7:   Seats Won by the SP and BSP at the Expense of Other Parties in the 1996 General Elections

	INC	JD or JP	BJP	BSP
SP	0	7	8	1
	INC	JD or JP	BJP	SP
BSP	0	4	2	0

The changing features of caste mobilization from one region to another have made it difficult for the BJP to build a stable base around the larger caste-groups in the whole state. The relative peacefulness of the political context in the 1996 campaign has also contributed to a loss in the regions where Muslims are numerous. It is indeed significant that in 10 of the 15 lost seats, the Muslim population is over 15 per cent and that 7 of them were won by the SP.

In terms of future mobilization, political volatility is the BJP's main liability. It is not simply due to the voters' difficulty to come to terms with the post-Congress political scene but it also springs

---

[29] As in Lucknow in the last elections, where it had gained the support of the *Maharishi Balmiki Seva Sansthan*, caste association of the Balmikis, or in central UP of the *Kurmi Mahasabha*.

from each and every party's withdrawal from the front of economic development, improvement of social conditions and crime control. In that sense, it is meanigful of a maturing of the electorate, which tends more and more to demand an assessment of the work of their representatives. This does not mean that accountable government has become an electoral winner in UP. Caste and community relations are still the two main concerns, as the fate of some absentee MPs shows, shifted to safer seats where the caste equation would favour them or where their image would win them votes.[30] UP society remains highly polarized by caste but community relations also remain a factor of political mobilization. Therefore, it is necessary to show to what extend this factor influenced the BJP's fate since 1991 and whether the decrease in communal tension and violence has contributed to electoral losses for the BJP.

Though the 1996 campaign took place in a very unemotional climate with Hindu–Muslim relations deliberately played down by the BJP leaders, the impact of the previous polarization lines (Mandal and Ayodhya) could still be felt. The stability demonstrated by upper-caste vote, and in particular Brahmins', stroke many commentators throughout UP: there seemed to be no other choice for them, whether in rural or urban areas, but to vote for the BJP as the sole representative of their interests. I have argued before that the adoption by the INC of pro-majority themes was a turning-point in the politics of UP, making these themes acceptable to Hindu voters who might not have dared to voice them until then. It seems to me that the Ram Janmabhoomi campaign, and above all the destruction of the Babri Masjid, was the consolidation of that tendency. While the Congress's attitude started the polarization of communities, the Ram Mandir movement further influenced the upper castes to conceive the possibility of asserting their ritual predominance also in political terms.

---

[30] The transfer of Sachidanand Sakshi Maharaj, former MP from Mathura, to Lodhi-Rajput dominated Farrukhabad is illustrative of both aspects of the strategy. A Lodhi-Rajput sadhu, Maharaj had vehemently campaigned against Muslims and for the handover of the Mathura Krishnajanmasthan. Once elected, he seemed to have dropped any interest for his constituency. In the 1996 electoral context, he may have lost his seat in Mathura, but won in Farrukhabad where Lodhs are numerous. Almora constituency is another exemple where the BJP chose to withdraw his Brahmin MP and field a candidate of the same Rajput caste as the Congress candidate and four times MP.

Though the construction of a Ram Mandir at Ayodhya, or the recovery of the shrines at Mathura and Varanasi, were only propagated by the extremists of the VHP and parts of the RSS, in 1996 the question of the status of Muslims in Indian society remained in the mind of many of UP's Brahmins. In the interviews I conducted with members of this caste throughout 1996 and 1997, they almost invariably described their withdrawal from the Congress as a rejection of 'its pseudo-secularism' and its 'appeasement of Muslims'. In my point of view, these reasons came to be identified retroactively as a justification to their attraction for the BJP. But this is not so important as the fact that they were offered to me by virtually every articulate Brahmin I interviewed, except in Uttarkhand. Most strikingly, they were to be found even among long-time INC supporters or ideologues, showing that the legitimacy of this discourse had come to be accepted across political lines within the Brahmin community. It does not imply actual militancy but that a significant rethinking of Muslims' position in Indian society—first of all, the adoption of a common civil code—figures prominently in the desires of a powerful and vocal part of the electorate.[31]

Since the 1993 elections which followed the destruction of the Babri Masjid, Muslims seem to have consolidated their political reasoning in UP, aligning more systematically with Mulayam Singh Yadav's SP. The antics of the Imam Bukhari, the Shahi Imam of the Jama Masjid in Delhi, who urged them to vote for the BSP and appeared at the BSP meetings during the 1996 general election campaign, have had as little impact on their votes as the Congress's belated projection of Muslim leaders, such as Salman Khurshid or Arif Mohammed Khan. The Muslims' animosity towards the Congress was focused on Narasimha Rao for his unability to defend the Babri Masjid, notwithstanding his own public pledge and all the freedom given to him by the secular parties. Obviously, during the general elections, Narasimha Rao was *persona non grata* in UP and the Muslims leaders in his party were having a hard time trying to draw voters' minds away from him. But this resentment has now taken the form of a positive association with the SP, which the BSP's current commitment with the BJP will probably

---

[31] See for a similar point of view, Robinson, Rowena, 'Losing (Hope) to the BJP', *Economic and Political Weekly*, 5 July 1997, pp 1579–80.

reinforce. Quite understandably, the BSP is seen by Muslims as an unstable party, bent on acquiring power at the price of any reversal of alliance, including passing from the Congress to the BJP,[32] and once in power, hardly keen on helping Muslims.[33]

Antagonizing the Muslims, as it did during the Ayodhya campaign, cannot bring the BJP to power in a fragmented society. It seems to have realized that and its attempts to play down the anti-Muslim discourse of the other members of the Sangh Parivar during the 1996 general elections point towards the exit of the Hindutva credo from the foreground of UP's political scene. The ideological gap between the BJP and the RSS/VHP combine sharpened during the campaign, with the VHP crusading against animal slaughtering in eastern UP and asking for the restitution of the Gyanvapi mosque in Varanasi. Meanwhile, L. K. Advani's rath yatra which passed through the highly Muslim populated districts of Faizabad, Ayodhya and Bara Banki was much more moderate. The 'visibility' of the BJP's hostility to Muslims has become an essential advantage which cannot be discarded in winning upper-caste voters. Paradoxically, for some Muslims, it has also become a synonym of the BJP's political uprightness—in the sense of adherence to an agenda—as opposed to the Congress's duplicity. Though the Muslims's rejection of the Congress was chiefly associated with Narasimha Rao, they still regard it as untrustworthy in spite of Rao's replacement by Sitaram Kesri. During the Assembly elections in October 1996, the Congress–BSP alliance could not win them back.

The tensions at work across the BJP's support base have found one channel of expression inside the party in the resistance of the Backward Caste section to a further commitment to the BSP and another one with the other components of the Sangh Parivar in dissatisfaction with the dilution of the Hindutva rhetoric.

Social engineering seems to have taken the lead over religious polarization in the BJP's strategy in UP or as the expression goes in Congress circles, 'the BJP is hesitating between Rama and Kanshi Rama.' Under the injunctions of Kalyan Singh, the BJP has been trying since the last elections not only to balance further the proportion of upper castes with members of other *varna*, but also

---

[32] The BSP had allied with the Congress during the Assembly elections of october 1996, only months before it chose to form a governement with the BJP.
[33] Interviews, Lucknow, April 1996 and Varanasi February–April 1997.

to give them wider responsibilities and hearing in the party. This seems like the logical sequel to the expansion started as early as 1989. However, the general context of OBC assertion has since then made some of the upper caste leadership of the party uneasy about the impact of this evolution. Thus sharp tensions have appeared between the general and Assembly elections of 1996, over the interpretation of the results, between Kalyan Singh's group and the upper-caste lobby headed by Kalraj Mishra and Lalji Tandon and supported by Murli Manohar Joshi. In the eleventh general elections indeed, nearly 80 per cent of the BJP backward-caste candidates were returned against 45 per cent of the forward castes. This, together with the nomination of new OBCs at positions of power in the party's organization in UP has contributed to a growing dissatisfaction among the upper castes, culminating in open criticism and even in some cases actual fight.[34] In addition, the new-comers generally originate from parties more unruly than the BJP and do not have the RSS background of discipline and group-achievement.[35] The results of the 1996 Assembly elections have led the central leadership of the party to introduce a counterweight to Kalyan Singh and to try to limit the dissensions born from his bias for the Backwards. Like the general elections, the Assembly elections were marked by rebellion and protest by the sitting MLAs who had been denied tickets and a 'total lack of coordination' was deplored as one of the causes of the failure to gain a majority.[36]

In addition to the problems brought about by OBC assertiveness, the confirmation that the Dalit political movement could not be written off has also contributed to fuel these disruptions. After the decline of the Congress and rise of the BJP, the BSP-led Dalit emergence has been the most striking feature of the recent political scene in UP. In just 12 years, the BSP has managed to become UP's

[34] See the stir in Kanpur after the nomination of a Nishad (OBC) new-comer as the Chairperson of the State Fisheries Corporation.

[35] The turmoil caused by the new BJP MP from Hamirpur (an ex-Janata Dal member, belonging to Kalyan Singh's caste) in trying to organize the OBCs across party-lines is significant of these instances, driving the RSS to organize sessions on party loyalty for the BJP MPs. *Pioneer*, 21 November 1996.

[36] In the words of party general secretary, K. N. Govindacharya who headed the study team set up after the defeat in the UP Assembly elections. Atal Bihari Vajpayee has also lamented the indiscipline and the factionnalism in the party. See *Pioneer*, 2 September 1996, 2 August 1996 and 9 November 1996.

third party in terms of vote and seats, displacing the INC, and more importantly, to take part in three governments in the last four years. Its achievements have been more symbolic than tangible, but in that sense, they have deeply transformed UP's political culture. With its concern for the Ambedkar villages, its statues of Dr Ambedkar on every street-corner and its scornful treatment of upper-caste bureaucrats, the BSP has managed to capture the imagination of UP Dalits, and to invigorate them with a sense of their own worth. This process is very similar to what has been happening in Bihar under Laloo Prasad Yadav's rule: though economic conditions have not changed for the JD's Scheduled Castes supporters, the later have been given some opportunity to stand up to their former upper-caste landlords because of the Chief Minister's attitude. Just as Laloo Yadav has dramatically transformed political rules in Bihar, Mayawati and Kanshi Ram are attempting the same: giving UP Dalits a sense of belonging to the BSP because it gives them more confidence, if not more resources.

The entrance of the Scheduled Castes into the political mainstream was achieved by Indira Gandhi through talks of *garibi hatao* and implementation of land distribution programmes, thus bringing economic backwardness, not status, to the foreground of political demands.[37] Yet as long as they supported the Congress, Scheduled Castes remained in the background of the organization, relegated to the position of a vote bank. The BSP's objective was to politically empower Dalits. Yet, by putting social identity first, it has also contributed to the downgrading of development issues. Contrary to the case of the Backward and Other Backward Castes, economic development has not been the fuel for Dalit political assertion, which makes it even more difficult for the BJP to get Dalit votes on its own. For the majority of Dalits, the BJP remains an upper-caste party and has no space to accommodate their new forms of expression and their demands.[38] Though the Rashtiya Swayamsevak Sangh has been striving since its creation to build social harmony and equality within its ranks, the Dalits have

---

[37] Incidentally, Muslims have been blaming the Congress for doing just the opposite in their case: refusing to tackle the issue of economic backwardness and segregation. See for instance, Hasan, Mushirul, *Legacy of a Divided Nation. India's Muslims Since Independence* (Delhi: Oxford University Press, 1997), pp 252–97.

[38] For that point of view, see the criticisms made by a member of the *Dalit Shiska Andolan* in *Economic Times*, 29 December 1996.

remained in small numbers in the organization, in particular at the top,[39] and the same applies today to the BJP.

The BJP leaders have been attentive to questions of representation in the party though, like in the Congress, its upper-caste urban constituents have been trying to maintain their prevalence over the party's apparatus. Since its inception, a large section of the OBCs have been successfully integrated into the party and their early association makes it possible for them to raise a significant voice. As UP politics evolves away from upper-caste dominance, this form of tension will certainly multiply. Again, the similarity with the Congress is apparent in the choices to be made to confirm the BJP's predominance over UP's political scene. The Congress's attempts at delinking social issues from its course, its confidence that it could strive on the image of its leaders and its heritage have failed because since the late 1980s, the rules of Indian politics have been sharply modified by the introduction of symbolic politics—whether based on religion or caste—and the focus on caste identity as the exclusive means of political assertion. The birth and the fast growth of new players like the BSP or the SP as well as the BJP's expansion after 1993 reflect the Congress's inability to come to terms with the transformations of UP's political code. But the effects of these changes are not limited to the decline of the Congress and the apparition of new players: they are having far-reaching consequences inside each party's organization. The tendency to structure parties around a solid core of members of the same castes (Yadavs in the case of the SP, upper castes in the case of the BJP or Chamars in the BSP) is now challenged. This has become necessary in order to develop patterns of support crossing ascriptive-based identity and aiming at tangible empowerment inside the party and no longer simple cooptation.

The evolution of the BJP's agenda since the last general elections is in that sense a reflection of the greater interaction between party and society.

THE POST-1996 SCENARIO

The Indian polity has been shaped by the long rule of the Congress party and its left-of-centre and secularist orientations. Following

[39] Jaffrelot Christophe, *Les Nationalistes Hindous* (Paris: Presses de la FNSP, 1993), p. 58.

the demise of the Janata Dal and the collapse of the Congress, sectional politics, whether caste- or community-based, have redefined the boundaries of UP's polity. In that sense, the 'middle-ground' which the Congress had circumscribed has exploded into a cluster of antithetic interests.

BJP's failure to gain power in the 1993 Assembly elections has changed the party's electoral approach. The image it projected in the 1996 campaign for the general elections reflects the change from sectional to national politics. The difficulties of controlling a religion-based mobilization as well as practicing caste politics have made it necessary for the BJP to develop a wider approach and try to reconcile the differentiated interests which had emerged and asserted themselves since the late 1980s. In its way, the BJP is reintroducing the notion of 'middle-ground' politics, which commentators had given up as dead after the series of Assembly elections between 1993–5. 'Middle-ground' politics corresponded to a dominant party system, as developed by Giovanni Sartori in the 1970s,[40] which revolved around the Congress as the only national party. The division of the opposition, both at the national level and in UP, helped the Congress to remain in power. Though the system cannot be revived under the same pattern, the expansion and strenghtening of its national network have been the chief aims of the BJP since the last elections. The forms of this very attempt are proofs to the impact of the last ten years' political reconfiguration. This is reflected in two striking changes from the BJP's previous strategies: the 'no compromise' approach has given way to a greater acceptability of external forces, as demonstrated by the alliance with the BSP, and the anti-Muslim stance has been softened and new arguments of equality before the law introduced.

The growth of the BSP in Uttar Pradesh is a by-product of the shattering of the former Congress vote banks, giving more individual weight to sectional interests and to the parties representing them, and transforming the original balance between parties. The polarization which emerged in the post-Congress years centred around the dynamics of secularism against Hindutva. The BJP's alliance with the BSP can be understood as an attempt at rebalancing UP's polity around new trends, displacing religious polarization

[40] Giovanni Sartori, *Parties and Party System. A Framework for Analysis*, vol. I,(Cambridge: Cambridge University Press, 1976).

from the centre of the political field and getting the full effect of the existing social polarization. The catch-22 results of the 1996 Assembly elections have compelled all political actors, except notably the Congress, to reconsider their social foundations, necessarily breeding tensions with older constituencies.[41]

The BSP's withdrawal of support to the government led by Kalyan Singh amid accusations of 'anti-Dalitness' is significant of the difficulty for any party in the post-Congress polity to associate widely differenciated constituencies. The iconography spree in which Mayawati's government engaged, the misdirecting towards Dalit constituencies of funds generally aimed at development of the state[42] and the massive transfers of non-Dalit officers have bred a feeling of discrimination in the upper castes. In joining hands with the BSP with the hope that it would help expand its electoral support among Dalits, the BJP actually run the risk of eroding its upper-caste base. The rejection felt by upper-caste members during the six months of Mayawati's government and their attention to Mulayam Singh's positioning in their favour[43] has introduced a new variable in the politics of the state. Upper-caste support for the BJP has long been taken for granted, as it had been for the Congress, because of the influence of that section inside the party and the party's own attitude to this 'favourite constituency'. It certainly remains overwhelmingly so, if only because the collapse of the Congress party has deprived them of any real alternative, yet an increased volatility cannot be written off.

The break-away of two-third of Congress legislators, chiefly from the upper castes, is also illustrative of their uneasiness. Acute factionalism between Jitendra Prasada and the newly nominated UPCC chief, N. D. Tiwari, has had its share in the outcome but the fear of upper-caste MLAs not to regain their seats in the advent of new elections is a further explanation to their decision. With upper-castes candidates finding it more difficult to win their seats,[44]

[41] The tensions inside the Samajwadi Party between Mulayam Singh Yadav and Beni Prasad Verma are a reflection of this trend, with Mulayam Singh trying to accommodate upper castes inside the party.

[42] *India Today*, 22 Sept. 1997, pp 22–8.

[43] Mulayam Singh Yadav has asked for instance for 10 per cent reservation to be granted to upper-caste students of poor economic background.

[44] Most of these Congress MLAs were elected thanks to the support of the Scheduled Castes.

their interest in supporting the government was very strong indeed.

These developments have proved that the Congress-style mobilization based on cooptation cannot operate anymore. Both the electorate and their representatives now expect material gains in return for their support.[45]

The BJP's agenda for the 1996 general elections had exposed a noticeable move towards the 'middle-ground', which was later denied by the other parties in their rejection of the confidence motion on the 13-days old Vajpayee government. In the field of the Sangh Parivar's staunchest ideological commitment, the reappraisal of Hindu-Muslim relations, the more recent efforts at propagating issues in constitutional and rational terms mark a clear tendency to decommunalize and dedramatize UP's political norms.[46] However, so far playing down the Hindutva rhetoric remains a political manoeuvre aimed at levelling the playing field. The recent statements made by L. K. Advani during his Swarna Jayanti rath yatra show that the BJP is not backing down on the Sangh Parivar's founding principles.

Strategically speaking, decommunalizing the political field has become particularly important in UP where the electoral expression of Muslims' consternation at the destruction of the Babri Masjid has compromised the party's chances of ever reseizing power. In that sense, consensual politics has become a necessity for the BJP, all the more so as divisions inside the Hindu electorate are sharpening.

However, the close interactions between the Sangh Parivar's members make it impossible for the BJP to stray too far from the RSS's founding commitment to Bharat Mata or the VHP's claim to construct the Ram Mandir. Electorally, it might have to be more receptive to the demands and feelings of its upper-caste base without antagonizing its OBC and Dalit voters. Thus the field of options opened to the BJP and the other parties remains limited by caste and community issues.

[45] All defectors have been accomodated in the new BJP government.
[46] This was voiced by several chief leaders of the BJP during 1996, see Pramod Mahajan mentioning a 'Problem of Articulation' in *The Pioneer*, 2 July 1996, or more significantly L. K. Advani's formulation during his Swarna Jayanti *rath yatra:* 'from Ram Bhakti to Raksha Shakti', *The Hindu*, 4 July 1997.

Ψ

3

Rajput Hindutva, Caste Politics, Regional Identity and Hindu Nationalism in Contemporary Rajasthan

ROB JENKINS

As in the late nineteenth century, a martial Rajput identity is being evoked only partly as a reassertion of caste unity; it is also being evoked as a rallying cry for all Hindus.[1]

Contemporary analyses of the Bharatiya Janata Party's (BJP) efforts to broaden its electoral appeal tend to highlight two clearly identifiable developments. First, the party, in concert with the organizations that make up the Sangh Parivar, has been reaching out to Dalit, OBC, and tribal groups in an effort to dispel its image as a movement dominated by the upper castes. Its grassroots developmental activities in this area,[2] spearheaded by specialized

---

[1] Radhar, Kumar, 'Gender, Politics and Identity at Times of Crisis: The Agitations Around Sati-Daha in India', *Discussion Paper 309* (Brighton, U.K.: Institute of Development Studies, 1992), pp 17–18.

[2] These have been extensive in Rajasthan, particularly in those southern portions of the state which have large tribal populations. The social-welfare work of organizations like the Vanvasi Kalyan Parishad (VKP), a tribal welfare council run by the RSS, was seen to have yielded electoral dividends for the BJP in the 1996 Lok Sabha elections. Operating in collaboration with like-minded local groups and sympathetic individuals, the VKP has in recent years become highly organized and extended its sphere of influence considerably. For instance, in the run up to the 1996 elections, the chairman of the Rajasthan Sports Council (an RSS man), with the help of VKP volunteers, organized massive sporting meets in tribal areas, partially at state expense. These became important occasions for electioneering. Along with the Hindu Jagran Manch (HJM), which also has a long history of social work in tribal areas, the VKP organized campaign tours

front organizations, have been accompanied by a set of broad ideological adjustments. These have centred on denunciations of caste divisions in society, equating them with a corrupted form of Hinduism that weakens Hindu unity. At the same time, the BJP is pursuing a second strategy, consisting of a series of region-specific mobilization campaigns. This represents an attempt to customize both the movement's message and its mode of organizing the wide variety of social and economic circumstances prevailing in India's states.[3] This second strategy (of regionalization), however, has not in general been accompanied by the type of ideological realignment one finds in relation to the party's efforts to woo subaltern communities, despite the very important fact that caste configurations vary widely from state to state (as well as between regions within states). The failure to supply the regionalization strategy with a complementary set of ideological underpinnings is attributable to a widespread belief within the Sangh Parivar that regionalization must proceed *sub rosa*, lest the Hindu nationalist movement should become fragmented along regional lines.[4]

Rajasthan represents an exception to this pattern. Both strategies (of social broadening and regional specificity) are not only in effect, but also supported by the elaboration of a set of corresponding ideological justifications. This is possible in Rajasthan because its history provides ample scope for strategists within the Sangh Parivar to wed nationalism to regionalism, and regional identity to a broadly (though not entirely) inclusive form of caste politics. The skillful exploitation of these historically contingent correspondences may explain why the BJP has had more consistent electoral success in Rajasthan than it has in other states. Of the four state governments dismissed in the wake of the destruction of the Babri Masjid in December 1992, it was only in Rajasthan that the party

---

throughout tribal areas which featured fiery orators from the VHP and the Durga Vahani, the Parivar's women's front. All of these activities were funded with what, in American political parlance, is called 'soft money'—funds that do not figure into the election commissioner's campaign spending limits.

[3] This is, of course, a complicated issue. To be sure, a large part of this process is a result of changes at the grassroots level. But we must also acknowledge the active role of the BJP party élites in crafting a strategy for 'regionalizing' the party.

[4] Interview with a senior politician who is active in the RSS lobby, 3 September 1996, Jaipur.

returned to power when fresh elections were held in November 1993.[5] While the party's fortunes have ebbed and flowed in Uttar Pradesh, Himachal Pradesh, Madhya Pradesh, and more recently in Gujarat, the BJP has maintained power at the state-level in Rajasthan, consistently captured half of the state's parliamentary seats, and continued to increase its share of the popular vote.[6] Unlike in Maharashtra, Punjab, Haryana, or Bihar the BJP in Rajasthan does not rely on a regional party as an ally. Because of the state's unique social structure and experience with democratic politics, *the Rajasthan BJP itself functions like a regional party.*

Whether a similar dynamics could take place in other states—subject to modifications tailored to each region's historical peculiarities—is an empirical question. By examining the Rajasthan experience, however, we can take the issue with arguments, put forth by usually very astute political analysts, that the rise of *regionalism* may presage the demise of the Hindu *nationalist* political force represented by the BJP. Like many other commentators, *Maharashtra Times* Editor Kumar Ketkar has extrapolated from the failure of regional parties to support the BJP's bid to form a national government following the 1996 general election, to argue that regionalism itself will cause a further unraveling of the BJP.[7] The *Economic Times'* Narendar Pani appears to have arrived at a similar equation. Like Ketkar's, Pani's analysis is unreceptive to the notion that the BJP might respond creatively to these trends, which themselves vary in intensity and character from region to region, by regionalizing its ideology, rather than making a few adjustments on points of policy:

[T]he ability of either the Leftist or Hindutva ideology to reach beyond their current allies to all the local groups that are now emerging must be in some doubt. Both ideologies tend to be preoccupied with just one aspect of Indian

---

[5] For an analysis of these elections, see Jenkins, Rob, 'Where the BJP Survived: Rajasthan Assembly Elections, 1993', *Economic and Political Weekly*, vol. XXIX, no. 11, 12 March 1994, pp 635–41.

[6] The BJP vote share rose from 41per cent in 1991 to 47 per cent in 1996. While much of this may be due to the virtual elimination of the Janata Dal and other centre-left parties from the state's electoral scene, it is still impressive, especially as the Congress was expected to be the major beneficiary of this development, having absorbed most of the important Jat leaders from the Janata Dal. In fact, the increase in Congress' popular vote was no greater than the BJP's: a 6 per cent gain, from 44 per cent in 1991 to 50 per cent in 1996.

[7] Ketkar, Kumar, 'Regionalism Will Do BJP in', *Economic Times*, 20 May 1996.

society, whether it is class or religion. Other aspects of Indian society like caste or regional identities are brushed under the carpet. And, whether we like it or not, the politics of some of the emerging local forces centres around caste and regional issues.[8]

And yet, because the BJP in Rajasthan has managed to link region, caste, and Hindu nationalism in a very compelling set of political narratives, we must not discount the prospects for similar developments in other states. Pani argues that the *ad hoc* way in which during the 1996 general election all-India parties went about 'wooing regional parties of all shades' indicates the poor likelihood of national parties adapting coherently and effectively to regional political forces. The problem with this view is that—again, like Ketkar's—it pays too much attention to indications emerging from national parties' strategies for building *alliances* with regional parties, and too little on changes within national parties themselves at the state level. The fact is that we do not know what the impact of regionalization on all-India parties will be, let alone what effect it will have on specific parties in specific regions at specific times. Once upon a time the Congress 'regionalized itself'. And clearly, at distinct historical conjunctures, certain regional parties have applied various degrees of saffron to their images, most notably the Shiv Sena, but in a very different way the AIADMK (All-India Anna Dravida Munnetra Kazhagam) in Tamil Nadu under a Brahmin chief minister Jayalalitha. Only additional detailed research will enlighten us on this question.

The Sangh Parivar in Rajasthan does not rely upon obscure points of theological doctrine or scriptural authority to denounce caste distinctions as a way of unifying the Hindu community. Instead, the emphasis is on exploiting a pre-existing regional identity—one heavily imbued with what has been called the Rajput ethic—and reinventing it for its own purposes. Lloyd and Susanne Rudolph define the Rajput ethic as 'valour without regard to consequences.'[9] The attributes of martial acumen and valour

[8] Pani, Narendar, 'Regional Nationalism: Challenge to National Parties', *Times of India*, 16 May 1996.

[9] Rudolph, Lloyd I. and Susanne Hoeber Rudolph, *Essays on Rajputana: Reflections on History, Culture, and Administration* (New Delhi: Concept Publishing, 1984), p. 4. It is also worth noting that the Hindu nationalist projection of the Rajput ethic in Rajasthan is not uncontested. As the Rudolphs note, there is at least one competing 'practical norm of conduct' also existing in Rajasthan (p. 44).

associated with Rajput warrior/princes[10] are not only venerated by all communities in Rajasthan, but they also conform closely to the sort of assertive nationalism that the Sangh Parivar is attempting to project as a homogenized form of Hinduism. The BJP's tendency to privilege the symbol of Ram, a deity by no means dominant in practices of worship in Rajasthan, nevertheless accords with the prevailing status yardstick of martial honour. It is not particularly relevant to many followers of the Hindutva movement in Rajasthan that the privileging of the Ram myth, particularly its martial aspect, runs contrary to the doctrinal diversity that is seen by many to define Hinduism. That the BJP is 'semiticizing' Hinduism is not a rebuttal that finds favour with the vast bulk of Rajasthan's people.

Of far greater concern to those activated by the emotive mobilization tactics of the Sangh Parivar is the extent to which Rajasthan is accorded a special role within this purported nationalist renaissance. In this construction, Rajasthan is cast as the preserver of the true faith, of the assertive, self-confident, martial tradition of Hinduism. Other regions, according to this interpretation, have seen this tradition subverted under the influence of foreign ideologies, both Muslim and Western. In Rajasthan the flame of honour has not yet been snuffed out. It is the 'sacred fire' from which the rest of India can reignite its sense of lost strength and vitality.

This narrative is a potent source of political mobilization for the Sangh Parivar. It is a manifestation of regional pride, but, crucially, one that does not rely upon regional exclusivism. Its specific character—in contrast to some other regionalist ideologies, like the Telugu movement in Andhra—need not pose problems for its integration into the nationwide organization, which is one reason why the BJP Chief Minister of Rajasthan, Bhairon Singh Shekhawat, is given a relatively free hand in running both state and party, despite his conflicts with the more doctrinaire elements in the RSS. This interpretation of the Rajput ethic is born of a belief in the special contribution of Rajasthan's history to a larger nationalist reawakening. The idea of Rajasthan as a repository of traditional values also has the merit of being able to appeal, in

---

[10] See Hitchcock, John, 'The Idea of the Martial Rajput', in Milton Singer (ed.), *Traditional India* (Austin: University of Texas Press, 1959), especially pp 8–10.

theory, to all sections of the electorate. However, in operation, as we shall see, it does bring to the surface conflicts within Hindu society, to say nothing of its effects on Hindu–Muslim relations.

RAJPUT HINDUTVA AND REGIONAL IDENTITY

The chain of reasoning through which communalist ideology links nationalism, regional identity, and caste politics tends to shift over time in response to the unfolding of political events. The spin also varies according to who is speaking and who is listening. But the basic story is fairly consistent, and is able to draw on the richness of Rajasthani history, with all of its ambiguities and contradictions. The central element is the Rajput community itself. The ideology runs something like this: Rajputana, by maintaining the ideal norm of Kshatriya rule, has always been the protector of traditional Hindu values. Preserving these against foreign influence—especially from holders of power in Delhi—has been and will remain a priority.[11] Congress rule in Rajasthan has been characterized by the subversion of Rajasthan's interests and distinctive identity to a form of pseudo-secularist nationalism that benefits insidious enemies of the Hindu people.

Hindu nationalist forces were greatly assisted in their efforts to portray Rajasthan as the preserver of traditional Hindu values by an incident that occurred in Deorala village of Sikar district on 4 September 1987. Roop Kanwar, a grieving young Rajput widow, performed Sati by, according to conflicting accounts, either jumping or being pushed onto her husband's funeral pyre. While the almost-extinct practice of Sati has never been unique to Rajasthan, the widely recounted (and highly romanticized) tales of devoted princesses hurling themselves to fiery deaths in times of war have helped to associate it with the region in general, and (even more significantly) with the Rajput caste in particular. Three-fourths of

---

[11] Most Rajput states, of course, were by most reckonings far from independent under both Mughal and British rule, and the degree of resistance of many rulers is open to question. The Sangh Parivar has focused its activities popularly associated with valiant military efforts to oppose 'the Muslim invaders': Prithviraj Chouhan and Maharana Pratap. The latter's 400th death anniversary in 1997 has spawned numerous public celebrations, including several organized around L.K. Advani's 900 kilometre yatra through Rajasthan in June. (See Sebastian, Sunny, 'Good Response to Rath Yatra in Rajasthan', *The Hindu*, 11 June 1997.)

all reported Sati-Dahas since Independence have occurred in the Shekhawati region of Rajasthan, comprising the districts of Sikar and Jhunjhunu. Sati is in many ways the supreme manifestation of an ethic which prizes honour above all else, and is cited frequently by Rajasthanis when discussing the unique features of traditional Rajput rule. Though the Congress state government of the time was widely criticized in the national press and the Parliament for allowing the traditional *Chunati-mahotsva* that marks the conclusion of the Sati ceremonies to go ahead twelve days after the Sati, in the eyes of many rural Rajasthanis its non-committal attitude marked it out as just the sort of pseudo-secular organization that the Sangh Parivar in Rajasthan had been making it out to be. The Deorala Sati galvanized the Hindu nationalist movement in Rajasthan, spawning pro-Sati organizations, such as the Sati Dharma Raksha Samiti. These and other offshoots continue to function to this day, organizing commemorative celebrations for well-known Sati episodes in Rajasthan history, making donations to temple trusts, and supporting educational activities.

There are several caste-related aspects to this particular form of reconstituted tradition. First, according to Shail Mayaram, the Samiti 'was a much needed excuse for a tightening of Rajput solidarity between lineages.'[12] The coming together of Rajput leaders across divisions of party, region, and clan was a clear political correlate of this process. A line-up of speakers at a public meeting organized by the Samiti in Jaipur the following month denounced an ordinance, hastily passed by the state legislature the previous week, designed to prevent Sati more effectively in the future. The Rajput leaders who spoke at the meeting all espoused the cause of Sati, while one political heavyweight from the Jat community who addressed the rally, Lok Dal leader Nathuram Mirdha (later of the Janata Dal, and then a Congressman until his death in 1996), stated that 'the institution of Sati had no relevance in the present age.'[13] Whether he supported the practice or not, Mirdha's assessment of irrelevance was clearly off the mark, for it had (and continues to have) an important place in the popular imagination and in the rhetorical armoury of the Hindu nationalist

[12] Mayaram, Shail, 'Communal Violence in Jaipur', *Economic and Political Weekly*, 13–20 November 1993, p. 2534.

[13] Pangariya, B. L., *State Politics in India* (Jaipur: National Publishing, 1988), p. 163.

movement in Rajasthan. (We shall return to the question of Jat–Rajput rivalry, and its connection to the unfolding of the ideology of Rajput Hindutva, in due course.)

Second, Sudesh Vaid has argued that a somewhat hidden dimension of this process has been the use of Sati by Shekhawati Rajputs, traditionally not a very influential or respected clan, as a vehicle for forwarding their claim of increased stature.[14] The basis of this claim lay primarily in their successful participation in electoral politics and the state services, both police and administrative, since Independence. Their association with Sati was, in this view, a symbolic accompaniment—one designed to bring their political and ritual status into better equilibrium. How effective this has been is open to debate, and will require further research, but Vaid's point helps to convey the close association between the political aspirations of specific subcastes and the mobilizational strategies of the Hindu nationalist movement.

The third caste-related aspect to this process concerns the role of trading communities as financial backers of these Rajput-orchestrated Sati mobilizations. The Rajput–Bania axis (in Rajasthan, sometimes called the Rajput–Mahajan or Rajput–Jain axis) has a long pedigree in Rajasthan. According to Kumkum Sangari, this has been revitalized and restructured through their collaboration in staging the Deorala Sati.[15] The implication is that the increasing influence of money-power on political conflict (and not just of the electoral type) has been sanctified in the form of a closer alliance between Shekhawati Rajputs and the state's many trading communities, including (interestingly) Jains and non-resident Rajasthani business figures (primarily Marwaris). Thus, politics both within the Rajput community and between Rajputs and other communities is represented within this particular cultural practice, which as we have seen also serves to link the region of Rajasthan to a particular conception of pan-Hindu identity.

According to the ideological construction promulgated by Hindu nationalists in Rajasthan, the defining feature of Rajputana—the special gift of the land of the Rajputs to the Hindu nationalist reawakening—has been its preservation of a stable social order

[14] Vaid, Sudesh, 'Politics of Widow Immolation', *Seminar*, no. 342, February 1988.

[15] Sangari Kumkum, 'Perpetuating the Myth', *Seminar*, no. 342, February 1988.

through Rajput rule. But, as is often stressed in communalist discourse, this social order is tolerant and accommodating, not exclusivist. Though divided by clan rivalries, the Rajput community, and the social relations in which it is embedded, are the embodiment of an ideology which uses the traits of honour and shame as yardsticks against which to measure social prestige. To the extent that this contrasts with the more prevalent scale of social status, which dichotomizes purity and pollution, the Rajput ethic provides for a more *just* social order. Because Rajput rule tended to enforce meritocratic standards in the realm of politics—a sphere which was elevated above both spiritual and material affairs in traditional Rajasthani society—it also helped to unleash human endeavour and undermine the insidious ideology of renunciation and passivity to which the Hindu nation has elsewhere been subjected.

The tolerance of the social order under traditional Rajput rule is a point that is stressed often by those sympathetic to Hindu nationalism in Rajasthan. 'Why are the Jains so rich in Rajasthan?' asked an editorial staff member of the heavily BJP-oriented *Rajasthan Patrika*, the state's leading daily newspaper. 'They have done so well here that we have become a major exporter of Hindu Banias [i.e. Marwari businessmen]. There has never been persecution in Rajasthan for any group that is loyal and plays by the rules. Only those that are out to harm the Hindu way have met with difficulties.'[16]

To summarize a view put forward by Iqbal Narain and P. C. Mathur, Rajputs in Rajasthan stand as the embodiment of martial values and perform the functional role played by Brahmins in other parts of India.[17] Instead of Sanskritization, lower-status groups in Rajasthan sought upward mobility engaged in a process of Kshatriyanization.[18] Thus, today in Rajasthan a range of Dalit, tribal, OBC, Christian, and even Muslim groups claim descent

[16] Interview, 22 October 1993, Jaipur.

[17] See Narain, Iqbal and P. C. Mathur, 'The Thousand Year Raj: Regional Isolation and Rajput Hinduism in Rajasthan before and after 1947', in Francine Frankel and M. S. A. Rao (eds), *Dominance and State Power in Modern India: Decline of a Social Order*, vol. II (Delhi: Oxford University Press, 1990), pp 1–58.

[18] For a succinct description of this concept, see Frankel, Francine, 'Introduction', in Francine Frankel and M. S. A. Rao (eds), *Dominance and State Power in Modern India: Decline of a Social Order*, vol. I (Delhi: Oxford University Press, 1989), pp 1–20.

from, or intimate historical association with, Rajput clans. As Raymond Jamous[19] has pointed out, Meo Muslims in Rajasthan view some of their adopted rituals (in marriage ceremonies and rules governing marriage alliances, for instance) as distinctively Rajput.[20] Interestingly, they do not consider these practices as possessing a particularly Hindu dimension. The implication is that 'Rajput' is an ideal, rather than a subset of Hindu society. It exists as a code of conduct which cuts across religion, class, and caste. Its *structural role* as a mechanism which provides a common yardstick for social behaviour, and which therefore upholds a stable, though by its own reckoning more just, social order, qualifies it for the more evocative term, the 'Rajput ethic'.

The self-identification of some segments of Rajasthan's Muslim community is just one reflection of the predominance of the Rajput ethic. The way in which historical events are reconstructed in political oratory and in the education of the RSS cadres reflects a distortion of this phenomenon. One example concerns the prominent role played by Muslims in high politics in the conflicts of the late eighteenth century between Rajput rulers and the Rajput nobility. Envious of the imperial prerogatives found in the more centralized Mughal model, a number of Rajput princes wished to escape the constraints of feudal rule, with its constant headache of disputed land rights and wars of succession. Standing in their way was the traditional reliance upon clan nobles for military services. To avoid this constraint, rajahs of a number of important states entrusted Muslim military commanders to recruit and lead mercenary armies. Arsi Singh of Mewar (Udaipur) gave one such commander, Abdul Rahim Beg, a status equal to that of the Salumber Chief in his court.[21] The Maharajah of Kota engaged in similar tactics, placing a fairly large army under the command of Dalel Khan and Mehrab Khan. The use of Muslim military men was not unusual in many parts of India ruled by Hindu sovereigns

[19] Jamous, Raymond, 'The Meo as a Rajput Caste and a Muslim Community', in C. J. Fuller (ed.), *Caste Today* (Delhi: Oxford University Press, 1996), pp 180–201.

[20] See also Sikand, Yoginder, 'Meonis of Mewat', *Economic and Political Weekly*, (11 March 1995), pp 490–2.

[21] Singh, M. S., *Emergence of Modern Rajasthan* (New Delhi: Wishwa Prakashan, 1993), p. 11. The text of the grant is reproduced in James, Tod, *Annals and Antiquities of Rajasthan* (Delhi: Motilal Banarsidass, 1987), pp 233–4.

during this and earlier periods. But the niche that they occupied in these cases, as instruments of political conflict within existing feudal hierarchies, and thus amounting to a challenge to the traditional order, has been exploited by communal forces in Rajasthan—and not only those officially linked to Sangh Parivar organizations.

In one interview, a prominent BJP politician mentioned the Muslim mercenary tradition, as an aside, when referring to a particular Muslim Congress MLA as a 'hired gun'.[22] This self-proclaimed party intellectual, who was not a Rajput, argued with a hint of irony that it was only 'the Jat–Brahmin axis in the Congress' that would engage in the hiring of mercenaries any longer. When pressed to explain, his revisionist view of the eighteenth century Muslim mercenaries was that they took advantage of the Rajput princes' 'distress', offering their services in an effort to undermine the traditional order. They were, he continued, 'mischievous agents of other forces', just as today's Muslims 'held secret allegiances to foreign powers'.

This may all seem a far cry from the day-to-day organizing of political movements in contemporary Rajasthan. But the point is that these historical fragments leave uncertain imprints that prove convenient in justifying political attitudes. They are in the air at the level of the political leadership. These are often not the hardline RSS men, but those of a more accommodating, moderate ilk in their style of political action. The committed activists are more systematic in disseminating such historical reconstructions, embellishing their accounts with loving details.

The Hindu nationalist movement's foot soldiers in Rajasthan, the grassroots workers in Parivar organizations (including the BJP itself), constantly invoke fragments of history for partisan purposes. Though not everyone in the Rajasthan BJP is content with projecting the party as a Rajput-dominated organization—and in many respects it is not one—the Rajput *ethic* is a legacy its members are willing to use as a tool in attracting political support. This takes many forms. When attempting to appeal to lower-caste groups, BJP politicians and party workers make much of the links between the former princes and their lower-caste lieutenants. During the November 1993 state assembly elections, campaign managers

---

[22] Interview with a former BJP MP, 9 December 1993, Jaipur.

waiting for an audience with party leaders at the BJP headquarters in Jaipur said that historical references were used routinely in candidates' campaign speeches. One episode that they felt was particularly effective as a rhetorical device in low-caste *mohallas* was the well-known story that Jaipur princes in the late eighteenth century had elevated members from lower castes, including barbers and elephant drivers, to important posts in their administrations. Though often crudely packaged hagiography, the essential message conveyed in these political parables was that traditional Hindu rule, under benevolent Rajputs, had been, and will continue to be, based upon a distinct sense of fair play and respect for innate talent. 'It is to spread the idea of equality to the rest of India that they must vote BJP, we tell them', said one of the waiting pair of campaign workers, both from Jodhpur district.[23]

In Rajasthan, the local BJP makes little effort to sell (or even to defend) the national BJP line stressing the need for a casteless society—that divisions of caste and sect have weakened the Hindu community and made it vulnerable to Muslim incursions. The emphasis is on the benefits of the traditional order, the reciprocity inherent in the practical functioning of hierarchical relations, and the flexibility displayed by traditional rulers. The selective version of history on which these notions rely may not reflect the complex reality of the past; but the sense of uncertainty found in contemporary social relations provides them a powerful resonance.

REACTIONS TO MIDDLE-CASTE ASCENDANCY: THE STALLING OF MANDALIZATION

One of the characteristics of the current political dispensation that lends strength to this rosy interpretation of the beneficence of traditional Hindu (i.e. Rajput) rule is the position of the Jat community. Indeed, the construction of Hindu nationalist ideology in Rajasthan has not only drawn selectively on history to support its claims, but has also *reacted* to other patterns of socio-political development, some of which have themselves been historical reconstitutions. The most important of the latter have been attempts by the Jat community of Rajasthan to 'reinterpret

---

[23] Interview with two party workers from Jodhpur district, 30 October 1993, Jaipur.

its traditional status in society to buttress its contemporary aspirations and develop a mythology about the same.'[24]

These efforts are most clearly evident in the Jat Krishak Sudharak, a social reform movement which began in the late 1930s. This movement, which ultimately fed into the Kisan Sabha organizations which fought exploitation by Rajput jagirdars, 'involved attempts at *achieving social mobility by subscribing to value orientations found outside the traditional order*. Emphasis was placed upon change and progress, participation in and adaptation to the wider world of social action.'[25] While extremely successful at gaining entry for large numbers of Jats into the police and administrative services of various princely states, these reform movements nevertheless failed to result in material or psychic benefits for other non-élite castes. This has provided communal political forces in Rajasthan additional ammunition with which to portray Jats as both the major cause and the selfish beneficiaries of the broader malaise represented by the decline of the traditional social order. The success at associating the Rajput ethic with Hindu nationalism is, in many ways, merely the reverse side of the failure of Jat political élites to build strong vertical or horizontal alliances with other castes and communities.[26] Having successfully reformed internal practices, and having reoriented the self-perception of a large portion of those in the community, the Jat leadership neglected the task of building an ideology that could draw other communities into an alternative to the Rajput ethic. While many Jats have demonstrated their skill at dispensing material patronage to other communities, as a group they have not constructed a competing vision of common historical purpose.

[24] Kothari, Rajni, 'Introduction', in Rajni Kothari (ed.), *Caste in Indian Politics* (New Delhi: Orient Longman, 1970), p. 10.

[25] Sisson, Richard, 'Caste and Political Factions in Rajasthan', in Rajni Kothari (ed.), *Caste in Indian Politics* (New Delhi: Orient Longman, 1970), p. 181, emphasis added.

[26] Indeed, the other side of the Sangh Parivar's successful mobilization campaign is the unconstructive behaviour of the Congress, which has been alienating Muslims for years, both before and after the destruction of the Babri Masjid. In 1993, for instance one of the few Muslim leaders of a Congress front organization was sacrificed at the altar of petty factionalism, despite being an active organizer and relatively uninvolved in political infighting. *The Hindu*, 20 August 1993.

Indeed, Jats are viewed with more suspicion by other communities now than are Rajputs. One manifestation of this was the high
level of speculation during the 1993 assembly election that Congress' reliance on Jat leaders (and hence the Jat vote) might lead
to apprehensions among other communities who see Congress'
social base as too narrow, and (for many) outright fear of what Jat
rule might bring. Throughout the campaign, Congress leaders
made it clear that if the Congress came to power a Jat would for
the first time be made the Chief Minister of the state. This was
openly stated by many leaders, though only tacitly acknowledged
by others. As one journalistic analysis put it, 'the probable danger
the Congress-I may face from this kind of Jat consolidation
[among the state's prominent leaders] is the ire of the rest of the
people. If there is a backlash from other communities, the
Congress-I may suffer to some extent....'[27] In contrast to the
1960s, Rajput dominance within the BJP is seen as less troublesome
now because *overt* Rajput social power is less in evidence. And
where it is on display it is viewed as exemplary—a sort of cultural
expression, something with which all types of communities can
identify. The acquisition of Jat social and economic power is seen
to have come too rapidly, and now voters are apprehensive about
the prospect of their dominating the highest levels of state politics
as well.

There are three main sources of this widespread antipathy, each
of which has been used by the BJP to build solidarity within the
chronically divided Rajput ranks.[28] First, Jats are seen to have
cornered a disproportionate share of the benefits of the massive
Indira Gandhi Canal project, which has irrigated large tracts of the
Thar desert in northern and western Rajasthan. In 1992, Chief
Minister Shekhawat capitalized on this perception by putting
forward a controversial proposal to amend the Land Revenue Act.

[27] *The Hindu*, 3 October 1993.

[28] Rajputs tends to be divided not only along lines of region and segmentary
kinship, but perhaps most important politically, between aristocratic and non-
aristocratic lineages. Bhairon Singh Shekhawat hails from a non-aristocratic
lineage, and uses this status to blur the edges between élite and non-élite groups,
making himself the link between the Rajput aristocracy and humbler peasant
castes. For an interesting account of the importance of these divisions in one region
during the transition to democratic rule, see Singh, Hira, 'Kin, Caste and Kisan
Movement in Marwar: Some Questions to the Conventional Sociology of Kin and
Caste', *Journal of Peasant Studies*, October 1979, pp 101–18.

It was immediately and savagely attacked by the Congress. Former Congress minister Surendra Vyas lodged a petition with the Governor, urging him to withhold his assent to the bill because of the *mala fide* intentions of the state government. His contention was that it favoured the former jagirdars and ex-rulers of Rajasthan, and that it would cost the state's exchequer Rs 10,000 crores. Most of all, Vyas argued, it was a blatant attempt by the Chief Minister to curry favour among Rajputs. While contesting the figure of Rs 10,000 crores, most observers agree that caste solidarity was indeed the motive behind the amendment.[29] Rajput leaders in the regions surrounding the Indira Gandhi Canal were able to appeal to local resentment against prosperous Jat farmers from the neighbouring states of Haryana and Punjab who had moved in and squeezed out deserving recipients of land grants. These sentiments regarding Jat assertiveness, which blended issues of caste and region, resonated deeply with people in other parts of Rajasthan. Associating Jats with the Congress and Janata Dal, the Rajput leaders projected the BJP as the only bulwark against the threat of increasing Jat hegemony.[30]

This on-again-off-again strategy of fomenting distrust of the Jats and Jat leaders is a thread that runs through the recent history of BJP-politics in Rajasthan. It has provided an important context to major events. As Shail Mayaram has argued, the 1990 riots in Rajasthan could not be understood without reference to the anti-Mandal agitations that preceded them in the autumn of that year.[31] While the protests against the implementation of the Mandal Commission's policy recommendations on positive discrimination served largely to galvanize the upper castes politically, full-scale polarization on this issue was avoided by casting the Jat community as the villain of the piece. The BJP and other organizations spread the word that the Rajasthan Janata Dal's support for the Mandal recommendations was motivated primarily by a desire to place Jats in the OBC category. This, they argued, was a way of depriving the deserving Scheduled Castes, Scheduled Tribes, and OBCs of their rightful share of reservations in government

[29] Interview with Sanjay Srivastava, *Indian Express* correspondent, 16 December 1993, Jaipur.
[30] Interview with Surendra Vyas, 22 April 1994, Jaipur.
[31] Mayaram, Shail, 'Communal Violence in Jaipur', *Economic and Political Weekly*, 13–20 November 1993, p. 2534.

employment and government educational institutions. While there is a kernel of truth in this, it largely ignores the fact that the Mandal recommendations represented an *overall* increase in the share of reservations which would not in theory have adversely affected the Scheduled Castes or Scheduled Tribes. Whether they would have negatively impacted upon other OBC communities is less clear, since it was not clear that demanding the inclusion of Jats within the OBC category was an official policy of the Janata Dal in Rajasthan.

That the BJP's rhetorical campaign achieved substantial success in the court of public opinion speaks volumes about the extent to which the Scheduled Castes in particular were mistrustful of the Jat community. One reason why this mistrust was so widespread was the ongoing conflict between Jats and Jatavs, a Dalit caste which had suffered humiliation and violence at the hands of both individual Jats and organized gangs. The latter were notorious for sowing terror in Jatav colonies. The complicity of many local police officers and Congress organizations further ingrained the impression that Jats in control of political power would provide the worst of both worlds: a decline in civility and the basis for regional pride, but without the sort of compensation in terms of social empowerment which might otherwise have justified such costly alterations to the traditional order.

Yet, politically shrewd Shekhawat understood the limits of the strategy of Jat vilification. He has always been a pragmatist, one of the qualities that makes him suspect in the eyes of the state's RSS lobby. In 1953, for instance when six of the Rajasthan Jana Sangh's eight MLAs opposed the party's support for the abolition of the jagirdari system, Shekhawat was one of the two who refused to join the revolt.[32] This served him well in his subsequent efforts to build a political following beyond the Rajput community. Thirty-five years later his pragmatic streak made him similarly unwilling to write off a community as large, prosperous, and vocal as the Jats. The BJP (during its time on the opposition benches in the late 1980s) played upon divisions within the Jat community in order to court those sections which, in its opinion, had reason to be disillusioned with Congress rule. One of the BJP's most consistent efforts of this type was the wooing of the Jats of eastern

[32] *India Today*, 31 October 1995.

Rajasthan. Time and again it was emphasized by party managers that the Jats of the western part of the state had gained at the expense of their caste fellows in the east. 'What have Marwar [Jodhpur] Jats done for our people?,' was the refrain of one BJP leader, a Jat from Dausa district.[33] Betrayal, particularly at the hands of the Congress, is a theme that has paid rich dividends for the BJP in selected eastern regions. The party's grassroots campaigns continue to stoke up the memory of a 1985 incident in which a police deputy superintendent shot and killed Man Singh, an Independent MLA and member of the erstwhile royal family of Bharatpur, which had been a Jat-ruled state. The shooting came a day after a reportedly inebriated Man Singh rammed his jeep into the Congress Chief Minister Shiv Charan Mathur's stationary helicopter and, soon thereafter, into the makeshift platform from which Mathur was to address a political rally. Mathur was blamed by the local community for ordering the shooting of this unlikely symbol of Jat pride, causing much damage to the party's fortunes in the region. Man Singh's daughter was elected first as the local MLA, and later as a BJP Member of Parliament, unseating Congress stalwart (and Union Minister for External Affairs under Rajiv Gandhi) Natwar Singh in 1991. The BJP recaptured the seat in 1996, again defeating Natwar Singh.

CONCLUSION

Rajput Hindutva, then, is that form of 'Hinduness' that idealizes martial acumen and personal courage and recognizes the virtues of the Rajput rule. The Rajput ethic, on which it is based, is a cognitive as well as a structural category, one that for many groups transcends its roots in the Hindu-caste hierarchy. There are, however, several conceptual tensions inherent in this ideology, that is, in this politically motivated reading of tradition. Three of them are worth mentioning. First, it is, as stated above, a regional nationalism. Though attempting to evade this contradiction through a narrative stressing the region's role as a preserver of the nation, the Sangh Parivar is not immune to the divisive effects of this tension. Second, to the extent that Rajput Hindutva represents an ideal of a traditional social order, the values of which are applicable

[33] Interview, Bharatpur, 14 November 1993.

to groups outside the Hindu community, it is a sort of ecumenical manifestation of religious orthodoxy. This can sometimes serve to bring members of different communities together, thus undermining the efforts of strident Hindu nationalists to keep them apart.

While it may be possible to characterize the first two conceptual tensions as paradoxes, the third is more of a contradiction, one that arises in the course of the communalists' reconstructions of the history of Rajasthan, as well as in their portrayal of the relationship between that history and the current Hindu nationalist movement. In the communalist narrative, Rajputana is somehow cast as both the preserver of ancient values, and yet a place in which the ancient social order has been upset—by (certain) assertive Jats, by Congress, by Muslims, and by other unnamed nefarious forces. Again, this is not an insuperable political obstacle for the mobilizational strategies of the Sangh Parivar: while it may be *logically* difficult to project traditional Rajput rule as impervious to foreign subversion and yet also the victim of enemies from within and without, this combination is ideologically very potent.

This brief overview of how a Hindu nationalist ideology is being constructed in Rajasthan raises four further issues worth pondering as we assess similar processes in other states. The first is that we must consider carefully what constitutes a 'religious symbol'. Surely, there is more to this than images of Ram and Bharat Mata. Indeed, it is worth asking whether an entire social and political order and the interpretation of its historical role can be considered a symbol around which an assertive nationalist political mobilization can in fact take place. The Rajasthan experience suggests that it can, but perhaps only when this order is centred around a community (such as the Rajput) which can credibly claim to embody virtues to which a broad range of communities might aspire.

Second, the issues raised in this paper may serve as a corrective to the dominant mode of thinking about political mobilization of religious identities in India, in which the Sangh Parivar and its many informal allies are portrayed as the only political actors mining the rich and complex seam of popular consciousness that exists in India. In fact, everyone from Gandhi to the local leaders of today's Congress have invoked religious symbolism to build a political following and cement intercaste alliances—though some have done so with a greater sense of thought and understanding than others. In parts of Rajasthan, the symbolic, material, and organizational resources of the Bishnoi sect are employed by enterprising politicians in order to construct and nurture political machines. The competitive nature of religious mobilization is as true of India as it is of the United States, where the 'religious right' is not the only political movement to draw on religious imagery and narrative in an attempt to construct a new popular understanding of the Judeo-Christian tradition. African–American civil rights leaders, in the tradition of Martin Luther King, Jr., appeal to Christian values of tolerance and brotherly love,[34] as do (in a different way) Bill Clinton and many other mainstream American politicians. The point of this caveat is not to equate all forms of religious mobilization—some are clearly more invidious than others—but rather to highlight the competitive context within which Hindu nationalism takes place, particularly in Rajasthan.

Third, there is ample reason to take issue with the argument put forward by Sudipta Kaviraj that 'fundamentalist' religion as a mobilizing strategy relies upon a 'thin' version of religion,[35] and that, ironically, this dilution hastens the process of disenchantment and tends ultimately to pave the way for a proliferation of secular attitudes. Clearly, the process of 'fundamentalizing' Hinduism in Rajasthan glosses over many of the nuances of doctrine and worship in an effort to forge a movement capable of maintaining solidarity and competing for political power. But in the process of reconstructing the historical fragments of the region's dominant religious tradition there is a countervailing tendency to generate (unwittingly, perhaps) further complexity. That the unsavoury politicization of the Deorala Sati, for instance will result in the demystification of Sati as a practice throughout the state is by no means clear. The visits of BJP politicians to Deorala to pay homage to the deed have created a new layer of local mythology over which neither the communalists nor the secularists will be able to exercise

---

[34] For a good account of the role of stories that are both recounted and embodied by leaders, see the chapter on Martin Luther King, Jr., in Howard Gardner, *Leading Minds* (New York: Macmillan, 1995).

[35] Kaviraj, Sudipta, 'Religion, Politics and Modernity', in Upendra Baxi and Bhikhu Parekh (eds), *Crisis and Change in Contemporary India* (New Delhi: Sage, 1996), pp 307–10.

control as it multiplies and informs new understandings of the meanings behind the practice of Sati.[36]

The fourth and final point worth considering is the extent to which Hindu nationalism in Rajasthan, as in a number of other states, has in fact taken on a local flavour, and the impact of this dynamics on other social processes unfolding in the state. Because what it is to be a Hindu varies from region to region (as well as between sects), local idioms are the vehicle through which notions of the good and the right are promoted by political movements. While it is possible to invent traditions, such efforts are more likely to meet with success when they build upon the raw material that is most accessible to the local political consciousness. Their fuel is the substratum of historical associations that lay dormant within the collective memories of diverse communities. In Rajasthan, this process has been taken to an even more complex level. Local beliefs, traditions, and patterns of social relations have not only been mined by various movements; they have been used to fashion a compelling narrative of Rajasthani culture's role in the renewal of the Hindu nation throughout India. To the extent that this can be portrayed as exemplifying a social order that is both more stable and more just—as well as resistant to the pernicious influence of outside forces—it tends to undermine the potential of competing social movements, particularly those based upon assertive lower-caste identity.

In this sense, the promotion of Rajput Hindutva can be considered the preventive antidote to Mandalization, which has been slow to penetrate Rajasthan. Cracks in the organizational armour have, however, become visible of late: the purported OBC elements involved in Gopi Chand Gujar's abortive leadership coup against Shekhawat and tribal demands for sixth-schedule status in southern Rajasthan, to name but two. The electoral sphere has thus far remained largely immune to such developments. The 1998 assembly elections, especially if Shekhawat departs the political scene, may open a new chapter in the Rajasthan politics.

---

[36] Pangariya, B. L., *State Politics in India* (Jaipur: National Publishing, 1988), p. 162; and interview with Mr. Pangariya, 16 December 1993, Jaipur.

PART II
A 'HINDI-BELT' PARTY OR
A NATIONAL PARTY?

4

BJP and the Politics of Hindutva in Maharashtra

THOMAS BLOM HANSEN

INTRODUCTION

In the light of the overall evolution of Hindu nationalism in India, the political-ideological formations in Maharashtra presents an interesting paradox. While the state historically has given birth to a persistent, if limited, constituency for a variety of Hindu communalist organizations and discourses, its diverse and rich range of non-Brahmin and lower-caste assertions, as well as the dominant Congress party in the state, have until recently prevented the Hindu nationalist forces from attaining political power.

To the strategist in the Sangh Parivar, Maharashtra remains a major irritant. The BJP only could win power in this important state by becoming the political junior-partner to a movement, the Shiv Sena, whose public style and political practices have more affinities with the 'Congress-culture' than with the ideals of austerity, discipline and ideological devotion nurtured in the RSS. Seen from a national perspective, the resilience of Congress' political machine in Maharashtra and the mounting strength of the Shiv Sena is, undoubtedly, an obstacle to BJP's further national expansion.

The electoral victory of the Shiv Sena and BJP in the State Assembly elections in March 1995 in Maharashtra must, therefore, be understood in the light of the disintegration of the 'Congress-machine' and the concomitant transformations of the political economy in the state which from the mid-1980s created certain strategic openings for the BJP and Shiv Sena in the realm of electoral and clientelist politics. The dominance of the Congress party was *de facto* already broken by the initial 'saffron-wave' in the state from the mid-1980s to 1992 where both the Shiv Sena and BJP consolidated their urban constituencies, and expanded out of Bombay, Pune and Nagpur and successfully established themselves as viable alternatives to Congress in the rural areas, especially in the regions of Konkan, Marathwada and Vidarbha. The process of gradual disintegration of the Congress-machine and a subsequent expansion of the Shiv Sena and BJP in rural areas and provincial cities continued and culminated in the electoral victories of these parties in 1995 and in the General Election in 1996.

IN THE BRAHMIN COCOON

Maharashtra was the birthplace of the RSS and most of the senior leaders in the movement were for decades recruited from among the Maharashtrian Brahmins, especially Chitpavan Brahmins. Prior to the assassination of Gandhi, the centres of vernacular Brahmin culture in the middle classes in provincial cities like Pune and Nagpur provided important centres for the RSS. The message and style of RSS was received with more apprehension by Bombay's business-minded élite and with outright hostility by the vast mill-districts in the city. The popularity of the RSS, as well as Hindu Mahasabha, in these provincial milieus were intimately related to the loss of status and power of the Chitpavan and Deshastha Brahmins in the social order.[1] This was exacerbated in the political field as Congress in the 1940s successfully captured the ideological constructions of the Maratha-ethos and the rhetoric of the *bahujan samaj* (the depressed communities) and incorporated these ideological elements into the mobilization strategies of the party. In the wake of the assassination of Gandhi in January 1948, Pune, Nagpur and many towns in western Maharashtra saw riots wherein

[1] Nandy, Ashish, *At the Edge of Psychology* (Delhi: Oxford University Press, 1980), pp 78–98.

thousands of Brahmin families lost home and property. The public stigmatization of Brahmins in general, and the branding of the RSS as a vehicle for Brahmin interests in particular, pushed away sympathizers and passive supporters of the anti-Muslim and Hindu communal construction built up by the RSS and Hindu Mahasabha and left only the 'hard core' of RSS intact. The RSS consolidated its base in Pune, Nagpur, Amravati and in certain places of the greater Bombay region where it gradually built up an embryo of an 'alternative civil society'; i.e. an autonomous network of organizations and activities under whose protecting canopy its members could live relatively secluded from the surrounding society which increasingly was pervaded by the dominant forces of capitalist modernization and the liberal political culture of the new Indian state.

In the political field, Jana Sangh was active in Maharashtra from the outset in 1951, but it did not get much success until the agitations of the Samyukta Maharashtra Samiti (SMS) commenced in the 1950s with enthusiastic participation of Jana Sangh workers. The party succeeded in getting five MLAs elected on a SMS platform in 1957 at the peak of agitation for a unilingual state for Marathi speakers. This agitation rallied communist union-activists, peasant-activists rooted in the non-Brahmin tradition and upper-caste urban middle class sections with Hindu nationalist leanings around a common populist platform against what was seen as an alliance between the Congress High Command and major industrial interests in Bombay determined not to let Bombay be 'swallowed' by the politics of a unilingual Maharashtrian state. Ideological differences notwithstanding, the main bone of contention within the SMS was the question of the status of the movement *vis-à-vis* its constituent parties. Many SMS activists saw the movement as a new opposition-party in the making, while especially cadre-based parties like the CPI and the Jana Sangh were reluctant to give up their distinct profile and their sovereign authority over their members and activists. These issues remained unresolved and an open conflict in 1958 regarding a new 'constitution' for the movement combined with a distaste for the ever more pronounced anti-capitalist slant of the SMS meant that Jana

---

[2] Phadke, Y. D., *Politics and Language* (Bombay: Himalaya Publishing House, 1979), pp 241–57.

Sangh left the movement for good the same year.[2] In the following years the state-unit of Jana Sangh tried to consolidate its networks and organization and tried to hone its distinct profile on clear-cut issues such as the agitation for the liberation of Goa, and a largely unsuccessful attempt to extend the high profile agitation against cow slaughter in North India in the late 1950s to towns and provincial cities in Maharashtra.

In the following election in 1962 the Jana Sangh fared rather badly both in the elections for the new State Assembly in Bombay and for the Lok Sabha. It was not until the State Assembly election in 1967 that Jana Sangh could start an independent parliamentary career in the state of Maharashtra by winning four seats (from Pune, Kalyan, southern Bombay, and rural Vidarbha).[3] In 1972, the party managed to win five seats in the Legislative Assembly and to further extend its support in a number of urban constituencies. In spite of a series of fairly successful agitations among cotton-growers in Vidarbha and some organizational expansion in the Konkan area and in Pune district in the 1960s, Jana Sangh remained almost exclusively urban-based.[4]

The deep-running ambivalence in the Sangh Parivar regarding electoral politics and patronage-politics, and its quest for ideological purity and principled stands, exacerbated this isolation for several decades. Most of the attempts to create a broader mass-following through various front organizations found few takers because of the condescending paternalism which characterized its approach towards poor and lower-caste groups. The RSS strategy of acculturation of 'the masses' to higher-caste cultural idioms

[3] V. M. Sirsikar's detailed study of the electoral process in the six Legislative Assembly constituencies in Pune City in 1967 demonstrates very clearly that Jana Sangh's seat in the Shukrawar constituency covering the middle-class and upper caste part of the Old city in Pune overwhelmingly was won due to massive support from the substantial number of educated Brahmins residing there. The party's rather efficient organization relied heavily on RSS-networks but was unable to reach out beyond this limited constituency. (Sirsikar, V. M., *Sovereigns without Crowns: A Behavioural Analysis of the Indian Electoral Process*, Bombay: Popular Prakashan 1973, (See especially pp 30–85).

[4] While Jana Sangh's share of the vote at the state-level was increasing at a slow but steady pace, the party's share of the popular vote at Lok Sabha elections was fluctuating according to the conditions of possibility in the political field in different periods. The share was in 1957: 3.4 per cent; in 1962: 4.4 per cent; in 1967: 7.4 per cent and in 1972: 5.2 per cent). Butler, D. Lahiri and Roy, *India Decides* (Delhi: VM Books, 1991), pp 171–81.

found few takers in Maharashtra. The historical legacy of the non-Brahmin movement, the presence of an active and assertive Dalit-movement, the legacy of a vigorous Left-movement in the Bombay region, and most of all, the sustained dominance of a strong, self-confident and well-organized Maratha-Kunbi peasantry in the rural areas, had made Maharashtra one of the most politicized states in India. The political climate in the state, especially in the politically dominant districts in western Maharashtra, was marked by a celebration of the peasantry and rural virtues and by an anti-hierachical discourse that reiterated and celebrated the defeat of centuries of brahminical tyranny of the Peshwas'. The BJP-leadership in the state gradually realized that to 'make it' as a political or social movement in Maharashtra required more than condescending offers of extending 'cultured habits' and middle-class norms to the so-called 'weaker sections'.

However, the strength and flexibility of the Congress-hegemony in Maharashtra did make oppositional politics rather difficult. The predicament of all opposition parties in Maharashtra in the 1960s and 1970s were a forced existence on the fringes of the Congress hegemony, mobilizing the smaller social groups that were not essential to the strategic alliances which the Congress so aptly forged and reproduced between the major social groups and communities in the state. The vertical split in Congress in 1977, when the rising star in the party, Sharad Pawar, left to form his own Congress-S, did thus provide a significant opening of the political field in the state to new players.

The Jana Sangh's merger into the Janata Party in 1977 produced a major breakthrough for the party in the 1978 polls where former Jana Sangh members in the Janata Party in Maharashtra occupied thirty MLA-seats and five seats in the Lok Sabha until 1980. Compared to northern India, the Janata Party was, however, quite weak in Maharashtra and remained dependent on the dynamic leadership delivered by Sharad Pawar in the Progressive Democratic Front coalition government ruling from 1978–80. In spite of difficulties in breaking the massive Congress-hegemony in Maharashtra, the Janata Party experience had given the Sangh Parivar an unprecedented public breakthrough in the state and the newly formed BJP was in 1980 able to win fourteen seats in the State Assembly in spite of the rather massive swing towards Congress in that election. The party managed to hold on to these seats and expand to sixteen seats mainly in urban parts of western Maharashtra, in Dhulia, rural Vidarbha, Nagpur and in pockets of influence in Marathwada (Jalna and Aurangabad) in the following State Assembly election in 1985.[5] More importantly, the BJP managed to extend its organizational network outside the cities in many smaller towns, taluka-places and in villages, especially in Vidarbha, Marathwada and certain places in Konkan, like the rural parts of Thane district.

Yet the party was haunted by its brahminical image as Arvind Lele, former MLA from Pune and treasurer of the BJP in Maharashtra, explained:

Congress had the power, strong economic networks, muscle power, caste appeal with the *Maratha-Kunbi* and *bahujan samaj*. It was a major factor that we were branded as a brahmin party, though Uttamrao Patil, a *Maratha*, and so many *bahujan samaj* people were with us. Uttamrao Patil was our president for so many years. Motiramji Lahane was our president. All our presidents were from the *bahujan samaj*. But the *bahujan samaj* image is more for Congress and not for us. Because a certain tradition in the state right from *Satyashodhak Samaj* and Mahatma Phule is with Congress and against us. Therefore, we are branded as a Brahmin party, as a 'new *avatar*' of Hindu Mahasabha'. In Maharashtra this non-Brahmin feeling was always a major obstacle. It is still so even now.[6]

The early 1980s was in Maharashtra, as all over the country, a period of decline and disappointment after the enthusiasm of the

---

[5] This expansion in seats was, however, accompanied by a waning share of the popular vote sliding from 9.4 per cent in 1980 to 7.3 per cent in 1985 during this period, where Congress all over country polled the most massive majorities ever seen in Indian politics. See Singh, V. B. and Y. Malik, *Hindi Nationalists in India. The Rise of the Bharatiya Janata Party* (Delhi: Vistaar Publications, 1995), pp 182–3.

[6] In Sirsikar's survey from 1967 the cross-section of voters in the sample were asked to characterize the main caste-basis of various political parties. It turned out that the image of Jana Sangh as a brahminical party was more pronounced than the actual composition of the group of voters indicating support for the party actually warranted (Sirsikar, op. cit., pp 216–7). Brahminical culture was broadly associated with the RSS and related organizations because of the way its historically produced antithesis the Marathas were associated with the rural and the 'popular'. The RSS-chief *pracharak* for western Maharashtra S. Shastri explained: 'RSS is very small in rural areas. It is not so much that RSS is a Brahmin organization as it is a non-*Maratha* organization. In rural areas it is made up by Brahmins and intermediate castes (OBCs). RSS will be stronger if the *Marathas* take to it. We don't even have five to ten per cent *Marathas*. That is the weakness of RSS here.' (Interview, Pune, 5 August 1992.)

Janata period. The attempt to turn BJP into an authentic successor of the Janata Party's centrist 'moral alternative' to Congress proved even less efficient in Maharashtra than in other states. The strongly anti-Congress and Hindu communal constituency built by the Jana Sangh and Hindu Mahasabha in the urban areas in the state did not easily accept Vajpayee's notion of 'Gandhian socialism'. A substantial number of party-workers and supporters openly denounced the party line as that of a 'pseudo-Congress party'—a tendency that coincided with RSS' public preference for Indira Gandhi's majoritarian stances and rhetoric. The BJP's modest success in expanding its share of seats in the State Assembly in Maharashtra and in expanding its share of the popular vote in the General Election in 1985 to almost ten per cent, thus expressed the existence of latent resistance to Congress and the fruits of persistent organizational work, rather than any swing in favour of the BJP in Maharashtra. But even becoming a stable pole of opposition to the ruling Congress was difficult. After Sharad Pawar's tenure as the Chief Minister for the Progressive Democratic Front between 1978–80, he and his Congress-S had emerged as the uncontested leader of the opposition to the dominant Congress-I in the state. These difficulties were demonstrated by the ease with which years of persistent efforts on the part of the BJP to win over Maratha support and organize OBC-cultivators in Vidarbha were overshadowed by the successful farmers movement, Shetkari Sanghathana, led by the charismatic Sharad Joshi from 1980 onwards.[7]

RIDING THE SAFFRON-WAVE: BJP IN MAHARASHTRA 1986–92

The Shiv Sena's adoption of a new aggressive communal populism from 1984 onwards and Sharad Pawar's return to Congress-I in 1986 presented a new set of strategic possibilities and compulsions to the BJP in Maharashtra. Shiv Sena's victory at the Bombay Municipal elections in 1985 and its subsequent expansion in Marathwada and other parts of the state suddenly turned the party into the most dynamic non-Congress force in Maharashtra. In this

---

[7] See Omvedt, Gail, 'The "New Peasants Movement" in India', *Bulletin of Concerned Asian Scholars*, vol. 20, no. 2, April–June 1988, pp 14–24. Lenneberg, Cornelia, 'Sharad Joshi and the Farmers: The Middle Peasant Lives', *Pacific Affairs*, vol. 61, no. 3, Fall 1988, pp 446–66.

period the Shiv Sena was the only political force in India which in election-campaigns and public debates employed the aggressive anti-Muslim rhetoric that had become still more widespread and accepted since the VHP and RSS launched the *Ekmata Yatra* campaign in 1983, and later the Ram Janmabhoomi agitation. This left BJP in Maharashtra in a strategic dilemma caught between the image of a moderate kind of 'loyal opposition' to Congress it had built up since the mid-1970s, and the strident communal campaign of the Shiv Sena which successfully occupied the better part of the political and discursive position previously associated with Jana Sangh. If the BJP was going to survive and grow into a significant force in Maharashtrian politics, some sort of understanding with the Shiv Sena was imperative. As Pramod Mahajan, the chief architect behind the BJP–Shiv Sena alliance related:

At this time (in 1984–5) the BJP could not anticipate what was happening in the Hindu mind, but the Shiv Sena was the first to see it. So Thackeray was the first person to go for the Hindu line. Slowly from 1985–7 Shiv Sena was solely in charge of the Hindu wave in the country. For the Shiv Sena it is very easy to assess the situation and take a line (...) But for me there is a long way to convince my leadership to go for it. Even having an alliance with the Shiv Sena created a great debate in BJP and as I told you we are culturally different in many ways. (...)
But my problem was that if I am not with the Shiv Sena then the Shiv Sena will slowly kill me and capture my entire constituency. If you cannot beat them you join them (...) It was a precise political expediency if you want.[8]

It was, however, the return of Sharad Pawar to Congress-I in 1986 which created the most significant opening for the ensuing 'saffron-wave'. The BJP had an elaborate organization all over the state and had for years systematically sought to articulate and organize grievances of petty-traders, small producers, unemployed youths and other groups which the accelerated economic growth in the rural areas threw up outside the realm of more stable structures of patronage. However, most of the younger Congress-S activists who had rallied around Sharad Pawar's projection of himself and his party as the incarnation of Maratha strength and honour spontaneously went to the Shiv Sena. Within a few years Thackeray emerged as the primary political mass-leader of the opposition,

[8] Pramod Mahajan, Joint General Secretary of BJP, responsible for Maharashtra. Interview in Delhi, 10 December 1992.

outstripping the BJP leadership who could not match his inciting rhetoric and his unrivalled capacity for attracting huge crowds.[9]

As a reaction against this sudden success of Shiv Sena, the Left parties and Janata Dal in Maharashtra joined forces and created an alliance with Shetkari Sanghathan from 1988 onwards. They hoped this could provide an effective bulwark against the expansion of the Shiv Sena but were proved wrong.[10] However, as long-standing BJP parliamentarian Ram Kapse, MP from Thane (urban) constituency, admitted, this sudden success of the Shiv Sena had everything to do with the regrouping of opposition-constituencies in the wake of Pawar's 'homecoming':

Hindutva was the additional factor and not the main factor. The real reason is that the opposition shrinked. Sharad Pawar who led the opposition for many years joined Congress-I. He was with us (the opposition) for eight years and a vacuum was to be filled in. This could be filled in only by two political parties, Shiv Sena and BJP.[11]

The BJP–Shiv Sena alliance was formed prior to the 1989 General Election as a relatively loose agreement on adjustment of seats among the two parties in order not to divide the pro-Hindutva vote. The election campaign was largely fought out by each of the parties on different programmes whose common denominator merely was the rhetoric of Hindutva. The alliance was able to win 10 seats in the Lok Sabha (four to Shiv Sena, six to BJP) based on almost 25 per cent of the popular vote. Though a meagre result

---

[9] For a more detailed analysis of Shiv Sena's strategies and rural expansion in the 1980s, see my article 'The Vernacularisation of Hindutva: Shiv Sena and BJP in Rural Maharashtra', *Contributions to Indian Sociology*, vol. 30, no. 2, 1996b, pp 177–214.

[10] Sharad Joshi admitted openly that his clear anti-communal stand in the Legislative Assembly elections in 1990 damaged his organization: 'Right now we have a problem, let's understand it. We suffered a major setback from the Ayodhya thing. Many villages which we thought were ours and we had worked there, suddenly we found that they were more interested in the Ayodhya temple than remunerative prices or waiving of loans. This is a fact. (...) But we preferred to have some kind of kamikaze operation. We knew that our direction—free economism—cannot survive if we have this communal thing. I didn't need to. In fact Thackeray was wooing me. He had offered publicly that I would become the Chief Minister if the Shiv Sena became the guard in power. But I picked up a fight. Shiv Sena is a monster which has no right to be in the arena at all.' (Sharad Joshi, Interview in Pune, 7 March 1993).

[11] Ram Kapse, Interview in Kalyan, 27 January 1993.

in terms of seats this marked a remarkable advance in the share of the popular vote for both parties. Besides, the belligerent campaign of the alliance compounded a feeling that Hindutva-wave was in the making. The Janata Dal, which at the national level experienced its best election ever and rode to power on a broad wave of anti-Congress resentment, could not win more than five Lok Sabha seats in the state in spite of the support from the extensive activist network of Shetkari Sanghathana. Interestingly, the imperative of uniting all opposition to counter Congress seemed in the election campaign in 1989 to override ideological differences between the Janata Dal and the Hindu-right. Barring a few rhetorical postures, none of the parties attacked each other too directly and they even made seat-adjustments in several constituencies. But the Congress-machine in Maharashtra once more proved its capacity for winning elections in the state and secured another massive mandate for Congress. Meanwhile, the BJP and Shiv Sena began to prepare themselves for the State Assembly Elections in the following year.

The alliance between the two parties was based on a straight-forward calculation. The BJP needed Shiv Sena which had an appeal in 'plebeian' sections in urban as well as rural areas which the BJP's more middle-class and upper-caste image hitherto had prevented the party from gaining access to. BJP was, therefore, still vulnerable to Congress' effective anti-Brahmin critique of the party as 'the new *Peshwas*'. The alliance with the Shiv Sena was a way to win elections, a way to consolidate a popular constituency but as importantly, a way to overcome the brahminical stigma sticking to the BJP and the Sangh Parivar in spite of the long-standing efforts to induce Marathas and OBCs into the front ranks of the party. Gopinath Mundhe, from the Vanjari-community(OBC) in Vidarbha, leader of BJP's group in the State Assembly from 1990–5 and today deputy Chief Minister in the Shiv Sena/BJP cabinet, is one of the most successful products of the BJP's systematic projection of lower-caste leaders as 'grassroots leaders with an uncanny knack of knowing the people's pulse.'[12]

There was also confidence in the BJP that the party, due to its superior organizational capacity for consolidating support, in the long run would benefit more from the alliance than the Shiv Sena.

---

[12] Admiring portrait of *Mundhe* in *Observer*, 8 March 1990.

In spite of persuasive arguments in favour of the political utility of the alliance, different interests and groups within the Sangh Parivar in Maharashtra and at the national level were either hostile or sceptical towards intimate ties with the Shiv Sena. Among the older cadres of the BJP, the Shiv Sena was widely mistrusted as a sort of 'shadow-Congress', whose anti-Congressism at best was a tactical move which could not be trusted. Among the more 'purist' adherents to the classical RSS-strategy of character-building, Shiv Sena was regarded as a crude, 'uncultured' plebeian organization whose commitment to Hindutva was shallow and opportunistic. However, the politically pregnant situation in Maharashtra in 1988–9 where Thackeray's communal populism generated so strong emotions and enthusiasm, finally convinced the leadership of the BJP that it had to compromise on style and rhetoric, and hand over a number of seats to the Shiv Sena in order to fully ride the 'saffron-wave' gaining ground in Maharashtra.

The Shiv Sena's leadership clearly expected that the alliance with the BJP would lend it some of the middle-class respectability which its political *dada'ism* threatened to do away with. Besides, the Shiv Sena counted on that it would benefit from the BJP's experience and skills in parliamentary work which at this point were largely absent within the Shiv Sena.[13]

The election campaign prior to the State Assembly election in March 1990 proved that the alliance was emerging as the most serious threat ever to Congress' undisputed hegemony in Maharashtra. In the high profile election-campaign it was especially Thackeray's rabid but effective public postures that made the Shiv Sena emerge as the major opposition to the Congress. In spite of elaborate and efficient organizational expansion, the BJP still played the role as 'junior-partner' in the alliance. The party tried to utilize the considerable response which the *Shilanyas Puja* in 1989 had evoked in the rural districts of Marathwada and Vidarbha,

[13] 'Shiv Sena has mass, BJP has class—we need each other' was a popular one-liner depicting the alliance within the Shiv Sena, and in its form characteristic of the directness of Shiv Sena's discourse. As typical for BJPs idiom were more circumscribed statements like 'we (BJP and SS) are cultural poles apart', 'we appeal to different sections', etc. At the ground level the relations between activists from the two parties were often rather cordial. Only in Pune where BJP saw the Shiv Sena as an irritant in what it regarded as its own 'heartland', the relations appeared strained.

but the rumours of the Shiv Sena's aggressive 'defence of the Hindus' during riots and communal disturbances in Bhiwandi and Bombay in 1984, and in Marathwada in 1988, had given the Shiv Sena a popular reputation which the Sangh Parivar's more respectable style could not match.

Leaders and activists in BJP were optimistic about the prospects of winning state-power in Maharashtra, and of getting rid of the stigma and marginality which Congress had stamped on them for decades. The BJP-manifesto for the 1990 elections targeted mainly developmental issues and sought to identify the Congress as a conspiracy between Bombay capital and the sugar lobby of western Maharashtra exploiting the poorer regions of the state. Nevertheless, the thrust of the campaign was conducted on highly communal lines. One of the BJP-pamphlets read:

The present election is a *Dharma Yudh* (holy war) (...) the BJP–Shiv Sena alliance is bound to sweep this election because Shri Krishna is on our side and Lord Ram's *dhanushya baan* (bow and arrow) and Goddess Laxmi's *kamal* (lotus), such sacred and holy articles are our election symbols.[14]

The Shiv Sena's rhetoric, less slanted towards the quasi-religious discourse celebrating Ram which dominated the Ramjanmabhhomi campaign in North India, instead transformed the Sangh Parivar's rhetoric of 'Ram versus Babar' into a direct communal and historical metaphor of the battles between Shivaji and the Moghul emperor Aurangzeb.[15]

The aggressive campaign of the Hindutva-combine did, however, also modify the economy of stances in the political field, which now was bifurcated with the Janata Dal, RPI, Left parties and Shetkari Sanghathana siding with their old foe Sharad Pawar against the Shiv Sena–BJP alliance. The Congress' and Janata Dal's main card against the Shiv Sena and BJP was a re-formulated version of the historical antagonism between Brahmins and Marathas. Especially the Congress managed with considerable skill and innovation to project itself as the protector and spokesman of the bahujan samaj by invoking Mahatma Phule, the

---

[14] Quoted from *Sunday Observer*, 11 November 1990.
[15] For a more systematc analysis of Thackeray's rhetoric, see Hansen, Thomas Blom, 'Recuperating Masculinity: Hindu Nationalism, Violence and the Exorcism of the Muslim "Other"', in *Critique of Anthropology*, vol. 16, no. 2, 1996a, pp 137–72.

Varkari-bhakti-tradition, and the Gandhian legacy—as opposed to the Sangh Parivar, still effectively branded the 'murderers of Gandhiji'.

Another strategy of the Congress was to file legal suits against a number of Shiv Sena and BJP candidates, demanding derecognition of their candidatures on the grounds that they were violating the restrictions on employing religious themes in election campaigns. Although this strategy failed to have any immediate impact on the election-campaigns or results, it demonstrated to the BJP that its alliance with Shiv Sena could cost the party dearly, and could jeopardise the painstakingly constructed image of a party respecting democracy and civic values—an image which even BJP's opponents at this point accepted. After the elections ten different legal suits were filed against newly elected Shiv Sena and BJP members of the State Assembly. Six months later the Bombay High Court ruled *prima facie* that a Shiv Sena MLA, Wamanrao Mahadik, known for his violent rhetoric and intimate connections with the underworld, had been employing religious themes in his election-campaign. A prominent BJP-member of the State Assembly, Ram Naik, demanded, hence, that the use of Hindutva rhetoric and the communal slant in the party's election campaigns should be downplayed in the future.[16]

The result of the election in March 1990 defeated the hopes of the BJP–Shiv Sena alliance winning a majority in the Assembly. In spite of the impressive gains by the alliance, the result also confirmed the uncontested leadership of Sharad Pawar in the Maharashtra Congress party. Congress lost its absolute majority in the Assembly and won only 141 seats out of 288 (with a 39.1 per cent of the vote), while the BJP–Shiv Sena alliance won 94 seats on 27 per cent of the vote.[17] Congress hence formed a

---

[16] The cautious attitude of senior MLAs of the BJP was, however, not shared by the leadership of the BJP–Sena combine. Thackeray had stated in a public speech in 1989, that court-rulings would be of no consequence for the campaigning style of his party. And according to the *Sunday Observer* an MLA from the BJP stated that 'a time will come when we will not have to care even about courts' (Ibid.).

[17] The BJP leadership, while praising the utility of the alliance, also pointed out that the 'percentage-performance' of BJP was far better than that of Shiv Sena. While Shiv Sena got 52 seats out of more than 16 per cent of the vote, BJP was able to win as many as 42 seats out of only 10.8 per cent of the popular vote. (Pramod Mahajan, op. cit., see, also Pravin Sheth, 1992: 174). The fact that BJP

cabinet in alliance with Republican Party of India (RPI-Athawale), one of the factions of the Dalit party and succeeded on the basis of the imperative of a joint front against the Hindutva forces, to reach important compromises with the Janata Dal in the state.

In spite of their exclusion from administrative power, the ascendancy of the BJP and Shiv Sena as the third and second largest parties in the Assembly signalled that the moderate left-of-centre rhetoric and policy-orientation which had prevailed in the state since the 1950s now had come to an end. The political landscape in the state was deeply divided and the alliance had emerged as the only effective alternative to the established Congress-rule. The alliance had made itself a vehicle of broad-based communal sentiments, of the assertions of ascending social groups hitherto excluded from political influence, as well as a vehicle for regional protests from the three relatively backward regions of the state, Vidarbha, Marathwada and Konkan, where the historical weakness of Congress had enabled the alliance to mobilize significant rural support.

Later the same year, BJP's commitment to the alliance was severely tested when the Shiv Sena activities and utterances embarrassed the BJP leadership on several occasions. The most evident example was the issue of the recommendations of the Mandal Commission. Thackeray had, to the annoyance of some of his lieutenants, criticized the entire idea of the Mandal Commission as 'casteist and divisive', thus jeopardising the position of the Shiv Sena as the potential beneficiary of a larger political mobilization of OBC communities in the state. The BJP state unit, keen on promoting itself as pro-OBC, immediately sensed a possibility of projecting itself more favourably to OBC-constituencies, and publicly supported the implementation of the Mandal Commission recommendations as an urgent political priority. The state-level leadership of the BJP deemed it necessary, in the political context of Maharashtra, actively to support the Mandal-issue, in spite of the objections within the BJP at the national level regarding the issue; and in spite of the outright opposition to the Mandal-reservations from the BJP-state governments in Madhya Pradesh, Rajasthan and Himachal Pradesh.

---

only improved its share of the popular vote with a few per cent, but tripled its number of elected MLAs testifies to the importance of electoral alliances and seat adjustments for the performance of smaller parties in the Indian electoral system.

To the BJP in Maharashtra, the specificity of the OBC-communities promised to be an instrument which could 'open' and
differentiate the bahujan samaj category and thus make it available
for Hindu nationalist intervention. The OBC-identity could
disentangle the notion of backward castes from that of the Maratha-
designation which for decades had been a powerful ideological pole
available to the Congress and lethal to the BJP in Maharashtra.
Gopinath Munde, the BJP leader from an OBC-background
attempted to enhance the credibility of the BJP among the OBC-
communities. The instrument was, as always, the communal
argument. Munde pointed out that the real bone of contention
lying behind BJPs scepticism regarding the Mandal-issue was the
question of whether Muslims should be included in the OBC-
category.[18] To the BJP, the difficult task was to display its
commitment to the Mandal-formula clearly enough to attract votes
from OBC-communities, while at the same time, to hold on to the
support from the upper castes and groups of Marathas which the
party required to consolidate its standing in the rural areas.[19]

Conveniently for the Shiv Sena–BJP alliance in Maharashtra,
Advani's Rath Yatra soon became a dominant theme which
overshadowed the political agenda, even in Maharashtra where
worship of Ram never was as popular and widespread as in
northern India. In Bombay, the Shiv Sena took charge of the
welcoming of the Rath Yatra and held a large public meeting with
Thackeray and Advani. As always, Thackeray outdid the alliance-
partner in rhetorical militancy, and left it to the BJP leaders at the
rally to repeat its assurances to the public that the Ram Janmabhoomi
agitation was a (respectable) matter of faith and not an electoral

[18] 'Those who embrace these religions believe that they are totally free of social
discrimination, why should they now seek the benefits of these recommendations?' (*The Independent*, 6 September 1990.)
[19] The chief organizer of the BJP in the Marathwada region, Sharad Kulkarni,
put the disjuncture between the RSS-ideology of integration and the ground
realities of caste-divisions and caste-politics in the following way: 'We are not
entering into caste-politics, we have to play due to some compulsions. Our elected
representative from a particular community does not identify himself with his
caste (...) People think he is of a particular caste and that we should go for him,
but we (internally) from the party-angle and the leadership always try to project
him as a leader of the whole society (...) higher thoughts must prevail in society
and smaller thoughts will go. You cannot eradicate it (caste, TBH) you will have
to replace it.' (Interview, Aurangabad, 19 January 1993.)

trick.[20] The BJP maintained that the yatra was an unquestionable, spontaneous expression of religious community unrelated to the 'impure' realm of the politics full of strategies, calculations and secular ideology open to debate and questioning. While the BJP in Maharashtra attempted to walk a public tightrope between democratic respectability and blatant communal majoritarianism, the Shiv Sena pursued, to the embarrassment of the carefully drafted BJP-statements trying to conceal the widespread communal attitudes within the party, a clearer militant and anti-democratic line. Thackeray reportedly called upon the *kar sevaks* to totally destroy the Babri Masjid[21] and female activists from Shiv Sena's *Mahila Agadhi* attacked a Janata Dal rally. Throwing stones, chairs and other things at the stage, the women prevented the Chief Minister of Uttar Pradesh, Mulayam Singh Yadav—a sworn enemy of the Hindutva-forces—from speaking in Bombay.[22]

In the campaign prior to the General election in 1991, the optimism of the BJP–Shiv Sena alliance was unhampered. BJP secretary P. Mahajan anticipated that BJP alone would be able to secure 25 out of the total 48 Lok Sabha seats in the state. The self-confidence of the BJP was higher than ever before as the party now without hesitation embarked on a campaign in which Hindutva was the main theme and where the entire inventory of communal myths and allusions was unfolded. Mahajan explained that the confidence of the party stemmed from the fact that the employment of the theme of Hindutva had been thoroughly rehearsed in Maharashtra in 1990:

Whatever is happening today at the national level, the experiment of the BJP, is in a way an extension of Maharashtra politics last year where the elections were fought on the basis of Hindutva.[23]

On this occasion, the BJP played down the Mandal-issue. The parts seemed to fall back on the conviction that 'the anti-Mandal and pro-Mandir vote is ours' as it was said again and again, and that a clear stand on these issues in itself would secure at least 40 per cent of the vote. Sensing that the party had improved its image in Maharashtra after the Rath Yatra the BJP went for a

[20] *Economic Times*, 8 October 1990.
[21] *Sunday Observer*, 4 November 1990.
[22] *Economic Times*, 8 October 1990.
[23] *Free Press Journal*, 23 March 1991.

tougher bargaining with the Shiv Sena on seat-distribution. Above all, the negotiations made it clear to the Shiv Sena that a still stronger BJP at the national level was not content with being 'junior-partner' in Maharashtra anymore.

In the ensuing election-campaign the Shiv Sena tried to outdo BJP's brand of communalism and released a video 'Flames of Patriotism' which probably is the single most communal and violence-inciting piece of election-material ever presented in Indian politics.[24] Thackeray's hailing of the murderer of Gandhi as a true national hero, and his earlier allegations that Dr Ambedkar had been financed by the (Muslim) Nizam of Hyderabad determined to splinter Hindu-society through a Muslim–Dalit alliance (a favourite demon of the Shiv Sena) proved, however, to be an unexpected asset for the Congress campaign in the state.

In an unprecedented relaxation of the otherwise tightly centralized selection of candidates for the Lok Sabha election, the Congress high command had given Sharad Pawar an almost free hand in Maharashtra.[25] After consolidating his support within the party, forcing warring factions together, and silencing dissent and public criticism, Pawar launched a rather effective and powerful election campaign.[26] On the one hand, Congress promised eco-

[24] The video was almost exclusively structured around metaphors of war and combat and the imagery dominated by flames, roaring tigers and Thackeray in heroic postures at mass-rallies. Though produced too quickly and without technical finesse, the staging of Shiv Sena as the fighting unit of the 'Hindu people' and the representation of this people through 'mass-aesthetics', carefully arranged rallies, the 'emperor of Hindu hearts' (Thackeray) as the sublime expression of the emotions of this massified people, the numerous references to past glory's of the Hindus, seem to have many parallels to fascist aestheticisation of the nation as the 'popular will'.

[25] Seth, Pravin, *The 1990 Poll and Politics: A Western Indian Perspective*, in Subrata Mitra and James Chiriyankandath (eds), *Electoral Politics in India—A Changing Landscape* (Delhi: Segment Books, 1992), p. 177.

[26] One of the rather effective means Pawar employed to galvanise his support base in the Congress party as well as in the political-administrative establishment, was the strategic allotment of flats, houses and land in some of the most exclusive residential areas of Bombay at concessional rates to MLAs, journalists, top-bureaucrats and other influential groups. The legality and precise circumstances of these allotments , the so-called 'land-scam', has never been fully established and continues to be a bone of contention in Maharashtrian politics which figured prominently in the resolutions and statements from the BJP state-unit in 1991. (Report from Fifth plenary session of BJP in Maharashtra, Jan 1991, *Indian Express*, 5 January 1991).

nomic stability and improved regional development, while it, on the other hand, tried to stigmatize the BJP and Shiv Sena as irresponsible troublemakers and upper-caste urbanites, good at rabble-rousing and creating communal violence and enmity, but unable to deliver development, governance and order.

The result of the elections was surprising, even to Congressmen. The Congress secured 48 per cent of the popular vote (45 per cent in 1989), and won as many as 37 out of 48 seats. The BJP lost votes and secured only 20.6 per cent of the vote (23.7 per cent in 1989) and lost half of its seats in Maharashtra. The party was only able to secure seats in Pune, Bombay North, Thane, but lost in all rural constituencies. The Shiv Sena fared slightly better, as it managed to hold on to two seats in Vidarbha (held by two defected Congressmen), and Moreshwar Save's seat in Aurangabad. But even the Shiv Sena lost votes and secured only 9 per cent of the popular vote (1989: 10.2 per cent).[27] Though the alliance still secured almost a third of the popular vote, and though the BJP clearly performed better in General elections than at the state-level in Maharashtra, the dismal election-result of 1991 was blamed on the uncomfortable alliance-partner Shiv Sena. Many BJP-leaders accused Shiv Sena of not utilizing its share of the votes properly and held Thackeray's unpredictable utterances responsible for the alliance's vulnerability to a well-oiled Congress campaign rehearsing the well-known warnings against the 'new Peshwa's'.

Congress hurled another series of blows at the Shiv Sena–BJP alliance by scheduling local elections for *Zilla Parishads* and Municipal Corporations in February 1992, and later by engineering the defection of long-standing Shiv Sena leader Chhagan Bhujbal and 12 MLAs from the Shiv Sena to Congress in December 1991. The idea behind coordinating Zilla Parishad and Municipal elections was to force the Shiv Sena to concentrate on Bombay, and hence make the rural districts an easy victory for Congress. Another device expected to reduce the influence of the Shiv Sena and BJP was the reservation of 30 per cent of all seats in local elected bodies for women. Given the male-dominance within both the BJP and Shiv Sena and their apprehensions regarding gender

[27] Chiriyankandath, James, *Tricolour and Saffron: Congress and the Neo-Hindu Challenge*, in Subrata Mitra, and James Chiriyankandath, 1992, pp 269–73.

equality, this new provision was expected to be detrimental to the alliance.[28]

The defection of Bhujbal provided a pretext to the BJP for breaking up the alliance which had become still more troublesome after the 1991 General Elections. The student-organization of the Shiv Sena *Bharatiya Vidyarti Sena* (BVS) and ABVP had repeatedly been engaged in violent clashes on several Bombay campuses in August 1991, and the increasing factionalism within the Shiv Sena made the alliance still more troublesome to the BJP and disconcerting to the RSS. After the decimation of the Shiv Sena, the BJP emerged as the largest opposition party and took over the influential post as leader of opposition in the State Assembly. The BJP state-unit, determined to fill in the vacuum created by the disintegration of non-Congress opposition in general, and the Shiv Sena in particular, made by the end of December 1991 an ambitious attempt to carve out its own independent identity. The party staged a *Upa*-yatra, a local yatra which would join the larger Ekta yatra moving under the leadership of the BJP president Murli Manohar Joshi from Kanyakumari in the south towards Srinagar in Kashmir. In January 1989, the Upa-yatra, led by a young Dalit, Sandesh Kondwilkar, state secretary of the BJP, and a Maratha, Vijay Kalke, municipal corporator from Pune, was moving through the Congress heartland in the sugar districts of western Maharashtra, in a bid to rid itself of the Brahmin stigma still hanging to the party, and in order to challenge the Congress power in these districts. The yatra was launched at the so-called 'Holy Pass' where a famous warrior of the Shivaji period was killed, and ended in Aurangabad (or Sambhajinagar in the parlance of the Shiv Sena and BJP) six days later. Carrying saffron-coloured urns with holy water and soil gathered along the route, playing patriotic film-songs and the yatra displayed 'all the necessary sentimental and religious ingredients that has now become associated with the BJP as a sarcastic journalist reported.[29] However, the lack of a developed infrastructure of the Sangh Parivar in the sugar-belt, barring Pune District, made the yatra a rather unsuccessful undertaking. The only well-attended mass-meeting was held in Aurangabad where both the BJP and Shiv Sena had a solid backing. Also the Ekta yatra failed to

---

[28] *Times of India*, 11 November 1991.
[29] *Times of India*, 31 December 1991.

attract public attention or arouse nationalist feelings in the predominantly rural districts of Marathwada and Vidarbha it passed
through in early January 1992.

The protracted negotiations in the same period between the BJP
and Shiv Sena concerning the distribution of thousands of local
candidatures all over the state, caused considerable dissent. Especially the Shiv Sena, severely hampered by the depleted authority
of Thackeray, experienced defections and open revolts in many
places in Bombay and Pune against the allotment of seats by
Thackeray and his lieutenants. Also the BJP experienced a significant pressure from ambitious upcoming candidates who wished to
run for municipal or panchayat offices. The two parties negotiated
throughout January 1992 until it became clear that both parties in
order to limit the level of dissent, had to allow more candidates
at the grassroots level to contest than a coordinated campaign with
joint candidates could accommodate.[30]

In the elections the Shiv Sena lost its strategically crucial
majority in the Bombay Municipal Corporation. The party's
communal populism could not compensate for the maladministra-
tion of the city, the decline in infrastructure and civic amenities,
and the systematic corruption which the Shiv Sena corporators had
carried to an unprecedented level, associating openly with builders
and underworld-dons. Congress' promise to make a Dalit the next
Mayor of Bombay also contributed to secure a large number of
Dalit votes for the Congress–RPI alliance in the city.[31]

The alliance between the Shiv Sena and BJP broke down at the
local level as it became evident that the Shiv Sena and BJP had
emerged as competitors for the same constituencies which were no
longer expanding and hence no longer offered sufficient room for
the accommodation of the interests of both parties. Local elections
are fought on the basis of the day-to-day performance of local
politicians as brokers of economic and symbolic resources, rather
than more elusive emotional waves or catchy slogans. In that
situation, the common ground of anti-Muslim stances and Hindu
communal rhetoric between the two parties ceased to be an
effective means of cohesion.

The BJP had in the course of its alignment with the Shiv Sena
successfully extended its influence to lower-caste sections in the

[30] *Independent*, 7 February 1992.
[31] *Times of India*, 1 March 1992.

urban as well as rural areas, while the Shiv Sena had gained a foothold in the urban middle classes outside the Bombay area. Leaders from both parties maintained, nevertheless, that the parties would form another alliance in the next State Assembly or General Elections, and that the breakdown of the alliance only was to be seen as a tactical and temporary move.

In spite of deep-running ambivalences regarding caste-based local patronage-politics and its still rather feeble rural base, the BJP emerged from the late 1980s as the most effective vehicle in extending the base of the Sangh Parivar in Maharashtra. The VHP and the entire Ram-agitation had not engendered the same response in Maharashtra as in north India. In Maharashtra, the discursive formation of Hindutva was received as a part of an ideological and political battle between the Congress hegemony and other political forces, such as the Shiv Sena. The unequivocal political character of Hindutva in Maharashtra—never able to parade as a religious matter and thus conceal its central preoccupation with politics and power—the BJP and Shiv Sena were also from the outset bogged down in the predicament of all oppositional forces in Maharashtra. They invariably had to function within the strategic possibilities of a political field whose rationalities, distribution of ideological stances, framing of 'legitimate problematics' and caste-arithmethics had been defined by the Brahmin-Maratha antagonism and the peculiarities of the Congress-machine in Maharashtra, anchored, above all, in the social organization of power and cultural symbols in rural Maharashtra. The 'saffron-wave' in rural Maharashtra did modify certain relations and communalized the political arenas in many villages, but it was also in important ways stalled and displaced by the resilience of the structures of patronage and the hegemonic 'maratha'ized' political culture prevailing in the villages.

It is indicative of the gap between the 'cultural narcissism' of the middle class milieus in which the Sangh Parivar had developed its base for years, and the dominant political culture in the state, that BJP only could begin to break out of its social and ideological 'cocoon' by an alliance with the hard-nosed 'maratha'ized' communal populism of Shiv Sena. The purist strategy of cultural reform and religious mobilization pursued by the VHP and other Sangh Parivar mass-organizations was largely confined to the cities and to paternalist campaigns among the tribals and the urban poor.

The prominence of the BJP–Shiv Sena alliance as the prime movers behind the 'saffron-wave' in Maharashtra has caused deep dissension in the Sangh Parivar in the state. Many RSS-cadres of a purist mould disliked the association with the Shiv Sena, and felt that the politicization and 'maratha'ization' of Hindutva in Maharashtra, made the entire organization vulnerable to the 'creeping Congress culture'.

Among the so-called pragmatic BJP-leaders and activists, committed to fine-tune the political strategy of the BJP as a political party (rather than as a Sangh Parivar subsidiary) the alliance with the Shiv Sena was regarded as a convenient and compelling electoral arrangement given the continued weight of the Congress party in the state. Running on separate platforms would be no less than suicidal to both parties. Besides, the alliance enabled the BJP to profile itself as a relatively sane and moderate party, promoting a 'respectable Hindutva', while at the same time reaping the electoral benefits of the radical rhetoric and 'reputation' for action of the Shiv Sena. Nowhere was this more evident than in the peculiar economy of public stances displayed by the two parties during the tense months of December 1992 and January 1993. After the demolition of Babri Masjid the Shiv Sena, battered on its home turf in Bombay by the Congress and searching for a come back, began circulating stories of how the demolition was undertaken by 500 specially trained Shiv Sainiks. The BJP was more than willing to disown the responsibility for the events in Ayodhya and found these rumours quite useful in their attempts to retain a respectable image in Maharashtra. Later in December when the Shiv Sena initiated the infamous Hindu mass-prayers (*Maha-aartis*) and in other ways whipped up communal sentiments in Bombay,[32] the BJP-leaders publicly called for moderation and peace, while large numbers of Sangh Parivar activists participated in the prayers and played an active role in the large riots that rocked the city in the second week of January 1993.

The active involvement of Sangh Parivar activists in the Bombay riots proved that the Sangh Parivar variety of cultural nationalism, however quasi-intellectual and ostensibly peaceful it may appear

---

[32] See Sharma, Kalpana, *Chronicle of a Riot Foretold*, in Sujata Patel and Alice Thorner (eds), *Bombay: Metaphor for Modern India* (Delhi: Oxford University Press). Also see Masselos, Jim, 'The Bombay Riots of 1993: The Politics of Urban Conflagration', in *South Asia*, vol. XVII, Special Issue, 1994, pp 79–95.

within its middle-class 'cocoons', needed to mobilize the fears, misrecognitions and ideological fantasies of the 'communal unconscious' in order to create a broader popular base. In Maharashtra, the Shiv Sena provided the communal frenzy and communal fantasies which remain the optimal habitat of the Sangh Parivar, somewhat like the way in which the Bajrang Dal activists and the VHP *sants* and *sadhus* in the very different political culture of UP prepared the ground for the BJP.

The alliance with the Shiv Sena gave the BJP access to popular audiences and constituencies it never could have accessed by itself. In order not to slip back in its middle-class cocoon in Maharashtra, the BJP and the Sangh Parivar were forced to remain aligned with the Shiv Sena and its capacity for operation and mobilization among the large and still more assertive popular groups, i.e. all those who RSS-swayamsevaks continue to depict as the lower castes without 'culture and good habits'.

A SLIM VICTORY

The alliance between Shiv Sena and BJP was mended in the last minute in January 1995 in the run-up to the State Assembly election in the state, and the alliance was able to secure 138 seats in the State Assembly, 74 for the Shiv Sena and 64 for the BJP. After negotiations with parts of the unprecedented number of MLAs elected as Independents in the state, the alliance could present a cabinet led by the Shiv Sena's leader in the Assembly, Manohar Joshi, as the Chief Minister, and the BJP's leader in the Assembly, Gopinath Munde, as the Deputy Chief Minister. Though a victory in seats, the performance of the Shiv Sena–BJP alliance was not very impressive in terms of increasing its share of votes or making advances into new areas. More than half of the seats won by the BJP–Shiv Sena alliance were won in urban constituencies and in areas where the alliance already had a strong standing.[33]

[33] The alliance won its clearest victory in the Bombay region where it secured more than 49 per cent of the total vote and won 30 out of 34 seats, while the hitherto UP-based Samajwadi Party won two seats in constituencies dominated by lower-caste groups and Muslims. In Pune, two MLAs were elected for the Shiv Sena (Shashikant Sutar in western Pune, and Deepak Paygude in the 'plebeian' side of the Old city (Bhawani Peth). BJP had two MLAs elected in Pune (Girish Bapat, and a Maratha, Dilip Kamble) another MLA in Pune district, an as many as three MLAs in Nagpur.

Congress was almost entirely ousted from all the major urban
centres in the state. The rural vote for the BJP and Shiv Sena came
from Konkan where Shiv Sena already established its dominance
in 1990; from Vidarbha where the BJP had established itself in 1990
also strongly, and from Marathwada where especially the Shiv Sena
had regained a strong foothold, particularly in Aurangabad district,
Jalna and Beed, whereas the BJP made a somewhat slower progress
in the region.[34] Scandals in Marathwada and Vidarbha, incidents
of police brutality in Nagpur, and the fatal mismanagement of the
earthquake in Latur affecting the southern districts of Marathwada
in 1993 had seriously damaged Congress' general image, while the
Sangh Parivar's ability to organize relief-work had left a lasting
impression here. Besides, the Shiv Sena's violent campaign against
the renaming of Marathwada University in January 1994 had once
more galvanized its popularity among Marathas and the OBC
groups in the region.[35] The BJP chose a strategy of distant support
to the renaming-issue as part of their larger, and not entirely
unsuccessful, strategy of attracting various Dalit groups to the
party. This reinforced benevolent paternalism of the Sangh Parivar,
obviously spurred by the fear of a repetition of the alliances
between the OBCs, Dalits and Muslims in Uttar Pradesh, contributed to give the BJP the largest number of reserved seats in the
State Assembly in Maharashtra.[36]

[34] In the rural districts as a whole, the alliance's percentage of the popular vote
decreased or remained at the same level as in 1990. In Vidarbha, the percentage
even slipped from almost 35 per cent to only 25.9 per cent in 1995, though the
number of seats increased from 22 in 1990 to 33 in 1995. The victory was here
mainly connected to devastating factionalism within the Congress party. In
Marathwada the percentage remained stable, and Haribhau Bagade was reelected
in Aurangabad east, and the BJP won another seat in Sillod taluka north of
Aurangabad. Shiv Sena regained its foothold in Paithan and in Aurangabad City.
(For an analysis of the election, see Guru, Gopal, Assembly elections in Maharashtra.
Realignment of Forces, *Economic and Political Weekly*, vol. XXX, 8 April 1995,
pp 733–6.
[35] In January 1994, Sharad Pawar who as everybody else was impressed by the
show of strength of the lower-caste assertion in UP and Bihar in the Legislative
Assembly elections in November 1993, decided to implement the renaming of
Marathwada University. This decision suddenly energized the Shiv Sena in the
region and bandhs, strikes and rallies were announced. The government sent
paramilitary troops to the area in mid-January 1994 and as the Shiv Sena realized
the determination of the government on this issue, it quickly backed down and
cancelled the actions.
[36] Out of eighteen seats reserved for the Scheduled castes in the Legislative
Assembly in Bombay, the BJP won seven (three Chamars, one Mahar, two

The remaining Congress constituency was in the election sharply divided between several warring factions and an unprecedented number of dissident Congressmen were running as independents. This allowed the somewhat 'normalized', and to the occasion sanitized, Shiv Sena and BJP to emerge as credible alternatives and win several seats with a rather modest number of votes, while it also allowed the alliance to point forcefully at Congress' weaknesses and incoherence. The series of allegations of corruption and mismanagement in 1994 had depleted the authority of Sharad Pawar, and made it feasible for the BJP and Shiv Sena to run a hard-hitting anti-Congress campaign.[37] Meanwhile, the Shiv Sena tried to conceal many inner divisions coming to the fore in the election-campaign. Provincial leaders like Moreshwar Save went out with public criticism of the emissary of the Bombay leadership supervising the campaign in Marathwada, and several of Thackeray's oldest allies and founder-members of the Shiv Sena, like Madhav Deshpande, ran as independents against the Shiv Sena in order to expose the rampant corruption, nepotism and *gharanashahi* (dynastic rule) in the party.[38]

Although the election-campaign at the level of slogans and speeches mainly was directed against Congress and corruption, the

---

Matangs and one from the sweepers' community) and the Shiv Sena four SC seats (which all went to Chamars). The remaining (mainly Mahars) went to the RPI, Left parties and Congress (see Guru, 1995: 734). What is truly remarkable is that a large share of the Dalit votes, for decades a stable support for Congress, seemed to have changed sides, at least temporarily. Although none of the reserved constituencies have anything near a majority of Dalit voters, and many highcaste voters do vote for the SC candidate of their preferred party, the reserved seats do, nevertheless, have a considerable value as signifiers of the egalitarian commiments which most parties try to espouse. There is clearly a shift in political loyalties among Dalits, a shift which obviously is connected to the general fragmentation of Congress and its failure to provide employment and educational opportunities for these communities. However, there is no doubt that the protracted attempts to 'Hinduize' SC communities 'back into the Hindu fold' has paid off just as the long-standing assertiveness and relative success of Mahars have engendered allegations of their 'monopolization' of the Dalit cause and thus contributed to push Chamars and Matangs in the direction of the BJP and Shiv Sena.

[37] For an overview of some of the issues in the election see *Sunday*, 22–8 January 1995. On the allegations against Pawar for large-scale corruption from high-ranking IAS officers, see reports in *Frontline*, 7 October 1994. For Thackeray's allegations that the Enron-deal benefited Pawar personally, see interview *Sunday*, 26 March–1 April 1995.

[38] For reports on various instances of dissent in Shiv Sena, see *India Today*, 28 February 1995.

massive victory of especially Shiv Sena in the most communally tense areas, testified to the sedimentation of anti-Muslim sentiments in what one may call the 'political unconscious' of large numbers of people. The total dominance of Shiv Sena in Bombay, Aurangabad and other places marked by communal tensions and bloody trajectories in 1992 and 1993 was hardly a coincidence. Similarly, it was no mere coincidence that Shiv Sena in its election-campaign in January 1995 was the only party which on several occasions employed a radical, communal rhetoric and tried to make the liberation of the Hindu shrines in Mathura and Kashi in Uttar Pradesh a part of its election propaganda. The Shiv Sena leadership was well aware that beneath its anti-Congress bravado, its most solid source of support both from the middle class and the more popular sectors, remained its image of being the 'ultimate defender of the Hindus'. The memories of high pitched communalism in the early 1990s, the post-Ayodhya riots, the Bombay carnage and the bomb blasts in 1993 were maybe tucked away, but certainly not forgotten.

Only two weeks after the voting in the election took place, a survey of voters preferences was made by political scientists from Pune University. The sample consisted of 1055 respondents in fifteen constituencies sampled in order to be representative and encompass the regional variations in composition and size of population, urban–rural differences etc. in the entire state.[39] Out of this survey, made at a conjuncture marked by widespread dissatisfaction with Congress, emerged a picture of the relative strength of Congress and the Hindutva-parties, and a social profile of their respective constituencies which in many ways confirmed trends and correlations identified through a survey conducted by this author almost three years earlier.[40]

Firstly, the Congress was clearly the most preferred party with 38 per cent of the respondents supporting it while the alliance only attracted 25 per cent of the respondents (Shiv Sena 10.5 per cent

[39] Palshikar, Suhas, 'Capturing the Moment of Realignment', *Economic and Political Weekly*, vol. XXXI, 13–20 January 1996, pp 174–8.

[40] Hansen, Thomas Blom, *The Saffron Wave. Democratic Revolution and Hindu Nationalism in India*, vol. 1–3, International Studies, Roskilde University, 1996, pp 639–887. Also see Hansen, Thomas Blom, 'Vernacularisation of Hindutva: BJP and Shiv Sena in Rural Maharashtra', *Contributions to Indian Sociology*, vol. 30, no. 2, 1996b, pp 117–214.

and BJP 15 per cent). In my own survey Shiv Sena did also consistently draw less overall support than the BJP. This indicates that the higher proportion of MLAs elected on the Shiv Sena tickets also has to do with its bargaining power *vis-à-vis* the BJP in the allotment of tickets to joint candidates, rather than the actual popularity of the party *per se*.

Secondly, the profile of the 'typical' Shiv Sena and BJP-voter emerging from this state-wide survey seems also to support earlier findings. The 'typical' BJP-voter is a middle-aged, urban, higher-caste voter with some education and modest or good salaries—in urban areas often non-Maharashtrians (from Gujarat or north India) while the profile of a 'typical' Shiv Sena voter is that of a slightly younger, less educated Maratha or OBC with modest income, rather evenly drawn from urban and rural areas. As my earlier survey also pointed to, the Congress supporters were drawn from all areas, classes and castes, with a slight over-representation of Marathas, rural dwellers and lower castes as compared to other parties.

The caste-composition of the 1995 State Assembly did not change dramatically with the relative decline of Congress and advances of the Hindutva parties. The Shiv Sena had clearly made itself the main alternative for dissenting or young rural Marathas opting for a career outside the Congress, and the dominant political position of this caste-cluster was reflected in the high proportion of Marathas in the 1995 State Assembly (more than 55 per cent of all members). The caste-composition of the 64 BJP MLA's reflected the party's systematic strategy of transforming its upper-caste image. Only 10 of the elected BJP legislators were Brahmins, 24 belonged to the Maratha-Kunbi caste-cluster and out of the remaining 30 most came from the Scheduled caste communities (7), nomadic communities (8) and the OBC-communities (6) and various non-Maharashtrian communities (9).

However, the urban slant of the alliance was reflected in the composition of the cabinet. The new cabinet had more Brahmins on vital posts (Chief minister plus two ministers) and less Marathas (only four against ten under Sharad Pawar), while only half of the ministers were elected in rural areas.[41] Whereas the BJP during its

[41] Vora, Rajendra, 'Shift of Power from Rural to Urban Sector', *Economic and Political Weekly*, vol. XXXI, 13–20 January 1996, pp 171–3.

campaign seemed eager to project itself as a rural party, and project Gopinath Mundhe as an idealist social reformer 'whose passion and goal it is to see that every village in Maharashtra has electricity, water and roads,'[42] the Shiv Sena made it a point during the election campaign to promise a solution to the many urgent infrastructural and housing-problems of Bombay and other major cities in the state.

GOVERNANCE IN MAHARASHTRA: CONTINUITIES AND CRISIS

Bearing the general RSS-vision in mind one could expect a pressure from the Sangh Parivar towards a somewhat more authoritarian relation between state and citizens, with the BJP trying to mould itself as a 'moral force' intervening deeper into social life and expecting a certain moral commitment from the citizens in compliance with cultural practices of the Hindu middle classes. The thrust of the ideological frame of the Sangh Parivar points in several ways towards such an almost nineteenth century vision of the Hindu nation as a cultural-civilizational unity expressed in a centralized, uniform and culturally homogenous nation-state with a strong self-reliant economy and technology and defended by a strong military force. This, combined with a pronounced distaste for the rehearsal of social splits and contradictions in the sphere of politics, has informed BJP's recurrent suggestions for a 'presidential system' that would produce strong governments instead of the 'instability of parliamentary democracy', as Vajpayee put it prior to the election-campaign in 1996.[43]

How did these visions fare when faced with Shiv Sena's very pragmatic political practices that hardly differed from those of Congress, and when faced with the populist style of governance refined by Congress for decades. During the election-campaign the Shiv Sena had made the question of 'illegal' Bangladeshi immigrants in Bombay a major issue; it had promised to re-christen Bombay as Mumbai, and it had once again made the slum-development scheme promising rehousing for four million slum dwellers a major issue. The BJP had concentrated on Congress-corruption in the

[42] Quoted from an admiring portrait of the BJP-leader in *Sunday*, 11–17 June 1995.
[43] See *Pioneer*, 2 February 1996.

cooperative sector, and it had made critique of Congress' 'sell-out' to multinationals—as the large American power company Enron— a major issue. The attitude to foreign investments soon proved to be a major bone of contention between the two alliance partners. Soon after the new cabinet had been sworn in, Thackeray went on national TV and assured that his party fully supported the economic policies of the previous government. Nevertheless, the cabinet immediately began a critical review of the disputed Enron project, which especially parts of the BJP and RSS claimed would subject the Indian consumer to foreign exploitation. In August 1995 the project was officially scrapped but pressed by Shiv Sena, the BJP finally agreed to resume the negotiations with Enron. In January 1996 this resulted in a final approval of a redrafted project. (For more details see my article on Swadeshi in this volume.)

The handling of the Enron-affair seems in many ways to be indicative of the mode of populist governance of the new cabinet: to achieve spectacular results on symbolic and high-profile issues, to make certain token actions—effectively supported by a press more than willing to quote ministers and officials at length—and to make a few determined actions in order to undermine or curtail the power of established strongholds of the Congress party in the state. Regarding the vital issues of economic policies and the intensity of state-regulation in most spheres, the cabinet seems, so far, only to deviate marginally from the practices of the preceding Congress administration. As it is well known, the prominence of symbolic management rather than substantial implementation was always an integral part of the populist style of governance created by Congress.

The high-profile promise of eviction of Bangladeshis resulted in a limited but widely publicized action where approximately one thousand persons without proper papers more or less randomly were rounded up in Central Bombay and put on trains out of the state in July and August 1995. Hereafter, no systematic action has been undertaken. The issue of 'cleaning up' Bombay took a grim turn with the state-government announcing that it would begin to deport all beggars in the city back to their native state (regardless of being born there)—ironically as response to a similar policy initiated by the BJP-administration in Delhi, which had sent 52 Marathi-speaking beggars and pavement dwellers to Bombay. This happened, as *Indian Express* reported with loyalty to the BJP, 'to reduce the increasingly sinister menace of beggary, intimidating citizens, and intruding on private property.'[44] Once in power, it seemed increasingly clear that both Shiv Sena and BJP would take the side of the 'civilized' middle class to oust and expunge the 'plebeian' from Bombay and other cities, whether in its Muslim or its *zopadpatti* incarnations, encroaching upon the comfort and physical security of the middle class.

In November 1995, the Shiv Sena–BJP cabinet finally managed to get the approval for changing the name of Bombay to Mumbai, and immediately proceeded to press for renaming of a range of provincial cities with 'Muslim names' such as Aurangabad, Osmanabad, etc.[45] Another of Shiv Sena's long-standing demands, to make Marathi a compulsory subject in all schools in the state regardless of their medium of instruction was put before the Supreme Court. This immediately raised the issue of classification of 'minority-languages' vis-à-vis Marathi. The Shiv Sena once again displayed blatant political opportunism by declaring that Gujarati was excepted from this rule.[46]

Another move which generated considerable doubts regarding the government's commitment to democratic procedures was the disbanding of the Srikrishna commission which had been set up in 1993 to probe into the question of responsibility for the Bombay riots in December 1992 and January 1993. Slowly and meticulously working its way through more than twenty out of the thirty-two police-districts in the city where incidents took place, the commission accumulated ever more evidence pointing towards active involvement of Shiv Sena at an early stage in the riots. The evidence

---

[44] *Indian Express*, 19 October 1995. In these reports as so many other in the press, the subtle distinction between 'citizens' inhabiting society, and 'beggars', 'slum dwellers' 'squatters' and other poor and marginalized groups 'outside society', is evident and characteristic of both liberal and Hindu nationalist analyses of social problems in India.

[45] The economic consequences of the change of name will be considerable if all official stamps, name-tags, documents, etc. in both the public and private sector are to be changed. Muslims in Maharashtra also complained about the 'attempt to obliterate the history of Muslims by targeting dates and places in the history of the state' (*Indian Express*, 23 November 1995).

[46] Shiv Sena has throughout the past decade systematically appealed to the Gujaratis, a large and affluent community in Bombay, among other things by launching large-scale public celebrations of the *Navratti* festival, a Gujarati celebrations of the artisan gods. For the details regarding the ongoing legal battle on the issue, see *Telegraph*, 23 May 1995.

also indicated that even the first round of riots in December 1992 in many ways involved the same systematic attacks by Hindus on Muslim neighbourhoods and property that had been so evident in the second round of the riots.[47] On the pretext that the commissions findings would be of no consequence and that the commission was too expensive, the Shiv Sena–BJP government decided to dissolve the commission, and it was stated that the government felt no obligation to make the findings public. The decision was immediately challenged on legal grounds, and the short-lived BJP interim cabinet under A. B. Vajpayee did in May 1996 put pressure on the Maharashtra government to reinstate the commission in order to 'establish our non-partisan approach in inter-community matters' as Vajpayee argued.[48] However, the BJP–Shiv Sena cabinet seemed determined to continue its inteference in the judicial process and to establish the Bombay riots as a kind of spontaneous, and fully justified, self-defence on the part of the Hindu population. In April 1997, the State Government decided to withdraw the cases filed against Thackeray by the previous Congress cabinet on the grounds that his editorials in *Saamna* in January 1993 had spread false rumours and had contributed to the atmosphere wherein the massive anti-Muslim pogrom took place.[49]

In a number of other fields the government has also launched symbolic raids specifically targeting Congress strongholds. In March 1995, a few days after forming the government in Bombay, the director of a cooperative sugar factory was removed and the government showed symbolic muscle in announcing that no corrupt practises would be accepted in this sector.[50] A new policy

---

[47] For the announcement of the disbanding of the commission see *Times of India*, 25 January 1996. See excerpts of the findings of the Srikrishna commission published in *Times of India*, 29 May 1996. The Shiv Sena–BJP government has on several occasions intervened rather blatantly in pending legal enquiries to protect its own interests. Firstly, the decision to give a more 'balanced' mandate to the Srikrishna commission by including the bomb-blasts in March 1993; secondly the withdrawal of eleven hundred cases filed by Dalits in Marathwada in connection with the atrocities committed under the renaming riots in 1978, under the 'Prevention of Atrocities Act. This withdrawal which also is legally contested was obviously a kind of 'revenge' for the successful renaming of Marathwada University in 1994, and a signal to the large Maratha constituency of the Shiv Sena in Marathwada. (*Economic and Political Weekly*, vol. 30, 7 October, p. 2465.)

[48] See *The Hindu*, 29 May 1996.

[49] *Frontline*, 18 April 1997.

[50] *Times of India*, 27 March 1995.

for the agricultural sector has been prepared since 1995 but the
pending corruption-charges against the Shiv Sena Minister for
Agriculture delayed the launching of the new policy. The main
pillars in this new policy will be privatization of a large number
of cooperative units and irrigation-schemes. In an effort to cut to
the heart of what is broadly seen as the centre of Congress' rural
power in the state, the privatization of a number of sugar-factories
were announced during the campaign prior to the local elections
in February 1997.[51] The Shiv Sena–BJP government has also been
able to curtail the activities of the cooperative banks considerably
by refusing to guarantee any new credits until they have recovered
some of their assets from rich farmers capable of repaying loans.[52]

Immediately after the new cabinet was sworn in, a host of
fanciful projects were suggested by the Shiv Sena leaders who
enthusiastically flirted with the idea of making Bombay the centre
for a new 'Asian Tiger' with Gujarat and Maharashtra as 'special
economic zones' in the Chinese style. Though the BJP had
apprehensions concerning the 'Bombay-centrism' of the Shiv Sena,
a series of high-profile infrastructural projects were floated in order
to modernize Bombay's strained and congested traffic system.
More than fifty major projects of flyovers, a system of underground metros, new express-ways, etc. have been proposed since
April 1995. In May 1996 a special Road Development Corporation
was formed to boost the construction of new roads in the Bombay
area and elsewhere in the state.[53] The government has also started
the planning of a large new airport, there has been discussion of
a helicopter service in the city, just as hoovercrafts have been tested
as alternative means of traffic around the peninsula. It is indicative
of the process of policy-making and the character of these visions
that the railways which are the most vital means of transport for
most people in the city—at present overloaded and in a rundown
condition—are given less attention because of the massive problems
surrounding expansion and renovation of the rail system. An
estimated 30,000 slum squatters live along the railway and many
have acquired semilegal rights on their plots. This makes any

[51] *Times of India,* 29 Febuary 1997.
[52] *Pioneer,* 18 March 1996.
[53] One of the stated objectives of the corporation was to privatize as many
projects as possible, just as it was stated that building of express-ways would be
given top-priority (*Indian Express,* 22 May 1996).

expansion of the tracks or acquisition of new land a rather sensitive issue.[54]

The most striking feature of most of these plans were, however, the extent to which they were marked by a distinct upper middle class view of the overwhelming part of the city—as vast expanses of slum or 'ordinary' neighbourhoods that had to be driven through by new expressways, driven under by a new metro, flown over in helicopters or altogether avoided in hoovercraft services that would take the upper middle class from their homes in the western suburbs to the city centre without passing through the congestions of the city. At the same time, the cabinet has announced extensive plans regarding the housing and removal of the hundreds of thousands of dwellers on the footpaths of Bombay and announced the reconstruction of thousands of dilapidated buildings in the city.[55] Especially Shiv Sena is committed to a change of the face of Bombay to make it a clean, green, and elegant city capable of claiming the status the city had in the 1950s, in the words of a Shiv Sena leader, 'the most elegant and modern city in South Asia—well maybe in the entire Asia.'[56]

The emerging style of Hindu nationalist governance in Maharashtra, more visibly influenced by the Shiv Sena than the BJP, seems to indicate a good deal of continuity from its predecessors: continuation of the 'investor-friendly' attitude, the practice of subverting the sovereignty of the judiciary, the firm belief in detailed regulation of various areas from education to quotas of cotton and sugar released for export. At the same time, the Shiv Sena's vision of a new Bombay seems to transcend the established rural populism in the Maharashtra Congress, or the moral discomfort with urban modernity in the Sangh Parivar. It seems committed to rapid urban development with fanciful projects full of action, grand scales and huge money which obviously is catching the imagination of many Bombay'ites. The Shiv Sena stands undoubtedly for a brutal, may be even philistine suburban petty-bourgeois vision of modernity. But it is a mode of appropriation of technology, assertiveness and masculinity that probably is more in tune with the actual forms of modern living and aspirations as they

[54] For an overview of Bombay's developmental problems, see special report in *Sunday*, 21–7 April 1996.

[55] *Indian Express*, 5 March 1996.

[56] Pramod Nawalkar, interview, op. cit.

unfold in the streets and chawls in Bombay and other cities and towns in the state than the high-caste notions of control, culture and austerity one finds within the Sangh Parivar.

After a number of initial successes in its first year where the sheer energy of the new cabinet in a number of policy-areas created a certain aura of resoluteness, the Shiv Sena–BJP cabinet ran into a series of crises in the latter half of 1996. Most of the strong criticism in the press, from social organizations and from civil-rights groups, revolved around ever stronger indications that the two parties in the government displayed open contempt for the judiciary and misused both the powers and the funds of the state to consolidate their own standing and clientelist powers. These allegations were in particular directed against the Shiv Sena, where especially the Thackeray family, according to a report from the 'Committee for the Protection of Democratic Rights' (CPDR), 'operate as extra-constitutional authorities in the state—answerable to no one'. The CPDR and an increasing number of press reports argue that the Shiv Sena in multiple ways used its power to cover up misdeeds committed by its cadres, to stall police-investigations, and to further the private economic interests of its leaders, many of whom are involved in the influential building and real estate industry in Bombay.[57]

The mounting pressure on the government and the many allegations of unlawful practices did not represent a serious political problem for the BJP as long as the allegations pointed towards the Shiv Sena and Thackeray. This enabled the party, once more, to play the part of the respectable and morally clean partner in the government. The BJP tried for instance to show this respectable face by arguing for some sort of compensation for sacked millworkers in the context of the much-debated closure of textile mills and sale of their attractive primeland in South-Central Mumbai to real estate developers.[58] The BJP also tried to hone its image of respectability by asking for fresh investigations in the controversial and hushed up Kini case where Raj Thackeray,

[57] See e.g. *The Autumn of the Patriarch: Bal Thackeray's Remote Control Tyranny in Maharashtra*, Committee for the Protection of Democratic Rights, Mumbai, 1996. Thackeray's oft-repeated comment about his personal 'remote-control' of the government turned out to be more like disdain for legal and administrative institutions on part of the Shiv Sena, than any hidden policy-agenda.

[58] *Indian Express*, 20 October 1996.

nephew of Bal Thackeray and groomed to be a part of the next generation of leaders in the Shiv Sena, was involved in the murder of a tenant in a real estate dispute. The strained relation between the two parties was also played out in the cultural field. The Sangh Parivar leadership felt provoked by the obvious bending of rules by the Shiv Sena when the tax-exemption which normally is extended to artistic 'high-culture' productions was granted to rather ordinary 'Bombay-masala' films produced by the members of the Thackeray family. Likewise, the RSS was enraged by the overnight decision whereby the company organizing the high-profile Michael Jackson show in Mumbai—attended by all the leading Shiv Sena figures, MLAs, etc. (many with cotton in their ears!)—was granted tax-exemption on the grounds that it was raising funds for social work among disadvantaged people in the state.[59]

The most damaging challenge to the BJP did, however, come from the noted Gandhian social worker Anna Hazare who in October 1996 started a campaign against the alleged rampant and systematic corruption in the Shiv Sena–BJP administration. Anna Hazare had been running a similar and quite efficient campaign against the previous Congress government, a campaign which the BJP actively supported and which beyond any doubt contributed to Congress' defeat in 1995.

Charges of high level corruption piled up in 1996 and the Shiv Sena–BJP cabinet decided to set up a high-level committee probing into these charges. Anna Hazare agreed to be a member along with Bal Thackeray and the BJP's Deputy Chief Minister Gopinath Mundhe. The inclusion of the respected and self-professed 'apolitical' figure of Hazare, who on several occasions made public statements regarding his belief in the sincerity and good intentions of the government, was obviously a significant victory for the cabinet.[60] Hazare and his assistants who saw themselves as a sort of 'ombudsman' institution, managed to get access to official files

---

[59] I discuss the many ways in which the Shiv Sena has sought to gain recognition and cultural legitimacy in Mumbai, and how the organization also has promoted its own 'plebeian' cultural forms, notions of violent masculinity, and visions of Mumbai's high-tech modernity in tune with global cultural flows, in my *Mumbai Dreams: Identities, Power and Governance in Bombay'*, Paper presented at SOAS, 26 Febuary 1997 (unpublished).

[60] See e.g. *Indian Express*, 21 September 1996.

and asked citizens and bureaucrats to submit evidence of corrupt practices in the government. After a few months it became clear that Hazare had done his work with more diligence than expected and that he was unwilling to fill in the legitimatory function carved out for him by the cabinet. In November 1996 Hazare broke off his cordial relations with Thackeray and Mundhe, demanded resignation of several ministers of state and went on an infinite fast.[61] The revelation of the corrupt practices of the BJP ministers, and the simultaneous press-reports on Gopinath Munde's extra-marital affairs, dealt a hard blow to the carefully nurtured 'clean' profile of the BJP in the state. On the behest of the BJP, two cabinet ministers, one from the Shiv Sena and another from the BJP, were forced to resign and the BJP did what it could to restore its somewhat battered image.

The necessary alliance with the Shiv Sena grew into an ever more problematic liability for BJP's public image in the following months, as Thackeray was sentenced to two weeks imprisonment for the open contempt of court (after allegations regarding corruption in the judiciary), and after Thackeray had made offensive remarks against a noted Marathi playwright and recipient of the state award for Marathi literature.

The political compulsion underpinning the alliance did nonetheless become crystal clear as the results of the municipal and panchayat elections in February 1997 revealed that the Shiv Sena in spite of massive criticism in the press and in spite of a somewhat ad-hoc'ish style of governance was able to consolidate and expand its electoral base and its representation in the local bodies. As before, the BJP remained dependent on this capacity of the Shiv Sena to defy and bypass most of the established rules in the political field and yet win elections.

ELECTORAL CONSOLIDATION AND PROSPECTS

For decades the Congress reaped the electoral benefits of being a very large and well-extended party because of the majoritarian slant intrinsic to the electoral system in India. The 'winner takes all' system favours big parties just as many years in power had given the party control over the huge clientelist resources that on innumerable occasions enabled the party to create and encourage

---

[61] See interview with Hazare, *Indian Express*, 24 November 1996.

defections of ambitious individuals from opposition parties to the Congress party. Being the central locus of power created certain self-perpetuating logics whereby money, influence and political talent invariably gravitated towards the large party in power. Judging by the results of the 11th General Election in 1996, the Shiv Sena–BJP alliance seems in the course of a couple of years to have been able to occupy this centre of political power in Maharashtra. The alliance was able to win as many as 33 parliamentary seats (out of a total of 48 in the state) with a joint percentage of votes of 38.5 per cent, while the Congress with 34.9 per cent of the vote only could win 15 seats.[62] This strong performance of the alliance stemmed from two factors. Firstly, there was a further consolidation of the strongholds of both parties in certain regions of the state. In Bombay, the alliance secured all six seats and polled 58.3 per cent of the votes; in Vidarbha, the alliance won nine out of 11 seats (40.2 per cent of the vote); in Marathwada, the alliance won six out of eight seats (39.4 per cent of the vote) and in the coastal Konkan strip the Shiv Sena swept the polls and the alliance won four out of five seats (46.2 per cent of the vote). Secondly, the Congress was ridden by deep-running dissent and factionalism in many regions. This produced a large number of independent candidates. In northern Maharashtra where neither the Shiv Sena nor BJP ever had a strong presence, Congressmen defected to the BJP and made it possible for the alliance to secure five out of six seats (45.6 per cent of the vote). Internal divisions in the Congress also produced independent candidates in many other constituencies in the state and enabled the Shiv Sena–BJP alliance to win comfortable victories on the basis of modest gains in votes, while the percentage of votes drawn by independent candidates in many constituencies went beyond 30 per cent.

As in previous elections, the agreement between the two parties gave more seats to the BJP (18) than the Shiv Sena (15) although the latter gained far more than the BJP and tripled its representation in the Lok Sabha as compared to 1991. It was clear, however, that Shiv Sena—sensing its own indispensability vis-à-vis the BJP in the state—went into a tougher bargaining with the BJP prior to

---

[62] Electoral figures kindly provided by V. B. Singh, the Centre for the study of Developing Societies, Data Unit, Delhi.

the election and that the party was able to take over several
constituencies controlled by the BJP for years (such as the Thane
constituency), and get seats allocated in rural Vidarbha where the
BJP through the 1980s had built up considerable strength and dense
political networks. Recognizing that it was rapidly losing ground
in Vidarbha, local Congress forces in the region decided to launch
attacks on the state government, charging it of neglect of the region
and in this fashion trying to capture the issue of a separate Vidarbha
identity which the BJP had deployed so effectively in their build
up in the region. By raising the issue of special grievances in
Vidarbha, the Congress also hoped to drive a wedge between the
Shiv Sena, who in the name of Maharashtrian identity is strongly
opposed to any prospect of dividing the state, and the BJP who
for years have been advocating the formation of more and smaller
states and who sucessfully have assumed the role as the primary
party representing Vidarbha's special interests. However, the BJP
was not alarmed by this attempt to take over their own policy:
'If Congress wants to create a Vidarbha state it is fine with us. It
will benefit us more than them (...) Besides it would leave us with
a clearer picture altogether. The Shiv Sena would dominate
Western Maharashtra, the coast and Marathwada, and we would
rule in Vidarbha. I don't even think the Shiv Sena would oppose
this if they gave it some thought...' a high ranking BJP organizer
in Maharashtra told me off the record in November 1996.

    The results of the 1996 General Election in the state thus
testified to the general weakness of Congress and indicated that the
BJP, at the price of concessions to the Shiv Sena, had consolidated
its standing in the state considerably and had broken out of its
urban higher-caste core-constituencies. The two parties have in fact
attracted a substantial share of votes from the Scheduled Caste
communities. While the BJP systematically has mobilized Dalits,
especially non-Mahars, the Shiv Sena's share of Dalit votes has to
do with the general 'plebeian' profile of the party, rather than its
espousal of a distinct Dalit identity. Throughout its thirty years
of existence the party has been involved in innumerable confrontations with Dalit organizations and the party has consistently, and
violently, opposed any concessions to Dalits, such as in the conflict
regarding the renaming of Marathwada University as 'Babasaheb
Ambedkar University' in 1994. In spite of recent official praise
showered on Dr Ambedkar by the Shiv Sena leaders, the party

continues a confrontationist style vis-à-vis Dalits. In July 1997 riots broke out in Mumbai, after the police, known for Sena sympathies and hostility to Dalits, shot dead ten Dalits in a slum colony. Instead of investigating the case, the Shiv Sena immediately blamed 'criminal elements conspiring to topple the government' for instigating the riots. A few days later, bands of Sena supporters attacked and ransacked the home of Congress leader (and ex Sena leader) Chaggan Bhujbal, in a retaliation against Bhujbal's strong criticism of the government's handling of the riots and the killings of Dalits.

Continuing disarray within the Congress, and mounting tensions between the BJP and Shiv Sena was evident during the local elections in February–March 1997. As in 1992, the two parties in the alliance failed to reach an agreement on seat-distribution for the civic polls. It was simply impossible to accommodate the many contestants and both parties experienced an unprecedented level of dissent and factionalism, not least in Mumbai where the stakes in terms of potential patronage and financial gains from a post as corporator are very high. The local elections in 1997 saw a larger number of independent candidates than in any previous election, and a very complex situation emerged after the polls as each party tried to win over, or simply purchase, as many of the independent candidates as possible.

In spite of the many political scandals and the massive public criticism of the Shiv Sena, the party was able to secure as many as 103 seats (out of 221) in the Brihanmumbai Municipal Corporation,[63] while the modest strength of the BJP in the metropolitan

---

[63] *Asian Age*, 27 February 1997. As it happened in the civic polls in 1985, the question of Bombay's (Mumbai's) status vis-à-vis the state of Maharashtra and the centre was once again cast in doubt in February 1997. In 1985 there were rumours of the possibility of Bombay being separated from Maharashtra and turned into a Union Territory. This rumour reactivated all the old themes and fears so prominent in the campaign for a unilingual Maharashtra and contributed undoubtedly to the Shiv Sena's first victory in the Bombay Municipal Corporation. In 1997, there were rumours that the Union Government deliberated a reverting of Mumbai to its old name Bombay to undo the damage which the change of name was alleged to have incurred on the financial markets and in India's international trade (*Times of India*, 17 February 1997). Unsurprisingly this rumour (which may have been 'planted' by Shiv Sena) gave Thackeray and other Sena leaders the opportunity to assert, once more, the sovereignty of the state government and to assert the Maharashtrian character of the city (*Times of India*, 19 February 1997).

area was revealed as the party only secured 26 seats. Congress candidates won 49 seats (as against 109 in 1992), partly because of the massive swing of Muslim votes towards the Samajwadi Party which was able to win 21 seats in the corporation, mainly from low-income and the Muslim areas in the Greater Mumbai area. In the other major cities in the state the Shiv Sena and BJP reinforced their hold on the urban electorate, except in Pune and Pimpri–Chinchwad where the Congress retained its hold on the civic body.[64]

A slightly different picture emerged from the *Zilla Parishad*, and *Panchayat Samiti* elections only a week later. The campaign prior to the elections had been marked by widespread factionalism and infighting between candidates especially within the Congress but also within and between the Shiv Sena and BJP. As a result the number of independents running for office was exceedingly high and made the electoral prospects in most districts very unpredictable. In Ahmednagar District, one of the most famous leaders of the cooperative movement Balasaheb Vikhe Patil turned against the Congress and worked in alliance with the Shiv Sena. In 12 out of the 29 districts of the state the seat-adjustment between the two alliance parties broke down—especially in districts where the alliance had a fair chance of actually winning a majority and where the stakes in the election consequently were considerably higher than in districts dominated by Congress.[65] In spite of these differences within the alliance, the result confirmed that the alliance parties never have been stronger in the rural areas, traditionally dominated by Congress for more than four decades, than now after two years of governance. Given the enormous attention Congress over the years has given to the structure of cooperatives, banking, development projects and channeling of

---

[64] In Pune, Congress won more than half of all seats while the BJP only improved its share of seats marginally to 20, while the Shiv Sena continued its slow expansion in the low-income areas of the fast-growing city and secured 15 seats in the civic body. In Thane city the Shiv Sena regained the dominance it had lost in 1992 and the alliance secured 50 out of 95 seats. In Nagpur the BJP secured on its own a majority of 64 (out of 129 seats) while Shiv Sena only won two seats. This was undoubtedly linked with the considerable flow of resources which the BJP minister of Public Works in Maharashtra (elected in a Nagpur constituency) had channeled to the city since 1995. (*Times of India*, 26 Febuary 1997.)

[65] *Times of India*, 27 Febuary 1997.

funds to *Zilla Parishads*, whose presidents were granted status equivalent to that of state-ministers in 1991, the results were rather satisfactory seen from the point of view of the ruling alliance. Congress did, predictably, win a majority in 11 out of the 29 districts in the state, most of them in western and northern Maharashtra, while Shiv Sena–BJP secured a majority in four districts (two in Konkan, Jalgaon in northern Maharashtra and one in Vidarbha).[66]

The relative success of both the Shiv Sena and BJP in the local elections seems to indicate that both parties have established effective local clientelistic structures enabling them to solve pending problems and to attract local 'social workers', i.e. brokers-cum-business-people with a considerable standing in towns, villages and neighbourhoods, to their respective parties. The combination of control over resources at the state and civic levels with networks of 'political entrepreneurs' in thousands of localities and institutions was always the backbone of Congress' power, and the Achilles heel of the opposition parties. It seems as if the roles have changed somewhat, and that especially the Shiv Sena, always more pragmatic and closer to the Congress in its practical approach to politics, has utilized its ascendance to state-power to build such networks and patronage-structures of a certain durability. The relatively weaker performance of the BJP at the local level indicates the continuing discomfort among party-cadres regarding the most 'profane' dimensions of the political field, such as corruption, thuggish methods, purchase of votes, and fund-raising through more or less explicit extortion. The BJP remains dominated by middle-class activists and long-standing members of the Sangh Parivar whose deep running notions of a purer 'value-based' political culture, less 'contaminated' by money and cynical self-interest, makes the party quite well suited and efficient in conducting election campaigns bent on emotional and general issues. Although the relations between the two alliance partners at local levels often are cordial, the internal organizational dynamics and languages of the two parties remain distinct—one respectable and middle class in complexion, the other 'plebeian', masculine and actionist. This difference tends to reproduce itself rather than converge because of the division of labour and constituencies

[66] *Times of India*, 5 March 1997.

which the alliance has institutionalized and corroborated over the years. It is in this perspective quite logical that it is the Shiv Sena rather than BJP which in substantial ways has begun the process of taking over not only the former constituencies of Congress, but also the major part of the political culture and mode of governance, developed and refined by the Congress for decades in the state.

It is probably too early to write off the Congress as a force to reckon with in Maharashtra. In spite of a poor performance in the Eleventh General Election, the party retained 34.9 per cent of the popular vote and remained the largest party in the state in terms of popular support. The party also still has an experienced leadership and a formidable cadre of experienced, if excessively cynical, local leaders all over the state. Above all the party also still has the most famous, and probably one of the toughest, political leaders in the entire country, Sharad Pawar, as an apex figure who still commands both awe and respect.

Ψ

5

Southern Discomfort: The BJP in Karnataka[1]

JAMES MANOR

If the Bharatiya Janata Party (BJP) is to obtain a parliamentary majority, it needs to break out of its confinement to roughly half of India—the western and north-central regions. It must win substantial numbers of seats in major states either of the east (Bihar, Orissa and West Bengal) or of the south (Andhra Pradesh, Karnataka, Kerala and Tamil Nadu). It has found it very difficult to do this, although its showing in Bihar in the 1996 general election offered it some hope. Bihar and the east are best left to other analysts. This chapter examines the BJP's prospects in the south—especially in the only southern state, Karnataka, where its chances are better than dismal.[2]

That last election suggested that the BJP may someday win a sizeable number of seats in a *national* election in Karnataka. But there are also good reasons to doubt this, and no present evidence, it has little hope of success in *state* elections there. Since its prospects in all of the other southern states remain wretched, at

[1] Research for this chapter was funded by grants from the British Economic and Social Research Council and the Nuffield Foundation. I am grateful to the *Times of India*, Bangalore for access to their indexed files of cuttings, and to E. Raghavan of the *Economic Times* for much valuable help.
[2] The discussion which follows consists of revised versions to two earlier studies—first of the BJP's performance in the southern states (especially Karnataka) in the 1991 parliamentary election, and then of its showing at the Karnataka state election in late 1994 (Manor, J., 'The BJP in South India: 1991 General Election', *Economic and Political Weekly*, 13–20 June 1992, pp 1267–73; and Manor, J., 'Still a Marginal Force: The Bharatiya Janata Party in Karnataka' in G. K. Prasad, D. Jeevan Kumar and K. C. Suri; *The Angry Voter: Assembly Elections in Andhra Pradesh and Karnataka, 1994* (Madras, 1995), pp 168–82.

this writing, the south continues to be a severe problem for the party.

THE PARLIAMENTARY ELECTION OF 1991

Many political commentators and politicians of various parties, not least the BJP itself, regard the south as a region that offers it some hope. During the 1991 election campaign, the party was accurately reported to be 'pulling out all the stops' in the south, devising special supplementary manifestos for each of the four southern states and redoubling its efforts there after the murder of Rajiv Gandhi.[3] But what was the outcome? Let us proceed state by state.

Kerala and Tamil Nadu

In recent years, the BJP and organizations associated with it (particularly the Rashtriya Swayamsevak Sangh or RSS) have invested more time and effort in Kerala and Tamil Nadu, especially the former, than in the other two southern states. It is therefore ironic that the party performed abysmally there in the 1991 election.

In Kerala, this is nothing new. In the years up to 1991, the BJP and its predecessor, the Jana Sangh, had never won a single seat in an election to the state assembly or the Lok Sabha—indeed, in parliamentary elections, they failed even to finish second in any single contest.[4] Before the 1991 elections, there was brave talk of winning two of the 20 Lok Sabha seats and four of the 140 assembly seats that were filled in 1991,[5] but they won none. The 4.7 per cent of the vote which they gained in the Lok Sabha poll was an increase of only 0.5 per cent over their total at the 1989 election, and this entailed a loss of 360,000 votes even from what one press report described as its 'dismal' performance in the district council elections six months earlier.[6] The extreme weakness of the BJP was apparent from its decision to revert to its 1989 role as covert supporter of the Congress-I against the Communist Party of India-Marxist. It is difficult to see why the party should have the slightest optimism about its future in Kerala.

---

[3] The quotation is from *Business and Political Observer*, 14 May 1991. See also, *The Times of India*, 31 May 1991.

[4] Singh, V. B., and S. Bose, *State Elections in India: Data Handbook on Vidhan Sabha Elections*, 1952–85, vol. 5, *The South*, (New Delhi, 1988), pp 50–3.

[5] *Newstime* (Hyderabad), 17 April 1991.

[6] *The Times of India*, 8 April 1991 and *Deccan Herald*, 19 June 1991.

Its position in Tamil Nadu is even worse. The BJP and Jana Sangh have always performed wretchedly here. All but one of the 60 candidates which they put forward at state assembly elections between 1952 and 1984 lost their deposits.[7] Only eight of their candidates at all Lok Sabha elections prior to 1991 managed to finish as high as third, and the largest share of the vote polled by any of them was 7.1 per cent.[8] In the 1991 election, the BJP gained only 1.4 per cent of the total vote.[9] If we are looking for signs of promise for this party in the south, we need to look elsewhere.

Andhra Pradesh

The BJP won one of its five southern seats in 1991 in Andhra Pradesh—in Secunderabad, a constituency which embraces roughly half of greater Hyderabad. The party also finished a close second in the neighbouring constituency of Hyderabad which extends over the other half of this conurbation and into some rural areas beyond. The detailed results from these two seats are worth noting. (See Table 5.1)

TABLE 5.1: The BJP in Andhra Pradesh (1991)

Constituency	Votes
Secunderabad	
Bhandaru Dattatreya (BJP)	253,924
*T Manemma Anjaiah (Cong-I)	168,924
K Pratap Reddy (Janata Dal)	9,350
G Suryanarayana (Samajwadi Janata Party)	1,665
Hyderabad[10]	
Sultan Salahuddin Owaisi (MIM)	459,886
Baddam Bal Readdy (BJP)	414,552
Indra Reddy Patlolla (Telugu Desam)	49,545
M Suja Shankar (Congress-I)	33,429
Others	18,108

*denotes incumbent.

[7] Singh and Bose, *State Elections...*, op. cit., pp 42–4. This excludes 1977 when the Jana Sangh formed part of the Janata Party.

[8] Bulter, D. B., A. Lahiri and P. Roy, *India Decides: Elections 1952–91*, second edition (New Delhi, 1991), pp 255–62.

[9] *India Today*, 31 October 1991, p. 20. The BJP has never been a remotely serious force in Pondicherry.

[10] *The Hindu*, 18 June 1991.

Polling for both of these seats occurred on 20 May, the day before the murder of Rajiv Gandhi. Had votes been cast after the assassination, the BJP might—ironically—have won them both. Their margin in Secunderabad was probably great enough to withstand the 8 per cent swing to the Congress-I which occurred between the two phases of voting. Congress-I organizers reckon that had all voting taken place after the assassination, they could have won any seat that opposition parties gained on 20 May with majorities of less than 100,000.[11] Secunderabad just falls into that category, but the swing to the Congress-I mainly came from Telugu Desam supporters and not from those who backed the BJP.

In Hyderabad, it is entirely possible that enough Muslim votes would have swung from the Majilis-e-Ittihad al-Muslimin (MIM) to the Congress-I to let the BJP candidate in. Indeed, the loss of votes to the Congress-I had always been the main fear of the MIM.[12] (It had withdrawn nine of its 11 candidates in Telengana in exchange for a Congress-I agreement to field a Hindu from the 'backward classes' rather than a Muslim in Hyderabad, so that a split of Hindu votes would hurt the BJP there. This probably tipped the balance in that constituency.)[13]

There must, however, be serious doubts about whether these two strong showings for the BJP indicate great promise for the future. Several things make it less impressive than it first appears. In Secunderabad, T. Anjaiah, the widow of the former Chief Minister and MP for this constituency, was a weak candidate. She was widely regarded as a sincere, pleasant person, but her poor performance as a constituency MP had antagonized many groups, and she seldom spoke from the public platform—others held forth

[11] This emerged from an extremely informative discussion with B. Subja Rao, a Congress-I MLA, Hyderabad, 11 August 1991.

[12] Interviews with Congress-I and MIM activists, Hyderabad, 8 August 1991.

[13] *The Times of India*, 8 May 1991. The BJP alleged that polling irregularities had occurred in this constituency, but after detailed and extensive discussions with officials who oversaw the elections there, I believe that these are largely unfounded. It is true that the MIM received 90 per cent of the votes cast at some booths. But in those areas, Muslims constitute nearly 100 per cent of the electorate. Given the highly polarized communal atmosphere in the city, such heavy backing for the MIM is not too surprising. The presence of 20,000 members of the security forces in the constituency on the election day was a clear counterweight to booth-capturing. The turnout in the urban areas of the constituency was around 90 per cent, as against 60 per cent in the predominantly Hindu rural sectors.

on her behalf while she sat silently by. She also faced an unusually serious campaign of sabotage by members of her own party. All but one of the Congress MLAs for the constituency worked against her out of loyalty to the recently ousted Chief Minister, M. Channa Reddy, because she had supported his successor.[14]

Much more important in both parliamentary constituencies were the prolonged and thoroughly ghastly communal riots that had taken place in and around Hyderabad in November–December 1990. These surpassed all previous communal conflicts there both in their duration—they occurred in two prolonged phases spread over more than a month—and in their intensity. Unprecedently wide curfews had to be imposed. Over 120 people, including a police constable and an assistant commissioner of police, died.[15]

The most alarming aspect of the riots was the character of the violence. A cycle of atrocity and counter-atrocity developed which was extremely difficult for the security forces to tackle. Even women and children under ten were murdered. During curfew hours, armed bands moved about the city, breaking into homes, dragging women into the street and stabbing them or burning them to death—actions the like of which had never been seen here. Killing continued on a major scale for more than a week after the army was deployed in early December.[16] Newspaper editorials stating that this 'gruesome' episode had raised communal tension to 'levels hitherto unknown'[17] were not exaggerating. In such circumstances, it is hardly surprising that the BJP did so well in parliamentary elections in the twin cities. In 1996, in more normal times, they could not do well again in constituencies where they had never won before.

When we look beyond Secunderabad and Hyderabad, to the other 40 parliamentary constituencies in Andhra Pradesh, the picture changes dramatically. The party was not a serious challenger for any seat, even those that were filled before the assassination. Indeed, it failed to come second even once and was usually a very poor third. The state general secretary of the party lost his

[14] Interviews with Congress-I and BJP workers in Secunderabad, and with a knowledgeable IAS officer, Hyderabad, 7–9 August 1991.

[15] *The Times of India*, 17 December 1990 and interview with a senior official dealing with law and order, Hyderabad, 8 August 1991.

[16] *Newstime*, 14 and 21 December 1990 and *The Patriot*, 26 December 1990.

[17] *Newstime*, 16 December 1990 and *The Hindu*, 17 December 1990.

deposit in Visakhapatnam. The BJP's particularly strenuous efforts in three predominantly rural constituencies in Telengana were to little avail.

Several developments had caused the BJP activists to believe that the party 'would do wonders, upsetting calculations' L. K. Advani's *rath yatra* had passed through Andhra Pradesh, and the party's campaign was quicker off the mark than those of other parties in several parts of the state. During the campaign, its national leaders sometimes attracted substantial crowds here. It also managed to recruit a number of prominent people to its ranks—a former chief secretary of the state government, the president of the National Forum on the Environment, former directors of police communications and the anti-corruption bureau, a senior officer at the Super Speciality Hospital in Tirupati and two Telugu actors.[18]

The BJP's two main rivals also had serious problems. The Telugu Desam was extremely short of funds and suffered from internal divisions that were aggravated by N. T. Rama Rao's indecision in candidate selection.[19] The Congress-I which had ruled the state since 1989 was plagued by scandals, such as Rajiv Gandhi's hesitations in choosing candidates which one Congressman described as a 'frustrating and bizarre drama', and defeatist remarks about Andhra Pradesh by Rajiv Gandhi which another Congressman called 'childish'. Rampant factional conflict within the Congress-I, including an unseemly and highly visible squabble between the chief minister and the president of the state party, had filled the newspapers for months.[20]

Despite all this, however, the BJP's performance at the election was very unimpressive. It polled 8.8 per cent of the vote across the state, which at first glance appears to represent a marked improvement over the 2.1 per cent it received in 1989. But much of that increase is accounted for by its showing in the twin cities, and by the fact that in 1989 it had fielded no candidates there, as a result

[18] *Indian Express,* 2, 13, 16–18 and 24 April 1991 and *Hindustan Times,* 22 April 1991.

[19] *Indian Express,* 19 April 1991 and *The Times of India,* 29 April 1991.

[20] Quotations are, respectively, from *Indian Express,* 4 April 1991 and 25 April 1991. See also *The Hindu,* 25 November 1990, 4 and 10 February 1991, 5 April 1991 and 19 June 1991; *Deccan Chronicle,* 21 February 1991 and 30 March 1991; *Indian Express,* 17 December 1990, 14 and 23 March 1991, 3, 10, 18 and 24 April 1991; *Deccan Herald,* 8 February 1991; and *Newstime,* 7, 15, 25 and 28–9 November 1990, 18 December 1990, 21 and 28 March 1991.

of an electoral agreement with the Telugu Desam. The rest of it was the result of the sharp increase in the number of seats the BJP contested—39 in 1991 as compared to two in 1989—rather than a growth of its popularity.

Its performance outside the twin cities in 1991 was broadly consistent with its poor record at previous elections. The BJP and the Jana Sangh had only succeeded in winning one Lok Sabha seat on earlier occasions, in 1984 with a candidate who had the support of the Telugu Desam which humbled the Congress-I in that year. (The defeated Congressman in that election was P. V. Narasimha Rao.) In state assembly elections, the largest share of the vote that it has achieved was 2.8 per cent in 1983. At six state elections between 1952 and 1983 (excluding 1978 when it fought as part of the losing Janata Party), 192 of its 296 candidates lost their deposits and only six won seats. In 1985 and 1989, it won eight and five assembly seats respectively, but on both occasions it had electoral understandings with the Telugu Desam.[21]

At the 1991 parliamentary election, many groups in this state were unhappy with the performance of the ruling Congress-I—mainly elements of the 'backward classes', including many Muslims outside the twin cities and the Kapu community which had backed the Congress-I in 1989 and is hugely important in coastal districts.[22] But they had available to them a convincing alternative other than the BJP, namely the Telugu Desam. Meanwhile the 'forward' groups and the Scheduled Castes stayed mainly with the Congress-I.[23] (This stood in radical contrast to the situation in Karnataka, as we shall see.)

All of this indicates that in Andhra Pradesh outside greater Hyderabad, the BJP's showing was 'dismal'.[24] Its claim that it might have won six seats in the state had the assassination not occurred[25] is absurd. Even if it maintains its strength in the twin

---

[21] Singh and Bose, *State Elections...*, vol. 5, op. cit., pp 26–8. The figures for 1952 are for old Hyderabad state.

[22] The Congress-I gave 'forward' groups a very large share of its tickets. It only nominated one Kapu candidate, and he stood outside the coastal belt where that group is concentrated.

[23] This is based on interviews with more than a dozen politicians and political analysts in Hyderabad, 7–13 August 1991.

[24] *Deccan Herald*, 21 June 1991.

[25] *The Hindu*, 19 June 1991.

cities, its performance at this election suggests that it will find it enormously difficult to become anything other than a minor force in this state.

Karnataka

This leaves Karnataka where the BJP's candidates received 28.8 per cent of the vote,[26] a dramatic improvement both on the 2.6 per cent that its five candidates received in 1989 and on its best showing of 4.7 per cent in 1984 with six candidates (standing in an alliance with the Janata Party). This placed it second to the Congress-I which gained 41.9 per cent of the votes, and ahead of the Janata Dal which had 18.5 per cent. The BJP had never before won a Lok Sabha seat here.[27]

This time it won four and would probably have won a fifth, had the assassination of Rajiv Gandhi not occurred. It finished a reasonably respectable second in a further six seats. In six others it was a remote second, and in 10 more a remote third. Four of those candidates lost their deposits.[28] (One of the 28 contests was countermanded after the death of a candidate.)

This was an impressive showing, but to understand it more fully and to see what it may imply for party's future, we need to look closely at the details of what occurred. Let us begin by considering the four contests that it won, and the fifth in which it nearly succeeded. (see Table 5.2.)

Bangalore South

Caste was an important element here. Unusually for Karnataka, this constituency has a significant number of Brahmin voters, but they are still outnumbered by Vokkaligas who from the most numerically powerful social group. Both the Congress-I and the Janata Dal nominated Brahmin candidates, splitting that vote, while the BJP nominated a Vokkaliga. This alone was enough to spell serious trouble for the BJP's two rivals, but several other things added to their woes.

[26] Butler, Lahiri and Roy, *India Decides...*, UM Books, op. cit., p. 177.
[27] I am grateful to E. Raghavan and the staff of *The Times of India*, Bangalore, for these statistics.
[28] I am grateful to E. Raghavan for these figures.

TABLE 5.2: The BJP in Karnataka (1991)

Constituency	Votes
Bangalore South	
K. Venkatagiri Gowda (BJP)	275,083
+ R. Gundu Rao (Congress-I)	247,835
V. S. Krishna Iyer (Janata Dal)	65,356
B. K. Sundarajan (SJP)	134
29 Independents	8,592
Tumkur	
S. Mallikarjunaiah (BJP)	255,186
+ G. S. Basavaraju (Congress-I)	236,269
D. Nagarajaiah (SJP)	73,597
Eight Independents	24,085
Mangalore	
V Dhananjaya Kumar (BJP)	274,814
+ Janardhana Poojary (Congress-I)	239,262
P. Ramachandra Rao (CPI-M)	23,794
H. Subbaiah Shetty (SJP)	3,751
Four Independents	8,961
Bidar	
Ramachandra Veerappa (BJP)	227,867
+ N. Suryavamshi (Congress-I)	111,642
K. Pundalik Rao (Janata Dal)	103,759
Four Independents	6,953
Davangere	
+ Channaiah Odeyar (Congress-I)	237,542
S. A. Ravindranath (BJP)	237,087
D. G. Basavana Gowda (Janata Dal)	105,260
11 Independents	16,150[29]

NB: In each of these contests, local factors provide much of the explanation for the result.

+ denotes incumbent.

The negative image which the Congress-I candidate and sitting MP, R. Gundu Rao, acquired during this time as Chief Minister (1980–3) persisted in the minds of many voters here and out-weighed any advantage that his massive personal fortune, upon which he drew heavily at election time, gave him. He also faced

[29] *The Times of India*, 22 May 1991 and *Deccan Herald*, 20 June 1991.

an attempt by people loyal to the Congress-I candidate in neighbouring Tumkur, whose campaign Gundu Rao's men were sabotaging, to return the favour.

Many Janata Dal activists deserted their candidate and travelled to distant Bagalkot to work for Ramakrishna Hegde who had drawn them into politics during his time as an MLA from one segment of this constituency. It was also true that many Brahmin voters here have always voted for the BJP, even when it had little hope of winning, and many of them stayed with the party this time despite the caste of the candidates. Finally, this is one of the few places in the state where the BJP and the RSS have strong organizations, and it is the only wholly urban seat in Karnataka which meant that the Congress-I could not benefit from its greater support in rural areas (see the discussion of Mysore below).[30]

Tumkur

The Congress-I unwisely renominated an unpopular MP who, as the party's official postmortem noted, had antagonized local Hindu religious leaders. Press reports also observed that he had 'treated party workers and party leaders with contempt.' This alienated nearly all of the party's local legislators and some of its major state-level leaders. Several of these legislators were close to Gundu Rao, and he encouraged and funded their efforts to defeat the Congress-I nominee. Disaffection was so serious here that the party's official investigation reported 'a near total lack of campaigning'.

The Janata Dal ceded this seat to the SJP as part of an electoral pact, and the latter chose a weak candidate. This caused fierce resentment among Janata Dal workers, many of whom left for Bagalkot to work for Hegde. It also drove anti-Congress-I voters to the BJP, which was also able to exploit communal tension in the wake of serious Hindu–Muslim riots here in late 1990. The BJP, unusually, had a strong candidate here—S. Mallikarjunaiah, Deputy Chairman of the legislative council, who finished a respectable second in this constituency in 1977 while a member of the Lok Dal.[31]

[30] *The Times of India*, 1 November 1990 and 8 April 1991; *Indian Express*, 19 April 1991; and *Deccan Herald*, 11–12 and 19–20 June 1991.

[31] Conversation with G. K. Karanth, Bangalore, 18 August 1991 and *The Times of India*, 11 October 1990 and *Deccan Herald*, 10–11 June 1991.

Mangalore

This constituency embraces both coastal areas in Dakshina Kannada district and hillier areas in which Coorgs (Kodavas) are numerically strong. The coastal segments of the constituency are the only places in the state where the Vishwa Hindu Parishad has any substance, and they are one of the few places where the BJP/RSS cadres are present in strength. The same cannot be said even of most segments of the adjacent coastal district of Uttar Kannada. Also unusually for this state, the presence in the hillier areas of a large number of Muslim plantation workers, recent migrants from Kerala, had heightened communal suspicion. Both the coastal and the hill areas had witnessed communal clashes in late 1990s, and the resulting polarization clearly assisted the BJP.

Once again, however, errors by the BJP's opponents enhanced its chances. The Janata Dal ceded this seat to the SJP and the implausible 'feather weight candidate' whom it put forward discouraged Janata Dal activists from campaigning and again thrust most anti-Congress-I voters into the BJP camp. Perhaps most crucially of all, there were a great many such voters, especially among the Coorgs, many of whom were furious with the Bangarappa government for intruding upon their long-standing 'jamma' rights to plots of forest land. Many residents of the coastal areas had ties with the banking profession, whose members were extremely unhappy with the 'loan melas' of the sitting Congress-I MP, Janardhana Poojary.[32] When we add to that a long-standing conflict between Poojary and Gundu Rao[33] and the all-too obvious strife between Poojary and another influential fellow-Congressman, state minister Veerappa Moily, the outlook for the Congress-I here was unusually grim.

Bidar

The BJP again benefited greatly here from self-destructive doings within the Congress-I. The incumbent Congressman was 'thoroughly unpopular' and his renomination was a grave mistake. He

---

[32] At an election rally in Coorg during the 1989 election campaign, Gundu Rao stated in Poojary's presence that the latter had done little for the constituency! *Indian Express*, 11 December 1989.

[33] Conversation with E. Raghavan, Bangalore, 16 August 1991 and *The Times of India*, 6 October 1990, 8 November 1990, 27 April 1991 and 11 May 1991; and *Deccan Herald*, 9 June 1991.

had seldom visited the constituency or even the state; open leading journalists had never seen him in Bangalore between 1980 and 1991. A personal feud between him and a family of great influence in the constituency immobilized one section of the Congress-I, and most of the party's other activists either remained inert or actively sabotaged his campaign.

The candidate had also alienated many Muslim voters, an important group here. They did not desert the Congress-I *en masse*, but enough of them turned to the Janata Dal to hurt the incumbent. Lingayats in Bidar, an even more formidable force, tended to sympathize with Veerendra Patil whose main base is in neighbouring Gulbarga. The Congress-I high command had ousted him as Chief Minister only a few months before, and he remained ostentatiously aloof from the party's election campaign. All of this added up to a recipe for disaster for the Congress-I, and disaster duly struck.[34]

Davangere

This constituency, which the BJP nearly won, had also witnessed severe communal violence consisting mainly of attacks by Hindus on Muslims, in late 1990, in which at least 12 people were killed. Many more Muslim voters here than in Bidar abandoned the Congress-I, which in their view had not given them adequate protection, and turned to the Janata Dal—partly because of V. P. Singh's stand on Ayodhya and partly because its electoral ally, the Communist Party of India, had assisted them during the riots.[35]

Sadar Lingayats, who are numerically and economically powerful here, were unhappy with the Congress-I for nominating a 'backward class' candidate in Davangere and for denying their group the ticket in neighbouring Shimoga as well. They were also alienated from both the Congress-I and the Janata Dal after what they perceived as affronts in their handling of this part of the state. Former Chief Minister S. R. Bommai, a Sadar Lingayat, might have attracted them to the Janata Dal. But he spent most of the campaign in Delhi, working with V. P. Singh whose policy on the Mandal Report alienated Lingayats. As a result of all of this, the two

[34] *The Times of India*, 7 October 1990 and 27 April 1991; and *Deccan Herald*, 12 June 1991.
[35] Interviews with I. Qureshi, E. Raghavan, two BJP and three Congress-I activists, Bangalore, 14–18 August 1991; and *Deccan Herald*, 11 and 27 June 1991.

influential Lingayat 'mutts' in this area supported the BJP in this campaign and took many Lingayat voters with them.[36]

The considerable importance of local factors in these five constituencies casts doubt on the notions that the traditional themes of the BJP captured the imagination of Karnataka's voters, and that it now possesses a solid foundation in this state from which it can rise to greater prominence. Let us now turn to state-wide trends. The message which they convey is complicated. On the one hand, they indicate that the BJP's gains were less the result of the party's positive achievements than of the Congress-I and Janata Dal bungling and unpopularity. On the other hand, if those other two parties continue to perform poorly, the future may hold promise for the BJP.

The three principal reasons for the BJP's advances at this election were (i) continuing problems and decline within the Janata Dal; (ii) the poor performance of the Congress-I's state government and severe factional conflict within it; and (iii) the belief among many Lingayats and Vokkaligas that both the Congress-I and the Janata Dal had abandoned them in favour of the 'backward classes'. These three things are difficult to separate, but let us consider each of them in turn.

The Janata Dal managed to forge an electoral alliance with H. D. Deve Gowda's SJP in Karnataka which, in theory, papered over the split that had occurred prior to the 1989 election when Deve Gowda had broken with the Janata Dal. The agreement gave six seats to the SJP, one of which Deve Gowda himself narrowly won in his stronghold of Hassan. In reality, however, this alliance broke down at district and taluk levels where intense bitterness between the two groups persisted. In constituencies where SJP candidates stood, Janata Dal activists remained inert or hostile, and vice versa. To make matters worse, Deve Gowda selected very poor candidates for the SJP's other five seats—mainly on the basis of personal loyalty, which has usually been his prime concern. All five performed very badly.[37] This was an important factor in two of the BJP's four victories.

[36] This is based on interviews in Bangalore with E. Raghavan and with two Janata Dal organizers, 16 and 17 August 1991, and on *Deccan Herald,* 11 June 1991.

[37] This is based on an interview with Imran Qureshi, Bangalore, 18 August 1991 and on *Indian Express,* 2 April 1991, and *Deccan Herald,* 2 April 1991, and 9 and 12–13 June 1991.

Leaders of the Janata Dal and the SJP also greatly overestimated Deve Gowda's pulling power among his fellow Vokkaligas, many of whom had been disillusioned at the state election of 1989 when he failed miserably in his stated aim of ushering in a new era of Vokkaliga pre-eminence in state politics. Their wariness towards him was intensified by their unhappiness over the stand which V. P. Singh, the Janata Dal's national leader, took on the Mandal Commission report. This would have been easier for the Janata Dal to bear had the Mandal issue attracted votes from the 'backward classes', including Muslims. But in most areas, the Congress-I competed well for support from these groups—especially 'backward class' Hindus.[38]

The Mandal issue also alienated members of the other dominant landed jati-cluster, the Lingayats. Indeed, both of these dominant groups took heart from the anti-Mandal agitation in north India which indicated that they had unexpected allies in their opposition to reservations. The Janata Dal might have had more Lingayat support had it succeeded in persuading the recently deposed Lingayat Chief Minister, Veerendra Patil, to defect from the Congress-I. But after considering this for a long time, he remained a nominal Congressman after gaining Lok Sabha tickets for his son-in-law and three other followers. The Lingayat votes had been important to the Janata Dal since 1978. Without Veerendra Patil (a member of the Banajiga jati), the long-standing difficulties of the national party president S. R. Bommai in appealing to voters beyond his Sadar jati (which had earned the resentment of other jatis by gaining a disproportionate share of spoils) became especially serious.[39]

The weakness of the Janata Dal's organization left it ill-equipped to cope with these problems. It had always lacked organizational strength, and various efforts by Ramakrishna Hegde and others to change this had, as he readily admits, failed. Even the state's system of *zilla parishad* and *mandal panchayat* institutions, which were created by Hegde partly to serve as a framework over which to construct a party organization, had been of little help. Indeed, it had sown a certain amount of dissension in the Janata ranks since

[38] I am grateful to M. N. Srinivas for stressing this point.

[39] Interviews with E. Raghavan, Narendar Pani and two Janata Dal legislators, Bangalore, 14–16 August 1991 and *Indian Express,* 12 April 1991.

legislators resented and opposed those who emerged from these institutions.

All of these woes, which produced what Hegde has called 'a kind of disgust for the Janata Dal',[40] help to explain why the party's workers gave up canvassing in many constituencies within 10 days of the start of the campaign. Many more abandoned their efforts once the assassination occurred, on the often dubious assumption that it had made the Congress-I unbeatable. Only Deve Gowda in Hassan and Hegde in Bagalkot had solid support from activists throughout. But the latter was narrowly beaten by a formidable young Congress-I newcomer who had organized the building of a barrage across the Krishna with money raised from the public, irrigating 30,000 acres of land in this drought prone region.[41]

As a result of all of these things, the Janata Dal in Karnataka, unlike the Telugu Desam in Andhra Pradesh, did not provide anti-Congress-I voters with a credible alternative. This was an enormous help to the BJP which, though not in all constituencies, managed to cast itself in that role.

Let us now turn to the Congress-I whose unpopularity also assisted the BJP. The chronic internal squabbling which has long afflicted the party in Karnataka was vividly apparent in its difficulties in capitalizing on the murder of Rajiv Gandhi. Since all voters in the state went to the polls after the assassination, it was impossible to measure the swing in votes here as we could in Andhra Pradesh where post-assassination elections gave the party about 8 per cent more than it had gained before. Nonetheless, the usually reliable MARG polls indicated that the Congress-I only gained about half as much benefit as it had in Andhra Pradesh from the sympathy factor after the murder.[42]

This is mainly explained by the extraordinary fact that factional strife within the Karnataka Congress-I actually *increased* as a result of the assassination. It is extraordinary because in many other states—quite famously, for example, in Maharashtra—the loss of Rajiv Gandhi drove Congressmen together, not apart.

In Karnataka, the logic of this went as follows. Before the murder, Congressmen there felt that they were fighting to win all

[40] Interview with Ramakrishna Hegde, Bangalore, 17 August 1991 and *Deccan Herald*, 17 June 1991.

[41] *The Times of India*, 3 May 1991.

[42] *Deccan Herald*, 12 June 1991.

27 seats for Rajiv Gandhi and the national party. Afterwards, they felt that by winning seats they would strengthen the hand of their Chief Minister, S. Bangarappa, within the party at the national level. The more such strength he had, the more power he would be able to exercise within the state. Since most of the five major factions within the state Congress-I preferred to weaken Bangarappa, more Congressmen took to sabotaging their party's parliamentary candidates after the assassination than before, and those who had been doing it all along intensified their efforts. Numerous Congress-I members of zilla parishads and mandal panchayats also worked to defeat their party's nominees in order to register their resentment at the state government's hostile attitude to these institutions. As a result, there are 'very few constituencies where Congressman hasn't fought Congressman.'[43]

Such divisions within the Karnataka Congress-I and the unpopularity of the party are further explained by the change of Chief Minister that occurred in November 1990. This meant that neither the deposed Veerendra Patil nor his successor Bangarappa had enough time to make the kind of impact that the party needed to win support. Among other things, infighting within the state Congress-I, and the interference and indecision of the party high command in New Delhi, prevented Bangarappa from forming a full cabinet and from making the appointments to various boards and corporations which might have gained the support of various key leaders and groups.

To make matters worse, these two men governed in different, indeed contradictory ways, and each sought his main support from a different set of social groups. Veerendra Patil was a staid, bureaucratic Chief Minister. He had last held the post in 1972 in a much more tame, well-ordered time before the emergence of the 'backward classes' and had been little involved in state politics in the interim. He thus seemed to be a latter day Rip van Winkle.[44] His cautious, by-the-book approach made him appear far too unresponsive. He made little effort to appeal to a wide range of

---

[43] The quotation is from *Deccan Herald*, 12 June 1991. See also, *The Times of India*, 12 October 1990 and *Deccan Herald*, 11 June 1991. On zilla parishad and mandal panchayat members, *The Times of India*, 26 February 1991, *Indian Express*, 2 April 1991 and interview with Narendar Pani, Bangalore, 15 August 1991.

[44] This characterization and much of this interpretation of state politics under these chief ministers comes from E. Raghavan.

social groups, and as a Lingayat who had been the last chief minister in the era of Lingayat dominance (1956–72), he was seen by many, with some justice, as a guardian of that group's interests.

By contrast, Bangarappa presented himself much more aggressively as the champion of the 'backward classes', and this persuaded many Lingayats that the ouster of Veerendra Patil was a severe blow to their interests. Both Lingayats and Vokkaligas were aggrieved at their under-representation in the state cabinet and in candidate selection for this election.[45] Bangarappa was the antithesis of the staid bureaucrat—posturing dramatically, taking risks, throwing his weight around and most crucially, engaging in dubious manipulation of the bureaucracy in the interests of 'fundraising'. This occurred on a scale unknown even in the Gundu Rao years, and for the first time it intruded severely into daily administrative and developmental activities.[46]

The radical nature of this change of chief ministers traumatized an already badly fragmented party, and sowed confusion in the public mind about what the Congress-I stood for. To have made this change when an early parliamentary election was likely was an act of political folly.

This brings us to the third and most important reason for the gains made by the BJP at this election. Both Bangarappa's Congress-I and the Janata Dal, which had previously been the only serious opposition party, gave many Lingayats and Vokkaligas the impression that they had largely abandoned them in favour of the 'backward classes'. Never before had both major parties done so at the *same* time.

The Congress-I gave this impression in several ways. We have already mentioned the ouster of Veerendra Patil, but he surprised the party high command by openly resisting the attempt to sack him, so that many Lingayats believed that he had been 'insulted by Rajiv Gandhi'.[47] Then came Bangarappa who was so preoccupied with the possible loss of 'backward class' and the Muslim votes to the Janata Dal, as a result of V. P. Singh's Mandal commitment, that he failed to see that his main worry was a loss of dominant

---

[45] See for example, *Deccan Herald*, 28–30 June 1991.

[46] This is based on interviews with six current and retired civil servants in Bangalore, 15–17 August 1991.

[47] The quotation is from *Indian Express*, 12 April 1991. See also *The Times of India*, 8 and 10 October 1990.

caste support to the BJP.[48] The most senior Vokkaliga in the state cabinet was K. H. Patil, but he was from the Reddi jati of northern Karnataka which many Vokkaligas regard as a marginal or even a dubious element in their jati-cluster—and in any case, he was visibly unhappy with the character of the new government.

The Janata Dal did its best to woo Vokkaligas by forging an uneasy electoral alliance with the state's leading Vokkaliga politician, Deve Gowda of the SJP. But the bitter and very public quarrels that had caused him to leave the Janata Dal three years earlier—and his refusal in 1991 to be drawn fully back into the party—made this rapprochement seem unconvincing. Deve Gowda was also locked in a tight struggle against a formidable Congress-I rival in his own constituency, so that he only appeared briefly outside it during the election campaign, and then in just two other districts.

We have noted that the Janata Dal had a very prominent Lingayat in ex-Chief Minister Bommai—indeed he was the party's national president. But by holding that post he caused the party problems in Karnataka in two ways. First, it meant that he had to spend most of his time outside the state, so the Janata Dal's main Lingayat connection was less visible than it needed to be. Second, his presence in Delhi at V. P. Singh's elbow reminded Karnataka Lingayats (and Vokkaligas) of the Janata Dal's commitment to the Mandal Commission recommendations. That alienated them from the party, since it made the Janata Dal seem—as V. P. Singh constantly stressed in his speeches—the advocate of the 'backward classes'.

For all of these reasons, many Lingayats and Vokkaligas felt that the two main parties in Karnataka had cast them adrift. It must be emphasized that while these two groups continue to dominate life at the village level, it has been impossible for them to dominate state-level politics since Devaraj Urs brought the 'backward' groups into play in 1972.[49] Those who argue that a 'reconsolidation of power by the dominant castes in Karnataka' has occurred[50] are

[48] *The Times of India*, 4 April 1991.

[49] Manor, J. 'Karnataka: Caste, Class, Dominance and Politics in a Cohesive Society', in F. Frankel and M. S. A. Rao (eds), *Dominance and State Power in Modern India*, vol. 1 (Delhi: 1989), pp 322–61.

[50] Kohli, A., *Democracy and Discontent: India's Growing Crisis of Governability* (Cambridge: 1990), p. 298.

mistaken. Nothing demonstrates this more vividly than the belief among Lingayats and Vokkaligas at this election that the two main parties had abandoned them. But while it is impossible to restore the dominance of these groups at the state level, it is also politically insane to alienate them both. They constitute, between them, nearly one-third of the state's population, and their social status and economic power give them influence far in excess of their numerical strength.

Many disgruntled Lingayats and Vokkaligas felt forced to seek an alternative to the two main parties, and there was only one place to turn to, the BJP, which carefully nominated many members of these groups for the parliament. It was this, rather than a widespread commitment to the Hindu nationalist ideals of the BJP, that mainly account for its increase in popular support at this election.

Indeed, in a reversal of the pattern found in much of western and north-central India, BJP voters in Karnataka were less committed than those who backed other parties. Witness the fact that on the morning of election day in Chikmagalur, activists from the Congress-I and CPI, were hoping for rain while those from the BJP wanted fair weather—because BJP voters were less determined to turn out.[51] Or consider that only in Mangalore did an old fashioned BJP/RSS activist win a seat; and even there the protest votes of the Coorgs were essential to his success. Elsewhere, such candidates lost. Those who won seats or performed well for the BJP tended to be recent recruits, often ex-Congressmen and always the types of people whom Congress has nominated for parliament.

The BJP turned to such people partly in order to shed its image as a party dominated by Brahmins (3.2 per cent of the state's population)—it fielded almost no Brahmin candidates[52]—partly because there was a distinct shortage of long-standing BJP/RSS cadres to choose from. The party had concentrations of such people only in a few small, urban pockets in this state, and in all but two of those places (Mangalore and Bangalore South), it failed to win at this election. It lacks even such small pockets in places where one might expect to find them.

[51] *Deccan Herald*, 10 June 1991.
[52] *Indian Express*, 23 April 1991.

Its organization in Bangalore North, for instance, was 'practi-cally non-existent'.[53] But the most startling example was the Mysore city were heavy concentrations of Brahmins are found. The Mysore parliamentary seat appeared to hold great promise for the BJP which managed to persuade the sitting Congress-I MP and son of the last Maharajah of Mysore, S. N. Wodiyar, to defect at the eleventh hour. The Congress-I countered by nominating Chandraprabha Urs—a state government minister, daughter of the late Chief Minister, Devaraj Urs and a distant relative of Wodiyar. She defeated him by just under 17,000 votes. Her victory was achieved because the turnout in the rural segments of the constitu-ency where her strength mainly lay averaged 59 per cent, against roughly 50 per cent in Mysore city. The low turnout there was a reflection of the serious weakness of the BJP's organization, as Wodiyar himself said openly.[54] Once again, we see an inversion of the typical situation in areas of BJP strength in western and north-central India—the party here and in most of Karnataka had a poorer organization and less committed voters than the Congress-I.

Another contrast with the BJP elsewhere worth noting is the absence from the Karnataka campaign of the hysterical, often violent anti-Muslim rhetoric that was offered on tape and in person in the west and north. The extreme doings of Vishwa Hindu Parishad and Bajrang Dal activists were scarcely in evidence in Karnataka. Instead, the state's Hindus heard the mildest of appeals to their piety. 'What is wrong' asked BJP campaigners calmly and quietly, with a temple for Ram?' This consistently low-key message was appropriate to a state where communal antagonism has seldom had any importance, and where it has never been sustained for long. This suggests that even if the BJP should entrench itself as a major force in Karnataka—and it has some way to go to achieve that—the character of the party there is likely to be much less aggressively communal and much more centrist than it is in the western and northern states.

[53] This was the view of Mumtaz Ali Khan, an extremely well-informed observer, *The Times of India,* 24 November 1989.

[54] The statistics are extrapolated from *Deccan Herald,* 16 June 1991 with help from E. Raghavan. See also *The Times of India,* 7 May 1991 and *Deccan Herald,* 17 June 1991.

The kind of people holding prominent places in the Karnataka BJP is also likely to differ from patterns in the west and north. Indeed, this is already apparent from the large number of ex-Congress and ex-Lok Dal members, and of people of that type, in its list of parliamentary candidates and party office-holders. This lent the BJP a degree of respectability at the 1991 election. But it is also posing severe problems. Long-standing RSS hard-liners who continue to dominate much of the state-party organization fiercely resent this and refuse to yield power to these newcomers. They have openly stated that they are 'worried about the party's health as it has not only admitted all and sundry, but rewarded many of them with party tickets.'[55]

This conflict for control of the state BJP is retarding efforts to build a minimally satisfactory state-wide organization. The party has a large handful of prominent figures at the apex of its state organization and among its MPs and state legislators. It also has a few small pockets of organizational strength at the grassroots, almost entirely in some (although not in most) urban areas. But it has little grassroots organization in rural areas, and the grassroots and the apex of the state party are linked by very flimsy intermediate-level structures. Party leaders may be glad to hear that in some areas, Amal Ray discovered people spontaneously organizing to support the BJP candidates in 1991—something that he had not seen since the days of the undivided Communist Party in West Bengal.[56] But it should also worry them, since their lack of organization compelled people to do this.

Internal conflict within the Karnataka BJP is also undermining its capacity to achieve one other important goal. Since extreme communal postures have limited appeal here, the BJP badly needs to show that it can take hold of a few concrete issues that matter to important interests and then use them to develop committed support.[57] Between 1989–91, it attempted this by pressing for concessions to farmers, such as the waiver of all agricultural loans up to Rs 10,000 and for the regularization of unauthorized cultivation in favour of cultivators. But the response from farmers

[55] *Deccan Herald*, 11 June 1991 and a comment by M. N. Panini, New Delhi, 23 August 1991.
[56] Interview with Amal Ray, Bangalore, 18 August 1991.
[57] V. N. Subba Rao made this point in *Deccan Herald*, 25 June 1991.

at public rallies was disappointing, and this campaign appears to have misfired.[58] Until it improves on this sorry record, its competence as a proactive force in Karnataka will be open to serious doubt.

The BJP's organizational weakness and its inability to seize upon issues that are tangible and sustainable was clear from the result of a Lok Sabha by-election on 16 November 1991, when both the Ram temple issue and the memory of the 1990 communal riots (the worst in the state's history) had faded. It occurred in Dharwad South, a constituency that borders on Davangere where the BJP narrowly lost, and Shimoga where pockets of BJP/RSS activists were available to assist in the campaign, and Dharwad North where the BJP finished a strong second in June, less than 22,000 votes behind the Congress-I.

A close fight was expected between the Congress-I and the BJP, particularly since the latter's candidate had lost narrowly on the Janata Dal ticket here in 1989, polling 46.8 per cent of the vote. It was not to be, however. The Congress-I won handily, with a much increased majority. The BJP candidate received only half as many votes as he had polled in 1989.[59]

It was clear in 1991 that if it did not strengthen its organization and found new and compelling issues in Karnataka, the BJP would need to rely for future gains on self-destructive behaviour by leaders of the Janata Dal and Congress-I. During the nine months that followed that election, these two parties continued their headlong rush in just that direction. On the Janata side, Bommai remained out of sight at the party headquarters in Delhi, the SJP's Deve Gowda resigned his seat in the parliament, Hegde openly sought a rapprochement with the Congress-I, and little organization building occurred. The state Congress-I was more visibly strife-torn than ever before, and its Chief Minister continued to encourage the kind of extravagant normlessness which has led many ruling parties to crushing defeats in state elections all over India. But as the state election three years later showed, the three Janata leaders eventually reunited and forced the BJP back onto the margins of Karnataka's politics.

[58] See for example, *The Times of India*, 18 March 1990, 19 February 1991 and 25 March 1991.

[59] *The Statesman*, 18 and 22 November 1991; and Butler, Lahiri and Roy, *India Decides....*, op. cit., p. 181.

THE KARNATAKA STATE ELECTION OF 1994

The 1994 state election in Karnataka was a major disappointment for the BJP. Its share of the popular vote declined dramatically from 1991 to a level well below that of the Congress-I. It won more seats than the Congress-I because its votes were more concentrated geographically, and it thus became the official opposition in the new State Assembly. But this was greatly outweighed by two other things. First, it won far fewer Assembly segments than in the 1991 parliamentary election. Second, the anti-Congress-I vote went overwhelmingly not to the BJP but to the Janata Dal which rebounded to a stunning victory. This left the BJP in a marginal, secondary role in the state—out of the running for majorities in the State Assembly and for a large number of Lok Sabha seats.

The result of the 1994 Assembly elections in Karnataka was hailed by India's much-read fortnightly, *India Today*, as a 'success' for the BJP which demonstrated its ability to do well by stressing issues other than Hindu chauvinism. It argued that this proved that the BJP was 'the only party with a pan-Indian character which can capitalize on people's disillusionment with the ruling (Congress-I) party.'[60]

This is, in fact, the *opposite* of the truth, since it is precisely this which did *not* happen in Karnataka. *India Today* then compounded its error by announcing that the party had gained 28 per cent of the vote in the state. That was what it had received at the parliamentary election of 1991, not of 1994 when its share of the vote plummeted. We also need to discount false statements by the state BJP leaders about the 1994 result—that, for example, they won seats in every district when they drew a blank in five of twenty.[61]

After this result became known, very little was heard from the BJP about their performance in 1991 Lok Sabha election. They found it far more flattering to compare 1994 to the last state election in 1989. They were quick to point out that they increased their share of seats from four in 1989 to 40 in 1994, and their share of votes from 4.13 per cent to 16.97 per cent. But they seldom added that they contested far more seats in 1994 (223 of 224) than

[60] *India Today*, 31 March 1995, p. 35.
[61] *Times of India*, 10 December 1994.

in 1989 (119), which accounts for some—though not most—of their increased share of the vote.[62]

If, however, we assess the 1994 figures alongside those of 1991, the picture changes dramatically. Their share of the vote fell steeply, from 28.8 per cent in 1991 to 16.97 per cent in 1994. Consider also the following figures on the number of Assembly segments in which the BJP finished first or second at each of these elections. (see Table 5.3.)

TABLE 5.3:   BJP Elections Results (1991 and 1994)

Year	First Place	Second Place	Lower
1991	59	69	126
1994	40	24	159

In 1994, the BJP failed to come even second in roughly 71 per cent of the constituencies. This was no 'success'.[63]

Still more worrying for them in 1994 were the *types* of areas in which their substantial losses and their modest gains (compared to 1991) occurred. They lost in 33 of the 58 Assembly segments where they came first in 1991, and at least 24 of these were in the rural

[62] Since states' reorganization in 1956, the Jana Sangh/BJP has performed as follows at state elections:

Year	% of Votes	Seats Contested	Seats Won
1957	1.3	20 (of 208)	0
1962	2.3	63 (of 208)	0
1967	2.8	37 (of 216)	0
1972	4.3	102 (of 216)	0
1978	Contested as part of the Janata Party		
1983	7.97	110 (of 224)	18
1985	3.84	115 (of 224)	2
1989	4.13	119 (of 224)	4
1994	16.97	223 (of 224)	40

On the 1989 election, see Shastri, S. and M. J., Vinod, 'The Dynamics of Electoral Politics: A Case Study of the Karnataka Assembly Elections, 1989', *The India Journal of Social Sciences*, 1991, pp 387–406.

Sources: Singh, V. B. and S. Bose, (eds), *State Elections in India 1950–85*, vol. 5, New Delhi, 1989, and Shastri, ibid., p. 18.

[63] Shastri, S. *Towards Explaining the Voters' Mandate: An Analysis of the Karnataka Assembly Election 1994*, Bangalore, 1995, p. 39, and election documents, *Times of India*, Bangalore.

maidan (plains) constituencies where elections in Karnataka are won and lost. Ten of the 14 constituencies which they *gained* in 1994 were either in urban areas (although they failed in several cities where they ought to have done well),[64] in the *malnad* (hill country) or in the two coastal districts, where the composition of society and much else differs radically from the rest of the state,[65] 18 of the 26 constituencies that they managed to *hold* in 1994, as in 1991, also fall into these three categories.

This brings us to the most crucial feature of the BJP's performance in 1994. They won only 12 seats in the rural *maidan* (plains) where any party that hopes to rule the state must gain at least seven or eight times that number. They *lost* twice that number of such segments which they had won in 1991. The 1994 result leaves the BJP as a party largely representing eccentric, marginal areas of the state. For the BJP, this is nothing short of alarming. It makes the 1993 predictions of party General Secretary K. N. Govindacharya that the party would win 'a majority of the 28 seats' in Karnataka at the next parliamentary election and that it would finish first or second in 'about half' of the seats in South India[66] appear ludicrous, as the results of the 1996 national election (discussed below) show.

The near-total exclusion of the BJP from the rural *maidan* in 1994 and the success there of the Janata Dal—which had won no parliamentary seats in 1991 and only 24 seats at the last state election in 1989—tell us much about the type of party system that had come into being by the early 1990s. This was a three-party system, but no one in which all of the parties competed on roughly equal terms. It was a system in which only two parties, the Congress-I and the Janata Dal, had a chance to win by attracting broad support in the rural *maidan*. The third party, the BJP, had to content itself with a geographically and politically marginal role in the opposition. Even when both the other parties made

[64] Examples include Davangere, Gulbarga, Belgaum, Kolar, Bhadravati and several parts of Bangalore where they won only two seats, against four segments in which they came first in 1991.

[65] For a full discussion of this, see Manor, J., 'Karnataka: Caste, Class, Dominance and Politics in a Cohesive Society', in F. Frankel and M. S. A. Rao (eds), *Dominance and State Power in India: Decline of a Social Order*, vol. 1, Delhi, 1989.

[66] *Times of India*, 10 April 1993. See, in the same vein, the report that Karnataka BJP leaders were 'very hopeful of being in a position to form a state government in the not too distant future'. *The Hindu*, 4 October 1993.

fundamental miscalculations, as occurred *uniquely* in 1991, the BJP could not hope for anything more than an enlargement of what was still essentially a peripheral role.

Two words of caution are in order at this point. First, in recent years, the political volatility which is evident throughout India has given rise to unexpected and sometimes dramatic changes in the party systems of several states.[67] We should therefore be careful not to presume that this system in Karnataka will necessarily persist indefinitely. Second, we should note the unprecedented severity of the Congress-I's defeat at the 1994 election. Consider, for example what for Congressmen is an appalling feature of the result—their failure to win *even one* seat in all of Mysore, Mandya and rural Bangalore Districts (they won one in Bangalore City).[68] They had never lost so badly before, and it is possible that they will fail to recover as they have in the past. Their share of the popular vote was an historic low for them, but it was almost precisely the same percentage gained by the Janata Dal at the last state election in 1989—and look how the latter recovered in 1994. Despite their small share of the votes, Congress-I still managed to win 36 seats, as against the Janata Dal's 24 in 1989.

Consider also the figures on lost deposits in 1994; Congress-I, 34; Janata Dal, 38; BJP, 134.[69] The Congress-I came either first or second in 158 constituencies, Janata Dal in 163, and BJP in only 64.[70] In 31 constituencies where neither the Congress-I nor the Karnataka Congress Party won, the combined total of their votes was greater than that of the winning candidate.[71] This is not to say that they would have won all of these seats had Bangarappa's Karnataka Congress not stood, but they would have done much better there. The long list of prominent politicians who remained associated with the Congress-I and the dissolution of the Karnataka Congress in late 1996—as Bangarappa rejoined the Congress-I—make it likely that it will remain the only potential rival to the Janata Dal for power in this state.

[67] See in this connection, Manor, J., 'Regional Parties in Federal Systems: India in Comparative Perspective', in D. D. Verney (ed.), *Federalism Compared*, Philadelphia, 1995.

[68] M. B. Maramkal called attention to this in a perceptive article, *Times of India*, 14 December 1994.

[69] Shastri, S., *Towards Explaining*, p. 42.

[70] Ibid., pp 21–2.

[71] Ibid., p. 44.

If we examine the reasons for the BJP's unimpressive performance in 1994, we will discover more reasons for doubting that it can break out of its isolation on the margins of the state party system anytime soon. Its fundamental problem was and is that Hindu nationalism has never captured the imagination of the voters in Karnataka or, for that matter, elsewhere in the south. Representatives from the BJP units in Karnataka and the other southern states themselves conceded this in 1993 when they 'virtually demanded' that national leaders talk about issues other than Ayodhya because a communalist message 'would not sell in the South.'[72] This basic difficulty for the BJP cropped up again in 1994, in a new form. Non-partisan observers and the BJP activists agree that the destruction of the Babri Masjid at Ayodhya in December 1992 damaged the BJP's electoral prospects in Karnataka in three ways. First, the mayhem at Ayodhya was fuelled by anti-Muslim fervour which very few Hindus in Karnataka can comprehend. Second, it appeared to settle the dispute over the existence of the structure. It therefore had the effect of removing this issue from the political agenda. That did not represent a major loss for the party, since this controversy never evoked strong public concern in Karnataka, but it deprived the BJP of an issue that had modest utility in appealing to some voters.

Finally and much more seriously, it made the BJP appear to be less mature, disciplined and responsible than other political parties. This struck at the heart of much of the support which the BJP had gained in Karnataka in recent years. Throughout the period from the 1970s to 1992 voters in the state expressed admiration for the Jana Sangh/BJP because their election meetings were much more orderly and carefully organized than those of other parties. Speakers advanced their arguments in a dignified, low key, eminently reasonable manner. Recall that this was how the BJP presented the case for the Ram temple during the 1991 parliamentary election campaign and they reaped a substantial reward for doing so. All of this suggested that this party was more responsible, constructive and mature than the others. These sentiments were expressed very frequently indeed in the period before the 1991 parliamentary election. The scenes of disorder and destruction at Ayodhya and the rioting across much of India which followed in

[72] *The Hindu*, 4 October 1993.

its wake shattered this perception.[73] The BJP paid a price for this in Karnataka in 1994.

The *basic* failure lay in its inability to defeat the Janata Dal in the battle to take advantages of the intense resentment against the incumbent Congress-I government in Karnataka (not New Delhi), a *determining* factor in the 1994 election.

The Congress-I also suffered from the timid and unwise decision of Prime Minister Narasimha Rao to renominate all but 38 of the 176 Congress legislators, despite a recommendation by an AICC observer that 50 to 60 per cent of these highly unpopular people be denied tickets.[74] In the event, only 26 (20 per cent) of the 130 sitting Congress legislators who stood at this election were re-elected.[75]

The Congress-I was also damaged by an unprecedented defection by Muslim voters, mainly as a result of the destruction of the Babri Masjid in late 1992. Here, unusually, was a national-level incident that *did* affect the result. The swing among Muslims is reliably reckoned to have been more pronounced than among other social groups.[76] It was facilitated by the widespread belief among Muslims and everyone else, as the campaign proceeded, that the BJP had no hope of winning, so that Muslims could safely abandon the Congress-I for the Janata Dal.[77] The outgoing Congress Chief Minister, Veerappa Moily, acknowledged this as an important factor in his party's defeat. Several other things intensified Muslim alienation. The state Congress-I government's attempt to compensate for Ayodhya by sanctioning a lethal police firing on Hindu nationalists at the Idgah Maidan in Hubli (Karnataka) on 15 August

[73] This was especially apparent in places with a substantial middle class population, such as Jayanagar in Bangalore where the BJP lost in 1994 despite coming first in 1991, and despite having a good candidate strongly supported by volunteer campaigners (*Times of India,* 30 November 1994). But disillusionment with the BJP after Ayodhya also occurred among rural voters especially in the socially conservative southern district which formerly comprised the princely Mysore.

[74] Shastri, S., 'The Karnataka Assembly Election, 1994: A Pre-election Analysis', *Southern Economist,* 15 November 1994, pp 17–19; and *Times of India,* 10 November 1994.

[75] Shastri, S., *Towards Explaining,* p. 28.

[76] For this and for much else in this discussion of Muslims, I am grateful to Imran Qureshi.

[77] See for example, *Hindustan Times,* 24 November 1994.

1994 backfired, in that the public reaction against it made Muslims feel more vulnerable to Hindu extremism. Moily, who had persuaded the national leaders to introduce news broadcasts in Bangalore in Urdu (spoken by many Muslims)—a decision that prompted anti-Muslim rioting in 1994—was blamed by the minority for putting them in still greater jeopardy.

In order to crystallize anti-Congress feeling among Muslims, the Janata Dal recruited (as late as October 1994) one C. M. Ibrahim, a Muslim Minister in earlier Congress-I governments, to go into centres in which Muslim voters were concentrated, to make 'rabid'[78] speeches about the threat which the reelection of Congress would pose to the minority. Allegations that Ibrahim, while a Minister, had been involved in the abduction and confinement of a young girl had triggered widespread demonstrations by feminists and others against him, but his chequered past was largely ignored in 1994. He made especially effective use of a raid during the state election campaign by the Intelligence Bureau on a Muslim college in north India. This, he claimed, demonstrated anew the Congress leaders' antipathy to Islam. His speeches so polarized several urban centres that they certainly helped the BJP to win several seats there, but they also enabled the Janata Dal to take crucial Muslim votes away from the Congress-I in many constituencies.[79] (After the election, Ibrahim was made president of the state unit of the Janata Dal, with an eye to securing Muslim support for the party at the next parliamentary election. When Deve Gowda later became Prime Minister, Ibrahim became his main trouble shooter.)

But despite all of these things, the *main* reason why the Congress-I was not reelectable in Karnataka in 1994 was that its wretched performance in power since 1989 had alienated voters in every section of society. The fractious, unstable character of the Congress-I was obvious from the fact that its government had been led by three chief ministers over its five-year term. None of them offered even semi-adequate governance. The first was an unresponsive, bureaucratically minded leader; the second led the most extravagantly corrupt and normless regime in the state's history; and the third was 'hopelessly disorganized' and alienated a huge

[78] This word was used by one of the state's most sober and judicious political analysts. Interview, Bangalore, 8 March 1995.

[79] See for example, the evidence on Muslim shift from Congress-I in Chamarajpet Constituency, *Times of India*, 31 November 1994.

number of his party colleagues by not consulting them, by bungling and by inconsistent words and actions which made him appear deceitful.[80] The insane faction fighting which defaces the Congress-I in nearly all states was constantly apparent in Karnataka, even within the state cabinet, throughout the five years after 1989.[81]

It was this unseemly scene at the *state* level and not economic liberalization or the image of the Prime Minister or any other aspect of *national*-level politics which doomed the Congress-I from the start in Karnataka.[82] It has long been obvious that the voters of this state are sophisticated and discerning. That was clear, for example, from the astonishing swing in support away from Congress candidates at the 1984 parliamentary election to Janata candidates and in the 1985 State Assembly election in no less than 105 of the 224 Assembly segments, in a period of just nine weeks. The electorate here is fully capable of recognizing wretched government when it sees it, and the Congress-I offered little else between 1989–94.

It would be wrong to conclude that the BJP lost to the Janata Dal because it failed to match the latter's populist promises to voters. The Janata Dal offered plenty of these, especially in a supplementary manifesto which Deve Gowda issued late in the election campaign,[83] but so did the BJP. Indeed, their most important proposal—to write off both the principal and the interest from most agricultural loans—far outstripped the Janata Dal's much publicized promise to write off interest alone. And yet, the BJP's most damaging failure was its inability to garner votes from owner-cultivators in *maidan* (plains) constituencies: the very people whom it targeted with this promise.

It is also important, however, to recognize that the BJP's lacklustre performance at this election owed something to

---

[80] Interview with a senior bureaucrat who worked with the Chief Minister, Bangalore, 10 March 1995.

[81] For evidence of the persistence within the Congress-I of mindless factionalism and breathtakingly normless behaviour even *after* its election defeat, see for example, *The Hindu*, 4 March 1995 and *Times of India*, 12 March 1995.

[82] An opinion poll just prior to the election showed the voters of Karnataka and Andhra Pradesh to be favourably disposed towards the Prime Minister, despite their intention to vote against the Congress in the state elections.

[83] These include rice at Rs 1.50 per kilo and grants to unemployed youth. *Hindustan Times*, 25 November 1994.

miscalculations and insensitive, undemocratic behaviour of the party's state-level leadership. Many BJP activists in Karnataka complain that their leaders made a monumental blunder in assuming that the Janata Dal was finished in the state after the disaster that it suffered at the 1991 parliamentary election. BJP workers at and near the grassroots could see that despite the ramshackle nature of the Janata Dal's organization, it enjoyed support from far more influential people and skilled operators in rural arenas all across the state than the BJP did. The BJP activists also knew that a great many Janata Dal politicians—Assembly members and potential candidates—remained very popular in their bailiwicks, despite the results in 1991. The BJP leaders in Karnataka curtly dismissed the anxieties which party activists repeatedly expressed over the intervening years. They naively assumed that after the last parliamentary election, anti-Congress-I votes would come inevitably to them.

Their complacency persisted even after all of Karnataka's Janata Dal leaders sank their differences in early 1994 and, indeed, after the three most prominent figures in their ranks—Deve Gowda, Bommai and Hegde (a Vokkaliga, a Lingayat and a Brahmin)—undertook a hugely successful tour of the state many months before the state election was due. They were greeted by large, enthusiastic crowds which, unlike those that later attended rallies of the Congress-I and Bangarappa's Karnataka Congress, were not paid to turn up. This persuaded large numbers of people in many parts of the state that the Janata Dal, and not the BJP, was *the* alternative to the ruling Congress-I.[84] The alarm among grassroots BJP activists grew as they saw the three Janata Dal leaders introducing candidates in most parts of the state well in advance of the election, candidates drawn heavily from the Vokkaliga and Lingayat communities. The Janata Dal, which had lost ground to the BJP in 1991 because it had appeared to abandon the two dominant land-owning groups, was now deftly mending its fences with these caste-clusters.[85]

[84] Interview with E. Raghavan, Bangalore, 9 March 1995.

[85] It was helped by the decline in the salience of the Mandal reservations issue which in 1991 had made the Janata Dal appear to be the enemy of the forward castes. Ramakrishna Hegde's decision not to seek a seat in the Assembly and his support for Deve Gowda as the next Chief Minister lent a useful clarity to the Janata Dal campaign. It also made Hegde appear more sincere than on some

The BJP footsoldiers appealed desperately for a similar pre-election campaign, but the state leadership—which has never engaged in the kind of systematic, long-term preparatory work for which the party is well known in many other regions—remained largely inert. They contented themselves with what the BJP activists call 'empty gimmickry and cosmetic touches', a few slogans and ploys announced from Bangalore and not carried into the rural heartland where most of the votes were. The BJP candidates remained unnamed until very late. When disgruntled voters in rural areas explained their problems to local BJP workers, the party's leaders refused to respond to pleas from those workers for protest meetings or local projects to assist people in their distress. This left many of the party's activists at the district level and below feeling 'sidelined, humiliated and disheartened'. The force with which these opinions were expressed should not be underestimated—some were driven to tears.

The despair which gripped many BJP activists in 1994 was not new. It had been building up for several years in reaction to efforts by the current state leadership to ensure its personal dominance over the organization. Activists insist that democracy within the state unit of the party is a sham. Meetings to elect the heads of low-level party committees often include only *some* of the members, to ensure that people who are deferential to the state leadership get chosen. Elections at higher levels of the party therefore tend to throw up people who are the state leaders' 'yes men'. The BJP's state executive committee is thus a 'dummy organization' which does not convey reliable information from above and which permits the leadership to behave in ways which 'demoralize and humiliate' party activists at lower levels.[86]

This has retarded the growth of the BJP's organization, even though it has always been far less strong and extensive in Karnataka than its counterparts in northern and western India. Indeed, party

---

previous occasions. The Janata Dal leaders wisely let Deve Gowda dominate the campaign in southern, mainly Vokkaliga districts. Hegde (a Brahmin) and the party's prominent Lingayats confined themselves mainly to the northern Karnataka.

[86] Similar problems appear to have afflicted the BJP in Andhra Pradesh where it was as always, embarrassed by the Assembly election result, partly because the personal animosities of the party leaders in charge of the campaign were given too much free play. *Times of India*, 10 November 1994.

activists provided detailed evidence to indicate that the organization had become *less* effective since the 1991 parliamentary election. It still failed to penetrate very far into most districts, and in areas where some headway was made in the late 1980s, the bullying and miscalculations of the state leadership undermined it. Many activists who felt shut out of the party remained largely inactive in the 1994 election campaign, since success for the party would only have strengthened the hand of leaders whom they heartily loathe.[87]

In many states, the main conflict within the BJP is between sangathanists with close RSS connections and others.[88] Party workers in Karnataka insist that this is not true here, and that the main conflict is between two groups which both include strongly RSS-oriented people. Groupism here is caused by actions for and against the leadership which packs the organization with its loyalists. Both groups also contain newly recruited members of the BJP, who have come in modest but significant numbers since the late 1980s. Many of these new members are said to be bewildered by this conflict, which they did not anticipate when they joined. They tend to stand aloof from the battle, making no meaningful impact upon it, adding thereby to the sense of purposelessness that has overtaken much of the party in Karnataka.

The message from state BJP leaders is that if party members just wait a while and don't rock the organizational boat within the state, then power will drop into their hands as the two other parties self-destruct. Many BJP workers find this unconvincing. The results of the 1994 election appears to them to have proved their point, and yet there was as little prospect as ever of shaking the complacency and autocratic inclinations of the state-level leaders after the election as before.

The BJP activists and nearly all senior journalists in Bangalore agree that when the party's state leaders finally got round, late in the day, to selecting candidates, they mishandled it badly. 'Merit didn't count' in the awarding of tickets. They picked people on the basis of their loyalty to particular leaders atop the party's organization in the state.[89] Journalists who had initially reckoned

[87] Interview with numerous BJP activists, Bangalore, 8–11 March 1995.

[88] See for example, Jaffrelot, C., *Les Nationalistes Hindous: Idéologie, Implantation et Mobilisation des Années 1920 aux années 1990*, Paris, 1993, Presses de Sciences Po., especially Chapters 9–11.

[89] Interviews with three BJP activists, Bangalore, 8, 9 and 11 March 1995.

that the BJP might win 70 or more seats (in a house of 224) scaled their predictions down drastically when they saw the names of those chosen.[90]

To make matters worse, the state party leadership then failed to exploit the promise of the remaining strong candidates in its list. One particularly striking example was Jeevaraj Alva, a late defector to the BJP in Bangalore who over many years had demonstrated formidable, if sometimes unedifying, skills at mobilizing voters, manipulating issues, deploying monetary and organizational resources, etc. After giving him the ticket for one seat in the city, the BJP leaders scarcely took note of him. He might have helped them win several other contests there, lest he should become strong enough to undermine the state leadership's 'stranglehold' (to use BJP activists' word) on the organization, his skills were left untapped. The most perceptive political observers in Bangalore are convinced that this and other such things occurred because those at the apex of the state BJP did not want anyone beneath them in the organization to gain prominence.

There were a few pockets in the state where the BJP was strong enough to do well despite such blunders, particularly in Dakshina Kannada and Shimoga Districts where the Jana Sangh, BJP and RSS have always been a significant presence. But elsewhere, many of their successes were attributable to two other things for which the party can claim no credit. The first, which will not recur, was the four-way split of the vote among the BJP, Janata Dal, Congress-I and Bangarappa's Karnataka Congress. In nearly all areas, the Karnataka Congress cut mainly into the Congress-I vote, although in a few places, it hurt the Janata Dal as well. It scarcely affected the BJP,[91] and this allowed that party's candidates to slip through in places like Mysore City (where two of their three victories were the result of extraordinary strokes of luck).[92] Since

[90] Interviews with numerous journalists, Bangalore, 8–12 March 1995.
[91] This is based on numerous interviews with journalists who observed the campaign and then did post-election investigations, Bangalore, 7–11 March 1995.
[92] In Narasimharaja, BJP leaders conceded (*Times of India*, 21 November 1994) that Aziz Sait, the long standing Congress MLA (and a Muslim) should have won hands down. He lost because: (i) a strong Muslim leader stood as an independent against him; (ii) the Janata Dal took some votes from Muslims angry at Congress' handling of Ayodhya; and above all (iii) because a ridiculous error with the candidate's nomination paper meant that Sait did not get the Congress Party's election symbol. In Chamaraja, a traditional Janata Dal stronghold, the party's

the BJP suffered so little from the presence of the Karnataka Congress, which no longer exists, its failure to make greater gains that it did should be a matter of concern to its leaders.

Second, the BJP benefited from huge blunders by Congress-I leaders. This was especially evident in Kodagu (Coorg) which the BJP swept. The Congress-I would have done far better there had the AICC General Secretary and former MP, Janardhan Poojary, not interfered in the nomination process so that 'all hell broke loose' within Congress-I ranks. Local party leaders were still said to 'breathe fire' long after the decision.[93]

The unwise actions of state BJP leaders damaged the party most severely in mainstream *maidan* (plains) areas where elections are won and lost. Party activists concede, for example that this was true in three northern districts. They were convinced that the BJP could win five or six seats each in Raichur, Belgaum and Bijapur districts,[94] but their actual totals were zero, zero and one, respectively, with many deposits lost unnecessarily.

They might have added neighbouring Gulbarga district where despite some 'anti-Muslim consolidation'[95] the BJP state leadership's selection of newcomers to the party for most tickets caused something close to a wholesale defection of the district party unit to the Janata Dal. The BJP won just one of the thirteen seats there.[96] They might also have mentioned nearby Bidar district where in 1991, they won the Lok Sabha seat while carrying five of the six Assembly segments. In 1994, they won just one of these. In Chitradurga district, on the cusp between northern and southern Karnataka, they lost everywhere, including four segments where they had led in 1991. Tumkur district, in the heartland of old Mysore, was almost as embarrassing. They won the Lok Sabha seat here in 1991 together with five of the thirteen Assembly

---

leader H. D. Deve Gowda wrecked its chances by secretly backing an independent candidate against the official Janata Dal nominee. This split the vote and let the BJP in. Interview with E. Raghavan, Bangalore, 8 March 1995.

[93] Interview with E. Raghavan, Bangalore, 10 March 1995 and *Times of India,* 24 November 1994.

[94] Interviews with BJP activists, Bangalore, 9 and 11 March 1995. It should be noted, however, that in Bijapur district, the BJP gained respectable share of the vote in about half of the races. *Times of India,* 14 December 1994.

[95] Interview with a perceptive political journalist, Bangalore, 7 March 1995.

[96] I am grateful to Narendar Pani for this information.

segments. It was one of the few districts in which the party had done solid organization-building in the years since then, but in 1994, the BJP won only two seats there.[97]

It is worth stressing that in the first six of the seven districts listed just above, Lingayats dominate village society and exercise disproportionate political influence. If the BJP were even a semi-credible force in mainstream rural areas, it should have done well there. It was the only party led by a Lingayat, B. S. Yediyurappa, and Lingayats loomed large in its candidates' list, especially in such districts. It was apparent to Lingayats that a Janata Dal victory would give the state its first *Vokkaliga* Chief Minister since 1956, H. D. Deve Gowda.[98] And yet the BJP fared particularly badly compared to the Janata Dal in these and other districts where Lingayats are the dominant group. This as much as any other feature of the election result demonstrates the huge distance which the BJP has still to travel if it is to move in from the margins of Karnataka's politics.

Despite the embarrassing failure of the state the BJP leaders at this election, and their destructive impact on the party's organization more generally, there was little chance that they would be dislodged at an early date. (They were still in place at the 1996 parliamentary election.) The autocratic grip which the state leaders had imposed on the organization beneath them ensured both that no serious challenge could emerge from below and that no one lower down in the party could accomplish enough to begin to look like an alternative leader.

The national leaders of the party were willing to permit the current leaders to continue, for several reasons. First, to change them would appear to be a concession that something is wrong and that the BJP's performance at the 1994 election was a serious disappointment. Both of these things are true, but the national leaders preferred to pretend that they were pleased that the 1994 election made the BJP the second largest party in the Assembly,

[97] I am grateful to E. Raghavan for calling these two districts and as usual much else to my attention.

[98] This was apparent both from the decision of former Chief Minister not to seek a seat in the Assembly and his indication that he would back Deve Gowda for the top job. Hegde then campaigned almost entirely in northern and coastal areas. This made it easier for Deve Gowda to convince his fellow caste men that he would head the new government.

with more seats than the Congress-I, 'the official opposition'. They also took heart from the notion that the party's dominant figure in Karnataka, Yediyurappa, was a highly aggressive performer on the floor of the House, despite his tendency to overplay his hand there, with embarrassing results.[99]

By clinging to the fiction that things were going their way in Karnataka, the national leaders of the BJP ensured that the widespread demoralization among party activists in the state would intensify.

THE PARLIAMENTARY ELECTION OF 1996

The BJP entered the 1996 national election with essentially the same internal problems that had afflicted it in 1994. Its state-level leaders continued to prevent organization-building and collective action to respond to the problems of important interests. They had been ineffective in the state legislature, although admittedly, they had faced a highly competent Chief Minister in Deve Gowda. The party's candidates in 1996 were similar to those who had stood in 1991 and 1994.

The BJP's performance in 1996 was an improvement over their showing at the 1994 state election, but it was a little disappointing by the standards of the previous parliamentary election in 1991. Table 5.4 shows the overall result in Karnataka.

TABLE 5.4:   Party-wise Results of the 1996 Election in Karnataka

	Seats	% of Vote
Janata Dal	15	34.91
BJP	6	24.85
Congress-I	5	30.29
Karnataka Congress	1	3.11

Voting was countermanded in one constituency, Belgaum. In a by-election later, the Janata Dal won it.

The six seats which the BJP won fell into two categories. On the one hand, they won two of the three seats in the coastal belt where they are now a formidable presence, but where the composition of society differs markedly from mainstream Karnataka; and one

[99] See for example, E. Raghavan's column, *Times of India*, Bangalore, 12 March 1995.

urban seat, Bangalore South. Three other victories, however, came
from mainstream *maidan* (plains) constituencies: Bidar, Davangere
and Dharwar North. All three of those were in areas where
Lingayats predominate. Their dissatisfaction with the Congress-I
and especially with the Janata Dal (whose then Chief Minister,
Deve Gowda, was a Vokkaliga) helped the BJP. But Vokkaligas
tended to support the Janata Dal, and Lingayats in many constituencies backed either the Janata Dal or the Congress-I. This
meant that the BJP could not profit, as it had in 1991, from a
widespread sense among *both* of these landowning groups that the
Congress-I and Janata Dal had abandoned them.

In four of these six contests, BJP candidates won by solid
margins. These results offer the party some encouragement, but the
wider picture was more worrying for them. The BJP finished
second in just five of the other 22 contests. It came extremely close
to winning the third coastal seat, Udupi, where the Congress-I
candidate's margin of victory was just 0.40 per cent of the votes.
They also came second in four mainstream constituencies—Gulbarga
and Bijapur in northern Karnataka, plus Shimoga and Tumkur
further south in old Mysore. These results were an improvement
on 1994, but the loss in Tumkur, where their candidate was the
incumbent and the Deputy Speaker of the Lok Sabha, was a serious
setback. The overall pattern of second-place finishes was as follows:

Janata Dal	7
Congress-I	15
BJP	5

This means that (counting the by-election for Belgaum) the three
parties finished either first or second in the following numbers of
races:

Janata Dal	23
Congress-I	21
BJP	11
Karnataka Congress	1

The BJP's 11 first- and second-place finishes in 1996 contrasts
unfavourably with the 16 that it achieved in 1991. This decline was
mainly the result of the failure of the BJP in 1996 to present itself
as the main alternative to the ruling party which, as we saw earlier,
it had done in many constituencies in 1991. The 21 first- and

second-place finishes of the Congress-I in 1996 indicate that it played that role far more often at this election.

It must be stressed that Karnataka's voters went to the polls without an inkling that their then Chief Minister, H. D. Deve Gowda, might become the Prime Minister if his Janata Dal did well at this election. His promotion to that post in mid-1996 came as a surprise to everyone, including the man himself.

Taken overall, the evidence from these three elections suggests that while the BJP might become a potent force at parliamentary (although not yet at state) elections, its prospects of scoring the kind of breakthrough that it clearly needs in the south on any future occasion are still open to serious doubt. A strong revival of the Congress Party in Karnataka during the year following the election of mid-1996 raises further questions about the BJP's future prospects there.

At this writing, it has not yet been possible to study the results of the 1998 parliamentary election in detail. But discussions with leading analysts in Karnataka suggest the following preliminary points. The BJP's success in winning 13 of the 27 seats contested in 1998 depended heavily upon its alliance with a regional party, the Lok Shakti (which won a further 3). If the Lok Shakti leader Ramakrishna Hegde, had allied with the Congress-I (as he nearly did), the BJP would probably have won only a tiny number of seats amid a sweeping victory for a Congress-I/Lok Shakti alliance.

Since the election, however, the ruling Janata Dal in Karnataka—which, with the Congress-I, has long been one of the two main forces in state politics—has begun disintegrating. If this trend persists, it will open up space for the BJP/Lok Shakti alliance to become the main alternative to the Congress-I in state politics. The BJP and the Lok Shakti might separate, but that would give the Congress-I a huge advantage. They both have far more to gain by remaining together.

Note that the future prospects of the BJP—in State elections, but not national parliamentary elections—still depend on what another force does. They still depend on the disintegration of the Janata Dal. The BJP is not yet strong enough to be the master of its own fate in Karnataka. But parties elsewhere have risen to sustainable positions of power by this route, by default. So despite its chequered past in this state, and despite its current (very real) limitations, its future may still be promising.

Ψ

6

Bounded Nationalism: Kerala and the Social and Regional Limits of Hindutva

JAMES CHIRIYANKANDATH

The failure of the Bharatiya Janata Party's attempt to form a government at the centre in May 1996 held salutary lessons for India's Hindu nationalists. In spite of the striking success it achieved in western and northern India between 1990 and 1995, winning power in half of the ten biggest states in the country (Uttar Pradesh, Maharashtra, Madhya Pradesh, Gujarat and Rajasthan), the BJP's electoral base remained too narrow to allow for the realization of the ambitious Hindu nationalist project—the transformation of a pluralist religious and cultural tradition into the political basis for the creation of a subcontinental Hindu nation. Much of southern and eastern India, as well as religious minorities and the majority of lower-caste Hindus throughout the country, remain either hostile or indifferent to the appeal of *Hindutva*. While this is so, the BJP's claim to national power will remain vulnerable to the countervailing forces represented by regional parties, and parties asserting the claims of the numerically powerful lower castes (the very elements that combined to form the United Front government that succeeded A. B. Vajpayee's embarrassingly brief BJP administration in June 1996).[1]

Against this background, an examination of the relatively unimpressive record of the BJP, and of the broad Hindu nationalist

[1] I have elaborated on this in *The 1996 Indian General Election* (Briefing Paper No. 31, June 1996, The Royal Institute of International Affairs, London).

Sangh Parivar (organizational family) centered upon the Rashtriya Swayamsevak Sangh (RSS), in Kerala can be revealing. The densely populated state on the south-western coast of India is not only more than two-fifths non-Hindu (see Table 6.1), it also features a powerful sense of regional (Malayali) identity, a Hindu population for whom caste identities have been politically significant for nearly a century, a formidable leftist movement, and a legacy of political mobilization on the basis of class as well as caste. In fact, it would not be an exaggeration to suggest that if Hindu nationalism could achieve a breakthrough in such an inhospitable setting as Kerala, it would demonstrate that it has the potential to do so virtually anywhere in India.

Yet despite more than half a century of sustained activity, Kerala remains the only state of any size[2] in India to have never elected a parliamentary or state assembly representative belonging to the BJP or its predecessor, the Bharatiya Jana Sangh (BJS). While the BJP registered a modest increase in its popular vote in the April 1996 Lok Sabha and State Assembly polls, it could hardly be described as a credible third force with barely 6 per cent of the total vote; the victorious communist-led Left Democratic Front (LDF) and the defeated Congress-led United Democratic Front (UDF) have each consistently won well over 40 per cent of the vote since their formation at the beginning of the 1980s (see Table 6.4).

COMMUNITIES AND POLITICS

The modern state of Kerala was formed in 1956 by merging much of the former princely states of Travancore and Cochin, united since 1949, with Malabar and Kasaragod, hitherto parts of Madras State. Although this created the most linguistically homogeneous state in India—95 per cent of Keralities speak Malayalam[3]—the development of Hindu nationalism was influenced by significant differences in the social composition and historical experience of the component areas.

More than two-fifths of Kerala's 30 million people are contained within the six districts of the erstwhile Malabar region and

[2] This excludes Goa and seven north-eastern states which had a population of under three million in 1991.
[3] *Census of India, 1981*, Series 10—*Kerala*, Paper 1 of 1987: *Households and Household Population by Language Mainly Spoken in the Household* (Delhi).

TABLE 6.1: Religious and Caste Groups in Kerala in 1981

(in percentages)

District	Hindu (excl. S.C./S.T.)	Scheduled Caste and Tribe	Muslim	Christian
Kasaragod	53.7	10.3	29.5	6.5
Kannur	60.3	4.8	24.0	10.9
Wayanad	29.5	21.1	24.6	24.5
Kozhikode	53.8	7.4	33.9	4.8
Malappuram	23.1	9.0	65.5	2.4
Palakkad	53.3	19.8	23.1	3.7
Malabar	46.3	10.8	36.5	6.4
Thrissur	47.5	12.5	14.9	25.1
Ernakulam	37.6	8.7	13.4	40.2
Idukki	32.6	17.7	6.5	43.1
Kottayam	39.6	7.9	5.0	47.5
Alappuzha	54.6	10.9	7.4	27.0
Pathanamthitta (Constituted in 1983. Included in figures for Alappuzha and Kollam.)				
Kollam	50.7	12.6	14.0	22.7
Thiruvananthapuram	58.3	11.5	12.5	17.7
Travancore-Cochin	47.6	11.2	11.3	29.8
Kerala	47.1	11.0	21.2	20.6
(1991 figures)	46.3	11.0	23.3	19.3

Note: Assuming an even rate of growth among non-S.C./S.T. Hindus, calculations based on the estimates used in the *Backward Classes Reorganisation Committee Report* (Trivandrum: Government Press, 1970) would give Ezhavas c.20 per cent, and Nairs c.14 per cent, of the population in 1991.

Sources: Census of India, 1981, Series 1—India, Paper 4 of 1984: *Household Population by Religion of Head of Household* (New Delhi), pp 296–324, 829–1062, and Series 10—*Kerala,* Paper 1 of 1985, pp 14–9, 26–9, 42–5; *Census of India, 1991, Series 1—India,* Paper 1 of 1995: *Religion* (Delhi), pp xii–xiii.

Kasaragod, an area where Muslims from nearly 40 per cent of the population and in which the Christian presence is not significant. The Mappila Muslims trace their origins to the eighth century when Islam came to the Malabar coast via the ancient maritime trade route to Arábia and the Gulf. There is a recognizably Mappila dialect of Malayalam and, unlike their coreligionists in the north, Mappilas possess no memories of Muslim imperium. However, although the pacific advent of Islam in Kerala was followed by nearly a millennia of interreligious peace, this was overtaken in the latter half of the eighteenth century by intercommunal bitterness arising out of the Malabar campaigns of Hyder Ali and Tipu Sultan of Mysore. This ushered in a period during which Mappilas tended to view both caste Hindu Nairs and Namboodiri Brahmins (often also their landlords) and the British colonial administrators with suspicion—the 1921 Mappila *lehela* (tumult) was a revolt that could be interpreted as both anti-British and anti-Hindu.[4]

In the wake of the 1921 rebellion, in which as many as ten thousand Mappilas may have died, the mass of Malabar Muslims became alienated from Congress. The pre-Independence Muslim League swept the Muslim reserved constituencies in Malabar in the 1945–6 Madras Legislative Assembly elections, and after independence, although a few Muslim leaders stayed with Congress and a more substantial minority of poor Mappilas were attracted by the powerful communist movement, political loyalties in the region continued to reflect communal patterns. With the Indian Union Muslim League commanding majority support among Muslims, and the Communist Party supported by many lower-caste Hindus, as well as radically-minded upper-caste people, Congress soon found itself relegated to third place, in terms of seats if not always votes.

The situation in erstwhile Travancore-Cochin is rather different. Here Christians, the majority of whom belong to ancient local Syrian churches that claim their origins from the missionary efforts of the Apostle Thomas in the first century, outnumber Muslims three to one (see Table 6.1). Pre-Independence politics in the princely states was characterized by an interplay of communal and

[4] Miller, R. E., *Mappila Muslims of Kerala. A Study in Islamic Trends* (Madras: Orient Longman, 2nd ed., 1992), pp 142–8. The 1921 rebellion still looms large in Hindu nationalist propaganda (see former BJP state president K. Raman Pillai's *Malabarile Mappila Lehela* ([Trivandrum, n.d.] for an example).

caste identity, class consciousness and political entrepreneurship.[5] The outcome was that party politics was complex and pluralistic with Congress losing its legislative majority as early as 1952.

While Christians were especially prominent within Congress (half the Congressmen returned to the Travancore-Cochin Assembly in 1952 and 1954 were Christians and A. J. John became the first Christian chief minister in India in 1952), many leading Hindu politicians, whether Congressmen or leftists, had a background of activity in the powerful caste reform associations that had been formed in the 1900s and 1910s—the Nair Service Society (NSS) and the Ezhava Sree Narayana Dharma Paripalana Yogam (SNDPY). Although these organizations also functioned in Malabar, their main base was among the Nairs and Ezhavas, respectively the largest *savarna* (caste) and *avarna* (outcaste) Hindu *jati* clusters, in the former princely states.

Attempts by the Travancore administration in the late 1930s to foster a sense of 'Hindu' consciousness that would supersede caste differences and counter the State Congress opposition to the autocratic rule of Dewan Sir C. P. Ramaswami Aiyar failed to make much political headway. But a decade later Mannathu Padmanabhan and R. Sankar, the leaders of the NSS and SNDPY, came together to oppose a Devaswom (Hindu Religious Institutions) Bill introduced in 1950 by the first Congress government of Travancore-Cochin. The measure barred them, as members of the legislature, from continuing to sit on the State Devaswom Board. Forming a Hindu Maha Mandalam in response to what they characterized as Christian interference in Hindu affairs, they also floated a political party—the Democratic National Congress. A mysterious fire at the famous Ayyappan temple at Sabarimala, a pilgrimage centre in central Travancore, fuelled the atmosphere of Hindu-Christian acrimony. However, the fall of the Congress ministry in 1951 defused the crisis and the politically expedient Mannathu–Sankar alliance dissolved.[6]

---

[5] See my '"Communities at the Polls": Electoral Politics and the Mobilization of Communal Groups in Travancore', *Modern Asian Studies*, 27(3), 1993, pp 643–65, and Jeffrey, Robin, *Politics, Women and Well-Being. How Kerala became 'a Model'* (London: Macmillan, 1992), pp 96–144.

[6] Jayaprasad, K., *RSS and Hindu Nationalism. Inroads in a Leftist Stronghold* (New Delhi: Deep & Deep, 1991), pp 139–40, 153, 179. Jayaprasad, sympathetic to the RSS, gives the RSS version of events but there is some uncertainty about

In the mid-1960s communal and personal rivalries within Congress resulted in the formation of a breakaway Kerala Congress. Though mainly led by Syrian Christians, it always included some Nairs. Of the fourteen Kerala Congress members, belonging to four splinter groups, elected to the State Assembly in 1996, two were Nairs and the rest Christians. Yet Christians continued to figure prominently in the mainstream Congress-I, providing 15 of the 37 Congressmen elected in 1996.

Both the NSS and the SNDPY sponsored their own political parties in the early 1970s, but these were electorally much less successful than the Kerala Congress and after 1980 it was the Marxist-led LDF that consistently returned the majority of the Hindu members of the Kerala Assembly. This reflected the support it commanded among the numerically strong lower castes: it won ten of the fourteen reserved Scheduled Caste and Tribe Assembly constituencies in 1996. Of the 78 Hindu members of the 1996 Assembly, 54 belonged to the LDF, while the UDF included 21 of the 37 Christians and 15 (including thirteen Muslim Leaguers) of the 25 Muslims.[7]

THE ORIGINS OF THE RSS AND BJS IN KERALA

The RSS activity in Kerala preceded Indian Independence with three Maharashtrian pracharaks (celibate full-time, and often life-long, voluntary workers) despatched to work in Thiruvananthapuram, Kochi and Kozhikode, the main towns in Travancore, Cochin and Malabar, in 1942. They included Dattopant Bapurao Thengade, later to found the Hindu nationalist trade union organization, the Bharatiya Mazdoor Sangh (BMS). Having to use English before they became conversant with Malayalam, their early efforts focused on secondary school students and enjoyed only limited success. The first batches of Malayali pracharak emerged in 1946–7 and by the mid-1950s none were being assigned to Kerala from outside the state.[8]

---

whether there was actually a fire (see Thomas, P. T., *Sabarimalai and Its Sastha* ([Madras: Christian Literature Society, 1973], p. vii).

[7] It is noteworthy that Muslim representation in the legislature has lagged behind their share of the population while the reverse has usually been the case with Christians.

[8] Interview with R. Hari, Kerala State pracharak, Ernakulam, 28 August 1992.

The young caste Hindus, especially in Malabar, who were attracted to the RSS were youths from traditional conservative families dissatisfied with the lack of dynamism and initiative of Congress but out of sympathy with the communist movement, the dominant current among their peers. These early recruits provided the core of the Hindu nationalist leadership in Kerala. They included T. N. Bharathan (b. 1925, pracharak 1946–52) and R. Venugopal (b. 1926, pracharak 1946), both of whom belonged to the Nilambur kovilam, a prominent royal landholding household (kovil—palace) in south Malabar, P. Madhavan (1926–88, pracharak 1946). P. Parameswaran (b. 1927, pracharak 1949), and R. Hari (b. 1930, pracharak 1951). Bharathan served as the first organizing secretary of the BJS in Malabar, later becoming its Kerala president; Venugopal became a local, then national, leader of the BMS; Madhavan, also from Malabar, was a prime figure in the development of the RSS in Thiruvananthapuram district and state vice-president of the state Vishwa Hindu Parishad (VHP) when he died; Parameswaran, achieved all-India prominence as an ideologue of Hindu nationalism, becoming national secretary of the BJS and director of the Deendayal Research Institute in Delhi before founding the Bharathiya Vichar Kendra in Thiruvananthapuram in 1982; and Hari became the first Malayali to be appointed State pracharak in 1983.[9]

Although M. S. Golwalkar, the second *sarsanghachalak* (supreme leader) of the RSS, visited Kerala at least thrice in the decade after it began its activity, the organization had little to show for the first 25 years of its work in the state. It claimed 650 *shakha*s (branches) and over 11,000 *swayamsevak*s (members) by 1967 but remained very much on the periphery of politics and public life, even opposing the formation of Kerala State on the grounds that it would encourage division. After discussions that Jana Sangh founder S. P. Mookerjee and Golwalkar had with the leaders of the short-lived Hindu Maha Mandalam on visits in 1951 and 1952 proved inconclusive,[10] the BJS also began to be active in Kerala.

---

[9] Jayaprasad, op. cit., pp 366–9; interview with Thiruvananthapuram District Pracharak Jayakumar, Thiruvananthapuram, 1 September 1992.

[10] Jayaprasad, op. cit., p. 140. RSS theoretician P. Parameswaran commented that while both Mannathu Padmanabhan and R. Sankar were 'good Hindus', their attempt at constructing Hindu unity was flawed, being a top-down rather than a grassroots consciousness raising exercise (interview, Ernakulam, 17 August 1992).

However, its efforts to develop links with the powerful Nair and Ezhava caste associations were stymied by their well-established links with the major political parties—Congress, the Communists and the Praja Socialists—and in the 1967 state assembly poll the BJS forfeited its deposit in all 24 (19 in Malabar), out of 133 constituencies, it contested, winning under one per cent of the total vote.[11]

THE GROWTH OF THE SANGH PARIVAR

Despite its long insignificant role in public life, the Hindu nationalist Sangh Parivar in Kerala developed rapidly from the late 1960s. Until 1966 the RSS and the BJS were the only bodies in existence (the RSS also published a Kozhikode weekly, *Kesari* (Lion), started by P. Parameswaran in 1951). But more than two dozen establishments emerged in the course of the next two decades. There were three distinct phases in the expansion of the Sangh Parivar: first, around the tumultuous period of the Marxist-led United Front ministry of 1967–9; second, during and after Prime Minister Indira Gandhi's period of Emergency rule in 1975–7; and third, after the formation of a Vishal Hindu Sammelan in 1982 and the launch of a political Hindu Munnani (Front) on the eve of the 1984 Lok Sabha elections (see Table 6.2).

In the view of P. Parameswaran, the expansion of the late 1960s was produced by a combination of factors. First, the natural maturation of a quarter century of activity. Second, the hostile reaction provoked by the influence being wielded in government by 'communal' parties (i.e. the Muslim League and Kerala Congress). And third, overlapping controversies relating to a dilapidated temple and the creation of the Muslim majority district of Malappuram.[12]

In November 1968 the RSS and BJS took the lead in conducting a successful agitation to force the United Front government to permit a recently formed Temple Protection Council to restore the Thali temple, allegedly destroyed by Tipu Sultan of Mysore, in the late eighteenth century. The Council won support that went far beyond the Hindu nationalists but another, year-long, agitation

[11] Baxter, Craig, *Jana Sangh. A Biography of an Indian Political Party* (Philadelphia: University of Pennsylvania Press, 1969). p. 323.
[12] Interview, op. cit.

failed to prevent the formation of Malappuram, the district within which the Thali temple lay.[13] The circumspect restraint shown by local Muslims helped defuse tensions stirred by Hindu nationalist references to 'Moplastan' and the Mappila Rebellion.[14]

TABLE 6.2:   Principal Sangh Parivar Establishments in Kerala

Period Initiated	Establishment	Field of Activity
1966–72	Vishwa Hindu Parishad (1966)	Religion
	Temple Protection Council (1966)	Religion
	Akhil Bharathiya Vidyarthi Parishad (1966)	Students
	Bharathiya Mazdoor Sangh (1967)	Trade unionism
	Adivasi Sangam (1970)	Tribals
	Vivekananda Medical Mission (1972)	Medical relief
1976–80	Tapasya (1976)	Culture
	Bala Gokulam (1977)	Children
	Bharathiya Vidya Niketan (1979)	Education
	BJP (1980)	Politics
	Rashtriya Sevika Samithi (1980)	Women
	Bharathiya Kisan Sangh (1980)	Agriculture
1982	Vishal Hindu Sammelan (1982)	Religion/politics
	Seva Bharathi (1982)	Social service
	Vanavasi Vikas Kendra (1982)	Tribals
	Bharathiya Vichar Kendra (1982)	Intellectual
	Hindu Munnani (1984)	Politics
	Janma Bhumi daily (1987)	Press
	Bharathiya Labour Party	Politics
	Samrakshana Samiti	Politics

Source: RSS State *Karyalaya* (Office), Ernakulam.

A second phase of comparatively rapid growth in Hindu nationalist strength followed the imposition of Emergency rule in 1975. With a martial ethos that emphasized tight discipline and obedience, the RSS found itself well placed to cope with being

[13] Most notably the veteran Gandhian and first president of the NSS, K. Kelappan (1890–1971), who founded the Malabar Temple Protection Council, the precursor to the Kerala Temple Protection Council.
[14] Miller, op. cit., pp 183–4.

driven underground. And after the 1977 general election erstwhile BJS members found the scope for their political activity widened as members of the Janata coalition that had won power at the centre. For instance, K. G. Marar, an RSS pracharak and former BJS state secretary, became a Janata Party district president, enjoying the backing of the Marxist-led front in the 1977 Assembly election, and of the Congress-I-led UDF in 1980. And O. Rajagopal, a former BJS state president, became state president of the Janata Party and was supported by the UDF in the 1980 Lok Sabha poll. The two men went on to serve in succession as president of the Kerala unit of the new BJP.

The impact of the expansion of the Sangh Parivar activities in Kerala should not be exaggerated—joining the RSS or BJP still represented a departure from the norm. However, the breadth of such activity exposed a wide cross-section of Malayalis to the RSS influence. The odd erstwhile Marxist writer or journalist joined the RSS-sponsored art and literary forum, Tapasya and a former vice-chancellor of Kerala University, and well-known political scientist, V. K. Sukumaran Nair, not only took part in the activities of P. Parameswaran's Bharatiya Vichar Kendra but also inaugurated an RSS camp.[15] This apparently spreading influence was enough, in May 1988, for the LDF Chief Minister, E. K. Nayanar, to warn government officials against taking part in RSS activities.[16]

The grassroots of political life were also affected. One reason for the clashes between the RSS and Marxist party workers when the LDF was in power in 1980–1, in which 46 people died, was the growth of the RSS-sponsored labour federation, the Bharatiya Mazdoor Sangh.[17] Its rise was assisted by the poor image of unions affiliated with the dominant Marxist Centre of Indian Trade Unions and the tacit encouragement of many wealthy business-men, including Christians, who preferred the former's emphasis on harmonious labour relations to the latter's reputation for heavy-handed militancy.[18]

---

[15] Seshadri, H. V., *RSS: A Vision in Action* (Bangalore: Jagarana Prakashana, 1988), p. 254; *Indian Express* (Kochi ed.), 27 April 1983, p. 5.

[16] 'Officials asked to keep off RSS', *Indian Express* (Kochi ed.), 19 May 1988.

[17] Jayaprasad, op. cit., p. 193.

[18] Interviews with Jayakumar, op. cit., and Poulose Mar Poulose, Bishop of the Chaldean Syrian Church of the East, Thrissur, 19 September 1992.

212 JAMES CHIRIYANKANDATH

HINDU CONSOLIDATION, CASTE IDENTITY AND NON-HINDUS

In Kerala, as elsewhere, the main thrust of the RSS activity was the integration of Hindus of the state into a united political and social bloc. However, such an endeavour faced formidable obstacles. Of these the most important were a regional tradition that to a significant extent transcended religious divisions; the presence of sizeable, and comparatively well-integrated, non-Hindu communities wielding considerable influence in public life; and the salience of both caste identities and class consciousness in shaping politics.

Until the 1980s the progress made by the Hindu nationalists in tackling these barriers was limited. In an attempt to make a breakthrough in April 1982 a Vishal Hindu Sammelan (VHS) was formed at a convention in Ernakulam that brought together a wide range of Hindu organizations with the slogan, 'We Hindus are One'. While the active constituents belonged to the Sangh Parivar, the participants included caste associations and influential religious bodies like the Mumbai-based Chinmaya Mission, whose Malayali Nair founder Swami Chinmayananda had played a prominent role in establishing the Vishwa Hindu Parishad (the World Council of Hindus) in 1964. The leading spirits were P. Parameswaran, who had returned to Kerala to set up the Bharathiya Vichar Kendra after more than a decade of activity at the national level (he became General Secretary of the VHS), and another veteran pracharak, P. Madhavan.

A distinctive feature of the proceedings was the deliberate effort made to project an image that was not caste-bound. Ezhavas, as well as Brahmins, officiated in the religious ceremonies and the *Shankaracharya* (chief priest) of Kanchi presided over the closing public function in an Ezhava-owned Ayyappan temple.[19] (The Shankaracharya was the custodian of one of at least four *maths* (monastic centres) reputedly founded across India by Shankara, the eighth century Kerala-born Brahmin philosopher credited with initiating the post-Buddhist renewal of Vedic Hinduism. These maths have become focal points for the expression of Hindu religiosity and their custodians are the nearest equivalent Brahminic Hinduism possesses to an ecclesiastical leadership.)

[19] Seshadri, op. cit., p. 127.

While public attempts to deny distinctions based on caste, such as the VHS, were symbolically significant, they were not entirely successful in overcoming the widespread perception that the Sangh Parivar institutions catered primarily for caste Hindus. This was despite the fact that, ostensibly, the RSS does not recognize caste in its functioning (P. Parameswaran claimed to not even know the caste of some of those boarding with him in the RSS karyalaya in Kochi).[20] Significant numbers of Ezhavas are found in the organization, especially in the Malabar districts, and the RSS leaders also point to their efforts among groups such as the tribals in the hill districts of Wayanad and Idukki, and the Dheevara (fishermen's) caste of the coastal districts of Travancore-Cochin, as evidence of the body's multicaste character.

The RSS and BJP sought hard to counter their identification with the upper castes. For instance, P. Parameswaran published an eulogistic biography of the Ezhava social reformer Sri Narayana Guru,[21] and the Kerala BJP decided to observe the birthday of Ayyan Kali, a pioneering Scheduled Caste (Pulaya) leader in early 20th century Travancore.[22] However, the local RSS leadership remained predominantly upper caste (Brahmin, Nair, etc.) in origin and the very proximity of Sangh Parivar facilities to temples[23] served to highlight their caste Hindu orientation in a state that had witnessed some of the most thorough-going social reform and uplift movements among lower castes struggling against not just untouchability but unapproachability (*theendal*) in the early part of the twentieth century.[24]

---

[20] Interview, op. cit.

[21] *Sree Narayana Guru, the Prophet of Renaissance* (New Delhi, 1979), Sree Narayana's portrait hangs alongside those of the RSS founder K. B. Hedgewar, his successor, M. S. Golwalkar, Swami Vivekananda and Sri Aurobindo in the RSS State Headquarters in Ernakulam.

[22] K. Raman Pillai, 'Sri Ayyan Kali, the Hero of Downtrodden', *Chithi*, 6 (12–13), October 1991 Special Issue, pp 10, 61.

[23] For instance, the state VHP headquarters in Kochi is located in the compound of a Sri Rama temple on the same road as the RSS state karyalaya and 'Samskrithy Bhavan'. The BVK headquarters is a converted traditional Nair *taravad* house in the environs of Sri Padmanabhaswami Temple in the Fort area of Thiruvananthapuram.

[24] After a visit in 1892 Swami Vivekananda had declared: 'These Malabaris are all lunatics and their houses so many lunatic asylums' (Swami Vivekananda, 'The Future of India', *Collected Works*, vol. 3 (Calcutta, 1960), pp 294–5).

Among the two major Hindu caste-groups, Nairs and Ezhavas, the efforts of the Sangh Parivar were hampered by the persisting, if gradually declining, influence of the caste associations, the NSS and the SNDPY, especially as the RSS insisted that swayamsevaks should always give primacy to their 'Hindu' identity. The position was further complicated when the two caste bodies set up their own political parties, the Nair National Democratic Party and the Ezhava Socialist Republican Party, both of which formed part of the Congress-led UDF in the 1980s. While the NDP demanded that the reservation of government jobs and educational places be based on economic criterion, the SRP favoured the retention of reservation for the Backward Classes as a social category. Such differences made sustained cooperation between the BJP and either party difficult.

Nevertheless, the BJP forebore from opposing NDP and SRP candidates in the May 1982 Assembly election. Seven months later the RSS was even accused of collusion with the NDP when it posed as the defender of Hindus during an unprecedented outbreak of Hindu–Muslim violence in Thiruvananthapuram (the violence followed a period of severe tension between the NDP and the Muslim League, uneasy partners in the UDF ministry).[25] Yet this tolerance of the caste parties did not last as Hindu nationalists grew impatient with their incessant factional infighting and their unwillingness to champion the Hindu cause in communal controversies. The entry of the BJP and the Hindu Munnani into the fray played a significant part in the severe electoral reverses suffered by the SRP and NDP in the 1987 Assembly elections (the SRP lost both its seats and the NDP, three of its four). Despite the fact that some BJP and RSS members continued to participate in NSS and SNDPY activities, this hostility was reciprocated. When the NDP abandoned the UDF on the eve of the 1996 Assembly poll, the NSS came out in support not of the BJP but of the Marxist-led LDF (the SNDPY backed the UDF).

Although the 1982 *Sammelan* did not usher in a period of dramatic Hindu 'consolidation', it marked the beginning of a fresh, more ambitious, phase in Hindu nationalist activity in Kerala, paralleling the new activism of the VHP at the national level. While

---

[25] Anon, 'Communal Backdrop to Trivandrum Riots', *Economic and Political Weekly*, 18(7), 12 February 1983, pp 209–11.

the latter culminated in the launch of the campaign to liberate the supposed birthplace of Sri Rama at Ayodhya in 1984, in Kerala the early focus was on local issues. In April 1983 controversy erupted over the alleged discovery of an ancient cross at Nilakkal on the route to the Ayyappan temple at Sabarimala. A decision by the UDF government to sanction the construction of a church on the site was strongly opposed by an action council convened by the VHS and a score of other Hindu bodies (VHS General Secretary P. Parameswaran called the proposed church 'a government church').[26] The government had come under pressure from the Catholic Church and local Christian legislators—Nilakkal lay in the planned new district of Pathanamthitta, constituted in June 1983 out of the Pathanamthitta taluk of Kollam district (43 per cent of the population of the taluk was Christian), the Tiruvalla taluk of Alappuzha district (51 per cent Christian) and adjoining areas.[27]

The affair evoked strong communal passions; sanyasins (holy men) led demonstrations by thousands of protesters and Congress Chief Minister K. Karunakaran was mobbed by women protesters seeking to prevent him from worshipping at the famous Vishnu temple at Guruvayur. After three months an interdenominational council of Christian bishops resolved to 'accommodate Hindu sentiments' and opted for a chapel to be built on an uncontested nearby site.[28] Hailed as a Hindu triumph, it was subsequently cited by the RSS leaders as a model of how such disputes should be resolved.[29]

Emboldened by their success at Nilakkal, the VHS leaders launched an overtly political Hindu Munnani to contest the 1984 Lok Sabha elections. Significantly, while retaining the association of many of the Hindu groups that had formed part of the *Sammelan*, the Munnani failed to get the backing of the NSS and SNDPY. Its platform, while echoing many of the recurring themes in BJP manifestoes, included demands that had a particular relevance to local Hindus, such as the creation of an autonomous

[26] *Indian Express* (Kochi ed.), 3 June 1983, p. 5.
[27] Nair, Adoor K. K. Ramachandran (ed.), *Kerala State Gazetteer*, vol. 1 (Trivandrum: Government Press, 1986), p. 34; *Census of India, 1981*. Series 10-*Kerala*, Paper 1 of 1985: *Household Population by Religion of Head of Household*, pp 38–41.
[28] *Indian Express* (Kochi ed.), 22 July 1983, p. 1.
[29] Interview with P. Parameswaran, op. cit.

state-wide Devaswom Board to run Hindu temples (in place of the existing Travancore and Cochin boards constituted of political appointees). In an effort to transcend caste divisions, its other demands included the retention of job reservation with an additional 15 per cent quota for the economically disadvantaged, irrespective of caste, and the institution of public holidays marking the birth and death anniversaries of the founder of the SNDPY, the Ezhava reformer Sri Narayana Guru.[30]

The Hindu Munnani was wound down after the 1987 election, most of its leaders being absorbed into the BJP. This coincided with the national BJP's increasing identification with the VHP-led Ram Janmabhoomi campaign centred on Ayodhya and a corresponding shift of emphasis on the part of Kerala Hindu nationalists. In October 1990, as BJP national President L. K. Advani's *rath yatra* wound its way to Ayodhya, state party president K. Raman Pillai conducted his own *jana shakti* (people's power) procession through Kerala. Ram *jyothi* (lamp) processions were also held and several thousand *kar sevaks* (volunteers pledged to construct the Ram temple) from Kerala travelled to Ayodhya.[31] Fourteen months later Advani's successor as BJP president, Murli Manohar Joshi, began the second stage of his *Ekta Yatra*, national unity march across India to Kashmir, from the Sri Padmanabhaswami Temple in Thiruvananthapuram.

The passions generated by such events contributed to a marked increase in clashes provoked by communal issues. Between October 1990 and December 1992 thirty people died in six such outbreaks compared to just five in the previous three decades.[32] While the toll was insignificant when compared to the far larger scale communal violence experienced in many other states, the fact that it was exceptional meant that it shocked the Kerala public, arguably costing the BJP the support of a substantial portion of its 1987 electorate.

Some of the worst clashes followed the emergence of a militant Islamic Sevak Sangh formed with the express aim of protecting Muslims against the RSS. Six people died when RSS volunteers were stoned in Thiruvananthapuram in July 1992, and four more

---

[30] Jayaprasad, op. cit., pp 246–7.

[31] *Malayala Manorama* (Kochi ed.), 4 and 12 October 1990.

[32] 1990–2 figure calculated from reports in the *Malayala Manorama* and *Indian Express* (Kochi): Jayaprasad, op. cit., p. 321, for the pre-1990 period.

died in and around Kochi in central Kerala after the ISS Chairman Abdul Nazar Madani was released from hospital in October 1992 (he had been injured in a bomb attack). Two months later, following the destruction of the Babri Masjid in Ayodhya by Hindu militants, twelve people were killed as both the RSS and the ISS were banned (the ban on the RSS was revoked by a judicial tribunal in June 1993).

The passions aroused by the Hindu nationalist campaigns of the 1980s, and the communal violence of the early 1990s, ensured that Kerala's non-Hindus would not be reassured by any attempt by the BJP to disclaim a Hindu chauvinist identity. When a sophisticated ideologue like P. Parameswaran could declare at a symposium on secularism that the stark choice before Muslims was to 'integrate or migrate',[33] it was not surprising that scarcely any Muslims could be found to stand as BJP candidates. The BJP leaders tended to be more circumspect in public but K. Raman Pillai, the party's state president from 1988–92, commented in an interview how easy it was for Muslim youths to be drawn to violence by the promise of *houris* in paradise if they sacrificed their lives for Islam.[34] The percentage of non-Hindus among the BJP Assembly candidates dropped steadily from 7.3 (four Christians and a Muslim out of 68) in 1982 to 4.7 (three Christians and three Muslims out of 127) in 1987, 3.6 (five Christians out of 137) in 1991 and 0.7 (a lone Christian out of 133) in 1996.[35] The 799 participants in the BJP State Council session in Thiruvananthapuram in January 1994 included only 22 Christians and three Muslims (3.1 per cent of the total).[36]

Claims by the RSS leaders that some Christians and a few Muslims attended shakhas were hard to substantiate,[37] but when it comes to the BJP what it is possible to say is that those non-Hindus active in the party were, almost by definition, unusual, if not eccentric, non-entities. The Christians included Professor

---

[33] *Malayala Manorama* (Kochi ed.), 28 May 1993.

[34] Interview, Thiruvananthapuram, 31 August 1992.

[35] Three Christians and a Muslim stood as BJP or (in 1984) Hindu Munnani candidates for the Lok Sabha between 1982–96. Even fewer non-Hindus stood in local elections (e.g. just three Christians out of 474 candidates in the 1991 District Council poll).

[36] BJP Press Release, Thiruvananthapuram, 4 January 1994.

[37] Interview with P. Parameswaran, op. cit. I met no non-Hindus on my visits to shakhas in Ernakulam, Thiruvananthapuram and Thrissur in 1992 and 1994.

O. M. Mathew, a Lok Sabha candidate in 1984 and 1996; Dr Xavier Paul, a party vice-president and managing editor of the BJP's Malayalam fortnightly, *Chithi*, in the early 1990s; and Dr Raichal Mathai, an Assembly candidate in 1987 and 1991. In an interview Dr Mathai, a Syrian Christian spinster in her sixties who joined the BJP after returning to Kerala following many years as a medical practitioner in England and Ceylon, conceded that her views were atypical of her community, suggesting that many Christians had 'closed minds'.[38] (Dr Mathai, along with Professor Mathew, was a special invitee on the BJP National Executive constituted in mid-1993.[39] Muslims were even more of a rarity in the BJP with less than a handful figuring of the BJP candidate lists in the 1980s and 1990s (the only one to appear more than once was V. A. Rahiman, a party vice-president in the early 1990s who stood for the Assembly in 1982 and 1987 and for the Lok Sabha in 1991).

THE BJP'S ELECTORAL PERFORMANCE

Historically, Hindu nationalists have always enjoyed greater strength in Malabar, with its concentration of Muslims and legacy of Hindu–Muslim tension, than in erstwhile Travancore-Cochin, with its complex mix of caste and class politics (see Table 6.3). The creation of the Hindu Munnani in 1984 was an attempt to make a breakthrough in the latter region.

To some extent it succeeded. The BJP contested both the 1984 Lok Sabha and the 1987 state Assembly poll in conjunction with the Munnani, registering the best results achieved to date by the Hindu nationalists in Kerala. And the fruits of their new activism were especially evident in the Travancore-Cochin region. Even in 1982 when the BJP fought 68 of the 140 Assembly seats, nearly three times as many as the pre-1977 BJS had ever done, it contested two-thirds of the constituencies in Malabar but only a little over a third of those in Travancore-Cochin. Yet in 1984 the Munnani candidate in Thiruvananthapuram, Kerala Varma Raja, related by marriage to the last Maharaja of Travancore, claimed a fifth of the vote (to date he remains the only Hindu nationalist Lok Sabha candidate not to have forfeited his security deposit).

[38] Interview, Thiruvananthapuram, 1 September 1992.
[39] *BJP Today* (New Delhi), 16 June–15 July 1993, p. 38.

TABLE 6.3:   The BJP in Assembly Elections—Seats Contested and
Percentage Vote

Year District	1982 Seats (% Vote)	1987 Seats (% Vote)	1991 Seats (% Vote)	1996 Seats (% Vote)
Kasaragod	3 (12.1)	5 (16.1)	5 (13.8)	5 (16.8)
Kannur	6 (2.9)	10 (5.3)	10 (3.6)	10 (4.9)
Wayanad	3 (5.9)	3 (6.1)	3 (6.2)	3 (7.0)
Kozhikode	10 (5.6)	12 (8.8)	11 (4.9)	12 (7.7)
Malappuram	10 (5.5)	12 (7.9)	12 (5.8)	12 (6.0)
Palakkad	4 (2.4)	9 (5.4)	11 (5.2)	11 (6.4)
Malabar	36 (5.0)	51 (7.8)	52 (5.8)	53 (7.4)
Thrissur	5 (1.9)	14 (6.0)	14 (5.1)	13 (6.0)
Ernakulam	9 (2.4)	12 (4.3)	14 (3.8)	14 (4.6)
Idukki	1 (1.1)	2 (2.2)	4 *(2.6)	3 (1.1)
Kottayam	5 (1.4)	5 (2.1)	9 (3.4)	10 (3.5)
Alappuzha	2 (0.4)	10 (3.6)	11 (2.7)	10 (3.2)
Pathanamthitta	3 (2.3)	7 (7.7)	7 (5.4)	7 (6.7)
Kollam	4 (0.3)	12 (4.8)	12 (2.7)	12 (3.5)
Thiruvananthapuram	3 (0.8)	14 (11.7)	14 (5.9)	14 (6.6)
Travancore-Cochin	32 (1.3)	76 (5.6)	85 (4.1)	83 (4.7)
Kerala	68 (2.7)	127 (6.5)	137 (4.7)	136 (5.7)

Notes: Includes constituencies fought by the BJP's allies—the Hindu Munnani
in 1987 and the Bharathiya Labour Party, the breakaway NDP(K) and the
Samrakshana Samiti in 1996.
Sources: Assembly Elections since 1951 (Trivandrum: Dept. of Public Relations,
Govt. of Kerala, n.d.); the 1991 statistics are based on data provided by the
Kerala Government Information Centre, Thiruvananthapuram, and returns
published in the *Indian Express* and *Malayala Manorama* (Kochi), 17 and 18
June 1991: and the 1996 figures use returns published in the *Malayala
Manorama*, 10 June 1996, p. 3.

Using its own symbols in preference to the BJP's lotus—officially
the locally ubiquitous coconut palm, though many of its posters
carried the representation of a Kerala temple—the Munnani succeeded in attracting many people who had never before voted for
the BJS or BJP (both had suffered from the perception that they
were essentially north Indian parties representing Hindi-speaking
Hindus). For instance, Kerala Varma's director of publicity in
1984, P. Ashok Kumar, though he had become an RSS swayamsevak
while being educated at Chinmaya Mission school, was a college

chemistry teacher who had only been drawn into politics during the Nilakkal agitation as the Mission's General Secretary in Thiruvananthapuram. He subsequently joined the BJP when it absorbed the Munnani.[40]

The Hindu nationalist vote quadrupled to over a million between 1982 and the 1991 district council elections. But much of this new support was thinly spread. The BJP consistently won over a tenth of the vote in only one of Kerala's fourteen districts, Kasaragod on the northern border with Karnataka, though it did attain this modest level of support in Thiruvananthapuram in 1987. Significantly, the other districts in which it consistently did better than in the state overall were Malappuram and Kozhikode, the two with the highest proportion of Muslims (see Table 6.1), and Pathanamthitta, where it gained support in the wake of the Nilakkal controversy in 1983.

Hindu nationalism's relative strength at either end of Kerala could be mainly explained with reference to subregional factors. An area that formed part of the South Canara District of Madras until 1956, non-Malayali Tulu, Kannada, Konkan and Marathi speakers constitute two-fifths of the population of the Kasaragod taluk of the district bearing the same name.[41] The district was created in 1984, partly in response to longstanding local demands for the merger of the area with Karnataka, and partly in recognition of its history of relative underdevelopment. It had the second highest proportion of illiterates of any district in the state[42] and BJP leaders accused successive state governments of being more concerned with placating religious rather than linguistic minorities.[43] For instance, one of the reasons why, in the early 1990s, Kannadiga students shunned a new local college and travelled across the border to Mangalore for their higher studies was because Calicut University, itself established partly in response to Mappila Muslim charges of neglect, refused to let them take examinations in their mother tongue.

[40] Interview, Thiruvananthapuram, 4 September 1992

[41] Census of India, 1981. Series 10—Kerala, Paper 1 of 1987: Households and Household Population by Language Mainly Spoken (Delhi), Table HM—6.

[42] Census of India, 1991. Series 12—Kerala, Paper 2 of 1991: Provisional Population Totals (Delhi), Table 1.1.

[43] Interview with K. G. Marar (1937–95), twice the BJP's state president, Thiruvananthapuram, 4 September 1992.

The BJP's strength was mainly among the non-Malayalis, who represented the majority of the Hindus in Kasaragod taluk, and local RSS shakhas were controlled by the Karnataka State Committee. Asked about this seeming anomaly, Kerala state pracharak Hari, drew attention to significant cultural differences, noting that in the area it was the festivals of Diwali, Dussehra (one of the few festivals officially commemorated by the RSS) and Ganesh *puja* that were celebrated rather than Onam, the main festival for Malayali Hindus. Politically, neighbouring Karnataka is the only state in south India where the BJP has made significant inroads; it emerged as the second biggest party in the 1994 state assembly elections, doing best in the Dakshina Kannada district adjoining Kasaragod.

Both the district *panchayat* seats, the only block *panchayat* and the three *grama panchayats* (village councils) in Kerala that the BJP won in the September 1995 local elections[44] were in the northernmost taluk of Kasaragod as was one of the two seats (out of 474) it secured in the 1991 district council elections (the other was in Palakkad on the Tamil Nadu border, like Kasaragod a district with a substantial number of non-Malayalis).[45] With its members well entrenched in institutions such as cooperative societies and banks, it represented the main opposition to the Muslim League in the area, emerging as the largest party in the Kasaragod municipal council in the 1995 poll and claiming 35 per cent of the vote in the two local Assembly constituencies, Manjeswar and Kasaragod, in 1996 (the BJP stands to gain both on a swing of under two per cent).

Local circumstances were also significant in Thiruvananthapuram. Among the most important of these, according to the RSS district pracharak, was its tradition of 'Hindu consciousness', a legacy of its past as the capital of the Travancore rulers whose chief title was Sri Padmanabha Dasa (servant of Padmanabha, an incarnation of the deity Vishnu).[46] In the 1988 elections to the City Corporation, the BJP won six seats (out of 50), all located in preponderantly caste Hindu (Nair or Tamil Brahmin) wards. But it was not just tradition that accounts for why Thiruvananthapuram District provided a

[44] *Malayala Manorama* (Kochi and Thiruvananthapuram eds), 28 September 1995.
[45] The 12 per cent Tamil and Telugu-speaking minority were concentrated in the city of Palakkad where the BJP won its seat.
[46] Interview with Jayakumar, op. cit.

third of all the votes won by the Hindu nationalists in Travancore-Cochin in 1987. There was also the pent up frustration felt by many caste Hindus belonging to families that had long depended for their livelihood on government service in the state capital. They had seen lower-caste people and Muslims (also classified as a Backward Class) taking advantage of educational concessions and the reservation of half of all appointments for them, with Muslims also benefiting disproportionately from the post-1970s boom in employment in the oil-rich Gulf.[47]

Thiruvananthapuram was the main focus for RSS activity in southern Kerala. The district claimed one in six of the RSS shakhas in the state in 1992 (there were some 300 shakhas with 6500 swayamsevaks in the city alone).[48] Concerned with broadening its appeal, the RSS undertook social service projects in poor areas, most notably adopting the coastal settlement of Muttattara to the south of the capital. In a deprived area that lacked a school, health centre, post office or market at the beginning of the 1980s,[49] the RSS, working principally through the Seva Bharathi (see Table 6.2), opened children's care centres and schools, conducted regular medical camps and undertook a range of other activities, including a drive against liquor outlets. (The area was close to the Poonthura locality that witnessed the worse of the RSS–ISS clashes in 1992.)

However, without the more deep-seated character of the elements fostering their strength in Kasaragod, the Hindu nationalists proved unable to sustain the momentum behind the advances made in the state capital. The BJP vote was almost halved in the 1989 Lok Sabha election and in the 1991 Assembly poll it failed to retain its security deposit in any of the constituencies in Thiruvananthapuram district (the Hindu Munnani had managed to do so in three, and the BJP in one, in 1987). Four years later it also lost half its representation on the City Corporation. Despite a partial recovery in the 1996 elections, the BJP failed to make good the greater part of its earlier losses through much of the Travancore-Cochin region (see Tables 6.3 and 6.4).

---

[47] See my 'Changing Muslim Politics in Kerala: Identity, Interests and Political Strategies', *Journal of Muslim Minority Affairs*, 16(2), 1996, pp 257–71.

[48] Interviews with R. Hari and Jayakumar, op. cit.

[49] *Census of India, 1981*, Series 10—*Kerala, District Census Handbook. Trivandrum District* (Trivandrum: Government Press, 1988), pp 54–5.

TABLE 6.4: Elections in Kerala 1982–96

(seats and percentage vote)

Front	1982 Assembly	1984 Lok Sabha	1987 Assembly	1989 Lok Sabha	1991 Assembly	1991 Lok Sabha	1996 Assembly	1996 Lok Sabha
UDF								
Contested	140.0	20.0	138.0	20.0	140.0	20.0	140.0	20.0
Won	77.0	17.0	60.0	17.0	92.0	16.0	59.0	10.0
% vote	48.2	50.9	43.6	49.3	48.1	48.6	45.6	46.6
LDF								
Contested	140.0	20.0	140.0	20.0	140.0	20.0	140.0	20.0
Won	63.0	3.0	78.0	3.0	48.0	4.0	80.0	10.0
% vote	47.2	42.3	45.0	44.4	45.9	44.3	46.7	44.6
BJP % allies								
Contested	68.0	11.0	127.0	20.0	137.0	19.0	136.0	20.0
Won	0.0	0.0	0.0	0.0	0.0	0.0	0.0	0.0
% vote	2.7	3.9	6.5	4.5	4.7	4.6	5.7	6.1

Source: See Table 6.3.

Unlike other parts of India, where Hindu nationalists often initially made striking electoral gains in the aftermath of the communal tension and violence of the Ram Janmabhoomi campaign in the late 1980s and early 1990s,[50] this was not the experience in Kerala. Though the BJP increased its vote marginally (to 7.3 per cent) in the January 1991 district elections, this obscured a pattern of declining or stagnating support in districts where it had done particularly well in 1987 (down to 14.3 per cent in Kasaragod and 7.6 per cent in Thiruvananthapuram).[51] The trend was confirmed in the Assembly and Lok Sabha polls five months later. In retrospect, the BJP leaders, while rejecting suggestions of collusion, suggested that an understanding in Malabar by which they supported a UDF-backed independent Lok Sabha candidate in return for UDF backing for an RSS-linked independent Assembly candidate (both lost), may have disillusioned some erstwhile BJP voters.[52]

It is certainly possible to discern a relationship between the fluctuating fortunes of the BJP and that of the UDF. The consistent pattern in three seats of Assembly and Lok Sabha elections from 1987–96 was—when comparing one Assembly poll to the next, and one Lok Sabha poll to the next—of the BJP picking up support when the UDF registered losses, and vice versa (see Table 6.4). In both 1987 and 1996 surges in support for the Hindu nationalists coincided with success for the LDF while in 1991 the drop in the vote for the BJP was crucial in the UDF's return to power.[53] Similarly, the decline in the BJP vote in the 1989 Lok Sabha poll

[50] See my 'Tricolour and Saffron: Congress and the Neo-Hindu Challenge', in S. K. Mitra and J. Chiriyankandath (eds), *Electoral Politics in India. A changing Landscape* (Delhi: Segment, 1992), pp 68–9, 73.

[51] Calculations based on *District Council Elections Reportage* (Dept. of Public Relations, Govt. of Kerala, n.d.).

[52] Interviews with K. Raman Pillai and K. G. Marar, op. cit. And despite the RSS view that 'splinter group politics was bad politics' (interview with P. Parameswaran, op. cit.), the BJP had no qualms in extending its support to a defector from the Communist Party of India (Marxist) who became Mayor of Thiruvananthapuram in 1991 with UDF backing (interview with P. Ashok Kumar, op. cit.).

[53] In fifteen of the twenty constituencies gained by the UDF the decline from the BJP's 1987 vote was precipitous—between twice and four times as much as the statewide average of 19 per cent.

followed a VHP call for Hindus to back the UDF candidates where the BJP stood no chance of victory (in the Kerala context this meant almost everywhere).[54] Together with the coincidence of the rise of the Hindu nationalists and the eclipse of the parties within the UDF sponsored by the Nair and Ezhava caste associations, electoral trends thus appear to bear out the widely held assumption that the predominantly caste Hindu voters for the BJP were far more likely to be erstwhile supporters of the UDF than of the LDF.

HINDU NATIONALISM AND PLURALIST POLITICS: THE FUTURE OF THE RSS AND BJP IN KERALA

Hindu nationalism in Kerala has come a long way since its meagre beginnings on the margins of political life. Whereas there were just 15 RSS pracharaks, 95 shakhas and 1200 swayamsevaks in 1947, by the early 1990s there were over 200 pracharaks, some 4300 sakhas and perhaps as many as 70,000 swayamsevaks.[55] Similarly, compared to the 12,000 members claimed by the BJS in 1967, the BJP boasted 415, 434 in 1992–3.[56] While such statistics indicate the rapid strides made by both organizations in the 1980s and 1990s, the BJPs electoral performance provides a more reliable guide to the limited mass appeal of Hindu nationalism (if the party's membership figures are accepted, it would mean that almost one in every two BJP voters in 1996 was a BJP member[57]—a remarkably high proportion for any political party in a competitive democratic setting).

A serious handicap for Hindu nationalist forces in Kerala was the paucity of political leadership in a context where they remained peripheral actors. While the commitment and ability of RSS pracharaks was grudgingly acknowledged even by those critical of

---

[54] Anon, 'Kerala. Temporary Communal Coalition', *Economic and Political Weekly,* 9 December 1989, pp 2685–6.

[55] Jayaprasad, op. cit., p. 151: interview with R. Hari, op. cit. Precise figures are difficult to come by given the shifting nature of shakha membership (between 15–25 swayamsevaks attend a shakha).

[56] Jayaprasad, op. cit., p. 209: Organizational Report to the BJP State Council session, Thiruvananthapuram, January 1994.

[57] The BJP candidates polled 883, 584 votes in the 1996 Lok Sabha elections.

their ideology,[58] the BJP leadership was widely regarded as medio-
cre and intellectually shallow. A rare exception was K. G. Marar,
state party president from 1984–8 and again from 1992 until his
death in 1995. A former Malayalam schoolteacher and RSS
pracharak from Malabar, he was an able orator known for his
cutting repartee.[59] Following his demise, leadership was mainly
provided by two lacklustre former state presidents in their sixties,
K. Raman Pillai and O. Rajagopal (Raman Pillai headed the party's
state election committee in 1996 and Rajagopal was a national vice-
president of the BJP and, as a Rajya Sabha Member of Parliament
from Madhya Pradesh, also a member of its Central Parliamentary
Board). An indication that Sangh Parivar leaders were conscious
of the dearth of political talent was that the local RSS *Sampark
Pramukh* (publicity convener), P. P. Mukundan, was appointed the
BJP's State Organizing Secretary on the eve of the 1991 elections.
He subsequently became the party's General Secretary and, after
Marar's death, assumed greater responsibility for determining its
local tactics.

While the BJP could well make its debut in the Kerala Assembly
in the not too distant future, thanks to its pocket of strength among
the non-Malayali minority in Kasaragod, this would not represent
a substantial political breakthrough for Hindu nationalism in the
state. The creation of the Hindu Munnani in the 1980s facilitated
limited expansion but the half-hearted attempt to replicate this
model in 1996 using the front of a Bharatiya Labour Party to appeal
to the Backward Class voters (the BJP contested ten Assembly
constituencies, as well as one Lok Sabha constituency), and a
Samrakshana Samiti to attract the support of the Scheduled Castes
(the Samiti contested one reserved Assembly seat), did not yield
similar dividends. To become a credible contender for power in
Kerala the BJP does not only need regionally sensitive channels of
expression, like the erstwhile Hindu Munnani, but also ways of

---

[58] For instance, the leading literary figure, Sukumaran Azhikode, well known
as an advocate of communal coexistence and social pluralism, praised P.
Parameswaran and wrote the foreword to the latter's biography of Sri Narayana
Guru (interview, Thrissur, 18 September 1992).

[59] For instance, he likened the UDF administration of the early 1990s to a
rickety old Kerala State Transport bus driven by a drunk on a road full of potholes
(interview, Thiruvananthapuram, 2 September 1992).

transcending the self-imposed limitations intrinsic to Hindu nationalism and coming to terms with the social and political realities of pluralism.[60]

However, this poses Hindu nationalists with an acute dilemma: How can they participate as secondary actors in the coalition politics of the state without seriously compromising their 'Hindu' credentials and becoming merely yet another minor sectional interest? Their experience elsewhere in India is of little help in this respect. When the BJP reached a limited national electoral accommodation with the National Front in 1989, or the Samata Party in Bihar in 1996, it did so as a major, if not superior, force, while its alliance with the Shiv Sena[61] in Maharashtra was girded by a shared (if far from identical) Hindu nationalist vision. Furthermore, the successful alliance formed with the Haryana Vikas Party in the 1996 elections, and that reached with the Akali Dal on the eve of the 1997 Assembly poll in Punjab, were not complicated by the kind of established patterns of multiparty politics antipathetic to the BJP that are found in Kerala. Neither the Congress-led UDF nor the Marxist-led LDF are likely to entertain any open arrangement with the BJP as it stands, and the party itself has tended to avoid accepting the position of a junior partner in any compact.

The main significance of the Hindu nationalists' experience in Kerala lies in throwing into sharp relief the social and regional factors inhibiting their emergence as a genuinely pan-Indian force. The dilemma the BJP faces in Kerala is not peculiar to the state. It highlights a choice it cannot indefinitely avoid making as a national party in a diverse federal polity—whether to remain a powerful factor on the margins of government or a party of government prepared to transcend the limits of its historical tradition.

[60] I have explored the nature of this pluralism in 'Hindu Nationalism and Regional Political Culture in India: A Study of Kerala', *Nationalism & Ethnic Politics*, 2(1), 1996, pp 44–66.

[61] The Shiv Sena made its electoral debut in Kerala in 1996 when its three Lok Sabha candidates won a total of 5609 votes.

Ψ

7

The Akalis and the BJP in Punjab: From Ayodhya to the 1997 Legislative Assembly Election

GURHARPAL SINGH

In the eleventh Lok Sabha elections (May 1996) the BJP emerged as the largest single political party. As speculation intensified about the possibility of the BJP forming its first ever national government, one regional party, the Akali Dal (Badal) [AD(B)], made a public declaration of support for the BJP's claim. This declaration surprised many observers. Why, they conjectured, was a party which was the premier representative of Sikhs prepared to give support to the leading Hindu nationalist party? Was there not something fundamentally irreconcilable in Sikh agitation [which the AD(B) had supported] for the Anandpur Sahib Resolution (ASR) with its call for political autonomy and the BJP's national agenda for Hindutva?

This chapter will analyse the emergence of the Akali–BJP alliance within the context of regional and national political developments since the early 1990s. It will examine the tactical, strategic and ideological factors that have enabled the two parties to coalesce and thereby unlock the 'Punjab problem', while simultaneously projecting an alternative agenda for national Indian politics. Particular emphasis will be given to post-1992 regional and national developments and the significance of the 1997 Punjab Legislative Assembly elections which resulted in a landslide victory for the AD(B)–BJP alliance.

THE AKALIS AND THE HINDU NATIONALISTS: ANTAGONISM OR AFFINITIES?

Although the recent minority national governments have re-kindled interest in coalition politics in India, combinations of ideologically opposed parties have been a common phenomenon at the provincial level. In the 1960s and 1970s the Communist parties [CPI and CPI(M)] developed the concept of 'United Fronts', 'Democratic Fronts' and 'Left Fronts'.[1] One of the leading practitioners of such fronts, Harkrishan Singh Surjeet, has coordinated the United Front combine of 13 parties that has successively been led by Deve Gowda (May 1996–April 1997) and I. K. Gujral (after April 1997) as Prime Ministers.[2] Surjeet initially perfected this art in Punjab after the 1967 Punjab Legislative Assembly elections when a combination of the Akali Dal, Jana Sangh (BJP's forerunner) and the Communist parties defeated the Congress.[3] Applying a Marxist formula, Surjeet rationalized these fronts in terms of developing the 'Democratic Front'; in reality, however, these fronts, especially between 1967–71, were ineffective in challenging the administrative regime of hegemonic control which included centrally imposed President's Rule. Nor does the Akali–BJP alliance of the 1990s appear to pose a serious challenge to the structure of hegemonic control: in conditions where Congress-I dominance has collapsed the Akalis are seeking to establish themselves as a pre-eminent regional political party, while the BJP views this arrangement as a precursor of regional pacts that would lead to national power.[4] This process may offer opportunities for the AD(B) to dismantle hegemonic control; it is equally likely to enable the BJP to establish the new ground realities of its eventual reconstruction in line with Hindutva.

These realities are embedded in how these two parties ideologically construct the other. For the BJP and its sister organizations

<hr>

[1] For detailed discussion of these fronts see Singh, Gurharpal, *Communism in Punjab, 1920–67* (New Delhi: Ajanta, 1994); and Nossiter, T. J., *Communism in Kerala* (London: Hurst, 1980).

[2] For the role of Surjeet as a backseat driver of the United Front, see *India Today* (hereafter *IT*) 31 December 1996.

[3] See Sharma, T. R., 'Diffusion and Accommodation: The Contending Strategies of the Congress Party and the Akali Dal in Punjab', *Pacific Affairs*, vol. 59(4), pp 634–54.

[4] *The Sunday Tribune* (hereafter *TST*), 23 February 1997.

Sikhism is essentially a militant Hindu sect, a 'martial face' of Hinduism. At the height of the troubles in 1984 a BJP resolution declared:

The Sikh Panth was born to protect Hinduism and the venerable Gurus sacrificed themselves and their dear children to protect Hindu honour. The Sikh contribution to the strength and prosperity of India is magnificent, and the nation is truly grateful.[5]

These words were backed by deeds insofar the BJP and its associated organizations offered a sympathetic ear to Akali politicians when the ruling Congress-I was condoning the pogroms against Sikhs in Delhi. At the same time because the BJP does not acknowledge *religious* separatism among the Sikhs, it is vehemently opposed to the claims of political separatism. Throughout the 1980s the BJP followed a hard line against Sikh militants waging an armed struggle for Khalistan; and like the Congress-I, it sees the Anandpur Sahib Resolution as potentially secessionist.

The BJP and its sister organization's outlook is, therefore, very much coloured by historical experience. Traditionally the Arya Samaj and, later the RSS, have been the most vociferous opponents of Sikh efforts to establish a distinct identity, particularly against Hinduism. The Arya Samaj project in Punjab to create a reformed Hinduism, included, amongst other things, arresting the increasing growth of Sikhism in the late nineteenth century under colonial patronage, especially recruitment into the armed services. Ideologically, animosities between the Arya Samaj and Sikh reformers declined in the prelude to partition but resurfaced with a vengeance in the new eastern province of Punjab in which Hindus formed an overwhelming majority, and their political influence on the mercantile Congress Hindus frustrated the Akalis' demand for a Punjabi-speaking province.[6]

Historically, the Akalis have had a long tradition of making alliances with ideologically opposed parties: Congress, Communists, Jana Sangh and the Unionists. Until 1966 as representatives of a political minority, such tactical coalition-building was a political necessity, and not an expediency. For the AD(B) the limits

---

[5] Quoted in Jaffrelot, C., *The Hindu Nationalist Movement and Indian Politics 1925–90s* (London: Hurst and Company, 1996), p. 345.

[6] For further discussion of this see Singh, Gurharpal, *Ethnic Conflict in India Politics: A Case Study of Punjab* (London: Macmillan, 1998 [forthcoming]).

within which the Sikh ethnic identity can be articulated in Indian politics—the ideological baggage of the BJP has been elided in the language of the 'older brother' and the party's anti-Congress-I credentials. Because ideological pragmatism has been the hallmark of the AD(B), its most stern critics of such an alliance have come from among Sikh radicals and militants, especially the Akali Dal (Mann) (AD[M]), which has consistently sought to project the Sikh question as an issue of minorities alongside the struggle of lower castes and India's Muslims. Thus, whereas AD(B)'s alliance with the BJP seems to pose the greatest threat to a distinct Sikh identity since the late 19th century with its potential for assimilation into Hinduism, political realists within the AD(B) seem to have calculated that this alliance provides the maximum scope for preserving Sikh identity and, indeed, advancing the agenda for political autonomy.[7]

PUNJAB AND POLITICAL DEVELOPMENTS SINCE 1992

The BJP has been the fastest growing political party in India. Its rise to national prominence in 1996 has been accompanied by the spectacular growth in the northern regions where it has ruled state governments in Uttar Pradesh, Delhi, Himachal Pradesh, Rajasthan, Gujarat, Madhya Pradesh, and in alliance with the Shiv Sena in Maharashtra. While there are many factors that have contributed to this rise,[8] the BJP's stance on internal insurgencies in Kashmir, Punjab and the north-eastern states have hit a chord with the anxieties of India's Hindu population. Yet in contrast to Kashmir the party's position on Sikh militancy and the Punjab question marked a distinct shift after the Punjab Legislative Assembly elections in 1992. These elections were boycotted by most leading Akali factions, resulting in a landslide victory for the Congress-I

---

[7] Since pre-Independence tactical alliances for the Akali Dal with political parties have been determined mainly by the possibilities they offer for advancing and protecting the interest of the Sikh community. For a classic case study of this see Nayer, Baldev Raj, *Minority Politics in the Punjab* (Princeton: Princeton University Press, 1966). Seen in this light the AD(B) in its embrace with the BJP is conforming to norm.

[8] See Jaffrelot, *Hindu Nationalism*, ch. 11.

in one of the lowest voter turnouts since 1947.[9] Under the fig-leaf of such legitimacy the Congress-I administration of Beant Singh intensified the strategy of violent control against both Sikh militant and moderate political leadership. Politically muzzled within Punjab, the moderates became active in Sikh politics outside the state. In the elections to the Delhi Assembly in December 1993 moderate Akalis encouraged Sikh voters in the capital to vote for the BJP. Delhi was one of the few successes for the BJP after the demolition of the Babri Masjid in Ayodhya (1992) and the presidential dismissal of its governments in four states. The new BJP government in the capital reciprocated this support by declaring Punjabi as a second language and launching cases against anti-Sikh rioters (mainly Congressmen) of 1984.[10] The rapprochement between the two parties, however, took time to consolidate: the proposal for an alliance against Congress-I took hold only after the May 1996 Lok Sabha elections in which AD (B) won eight of the 13 seats from Punjab.[11]

The fortunes of the Congress-I has been in sharp decline since the late 1980s and only the assassination of Rajiv Gandhi in 1991 prevented the party's defeat in the tenth Lok Sabha elections in June that year. For the new minority national government headed by Rao, victory in the Punjab Legislative Assembly elections was also accompanied by the success of 13 Congress-I MPs for the Punjab Lok Sabha seats. These additional MPs provided a critical boost to a party at a time when it was desperately seeking to establish an overall majority in the Parliament. In Punjab the victory was used to intensify counter-insurgency operations against Sikh militants as the new administration gave a free reign to the security services to crush armed resistance, though this resulted in high casualties among the non-militant civilians.[12] By early 1993 most of the leading militant organizations had been smashed. But the Congress-I was unable to transform this achievement into an enduring legitimacy. With a crippling fiscal debt—the fight against militancy had left the state government with a cumulative debt of nearly Rs 60,000m to the centre—and the reluctance of the national

[9] See Singh, Gurharpal, 'Punjab Elections 1992: Breakthrough or Breakdown?', *Asian Survey* (November, 1992), pp 410–21.
[10] *Des Pardes* (Southall), 17 December 1993. (Hereafter *DP*.)
[11] *India Today*, 31 May 1997. (Hereafter *IT*.)
[12] *Jane's Defence Weekly* (London), 23 June 1993.

government to deliver the outstanding provisions of the 1985 Rajiv–Longowal Accord, the administration was compelled to sustain ideological warfare against Sikh militancy by also proscribing the activities of Sikh moderates.[13] This policy was best personified in the Chief Minister Beant Singh and the Chief of Police KPS Gill. The assassination of Beant Singh in August 1995 by a suicide bomber, however, deprived the Congress-I of his firm leadership, while the implicating of Gill in security lapses resulted in his subsequent removal from Punjab. Harcharn Singh Brar, Beant Singh's successor, was reluctant to wage an ideological war against Sikhdom, preferring instead to reopen issues within the Rajiv–Longowal Accord, in particular the vexed question of sharing water with neighbouring states over which Beant Singh had maintained remarkable consistency since 1992. Even Brar's moderate leadership failed to lift the Congress-I as the party became increasingly associated with decay, corruption and systematic abuse of human rights. When the party suffered a humiliating defeat in the May 1996 Lok Sabha elections in Punjab, retaining only two of the 13 seats, the new leadership of Sitaram Kesri in New Delhi ousted Brar and replaced him with a loyalist Rajinder Kaur Bhattal.[14] But Bhattal's plan to revive the fortunes of the Congress-I with a populist 51-point programme on the eve of the elections backfired as the Election Commission, suspecting a pre-election spending spree, advanced the date of the polls.[15]

Within Sikh politics the move from violent control to hegemonic control eliminated the militants, marginalized the radicals and ultimately succeeded in strengthening the moderates. As counter-insurgency operations after 1992 eliminated the armed and democratic militants, their political residue sought refuge with the radicals. Between 1992, as in the years between 1985–7,[16] the factional struggle for dominance was largely conducted within the SGPC, the 'Sikh political system'. Confronted with the onslaught of the Beant administration, the radicals and the Shiromani

---

[13] See Singh, Gurharpal, 'Punjab Since 1984: Disorder, Order and Legitimacy', *Asian Survey* 34 (4) (April 1996), pp 410–21.

[14] *IT*, 15 December 1996.

[15] *IT*, 31 January 1997.

[16] See Singh, Gurharpal, 'The Punjab Problem in the 1990s: A Post-1984 Assessment', *Journal of Commonwealth and Comparative Politics*, 25(2) (July 1991): pp 175–91.

Gurudwara Prabandhak Committee (SGPC) leadership of Gurcharan Singh Thora sought to forge a united front of Sikh politics by employing the ideological, institutional and factional resources of Sikhdom.[17] In this endeavour they inducted the services of the Jathedar (head priest) of Akal Thakt. In May 1994 under his sponsorship six moderate and radical Akali factions merged to form the Akali Dal(Amritsar) (AD [A]). This merger was followed by adoptation of the Amritsar Declaration which called for the formation of 'an independent Sikh homeland wherein the community would be free to profess and propagate Sikhism without interference from any quarter.'[18] Notably the AD(B), the main moderate group, remained aloof from the AD(A) and the efforts of the SGPC leadership and the Jathedar of the Akal Takht to ensnare it in a unity dialogue. Subsequently the AD(B) demonstrated the strength of its political machine in the successful Punjab Legislative Assembly bye-election of May 1994 and, as the AD(B) emerged as the leading political representative of the Sikh community, it acquired significant factional defections from the AD(A) and, perhaps more importantly, moderated the antics of Thora who had engineered the unity moves. Thora and the leader of the AD(B) Parkash Singh Badal reached a compromise in February 1995 where the former agreed to restrict his activities to religion while the latter to lead the political programme. Thora's ambitions were further clipped by the AD(B)'s victory in the SGPC elections in 1996. Overall these developments further enhanced the status of the AD(B) and together with the success of the party in the May 1996 Lok Sabha elections appeared to vindicate its slogan of 'panth, Punjab and Punjaniat' (Sikh community, Punjab and Punjabiness).[19]

THE PUNJAB LEGISLATIVE ASSEMBLY ELECTIONS

In the prelude to the actual election campaign nearly all political parties in the state felt it prudent to make seat adjustments with the rivals in order to mitigate the large seat swings inherent in the first-past-the-post electoral system. The AD(B) with its base in the

---

[17] For a discussion of the Sikh political system see, Wallace, P., and S. Chopra (eds), *Political Dynamics of Punjab* (Amritsar, 1981), pp 1–32.

[18] *The Hindu* (International edition), 7 May 1994.

[19] *TST*, 16 February 1997.

Sikh peasantry allied with the BJP with its urban Hindu constituency. The Congress-I was unable to attract a major partner and had to be content with the support of the CPI. The CPI(M) under the tutelage of Surjeet floated a much publicized 'third front' which also included the Janata Dal and the Samajwadi Janata Dal. The Bahujan Samaj Party (BSP), a key player in the 1996 Lok Sabha elections, was unable to strike a deal with either the AD(B) or the Congress-I. It fought the election in alliance with AD(M), a remnant of AD(A).

The AD(B)'s manifesto for the elections was a mixture of rural populism and a reassertion of the demands predating the Rajiv–Longowal Accord tempered with the need to emphasize Hindu–Sikh unity. The party pledged to fight for 'true federalism as contained in the Anandpur Sahib Resolution of 1978'. This commitment also included the repudiation of all previous accords on the adjudication of interstate river waters, the postponement of the Sutlej–Yamuna Link project, the transfer of Chandigarh and other Punjabi-speaking areas to the state, and the proposal to set up a human rights commission in the state. For the peasantry the party promised free power for tube-wells, free canal water for irrigation and a hike in the procurement price of the agricultural produce in line with the price index. A range of other measures were also proposed to attract industry, encourage development and further democratization. The manifesto concluded with the need to 'maintain peace in Punjab at all costs'.[20]

The Congress-I in turn repudiated the Anandpur Sahib Resolution as secessionist but promised to work for the implementation of the Rajiv–Longowal Accord as the framework for resolving the outstanding issues of river waters, Chandigarh and the Punjabi-speaking areas. As well as proposals targeted at the poor and the reservations for women, the party sought to frighten voters by pronouncing that the Akalis had 'formed a suicide squad of one lakh (one hundred thousand) persons whose main target was to kill Hindus'.[21]

The BJP's manifesto for the elections echoed in many ways the promises of the AD(B), but differed in one significant respect: while maintaining its opposition to the Anandpur Sahib Resolution the

[20] *TT*, 28 January 1997.
[21] *TT*, 29 January 1997.

BJP proposed to implement instead the report of the Sarkaria Commission to increase powers of the states and stop the misuse of the article 356 which had perpetuated the 'Congress Raj'. In place of decentralization and federalism the BJP document spoke of 'devolution' consistent with the 'unity and integrity of the country'. This main policy disagreement between the two parties, however, was not a major stumbling block. Vajpayee insisted the AD(B) had, after all, committed itself to 'guaranteeing peace, national integrity and communal harmony'.[22]

The election campaign itself was limited to only two weeks. Almost 70,000 police personnel and 100,000 paramilitaries were deployed across the state to ensure free, fair and peaceful polling at 18,097 polling stations of which 1,057 were identified as 'hyper-sensitive' and 2,744 as 'sensitive'.[23] In spite of the heavy presence of the security personnel, electioneering was marked by colourful campaigning traditionally associated with Indian elections. Turn-outs were high in areas which had been the hotbeds of militancy in the Amritsar and Gurdaspur districts. The strict enforcement of the Code of Conduct by the Election Commissioners resulted in, among other things, an alcohol ban during the campaign itself.

In total 693 candidates contested the Punjab Legislative Assembly elections. The result marked a landslide victory for the AD(B)–BJP alliance which captured 93 seats in the assembly of 117, and almost 48 per cent of the votes polled. The AD(B) did particularly well in rural (70) and semi-rural (24) constituencies making a virtual clean sweep in the Malwa region with a strong showing in the Majha and Doaba. The potential threat from AD(M) failed to materialize as the party secured only one seat despite fielding 29 candidates. The AD(B)'s share of the popular vote was slightly less than the record 38 per cent achieved by Akali Dal (Longowal) in the 'friendly' Punjab Legislative Assembly elections of 1985.[24] (see Table 7.1.)

The BJP also did better than was expected, winning the highest number of seats since the linguistic reorganization. The party's performance was strongest in urban and semi-urban constituencies where it had traditionally competed with the Congress-I and BSP.

---

[22] *TT*, 29 January 1997.
[23] India News Network Digest, Bowling Green, Ohio, USA, 6 February 1992.
[24] *Ajit* (Daily, Jalandhar), 11 February 1997.

As the Hindu vote swung behind the BJP, the Congress-I's position was undermined by the competition from the BSP. BJP's share of the popular vote, on the other hand, actually decreased by nearly 6 per cent compared to that of the 1992.

TABLE 7.1: Punjab Legislative Assembly Elections 1997 Result
(Turnout: 69.9%)

Party Polled	Candidates	Seats Won	Vote %
Akali Dal (Badal)	92	75	37.2
BJP	22	18	10.6
Congress-I	105	14	26.4
Bauhjan Samaj Party	67	1	7.5
CPI	14	2	0.9
Akali Dal (Mann)	29	1	2.9
Independents and Others*	364	6	12.8
TOTAL	693	117	100

Note: * Others also include the CPI(M), Janata Dal, Samajwadi Party and Samajwadi Janata Party.
Source: India Today, 28 February 1997; *The Tribune*, 11 February 1997; *Daily Ajit*, 11 February 1997; and *Des Pardes*, 21 February 1997.

The biggest loser was the Congress-I. Its share of seats collapsed from 87 to 14 in 1992; the party's share of the popular vote also fell dramatically to 26 per cent. The Congress-I was virtually wiped out in its traditional stronghold in the Doaba where its vote collapsed from nearly 40 per cent to 26.7 per cent in the Lok Sabha elections. Its performance in the Majha region was also unimpressive without a single victory in the region—many leading Congressmen in the Majha region simply refused to participate in the contest. In the Malwa region the party relied heavily on localized support, retaining only nine of the 63 seats in this area with its total share of the vote around 25.8 per cent. The expulsion of the former Chief Minister Brar based in the Malwa region just before the elections resulted in widespread dissent allegedly undermining the party's position in some two dozen constituencies.[25]

The minor parties were spectacularly unsuccessful. Whereas the Communist parties relied on localized support, the BSP was the

[25] *TT*, 2 February, 1997; *Ajit*, 11 February 1997.

main victim of failing to ally with a major party before the elections. The party's share of seats collapsed from nine to one in 1992, and its share of the vote declined from 16.2 per cent to 7.5 per cent. The leader of the BSP, Kanshi Ram, who had hoped to become the 'king-maker' between Congress-I and the AD(B), proved particularly inept at managing to acquire an effective partner. Had he been able to do so, the 28 per cent Dalit vote in the state could have been decisive in determining the outcome in at least 26 constituencies.[26] In the event the party's stance frustrated the Congress-I while rewarding the BJP.

PROSPECTS FOR THE FUTURE: THE BJP–AKALI DAL(B) ALLIANCE AND THE LIMITS OF HEGEMONIC CONTROL

The emphatic victory of the AD(B)–BJP alliance marks a decisive turning point in the configuration of political forces that have been party to the 'Punjab Problem': previous efforts by the AD(B) and its predecessors to build a regional anti-Congress coalition have been frustrated by the regular defection from such coalitions by the minor political parties, communists and the BSP, as well as the factional penetration of Akali legislators by the Congress-I. For the first time the alignment of the AD(B) with a dominant anti-Congress-I national party appears to foreclose the prospects of such a development while providing a model for the BJP to emulate in other states.[27] In contrast because the Congress-I and the minor parties in Punjab have always looked towards their patrons in New Delhi to influence events in Punjab, they are likely to lobby hard to make the life of the Akali–BJP administration difficult. No Akali administration has completed its full term and the President's Rule has been regularly imposed to oust Akali governments. Given the strength of the AD(B) and the BJP it is perhaps premature to assume that President's Rule will be imposed in the immediate future, especially as the defeat in Punjab was identified with the new national leadership of Kesri. But as Congress-I's influence extends over the national United Front government and the latter itself may implode, it will be difficult for the Congress-I and the

[26] *IT*, 31 January 1997.
[27] *TST*, 23 February 1997.

United Front leadership to resist the temptation of interferring in Punjab particularly if the new national elections bring a Congress-I government to power. In the last two decades the pretext for such intervention has been the mismanagement of law-and-order by the state governments. Hence, the law-and-order record of the coalition government in Punjab will be crucial for its future prospects. In addition the ministry's fortunes will be influenced by its ability to fulfil its economic promises, the resolution of the outstanding Punjab issues, and the short- and medium-term calculations of the alliance for regional and national power.

The issue of law-and-order was pushed immediately to the fore in the months after the coalition came to power. In opposition the AD(B) had promised a thorough review of the 'security state' which had waged the war of counter insurgency against militancy. In fact as 'violent control' was dismantled after 1995, the individual petitions against police excesses began to be heard with greater frequency in the High and Supreme Courts. Since then allegations against the Punjab police have accelerated with nearly 1,200 cases registered against serving police officers and overall one-sixth of the total police force vulnerable to being indicted.[28] This situation has arisen as a result of the political failure to find an effective settlement to the end of violent control that should have compensated the victims and protected the security services alike. In the event police officers who were at the forefront of counterinsurgency have, in the words of Gill, now become the new victims in which 'public interest litigation has become the most convenient strategy for vendetta'.[29] The suicide of former police officer SSP A. S. Sandhu, who waged a ruthless war against Sikh militancy in the border area, became a cause celebre which was taken up by K. P. S. Gill as a spokesman of the beleaguered police officers.[30] His call for a constitutional commission to examine the issue has been echoed by human rights organizations in Punjab for a parallel commission—along the lines of South Africa's Truth and Reconciliation Commission—to examine the whole dimension of counterinsurgency. Interestingly, the AD(B)–BJP government while committed to preserving the peace and law-and-order is suspicious

[28] *IT*, 9 June 1997.
[29] See *KPS Gill's Open Letter to the Prime Minister*, *TST*, 1 June 1997.
[30] *Economic and Political Weekly*, 21 June 1997.

of the recent spate of bombings in Punjab: with militancy eradi-
cated it suspects that disgruntled elements within the security
services may be continuing to play the role of agent provocateurs,
a role that they so effectively perfected during counterinsurgency.
Timely acts of terror have destabilized previous administrations in
Punjab; the AD(B)–BJP alliance is very conscious of this fact and
that the assassination of chief ministers is not uncommon in Punjab.

The development plans of the alliance have also had to confront
the reality of a debt trap that has increased since early 1990s. At
the end of March 1996 the debt of special outstanding loans to the
Centre was nearly Rs 60,000m. Special pleas for this loan to be
cancelled notwithstanding, the previous Congress-I administration
succeeded in obtaining only a waiver in the annual liability on the
loan of nearly Rs 8,000m. Estimates suggest that this lability
will increase to Rs 8,500m in 1997–8 and rise to Rs 10,180m in
2001–2.[31] For the Punjab government servicing this loan has
created a fiscal debt ratio of nearly 30 per cent.[32] Only recently
has the Centre decide to cancel some of these special loans but this
high rate of indebtedness meant that in the first budget introduced
by the alliance in June 1997 taxes were actually *increased* while the
budget recorded an overall deficit of Rs 3,520m. Apart from a few
symbolic acts, such as reducing the police budget by Rs 270m, little
headway has been made in fulfilling the alliance's generous promises to industry or agriculture.[33] Perhaps the most remarkable of
all the chief ministers has been unable to secure an upward revision
of agricultural procurement prices, set annually by the Centre,
which have deflated agricultural incomes and are, for example in
the case of wheat, considerably below the market price.[34] The
initiative to set up a special cell for attracting NRI investment,
which is pitifully low in the state may make some impact, but it
is unlikely to generate the level of resources required for meeting
the promises made to the agricultural sector or provide for further
development. The debt trap, like the issue of law-and-order, will
reinforce the mechanisms of hegemonic control.

Facing a high degree of indebtedness the alliance, in particular
the AD(B), may be inclined to revive the agitation for the

[31] *TST*, 2 March 1997.
[32] *TST*, 23 March 1997.
[33] *DP*, 20 June 1997.
[34] *TST*, 23 Febrary 1997.

settlement of outstanding Punjab demands over the transfer of Chandigarh, the Punjabi-speaking areas and the river-waters dispute. Such a mobilization, as in 1982, is open to outflanking by an ideological challenge by militants and radicals from within the Sikh political system; and a challenge of this sort could become reality if the alliance proves unable to deliver following such a mobilization. The vanquished and disgruntled factions within Sikhdom are only too eager to wage the ideological battle, and their fires might be easily stoked, as in the past, by a Congress-I in opposition.

For the BJP, in contrast, championing the demands of the Punjab is latent with potential dangers. Apart from being at odds with the AD(B) over the reform of centre–state relations and the Anandpur Sahib Resolution, the party would have to placate its government in Rajasthan and its partners in Haryana and Himachal Pradesh, who would be disadvantaged in any agreement favouring Punjab. For over a decade, the Congress-I deliberately stalled the implementing of the Rajiv–Longowal Accord because of its fear of destabilizing Congress-I governments in these states; the BJP is likely to follow suit given the *national* benefits of assuaging its units and allies in these states at the expense of the AD(B). Since 1985 no national government—even one with an overwhelming majority as the Congress-I under Rajiv—has been able to implement even parts of the Rajiv–Longowal Accord. Any future commitment by the BJP to effect such a package must be seen against this background and the coded misgivings it expressed about the Anandpur Sahib Resolution.

If a national BJP government were able to deliver a Punjab package the AD(B)–BJP alliance certainly has the potential to become strategic. The differences between the two parties may be overcome by political symbolism such as the BJP's support for the AD(B)'s candidate (Surjit Singh Barnala) in the elections to the Vice-Presidentship of India.[35] Political rhetoric, after all, is rarely the stuff of Indian politics, and if the BJP is twin-tracking in a tactical accommodation of the AD(B) (and other regional parties) to capture *national* power, then these parties and the AD(B), as the reconstruction of the United Front government (April 1997) demonstrated, are aware of the potential bargaining power they can wield in New Delhi. Yet such independence for the AD(B) is

[35] *IT*, 14 July 1997.

unlikely to produce results given the record of non-BJP governments on the Punjab issue. In the long term, therefore, the strategic advantage to the AD(B) of an alliance with the BJP lies in the possibility of the BJP, its rhetoric apart, managing the contraction of the Indian state to the borders of the Hindu ethnic core regions. Such contraction is possible given the increasing propensity to 'rightsize' the state. If there is 'growing realization within the BJP leadership that the objective of coming to power in New Delhi cannot be achieved until the party is ready to constructively integrate regional sentiments and aspirations',[36] then regional sentiments will also determine the degree of accommodation as well as the BJP's agenda. The paradox of BJP's drive towards majoritarianism is that the ideological agenda of the party may be practical only in its core 'Hindi-belt'.

CONCLUSION

It is tempting to see the AD(B)–BJP alliance as pragmatic, opportunistic and tactical. In reality it has been forged as a consequence of ideologically charged politics of violent control practised by national and regional Congress-I governments in Punjab which fostered Sikh militancy and, ultimately, castrated the political activities of Sikh moderates. Notwithstanding the ideological differences between the parties—differences which are in many ways more apparent than real—they have much in common in shaping a new regional and national dimension to Indian politics. For the AD(B) the basis of this dimension is to establish regional political ascendency alongside the restoration of Sikh pride. For the BJP its national project is to establish a new framework of hegemonic control that would promote Hindutva in place of the Congress-I's 'pseudo-secularism'. Both parties may well be excluded from political office by the powerful political combinations arrayed against them. But whereas, for the BJP the Punjab model of alignment with a regional party offers a tantalizing vision of power in New Delhi, for the AD(B) the physical elimination of militant Sikh nationalism in the early 1990s has fostered a new realism in which the BJP offers the best hope for maintaining a distinct Sikh identity and achieving maximum political autonomy within the Indian Union.

[36] *TST*, 23 February 1997.

PART III
DIVIDED THEY STAND

8

The BJP's Riddle in Gujarat:
Caste, Factionalism and Hindutva

GHANSHYAM SHAH

The Bharatiya Janata Party (BJP), Rashtriya Swayamsevak Sangh (RSS), Vishwa Hindu Parishad (VHP) and other partners of the Sangh Parivar aim at building a *de facto* Hindu rashtra, if not a *de jure* theocratic state. The BJP is their political front which strives to capture power through electoral politics while aiming at reviving the Hindu social order and traditions in order to reinforce and distinctively establish the dominance of Hindus in the country. To attain these objectives, the constituents of the Sangh Parivar individually and collectively make endeavours for building unity among all Hindus irrespective of their socio-economic status and cultural heritage. Various strategies have been evolved to coopt and appease both the backward castes as well as Dalits, the victims of Brahminism, who together constitute nearly 70 per cent of all Hindus. The theorists of Hindu nationalism construct and reconstruct certain values and institutions as a Hindu cultural heritage and redefine the Hindu social order, Hinduism and its 'others' (non-Hindus). This particular construction of the social order wishes away hierarchical relationships and uneven distribution of resources among various social strata. It is their assumption that unity among Hindus will eradicate caste-based differentiations.

The major challenge facing the BJP is how to build unity among Hindus and at the same time keep diverse interests together once the BJP holds power. The Sangh Parivar has developed a set of strategies and mastered skills in arousing emotions for Hindutva against 'others'. But this emotional momentum can never be sustained for long. It is, for instance, more difficult to sustain when the party is in power than when it functions in opposition. The BJP seems unable to resolve conflicting socio-economic interests and the greed for power among many of its members. Moralizing directives and sermons are simply not enough as the recent internal crisis of the BJP in Gujarat demonstrates.

The Sangh Parivar has disseminated Hindutva ideology in Gujarat over many decades. The party and its allies have built the organization brick by brick. It began to reap the benefits of these endeavours in the early 1990s and captured power in 1995. After this clear victory the party projected that it would build Gujarat as BJP's model state of governance. But these dreams were shattered sooner than anyone expected as the party was dethroned from power in less than eighteen months by its own members. The party's perspective and theory on Hinduism and Hindu social order could not come to its rescue to resolve the contradictions that have emerged. This article seeks to explore the reasons for the reversal of the BJP's fortunes in Gujarat.

IDEOLOGY AND RIOTS

The state unit of the Jana Sangh, the forerunner of the BJP came into existence in Gujarat within six months of the birth of the party in 1951. The founders of the party in Gujarat were volunteers of the Rashtriya Swayamsevak Sangh. The 1950s was its formative period. Being the proponents of an 'Akhand Bharat' with central-ized power, the party kept distance from the influential Maha Gujarat movement which demanded a separate Gujarati state on linguistic grounds. During this period, the party's activities were largely confined to participation in programmes organized by the RSS related to the celebration of cultural festivals mainly of the upper castes, such as Dussehra, Raksha Bhandhan and Guru Purnima. Party leaders occasionally held public meetings on larger national issues related to the Kashmir border, the Indo-Chinese conflict and the Indo-Pakistan wars. The main thrust of their speeches on these occasions were anti-Muslim in tenor and they bemoaned the degeneration of Hindu culture. The meetings rarely attracted a crowd of more than one hundred persons. However, strained Indo-Pakistan relations in the early 1960s and the subsequent war of 1965, helped the party to get the attention of sections of urban middle class. The initial leaders of the party were mainly Maharastrian and local Brahmins, while Rajputs from the Saurashtra region joined the party later.

The anti-Muslim feelings which prevailed among the upper-caste Hindus—mainly the Rajputs, Brahmins and Vanias—were nurtured by the Jana Sangh and RSS in the 1960s. Local party functionaries fuelled these sentiments through speeches, circulation of rumours and attachment of charged symbols to localized conflict between the two communities, efforts which often resulted in violent clashes. According to official figures there were as many as 2,938 instances of communal violence between 1960–9 in Gujarat. Some of them were major riots in Saurashtra and Kutchha. The Indo-Pakistan war in 1965 further aggravated tensions, and provided fertile ground for rumour mongers. The death of Balwantrai Mehta, the then Chief Minister of Gujarat, when his plane was shot down by Pakistan, strengthened anti-Pakistani sentiments within the urban middle class. More often than not, anti-Pakistan sentiments got transformed into hatred against local Muslims. Communal speeches of the RSS and Jana Sangh leaders added fuel to the prevailing communal tension. In 1968, the RSS organized a rally, attended by 1,615 volunteers from different districts of Gujarat. Addressing it, M. S. Golwalkar emphasized that only Hindus were secular because they had tolerated all sorts of suffering at the hands of various 'others'. He pleaded for the making of a 'Hindu Rashtra', a concept on which there had already been extensive discussions in the press in Gujarat. The major thrust of the debate was that Muslims had destroyed Hindu culture and now enjoyed special favours in the country and further that Hindu rashtra was synonymous with Indian nationalism. In the following year, the Jana Sangh played a leading role in retaliating the protests of Gujarati Muslims against the attack on the Al-Aqsa mosque in early 1969. Balraj Madhok, a Jana Sangh leader addressed a number of meetings in Gujarat in 1969. He criticized Muslims for raising hue and cry over a mosque which was thousands of miles away from India. He asserted that the same people did not utter a word when

Pakistan attacked the Dwarka temple during the Indo- Pakistan war. 'Do you think that Hindus have no feeling for their religion?' Madhok asked. Some religious leaders and Jana Sanghis formed the 'Hindu Dharma Raksha Samiti' (Committee to defend Hindu religion) in Ahmedabad in 1968. The Committee played a very important role in mobilizing anti-Muslim feelings in the city before the 1969 communal riots. A procession was organized in which slogans like, 'Protect Hindu Dharma, and let the irreligious perish' were shouted. The tension between two communities culminated in the large-scale communal riots in September–October 1969 which spread to several cities. The Jana Sangh and RSS workers were actively involved in the riots either by provoking the people, taking initiative in leading mobs, or simply by providing money or material to the rioters.[1] The Congress which was in power not only failed to control the riots but its leaders also shared a good deal of the Hindu communal outlook. They not only shared anti-Muslim attitudes with the Jana Sangh but they also participated, directly or indirectly, in the strife, thus helping this party to expand its support base in urban areas.

A lull with respect to communal riots followed in the 1970s, during which issues of corruption, price rise and the emergency were in the forefront. The Jana Sangh and particularly the students front of the Sangh Parivar, the Akhil Bharatiya Vidyarthi Parishad, which was dominated by upper-caste urban students, participated actively in the 1974 Nav Nirman student movement. It highlighted the issue of corruption rather than the price rise and scarcity of essential commodities.[2] The Jana Sangh forged an alliance with the Janata Morcha in order to defeat the Congress; and it also joined the anti-emergency campaign. This helped the party to broaden its base among the urban middle class in Ahmedabad, Vadodara and Rajkot.

Once again, in the 1980s, Gujarat was engulfed by communal strife. The anti-reservation agitations of 1981 and 1985 often turned into Hindu–Muslim riots in which both intraparty factional fights within the Congress and the BJP's call for Hindu unity played significant roles. Non-party organizations like the Gujarat Biradari,

---

[1] Shah, Ghanshyam, 'Communal Riots in Gujarat', *Economic and Political Weekly*, 5 (3–5), Annual Number, January 1970.

[2] Shah, Ghanshyam, *Protest Movements in Two Indian States—Study of Gujarat and Bihar Movements* (Delhi: Ajanta, 1977).

which was dominated by Sarvodayists, not only articulated a need for developing Gujarat's *Asmita* (culture, tradition and identity) but also exaggerated the role of Pakistani infiltrators across Gujarat's boarder in the communal riots. This was interpreted and tacitly encouraged and legitimized by the media to mean that the infiltrators and the Muslims in Gujarat were hand-in-glove with each other. The Hindu fanatics stressed the Gujarati identity with a view to bring all Hindus under one umbrella and to treat Muslims implicitly, and at times even explicitly, as outsiders.

Besides Ahmedabad and Vadodara, the centres of recurring riots, communal disturbances now spread to south Gujarat, which was not affected by the riots in the 1960s and early 1980s. Moreover, communal conflicts spread to rural areas. A number of small towns and medium-sized villages even in the tribal areas were engulfed by communal passions, resulting in killing and looting of Muslim households. In a number of places, 'agents provocateurs' associated with the Hindu nationalist movement slowly but meticulously instigated violence over local intra-community conflicts, which then had a chain effect.

The tension between Hindus and Muslims was at high emotional peak in the late 1980s on the issue of Ram Janmabhoomi. In 1989, the Sangh Parivar organized the *Ramshila Pujan*, a campaign aiming at collecting and consecrating foundation bricks for the future temple in Ayodhya. Religious sentiments were fanned by recitals of bhajans, slogans, legends, myths, movies and rituals.

The Sangh Parivar asserted that Ram was the life of the Bharatiya *sanskriti*, i.e. culture, and Babar was an invader. It was not the question of individual religious faith, it was essentially a question of Indian unity and culture, national pride, nationalism and patriotism, they said. This religious fervour was used for political purposes to broaden the base of the BJP and to recruit volunteers for the *kar seva*, i.e. labour for religious activities in Ayodhya. Bricks for the 'Ram mandir' were collected from villages as a token of solidarity. In some places each household was persuaded to contribute Rs 1.25 towards the construction of the temple. People were asked by the RSS and Bajrang Dal activists: 'Are you a Hindu? If you are, then prove it by contributing Rs 1.25 for the *Ramshila pujan*. If you do not contribute, you prove that you are from a Muslim womb!' Later volunteers were recruited for the kar seva in building the temple, and those who could not participate were asked to donate money for the cause. Exaggerated news and rumours about the kar seva were spread by the media. The Sangh Parivar circulated on a large-scale concocted news stories and video films showing the 'bravery and sacrifice' of the kar sevaks in the face of allegedly 'brutal repression' by the State Reserve Police of Uttar Pradesh. Further, in order to gear passions to a high pitch, Hindus were told: 'The blood of the innocents shed in Ayodhya should not be allowed to go waste.' Communal clashes followed.

L. K. Advani began his dramatic *rath yatra* from Somnath in Saurashtra in September 1990, and several mini rath yatras were organized by the BJP to spread the message of Ayodhya. Trishuls, saffron flags and caps, stickers inscribing slogans like, 'Say with pride that I am a Hindu', and slogans swearing by Ram that the temple would be constructed at the same place appeared in the cities and towns and captured the public imagination for Hindu unity and nationalism. During the rath yatra communal riots occurred at 26 places, killing 99 persons between 1 September and 20 November 1990. Repeated communal clashes, high-pitched campaigns for Hindutva and the issue of the construction of Ram mandir at Ayodhya helped the BJP a great deal in the 1991 Lok Sabha elections.

The next phase of the campaign for the demolition of Babri Masjid and construction of Ram mandir at Ayodhya was set in November 1992. Several hundreds of kar sevaks from various castes including the OBCs, Dalits and tribals were deputed from Gujarat for Ayodhya. The Sangh Parivar called for a 'Dharma Yudha' (holy war) on 6 December 1992, and projected the cause as a matter of do or die in Ayodhya. In December 1992, the VHP not only published posters but also brought advertisements in the newspapers appealing people to be ready for holy war for the construction of Ram mandir. It also said:

Apani apani hesiyat sabko dikhadi jayegi
Delhi me sonewaloki nind uda di jayegi
Sar uthake hi hame rehna hai Hindustan me
Sar uthane ki jo hai kimat chukai Jayegi.
[Everyone will be shown their place,
Those who are sleeping in Delhi,
Their sleep will be disturbed,
We have to live in Hindustan with respect, we will pay
the price for maintaining our dignity.]

Walls were painted with slogans to raise Hindu militancy, calling for a Dharma Yudha and abusing Muslims. *Garva Se Kaho Hum Hindu Hai* (Say with pride that I am Hindu), *Ek Do Babari Masjid Tod Do* (Demolish Babri mosque), and *Muslim Babar ki Aulad* (Muslims are progenies of Babar, who was an invador) were common slogans. In the rallies organized by VHP, people were told:

Hinduoki katal karneka farman aya hae dekho
Delhi me firse Mughal shasan aya hae.
[There is a dictate to murder Hindus, see, once again Mughal rule has come to Delhi.]

Following the demolition of the Babri Masjid communal riots took place on a large scale in different parts of Gujarat. They were most intensive in Surat, continued intermittently for nearly six months and claimed more than 200 lives. The whole of 1993 was an emotionally highly charged year, a fact that undoubtedly helped the BJP to sweep the State Assembly elections in 1995.

It may be immaterial whether these communal riots were engineered in all details or not by certain parties or groups, but it is certain that widespread anti-Muslim mobilization was effectively carried out prior to the riots by the BJP and other organizations of the Sangh Parivar through fiery speeches, slogans, processions and public meetings. Anti-Muslims passion clearly worked in favour of the BJP in elections and in the process of recruiting cadres. During this campaign, no dissenting voices, neither within the party nor outside it, were tolerated. Critics of communal politics and of the Ram mandir issue were ridiculed, harassed and occasionally physically assaulted. No discussion was possible with those—often petty businessmen and unemployed youths—who were in the forefront of this rather fanatic campaign. They had no inhibitions regarding the use of any means to intimidate their enemies—largely Muslims but also those Hindus who held different views on Hinduism. Moreover, in the riots and in the Ram mandir campaign organizations like the VHP, Bajrang Dal, Shiv Sena, Bhavani Sena and RSS played a leading role and the BJP often had little control over these organizations. The larger agenda of the Sangh Parivar was to invigorate and rejuvenate 'our traditional Hindu culture'. The RSS and VHP consider themselves to be in a commanding position in the larger society, and as

protectors of morality and religion. They also assume the responsibilities as torch-bearers and guides for party activists in order to
maintain their hegemonic position within the larger movement.

HINDUTVA AND CASTES

Communal riots arouse emotions and mobilize one community
against the 'others' in the streets. But hysterical emotional outburst
expressed in rioting situation can hardly be sustained for long and
cannot override other aspects of life. Passions may facilitate
electoral politics but cannot in themselves win elections where
voters also consider socio-economic issues and the ability of
governance of various parties. Electoral politics requires an organizational set up and worked-out programmes to resolve the day-
to-day problems of the voters. The Jana Sangh and RSS were aware
of the limitations as well as the advantages of communal riots.
Therefore, from the beginning they paid attention to the building
up of the party organization.

The feudal agrarian structure and the conservative character of
social life of Saurashtra was conducive to the efforts of Jana Sangh
at building an organizational network. Saurashtra, i.e. peninsular
Gujarat, was fragmented into 499 politico-administrative units—
including small states, estates and *jagirs* before their integration into
the Indian Union in 1948. Rajputs constituted the majority of the
chieftains and petty rulers of various states. They considered
themselves to be the owners of the land. Kanabis, now known as
Patidars, Kolis and others were tenants on the land. After the
integration of the princely states and subsequent enactment of
legislation which abolished the *zamindari* system and its interme-
diaries, Rajputs lost their political as well as economic power. They
were, therefore, against the Congress party which was responsible
for land reforms as well as the moving force behind consolidating
a democratic political system. Rajput organizations were formed
in order to launch direct actions against the state and to fight
elections but the results were not encouraging. Several Rajput
leaders realized that they could not survive in politics merely on
the basis of their caste which does not have any numerical strength
but mainly an aura of past glory. A few of these notables joined
the Congress and some joined the Swatantra Party in the early
1960s. The ideology of the Jana Sangh did attract some but the

party was at an incipient stage and could not promise immediate access to power.

The Jana Sangh fought all elections in the 1950s but its performance was poor and it could hardly secure even one per cent of the votes. However, its political clout began to develop in the 1960s under the leadership of Harisinh Gohil, a Rajput from Saurashtra, who became the president of the party in early 1960s. The Jana Sangh captured 21 out of 25 seats of the Botad municipality in Saurashtra in 1965, and the party opened its account in the State Legislative Assembly by capturing the Rajkot seat in the 1967 elections. Five years later, with the decline of the Swatantra party the tally of assembly seats of the Jana Sangh increased to three.

After the Navnirman movement in1974, the Jana Sangh consolidated its base in urban areas, Rajkot, Ahmedabad and Vadodara. It captured 18 seats in the 1975 elections and became a coalition partner of the Janata Morcha in the United Front government. The Jana Sangh was then rechristened the BJP in 1980, and it slowly developed a strategy for broadening its base among different castes in Gujarat.

One of the important strategies of the BJP has been to spread Hindutva ideology and forge unity among Hindus. Such unity is not possible without mobilizing backward castes, Dalits and tribals. In the BJP's discourse, the theme of Hindu unity is harped upon and concern for the deprived communities is often expressed. For the VHP 'Hindu' refers to nationality; it is not a *majahab* sect or opinion. The VHP argues that 'those who believe themselves to be Hindus are also Hindus'. The theme of unity among the Hindus is repeatedly found in *Vishva Hindu Samachar,* the organ of the Gujarat unit of VHP edited by K. K. Shastry, an ex-President of the Gujarat Sahitya Parishad and receiver of the title of Vidya Vachaspati (a pre-eminent learned person). The journal often exhorts its readers: 'All Hindus should unite against *vidharmis* (people of other religions, obviously a reference to Muslims). Outmoded feudal values still prevail in our villages which have kept the caste pollution intact and thus resulted in fraction within the Hindufold. Savarna (non-Dalit castes) Hindus should now become alert and not widen the gap between the castes, they must compromise with Dalits and not continue to remain selfish.'

The Bharat Sevashram (BS) and Hindu Milan Mandir (HMM), both started in the 1920s and working on an all-India scale, have been active in Gujarat since the early 1970s. Besides undertaking activities to unite various sects and organizing Ganesh festivals, they carry out welfare and relief measures among the backward castes. Although they invite political leaders of all parties to their functions, they are ideologically close to the VHP, they subscribe to the theory of Hindu rashtra and share a platform with the BJP on the Ramjanmabhoomi issue. During the 1991 Lok Sabha and the 1995 Assembly elections, the leaders of these organizations issued a public appeal to Hindus to vote for that party which works to protect their interests.

The main thrust of the activities of both organizations is to build unity and harmony among the upper- and lower-caste Hindus. It is argued that despite the fact that the Hindu samaj is several times more powerful than that of the Muslims, it suffers humiliation and discredit because of its lack of internal cohesion, community feelings and faith in religion among the members. The organizations reject the notion that Shudras occupy an inferior and degraded position, and although they do not reject the caste system they call for cooperation and unity of upper and lower castes for the protection of the Hindu dharma and the Hindu samaj.

According to these organizations, the low-caste Hindus are hard working, strong and able but bear much suffering. 'Because of their numerical strength, they are truly the spinal cord of the Hindu jati (race). Lakhs and crores of these people are getting dissociated from the Hindu samaj because they are humiliated and looked down upon. As a result, the Hindu jati is becoming weak and powerless,' it is argued. The backward castes are seen as the real Kshatriyas, i.e. the warriors who protected the Hindu samaj in the ancient period against all calamities, aggressions and shocks. The Hindu jati can only become strong by uplifting the lower castes who should be brought forward by imparting knowledge to them in ethics, good behaviour, education and other fields. 'They have to be made human beings in the true sense of the term (sic!)' these proponents of the Hindu unity argue.[3]

Many of the OBCs, particularly Kolis, Machchis and several artisan castes have often followed the path of sanskritization for upward mobility by imitating customs and rituals followed by the upper castes. In the past, process of sanskritization was encouraged,

[3] Shah, Ghanshyam, 'The BJP and Backward Castes in Gujarat', *South Asian Bulletin*, 14(1) 1994.

facilitated and legitimized, not only by the British colonial rulers, but also by nationalist social and religious reformers. It has continued in post-independent India but with notable differences. It is no longer an imitative process as it was in the past in which the upper castes remained the model to be followed. Now, lower-caste groups are increasingly in competition with the upper castes and desire to replace and defeat them. In this process, the lower-caste Kolis do not find it insulting to be called Koli. What they want is respect and dignity but without challenging the caste framework. They not only want equality with those who are presently above them in the hierarchical social and ritual order, but they also wish to replace them. Especially the urban middle class among Dalits and the OBCs have education and somewhat improved economic conditions, and they want *swaman*, i.e. self-respect and dignity, as well as status and recognition from the larger society.

The quest of Kolis to be Kshatriyas has been used by Rajputs who formed the Kutchcha, Kathiawar, Gujarat Kshatriya Sabha in 1947, which later, in 1950, was confined to the Gujarat region only and called the Gujarat Kshatriya Sabha. The Rajputs of Kutchcha and Kathiawar were at this time not willing to align themselves with Kolis, even less to accept the Koli claims to the Kshatriya status. They organized the Suddha (pure) Rajput Samaj, which, however, did not acquire political significance but merely articulated a certain sentimental longing for the past. Political-minded Rajputs who realized the importance of numbers in electoral politics, began to focus on how they could broaden their base. For them, Patidars who gained land from them and opposed Rajputs during the freedom movement, appeared to be the real adversaries, rather than the Kolis. Patidars were also the rivals of Kolis, particularly in central and north Gujarat, where Patidars encroached on the Koli land and reduced them to the status of labourers or tenants. Thus, for both Rajputs and Kolis, Patidars seemed to be a common enemy. Further, both groups needed each other: Kolis aspired for the Kshatriya status and political power; and Rajputs were in need of widening their support base to counter the dominant Patidar caste. In the 1950s a politically active Rajput said:

By accepting Thakardas (Kolis of central Gujarat) as Kshatriyas, many of my jati-fellows have cut off relations with me...nevertheless, it is necessary to accept them as Kshatriyas. (why?) In the new political system we lost land, property and privileges. Now we can get importance only through our numerical force. Though I do not like the adoption, I accept it on political grounds only. This is the only way of getting importance.[4]

For the Gujarat Kshatriya Sabha (GKS) leaders there was no contradiction between unity and interests of their caste and that of the Hindu religion. With their glorious past and separate cultural identity, they consider themselves to be the protectors of Hindu religion and culture. While mobilizing Kshatriyas and building the organization, the leaders invoked traditional symbols like sword, saffron-colour flag and turban; and revived rituals and festivals. One of the leaders said, 'Goddess Bhavani is displeased with us because we are not defending Hindu religion. Therefore we should worship the sword.'[5] The BJP and Sangh Parivar also invoked such symbols and rituals. One finds, therefore, a great deal of similarity between the language of the GKS and that of the BJP, though the former supported various political parties, such as the Congress in the 1950s and 1970s, the Swatantra Party in the 1960s and the BJP in the late 1980s. In fact, the BJP leaders formed the Kshatriya Sabha as alternative to the Congress dominated GKS in the early 1980s. Shankarsinh Vaghela, then the president of the BJP, was the architect of the pro-BJP Kshatriya Sabha. Recently Vaghela asserted that, 'OBCs supported the BJP because of me. I can cite so many instances when Dalits and OBCs extended support to me and my leadership.'[6]

Besides wooing the OBCs, the BJP also mobilized among Dalits and the tribals. The RSS floated the organization *Samajik Samrasata Manch* (SSM), i.e. Social Assimilation Platform, to attract followers of Ambedkar and other Dalits for the purpose of extending Hindu unity. The organization was launched on 14 April 1983, the birthday of both Dr Ambedkar and Dr Hedgewar (the founder of the RSS). Dr Hedgewar, according to the proponents of the SSM, did not support caste and class divisions. Caste-based divisions should be given up or ignored: 'We are one'. He emphasized: 'We are Hindus, where is untouchability? For us all are Hindus and nothing else. There is no varna of the Chaturvarna or of caste. Today we have only one varna and jati, that is Hindu.' The RSS

---

[4] Shah, Ghanshyam, *Caste Association and Political Process in Gujarat* (Bombay: Popular Prakashan, 1974).

[5] Ibid.

[6] *Frontline*, 20 September 1996.

leader underlined the inculcation of brotherhood among all Hindus and asserted that society survives on the basis of person-to-person bonds.

According to the promoter of the SSM, the central thrust of Ambedkar's ideology is dharma. Ambedkar was a strong critic of the Brahmin caste (not brahminism) that exploited society in the name of religion. But according to the RSS leader Dattopant Thengadi, Brahmins were to blame for the state of affairs and not the religion. Giving a twist to Ambedkar's decision to adopt Buddhism, it was asserted that Dr Ambedkar did not accept Islam or Christianity because he feared those religions would make people anti-national. With such assertions, the RSS tries to support its position that the true Indian nationalist only can be one whose *punyabhumi*, i.e. holy land is India. To strengthen this argument further the RSS quotes Ambedkar, thus: 'I would support a movement for the saffron flag.' Ambedkar's 'Thoughts on Pakistan' are also highlighted to show that he was anti-Muslim. According to the RSS' interpretation, Ambedkar believed that as long as a Muslim believes himself to be a Muslim, he cannot become an integral part of Hindustan. Besides, the RSS believes that aggressiveness is part and parcel of the Muslim culture and that Muslims misuse the weakness of the Hindu samaj. Such a situation, according to the SSM, calls for assimilation of Dalits into the mainstream of Hindu society and the nation.[7] In the 1980s, the BJP supported the protests made by Dalits against the atrocities committed by the upper castes. It also organized processions in several district headquarters and submitted memoranda to the collectors urging them to give protection to Dalits. The party organized a *Nyaya Yatra*, i.e. a pilgrimage for justice, which began on Ambedkar's birth day, 6 December 1995, and ended on Vivekananda's birth day, 12 January 1996. A group of party workers toured 118 taluks and 15 districts covering 26,000 km in 38 days. The RSS, VHP and BJP also organized relief camps and distributed foodgrains, medicines and clothes in tribal areas during the drought of 1985–6. Later, the party made special efforts to recruit Dalits, tribals and OBCs for kar seva in Ayodhya, and for the various processions organized in connection with the Ram Shila programmes.

[7] Thengadi, Dattopant, *Samajik Samrasta* (Ahmedabad: Samajik Samrasta Manch, 1994).

Shankarsinh Vaghela—who is a Rajput by caste but has cultivated close relationship with the Thakurs, other Koli castes from
northern Gujarat and Panchamahals—was the president of the
Gujarat unit of the BJP for nearly ten years throughout the 1980s.
He was succeeded by Kashiram Rana from south Gujarat, belonging to another OBC community. The party formed Harijan and
Vanjati (tribals) cells in 1980 in order to take up the problems of
these social groups. A number of Dalits and tribal leaders were not
only recruited by the party but were also given important positions
in its organization. One of the Dalit leaders, who has imbibed
middle class values, but claims to be radical in his ideology said:

The BJP subscribes to brahminical ideology but the Congress is in practice
no way different. Moreover I worked in the Congress for more than ten years
but I did not get a position whereas the BJP has given me a party position.[8]

There is a number of such individuals from the Dalit, tribal and
OBC communities who did not support the party's ideology of
Hindu unity, except its anti-Muslim component, and who were not
comfortable with the attitude of the upper-caste party bosses.
Nonetheless, they remained in the party because they got positions
which satisfied their desire for gaining some importance and
acceptance in the organization.

The BJP has frequently declared that it does not believe in caste
differentiation. But at the same time, it maintains that the varna
system is an ideal Hindu social order from the point of view of
division of labour and social harmony. Moreover, it does not
oppose caste practices in day-to-day social behaviour. The leaders
have no inhibitions in sponsoring and attending caste organizations
and their functions in which distinct caste pride is articulated. Most
of the BJP leaders, not to speak of the VHP leaders, do themselves
adhere to caste rules and observe rituals in social and religious
functions in which a hegemony of brahminical practices, and
notions of purity and pollution, are often strictly maintained.
'After all, there is something like blood and *sanskar*, i.e. cultural
heritage and we have to have marriage relationship within castes.
Norms of caste have to be respected,' said a district level BJP leader.
He was echoing the views of many of his party colleagues. Except

---

[8] Shah, Ghanshyam, 'Tenth Lok Sabha Elections: BJP's Victory in Gujarat',
Economic and Political Weekly, 16(51), 21 December 1991.

repeating that 'we do not believe in caste differentiation' the party does not seem to have any strategy for eliminating them.

The party did give weightage to caste in selecting party candidates in Lok Sabha as well as Vidhan Sabha elections. It fielded between 30 to 35 per cent candidates belonging to the OBCs in the last three Vidhan Sabha elections in Gujarat. Moreover, the party has put the Dalit, tribal and OBCs members in the forefront in various campaigns. But, at the same time, the party was never strongly in favour of job reservations for the OBCs, SCs, and STs. Upper-caste BJP members, like their caste fellows outside the party, complained about the Congress 'giving too much importance and favour' to the SCs, STs, and OBCs. In informal conversations they look down upon backward castes and many of them regard the lifestyle of the lower castes as immoral and unbecoming. A strong supporter of the BJP and Hindutva said, that 'next to the Muslims, backwards are responsible for most of the problems of our society.'[9] These views are shared by the many upper-caste members of the BJP who also control and dominate the party organization.

In 1991, as many as 63 per cent of the state and district level leaders were from the upper strata of Hindus—Brahmin, Vania, Patidar and Rajput. At the state level, the SCs–STs constituted 14 per cent, while their proportion was only six per cent at the local levels. The party leaders drawn from the ranks of OBC-communities were 17 and 30 per cent at state and district levels, respectively.[10] Within the party, there is a vocal and assertive pressure for more political posts from the members of the OBC communities who are in relatively large numbers at the local level.

THE ELECTORAL SURGE

In the 1991 Lok Sabha and the 1995 Vidhan Sabha elections, the BJP did raise several socio-economic issues before the electorate, but its poll campaign was focused on two issues: firstly, on Hindutva and the construction of a Ram mandir in Ayodhya, and secondly, on the price rise and spread of corruption under the Congress rule. Highlighting Hindu *asmita*, i.e. culture and tradition

[9] Personal interview.
[10] Shukla, Gajendraprasad, *Rajkiya Pakshani Vicharsarani Ane teno Adhar*, (unpublished Ph.D. thesis) Surat: Centre for Social Studies, 1991.

the Sangh Parivar actively canvassed for the BJP. Various Hindu sects also extended support to the BJP and appealed to their devotees to vote for the party which would protect Hindu interests. The message was clear—only the BJP could do that. Soon, Jain *munis* were seen joining hands with Hindu *sadhus* and saints in support of the BJP candidates.

The VHP and other RSS front organizations insisted that the construction of the Ram mandir was a matter of right to correct the injustice done to them in the past by Muslim invaders. It was a question of faith and 'national pride', i.e. Hindu pride. Among many others, the saffron-clad *sadhvi*s, Ritambhara Devi and Uma Bharati who were both extremely popular orators, gave fiery speeches arousing emotions on the issue of Hindutva. Along with other leaders, like L. K. Advani and Murli Manohar Joshi, they declared in public meetings that no power in the country could stop the construction of the Ram mandir in Ayodhya. The VHP told people that voting for the BJP in the election was equivalent to performing kar seva. Services and sacrifices of the karsevaks in 1990 were glorified. The 'martyrs' of the Ayodhya demand, they said, 'to form the government of the Rambhaktas (i.e. devotees of Ram)'. The implication was that only the BJP candidates are the Rambhaktas and only they could perform the task of constructing the temple.

The BJP and Sangh Parivar leaders repeatedly asserted before and during the election campaigns that the Congress as well as the Janata Dal had pampered Muslims and other minorities, and that the country was now facing the problem of terrorism from Muslims in Kashmir and Sikhs in Punjab. The VHP claimed that the Congress would demolish the Somnath temple in Saurashtra which was once destroyed by Mohammad Ghazani. Thus, the effort of the VHP and its allies was to identify the BJP as the only Hindu party willing to protect the interests of Hindus in their 'homeland'.

The Congress appeared defensive and unable to counter the arguments of the BJP and VHP. It only asked people to vote against communalism. Some of the Congress leaders asserted that the BJP was not interested in constructing the Ram mandir, but only in capturing power. Such arguments had little effect, especially because they came from leaders whose greed for power was all too well known.

The BJP posed itself, with considerable success, as a cadre-based party whose leaders were honest and devoted to the national cause. They stood for moral values that would build 'Ram Rajya'. The voters were told that they had tried all parties and received nothing but unhappiness. These parties had not only failed to solve their problems, but had allowed the people's identity to be threatened in their own motherland. Various outfits of the party, such as peasants', labourers' and women's organizations, and cells for the Scheduled Castes and Scheduled Tribes tried to appeal to different sections of society, promising that the BJP would take their grievances seriously and protect their interests. During the Vidhan Sabha election campaign in 1995, the BJP promised that it would create a *bhay*, *bhook*, *mukta* (free from fear, hunger and corruption) Gujarat under its rule.

The BJP won 20 out of 26 Lok Sabha seats from Gujarat in 1991 and later swept the 1995 state assembly elections securing 43.3 per cent votes and 122 seats out of 182. The Congress was reduced to a minority with 44 seats, though securing as much as 33.6 per cent of the votes. The BJP increased its share of votes especially in urban areas, but also in the rural areas and in the predominantly tribal regions of the state. Its performance in urban constituencies was particularly impressive (see Table 8.1).

TABLE 8.1: Percentage of Votes Secured by the BJP and the Congress by Regions

Regions	Party	
	Congress	BJP
Gujarat	33.6	43.3
Tribals	34.1	39.1
Rural	34.8	41.4
Semi urban	33.6	45.9
Urban	30.2	53.2
Saurashtra	35.8	43.4
North Gujarat	31.8	46.9
Central Gujarat	34.1	36.4
South Gujarat	31.6	46.4

The BJP won the elections not just because of its Hindutva rhetoric, although it was important in raising emotions and creating the pro-BJP wave. An earlier study of the voting behaviour

carried out soon after the assembly elections in rural constituencies
showed that only one-tenth of the BJP voters in the sample
explicitly preferred the party because it was pro-Hindu.[11] The
majority of the BJP's supporters had far more mixed considerations
(see Table 8.2). The party's promise to curb corruption and prices,
and its image of being a disciplined party different from others
attracted nearly one-third of its voters in the sample. Eighteen per
cent of its voters had wanted to try out the BJP as an alternative
to other parties without being committed to the party's ideology.
The broader quest for an alternative to the Congress and the pro-
Hindu atmosphere created by the BJP and the Sangh Parivar
seemed to influence around one-fourth of its voters in the sample
who gave no specific reasons for their vote for the party. It is likely
that they favoured the BJP because others did so.

TABLE 8.2: Distribution of Respondents in Rural Areas by Party
Preference and Reasons

(in percentage)

Reasons	Congress	BJP
Pro-poor	37	4
Pro-Hindu	*	9
Hope to check prices/corruption	*	16
Good manifesto	*	4
No discrimination/secular	4	*
Old and experienced party/supporting the party from the beginning/family tradition	15	2
Good party/disciplined party/listens to us	16	18
Good candidate	*	4
Let us give them a chance/let us try again	10	18
No specific reason/because others supported	15	25
%	97	99
N =	426	493

* Less than 0.5 per cent.

During the 1980s, the BJP evolved various strategies to expand its
social base, and it did extend its influence to different sections of
society. It managed to win over large groups of the OBCs, Dalits

[11] See, Shah, Ghanshyam, 'BJP's Rise to Power', *Economic and Political Weekly*,
31(2–3), 13–30 January 1996. 1128 Voters from 27 villages in nine rural constituencies were interviewed in March–April 1995.

and tribals in rural areas. The OBC voters such as Kolis who constitute nearly 22 per cent of the population, were equally divided between the Congress and the BJP (see Table 8.3). The largest number of its supporters were from the upper and middle castes such as Brahmin, Vania, Rajput and Patidar. It also won over several upwardly mobile artisan castes such as Suthar, and Prajapati in rural constituencies, and in urban areas it succeeded in winning over large groups of the OBCs and Dalits.[12]

TABLE 8.3: Caste/Social Group by Party Preference in Rural Areas
(in percentage)

Castes/Social Groups	Congress-I	BJP	Others	Non-voters/ Refuse to Reveal Party Preference	N
Upper, and middle	20	67	3	10	319
Artisan	7	67	13	13	60
OBCs	38	38	10	14	344
Scheduled Castes	61	17	7	15	107
Scheduled Tribes	59	29	6	6	107
Muslims	47	7	–	6	239
Jains	37	50	13	–	8
Others	42	39	3	16	31

THE VAGHELA FACTOR

Power struggles within the party for various offices accelerated as the party's prospects for winning power in the state became bright after the 1991 Lok Sabha elections. Internal squabbles surfaced on the eve of the Vidhan Sabha elections in early 1995. There were three contenders for the office of Chief Minister: Keshubhai Patel, Shankarsinh Vaghela and Kashiram Rana. Keshubhai Patel represented the Patidar lobby, particularly Leo Patidars from Saurashtra, and the latter two represented backward castes. Though Vaghela belongs to the Rajput caste he has a strong base among the Kolis of north Gujarat. Each of them manoeuvred to see that members of their faction got nominated as the party candidates in the elections. The RSS and VHP pressurized the party to give tickets

---

[12] *Ibid.*

to their favourites. The dominant leaders of the RSS backed Keshubhai Patel as the Chief Minister and also L. K. Advani endorsed his candidature. In order to prevent Vaghela and Rana from competing with Patel, the central leadership in the BJP decided not to field them in the Vidhan Sabha elections as party candidates on the grounds that they were already members of Parliament.

With the support of Advani and the RSS, Keshubhai Patel became the Chief Minister in March 1995 and, a new chapter of the intraparty power struggle hence, opened, bringing home the hollowness of the BJPs claim to be a united and disciplined party with a culture different from that of the Congress. In less than a month's time, Patel was forced to expand his ministry to accommodate several aspirant members from the group of the BJP legislators. In order to consolidate his position, he slowly sidetracked supporters of the rival camps of Vaghela and Rana. The mastermind his strategy was Narendra Mody, a RSS leader in Gujarat who gave directives on several matters and enjoyed considerable influence in the government. The remote control of Mody over the functioning of the government was resented among party cadres and dissatisfaction increased in the ranks of the party; dividing party workers into the RSS and non-RSS factions, a divide which to a large extent coincided with the cleavage between Patidar and OBC factions. The dissident OBC leaders felt increasingly frustrated and humiliated; they alleged that the party was controlled by Patidars and a few self-righteous RSS leaders. The fact that their grievances were ignored by the central leadership only added fuel to the fire. The situation grew into a dramatic revolt by Vaghela and his supporters against the government in September 1995. Vaghela airlifted 47 MLAs to Khajuraho in Madhya Pradesh and asserted that Keshubhai Patel no longer enjoyed the support of the majority of the members of the party. The unorthodox manoeuvre aimed at unseating Patel. The RSS leaders considered Vaghela's action as unethical and one that amounted to a serious breach of the party discipline. They demanded his expulsion from the party even if that would result in the loss of power in the state. Supporters of Keshubhai Patel, mainly Patidars, saw the entire revolt as an anti-Patidar conspiracy. Leo-Patidars of Saurashtra and central Gujarat closed their ranks to fight back at the Kshatriya and OBC lobbies, thus recasting the traditional rivalry between Patidars and Rajputs-cum-Kolis.

Later, after the high drama the party back-tracked somewhat, and a compromise was reached thanks to the intervention of Atal Bihari Vajpayee and other pragmatists. Vaghela was persuaded to put down the banner of revolt, Patel stepped down for 'the sake of the party', and Suresh Mehta, a compromise candidate, was appointed as the chief minister. In order to accommodate different factions, a big ministry with more than 45 members was formed. But that did not satisfy everyone, and several party members immediately joined the race for positions as chairpersons of various boards and committees in the state government.

The patch-up did not last long. Keshubhai Patel and his supporters were deeply hurt and only waited for their turn to take revenge. The RSS and some leaders of the VHP began to humiliate Vaghela and his supporters at various levels. A battle between both the factions called Khajuriya (rebels) and Hajuriya (loyalists) was fought openly in the Lok Sabha elections of May 1996. Though Shankarsinh Vaghela initially did not want to contest elections for the Parliament, he eventually did so under the imposition of directives from the party leadership. A section of VHP sadhus under the leadership of Sant Avichaldasji (though sadhus renounce their caste, he was incidentally a Patidar) made all efforts to see that Vaghela and his associates got defeated. Vaghela mobilized other sadhus to counter them, and Patidars from Saurashtra residing in Surat launched campaign against Kashiram Rana who was the party candidate from that constituency.

Vaghela lost the election from the Godhara constituency. His defeat was hailed by both the VHP and RSS functionaries and Keshubhai Patel's supporters as their moral victory, and it was reported that sweets were distributed in the party's office in Ahmedabad when the result arrived. However, such acts did not receive adverse criticism as breach of party discipline from the party leadership at the national level.

Further, the same group stripped naked and severely beat Atmaram Patel, one of the senior supporters of Vaghela from north Gujarat at a public meeting at Gandhinagar. Some other prominent leaders of the dissident group were also systematically identified and assaulted. Various evidence suggests that the attacks 'were pre-planned and sanctioned by someone fairly high up in the party hierarchy.'[13] Similar incidents, though on a smaller scale, took place at a public meeting in Surat where Kashiram Rana and his followers were attacked. The *modus operandi* of the disturbance in the Gandhinagar meeting was in many ways similar to what is often practised during communal riots. Vaghela demanded action against all the workers who had attacked Atmaram Patel, but it was not contemplated seriously. Moreover, Kashiram Rana was unceremoniously removed from the presidentship of the BJP state unit and replaced by a supporter of Keshubhai Patel from Saurashtra.

The public humiliations of Vaghela and his associates continued without interference from the central leadership who were either helpless or were directly backing the Hajuriyas and the VHP leaders in their efforts to oust Vaghela from the party. In order to assert his position, Vaghela eventually formed *Mahagujarat Ashmita Manch,* a platform designed to assert the identity of local leaders and traditions. He spoke out against the centralized power structure of the party and the partisan attitude of the party leadership in Delhi. A rally was organized on 20 August to demonstrate his strength but the BJP expelled him from the party two days before the date of the proposed rally. At the rally, Vaghela declared the formation of the Rashtriya Janata Party (RJP).

Later, a high drama took place in the assembly between the BJP legislators and the rebel MLAs whose number was 48. The outcome was that the BJP lost power and Shankarsinh Vaghela formed a new government with the support of the Congress. Six months later Vaghela also got elected as a member of the Vidhan Sabha from Palanpur constituency in north Gujarat. His old foe, Narendra Mody, was put in charge of the BJP's election campaign in order to see Vaghela defeated. To this end the BJP sought support of different castes and once again raised the issue of Hindutva. The BJP campaigners depicted Vaghela as a traitor and an immoral person; the VHP sadhus and RSS volunteers camped there for several days and campaigned against him. The election battle in Palanpur was in many ways a battle between Hinduism and castes, a battle that the BJP lost. Vaghela tried with some

[13] *Times of India* (Ahmedabad), 23 May 1996.

success to emerge as the leader of the OBCs in Gujarat; the
Congress is worried about losing its support base among these
groups, and the BJP is forced into a rethinking of the future balance
between the party's mobilization strategies bent on religious and
communal sentiments, and those aiming at mobilization through
caste alliances.

CONCLUSION

In spite of various ideological efforts towards rejuvenating Hinduism, stressing Hindu unity and the eradication of caste-based
hierarchical social divisions, along with a protracted campaign for
the Ram mandir and the accompanying bloody rounds of anti-
Muslim communal riots involving all strata of Hindus, the significance of caste distinctions and caste loyalties among the Hindus
has not receded. Caste still remains the first and primary symbol
of identity for most Hindus. For many, caste identity is not just
notional and remote from day-to-day material interests, it is linked
with their economic status and availability of opportunities for
livelihood. It is more so in the case of the deprived groups such
as the OBCs and Dalits.

This does not mean, however, that religious community identity as a Hindu does not exist at one level of collective consciousness. It does. Identifications with a particular caste as well as with
the wider Hindu community do coexist. The efforts of Sangh
Parivar and various religious sects aiming at reviving and reforming
Hinduism have certainly contributed to the moulding of this larger
Hindu consciousness. In Gujarat, the BJP has effectively activated
this consciouness and has thereby enabled the party to win
elections. To some extent the party also built its political success
upon various strategies that sought to establish it among the OBC
and Dalit communities. However, this following is neither stable
nor strong, and even less so after the exit of Shankarsinh Vaghela.

One clear lesson one can learn from the career of the BJP in
Gujarat is that when conflict on secular interests, economic
opportunities, education, political position, etc. arise between
dominant upper and middle castes and deprived castes, the pan-
Hindu consciousness tends to recede. The upper- and middle-caste
members of the BJP still dominate its apparatus and constitute a

hard core that resists the late comers from the Dalit and OBC communities. Whether in the name of values and principles, or invoking efficiency and seniority, this core group creates numerous obstacles for a true integration of the OBCs and other lower-caste members into the party structure. Hereby, the BJP also cuts itself off from influencing and shaping the dynamic political ascendency of the lower castes which is so decisive for Gujarat's political future.

Ψ

9

BJP and the Challenge of Factionalism in Madhya Pradesh

CHRISTOPHE JAFFRELOT

In a general sense, factionalism can be defined as a competition for power between organized groups within a political party.[1] In his typology, which is more specific, Bruce Graham differenciates factionalism from 'sectarian conflicts' (based on opposition of different doctrines) and 'sectionalism' (contest between representatives of different social groups), mainly on the basis of its *personal* character.[2] He convincingly argues that the process of factionalism

> depends above all on personal commitment, and for this reason recruitment to a faction takes the form of a series of one-to-one engagements between individuals: in its simplest form, therefore, a faction consists of a leader and a diversity of followers, each of whom has formed a vertical tie with him and offers his personal loyalty in return for some specific promise of future recompense.[3]

Factionalism is a major element of Indian politics since it was already affecting the Congress before the Independence. In one of his first studies of Congress factionalism in Uttar Pradesh in 1964, Paul Brass identifies the following set of features as being inherent

---

[1] See, for instance, Beller, D. C. and F. P. Belloni, 'Party and Faction: Modes of Political Competition', in F. P. Belloni and D. C. Beller (eds), *Faction Politics: Political Parties and Factionalism in Comparative Perspective*, Santa Barbara, ABC-Clio, 1978, p. 419.

[2] Graham, B. D., *Representation and Party Politics* (Oxford: Blackwell, 1993), p. 156.

[3] Ibid., p. 156.

to this phenomenon: factional groups had a 'predominantly personal nature';[4] alliances and secessions between and/or within factions were very volatile; factions were organized on a vertical basis as 'very loose coalitions of local, district faction leaders, tied together at the state level partly by personal bonds of friendship, partly by caste loyalties, and most of all by political interests.'[5] Apparently, the two major criteria defining factionalism in Uttar Pradesh, as well as in theory, are its personal character and its vertical arrangement relying on clientelistic relations.

These characteristics are also in evidence in the Congress party in Madhya Pradesh. The factions headed by Arjun Singh, the Shukla brothers, Madhav Rao Scindia, Digjivay Singh and others have been illustrating this pattern for years. More recently, the notion of factionalism has begun to be used by press reporters in reference to the other main party in the state, the Bharatiya Janata Party (BJP).

The BJP, and before it the Jana Sangh, always claimed that they were parties with a difference as far as their cohesion was concerned. They had certainly inherited a strong sense of discipline from the Rashtriya Swayamsevak Sangh (RSS). Indeed, in Madhya Pradesh, as elsewhere, the Jana Sangh and the BJP developed according to a party-building pattern which tends to restrain factionalism. But the 1990 accession to power of the BJP favoured the exacerbation of dissensions probably to a larger extent than in any other state unit of the party (with the exception of Bihar) at that time. While containing an element of factionalism these dissensions seemed to be of a different nature since the opponents to the dominant group were not always headed by a definite candidate to power nor were they vertically organized. Nevertheless, the criteria of factionalism came gradually to be fulfilled to such an extent that the 'sangathanist' party-building pattern was challenged. In the process the development of groupism as well as the rebellion of a large number of activists against their leaders brought into question the traditional coherence of the BJP.

---

[4] Brass, Paul, 'Factionalism and the Congress Party in Uttar Pradesh', reprinted in Paul Brass, *Caste Faction and Party in Indian Politics* (Delhi: Chanakya, 1984), p. 143.
[5] Ibid., p. 144.

FROM SANGATHANISM TO GROUPISM

The Sangathanist Party-building Pattern

While the 'aggregative' party-building pattern (mainly represented by the Congress in India) consists in obtaining the support of local notables heading 'vote banks', the Jana Sangh leaders and subsequently the BJP leaders, in accordance with their RSS background, put the emphasis on the formation of a strong organization (*sangathan*). The keystone of this undertaking was the corps of *sangathan mantris* (organizing secretaries), very often RSS *pracharaks* deputed by the mother organization to its political front.

In Madhya Pradesh, the network of sangathan mantris of the BJP was initiated in the early 1950s, at the time of the Jana Sangh. Its main builder was Kushabhau Thakre who for forty years remained the most important figure in the state party. Thakre had first operated as an RSS pracharak in the 1940s in Ratlam, Chittor and Mandsaur districts. He had served as a sangathan mantri for the Jana Sangh from 1951 in Malwa and 1953 in the State of Madhya Bharat, today the western province of Madhya Pradesh. He was replaced in this region by Moreshwar Rao Gadre and then Pyarelal Khandelwal (two other pracharaks) when he became sangathan mantri in 1956 for the whole of the newly-established state of Madhya Pradesh. The state sangathan mantri, an ex-officio member of the party's National Council, was then the most powerful officer in the state unit of the Jana Sangh. By virtue of his position Kushabhau Thakre exercised virtual command over the Madhya Pradesh unit of the Jana Sangh and, eventually over the state unit of the BJP.

His party-building technique was similar to that used by the RSS in extending its organization. His priority was to establish a dense network of local committees (and even village-based power centers—*shakti kendras*) by utilizing the existing RSS network and sending sangathan mantris into the countryside (in the same way as the first RSS pracharaks were sent out from Nagpur). For instance, in the 1960s, Gadre was sent to Chhattisgarh (where he died during the Emergency) and Narayan Prasad Gupta to Mahakoshal. A pracharak from Bhopal, Gupta built bases particularly in Jabalpur, Sagar and Betul districts.[6]

---

[6] Interview with N. P. Gupta, 17 November 1990, Bhopal.

Certainly, the Jana Sangh unit in Madhya Pradesh resorted to alliances with the notables and princes. In 1966, the Jana Sangh made a pact with the Rajmata of Gwalior, Vijaya Raje Scindia, who soon thereafter became an all-India figure of the party and then of the BJP. Despite this use of a more aggregative method of party-building, Thakre, Gadre, Khandelwal and Gupta held tightly in their own hands the reins of the Jana Sangh. The priority given to organizational affairs in the RSS combine, at least in the 1950s–60s, enabled the sangathan mantris to remain the most important figures in the party, taking precedence not only over notables and former princes but also over activists involved in elections and power politics in terms of ministerial responsibilities.

Indeed the main asset of the sangathanist pattern of party-building lies in the dual power structure, comprising organizational leaders and electing, more public figures. The 'infrastructure' is mainly embodied in the team of sangathan mantris headed by K. Thakre. Such men are not expected to face the electorate[7] or to assume ministerial responsibilities but rather to devote themselves exclusively to organizational work.[8] Their main task is to maintain the cohesion of the party and to mobilize it in the framework of the strategies shaped by the high command (or by themselves). In this perspective, they usually enforce a sense of discipline inherited from the RSS.

After Patwa had formed his government in 1990, the dual party structure was, in a sense, consummated by the formation of a cell, separate from normal political activity, which was designed to oversee the conduct of ministers. The key member of this 'core group' was Kushabhau Thakre, even though the Chief Minister usually took part in its meetings.[9] This arrangement should have helped the team of sangathan mantris to contain the development

---

[7] Kushabhau Thakre stood only twice in Khandwa—the first time during a critical by-election in 1979 which the Janata Party needed to win. N. P. Gupta contested elections in 1952, 1977 and 1980, and P. Khandelwal in 1989, 1991 and 1996.

[8] After the defeat of the BJP in the 1984 general elections (the party could not win a single seat in Madhya Pradesh), the organizational cadres initiated a new type of meeting which revealed the specificity of their task. The most important office-holders of the state BJP met at Gwalior in 1985 in order to analyse past mistakes and make plans for the future. Subsequently these 'Gwalior meetings' became an annual event. (Kushabhau Thakre, 'Madhya Pradesh Main Bhajpa Sarkar', *Swadesh Madhavi*, 19).

[9] Interview with Kushabhau Thakre, 11 August 1992, New Delhi.

of rivalries among the office-holders involved in electoral and government politics but its efficiency was soon affected by the accession of the party to power.

Where are the Faction Leaders?

In 1990, three personalities who had each occupied the post of the chief minister during the Janata phase could be considered as rivals: Virendra Kumar Sakhlecha, Sunderlal Patwa and Kailash Joshi. These three belong to the category of the RSS members, seconded by the mother organization to the Jana Sangh to contest elections and, eventually, to assume ministerial responsibilities. Sakhlecha and Patwa joined the RSS in Mandsaur district in the early 1940s when Thakre was operating there as a pracharak. They were elected for the first time as MLAs in 1957 from Mandsaur district. Sakhlecha became the leader of the opposition in the Vidhan Sabha in 1962 and Deputy Chief Minister in the Samyukta Vidhayak Dal (SVD) government of 1967–9. Patwa acted as the Chief Whip of the Jana Sangh group from 1962–7. He was defeated in 1967 and 1972 at Manasa but became the General Secretary of the Janata Legislative party in 1977 after being returned from Mandsaur. In contrast to this, Joshi has remained an elected MLA since 1962, without a break, in the constituency of Bagli (Dewas district), where he had joined the RSS in 1943.[10] He became the Secretary of the Jana Sangh group in the Vidhan Sabha in 1970 and the leader of the opposition in 1972 when Sakhlecha's election to the Vidhan Sabha was questioned in court and he was accused of malpractices. In spite of this temporary setback, Sakhlecha's ability as an administrator was widely acknowledged within the party.

Tensions emerged between these three men in the late 1970s when the Janata Party was in the office. The rivalry between K. Joshi and V. K. Sakhlecha came to a head in 1977. It seems that Thakre wanted Sakhlecha as the Chief Minister, but the socialists in the Janata Party were in favour of Joshi, who was finally chosen. In January 1978, Joshi resigned and Sakhlecha succeeded him. Later on Sakhlecha took exception to his replacement in January 1980 by Patwa, who had kept aloof from the two previous governments. The antagonism between Sakhlecha and Patwa, who had originally worked together in Mandsaur district, intensified after cases of

[10] Interview with K. Joshi, 24 November 1989, Bhopal.

corruption were registered against the former in 1982 and the latter in 1984.[11] In 1984 Sakhlecha was suspended from the party membership—the rivalry between Patwa and him being one of the causes underlying this decision. In 1980 Patwa became the leader of the opposition in the Vidhan Sabha and then, in 1985, succeeded K. Joshi as the President of the BJP in the state, whereas Sakhlecha resented the fact that he had no post in the party apparatus.[12] Sakhlecha then set up his own party during the 1985 elections, but did not succeed in winning a single seat.

The failure of Sakhlecha in his efforts to attract followers from the ranks of the BJP is indicative of the limitations, in the context of such a party, of any personal, secessionist strategy and, by implication, of the non-fulfilment of one criterion of factionalism, the strength of the allegiance of followers to one or another rival leaders. To be sure, Sakhlecha and Joshi both tried to win over the largest number of followers through 'one-to-one' contact. However, building a personal network was difficult because the party was not structured along such lines. The activists were used to a majoritarian discipline and gave their allegiance to the organization personified by sangathan mantris, such as Thakre. In 1989, Sakhlecha applied for, and was granted, readmission to the BJP.

Joshi's evolution was somewhat similar. When in March 1990 Patwa was appointed the Chief Minister, Joshi refused to join the government. Eight months later, however, he agreed to accept the post of the Minister of Industry and Energy. Like Sakhlecha, he probably realized that by being outside the party or on its fringes he was losing his influence. The strength of men such as Sakhlecha and Joshi derived not so much from their personal appeal or following, but rather from a network of activists paying allegiance to organization leaders. In these circumstances, Sakhlecha and Joshi decided to fight Patwa from within.

In 1990 Sakhlecha, who was not given the party ticket for the Assembly election, contested the internal election for the party presidentship in Madhya Pradesh against Lekhiram Aggarwal, the 'official' candidate supported by Patwa and Thakre. A swayamsevak since 1946, Aggarwal was primarily promoted in the party's

[11] The editor of *The Hitavada* in Bhopal was approved of by Patwa in his campaign against Sakhlecha, whom he accused of land grabbing among other things.
[12] Interview with Sakhlecha, 12 October 1991, Bhopal.

hierarchy by Thakre and Patwa, probably because of his financial resources and influence in Bilaspur and Raipur divisions. In these areas where the BJP remained comparatively weaker, this business-man had big concerns, notably in the trade of the *tendu* leaves used in the making of *bidis*. In 1990, Sakhlecha received 68 votes from the local delegates as against 123 for Aggarwal (there were 132 abstentions). Hereafter, Sakhlecha became a member of the BJP State Executive Committee, where he pointed out the shortcom-ings in the performance of the government.

In 1993, K. Joshi took over from him as the main opponent to the Patwa camp at the time of party elections, which were to take place at the local level in late 1992 as provided for in the regular schedule, but which had been then delayed by six months follow-ing the Ayodhya events of December 1992. L. Aggarwal was again in the fray with the support of Patwa and Thakre. He polled 224 votes, while K. Joshi received the support of 98 delegates. While forming its executive committee, L. Aggarwal retained Joshi but dropped Sakhlecha. However, Joshi had actively contested the functioning of the Patwa government, if not publicly, at least from behind the scene. For instance, he was the first leader to write to Patwa to criticize the allotment of prime land at a throwaway price to 'friends' and sister organizations in Bhopal.[13]

At first sight, the fight between Patwa, Sakhlecha and Joshi illustrates a factional process which is commonplace in Indian politics, even though the latter two did not aim for the office of the chief minister and contented themselves with the party presidentship. However, we have already seen that personal allegiances, which are criteria of factionalism, were not observed since leaders such as Sakhlecha and Joshi had no strong personal appeal. Indeed, the rise of indiscipline in the BJP's Madhya Pradesh unit did not really work along the usual lines because of the party's 'dual structure'.

Sangathan Mantris as Group Leaders

Until the early 1990s, the fight between personalities did not matter very much because the leaders involved—Patwa, Joshi and Sakhlecha—did not belong to the organizational infrastructure of the sangathan mantris. The sangathan mantris remained united and

[13] *National Mail* (Bhopal), 25 November 1994.

could, therefore, cope with such personal rivalries. It is this very 'sangathanist' architecture which fissured in the early 1990s and nourished groupism.

The formation of the 'core group' signified a calling of the old collective mode of leadership into question. Senior leaders such as N. P. Gupta and P. Khandelwal were sidelined. What they resented most was the defence of Patwa and Aggarwal by Thakre after the electoral setback suffered by the BJP in 1991. The reversal (from 27 to 12 Lok Sabha seats) mainly occurred due to the voting pattern in the tribal areas and rural constituencies where the BJP's credibility had been eroded because the loan-waiving policy in favour of the peasants was restricted, for reasons of financial constraints, to debts up to Rs 10,000, while, during the election campaign, the party had promised to free all of the peasants of all their debts.[14]

After the 1991 elections, sangathan mantris such as N. P. Gupta and P. Khandelwal, who had coordinated the loan-waiving campaign in 1988–90, protested against the shortcomings of Patwa's policies.[15] Thakre's obstinacy in continuing to support Patwa can only be explained in terms of his personal relationship with him, since as a pracharak he had initiated him into the RSS forty-five years ago and had remained his mentor since then.[16] Another prominent sangathan mantri who had been deeply influenced by Thakre was Kailash Sarang. He supported Patwa, who had been in charge of the Bhopal office of the Jana Sangh between 1960–77 and was appointed as the Vice President of the BJP in Madhya Pradesh by L. Aggarwal in 1991, and then the Treasurer in 1993.[17]

Gupta and Khandelwal naturally resented the way they had been marginalized by Thakre and Sarang. In 1993 Gupta headed a petition campaign urging the partymen to elect Kailash Joshi as party president with whom he certainly aspired to establish the same kind of relationship Thakre entertained with Patwa (and Aggarwal). This was not really a case of factionalism because the groups involved were not headed by candidates to power positions:

[14] The negative impact of this policy has been acknowledged by Bherulal Patidar, the then chief of the Kisan Morcha of the BJP in Madhya Pradesh (Interview in Bhopal, on 17 February 1994).
[15] Interview with P. Khandelwal, 30 August 1992, Bhopal.
[16] Interview with Patwa, 17 February 1994, Bhopal.
[17] Interview with K. Sarang, 16 February 1994, Bhopal.

Thakre on the one hand and Gupta (in tandem with Khandelwal) on the other were more organization men. It was rather a case of 'groupism'. While this word is less precise, it is more relevant since it reflects the collective nature of the fight between teams of leaders and suggests pertinently that only a limited number of people were implicated in this fight. Indeed, the groups in question had few ramifications at the local level. The criterion of vertical linkages, therefore, was not fulfilled.

However, the impact of this division is not to be minimized. The confrontation between Gupta and Khandelwal on the one hand and Thakre and Sarang on the other indicated that the equilibrium of the whole sangathanist ordering was at stake. After the 1993 party elections, not only Sakhlecha but also Khandelwal and Gupta—who had been the state party vice presidents—were dropped by L. Aggarwal from the newly constituted 110 strong executive committee.

The marginalization of Khandelwal and Gupta was the touch-stone of a reaction from the high command and the RSS. In July 1993, Thakre was divested of the charge of the BJP in Madhya Pradesh. He was called to Delhi and instead given charge of the party's organization. Sunder Singh Bhandari was appointed to replace him. Simultaneously, Khandelwal was shifted to Haryana, where he became the organizing secretary of the state BJP unit. This surgical operation reflects the prime importance of the party cadre in the sangathanist system.

Thus, till 1993 the dissensions in the state BJP cannot be analysed purely in terms of factionalism because such a notion implies a struggle *between individuals to whom local activists pay allegiance*, which is not in evidence here. Certainly, Patwa, Sakhlecha and Joshi acted as rivals for the post of chief minister and their fight was contained for so long as organizational cadres were not involved. It was the decision of Khandelwal and Gupta to openly criticize Patwa which made the difference. It is difficult to speak of factionalism here because they did not try to rally local support and were not candidates to any official post. The so-called 'faction leaders' were not the important personalities. Patwa was largely a creation of Thakre and Sarang, while Sakhlecha and Joshi did not matter very much as compared to Gupta and Khandelwal, who enjoyed enough prestige and authority to question the dominant group's style of governance, and to ask for more power for their group rather than any particular post. Thus 'groupism' and rebellion appears to have been more important than 'factionalism'. However, inner conflicts became more profound in 1993 and took a more personal and factional turn. First, the transfer of Thakre led Patwa to come to the forefront as a group leader and contender for the party leadership. Second, as the party had fallen victim to the growing indiscipline at the local level, it became easier for state leaders to establish vertical links.

GROWING INDISCIPLINE AND FACTIONALISM

The Spread of Dissensions

As a cadre-based party the BJP relies more heavily on a network of activists than the 'aggregative parties', which cash in on the influence of local politicians and notables. Hence, the great impact of the way its top leaders alienated some of the grassroots workers when after the inception of the government, the ministers tended to become estranged from the activists. Their resulting discontent favoured the spread of indiscipline.

An interesting instance of conflict between local activists and party leaders who had become MPs or ministers took place in the heartland of the BJP, in Indore–Mhow. The Indore district BJP vice-president and in the city of Mhow the BJP president, along with hundreds of activists left the party because they resented the haughty attitude of Bherulal Patidar (the Panchayat minister and the MLA of Mhow) and Sumitra Mahajan, the Indore MP whom they accused of being indifferent to her party workers except at the time of the election campaign.[18]

Such criticisms were seldom seen as constructive by the ruling group who reacted with harshness. Its distance from the party workers contributed to the diffusion of groupism among local cadres and activists. Until then, groupism had been apparent only at the time of party elections when the members entitled to vote

[18] *National Mail*, 8 April 1991. A similar estrangement arose between local leaders and the Parliamentary Secretary, H. P. Garg in Rajgarh. K. Joshi and the BJP MP from Bhopal S. C. Varma attributed the 1991 setback to the failure to enthuse the party workers for closer rapport with the people at the grassroot level (Ibid., 20 June 1991). After the 1991 elections, local party cadres, including the General Secretary of the BJP in Khandwa district, demanded the resignation of Patwa and Aggarwal because of their 'utter neglect' of party workers (Ibid., 20 June 1991).

had to choose between two candidates. Now, opponents to the dominant group began to express themselves in ways other than playing the institutional rules. In September 1992, 71 MLAs were involved in a signature campaign against Patwa. Less than three months later, the state government was dismissed in the aftermath of the demolition of the Babri Masjid.

Electoral Damages

When elections were announced in September 1993 the BJP high command decided that Kushabhau Thakre would return to Bhopal for the time of this poll since he could assess the situation better than Bhandari. The party did not renominate 56 former MLAs, among whom one found signatories of the representation against Patwa. As a result of the ticket distribution a dozen rebels decided to contest as independents.

In Susner (Shajapur district), for instance, Haribhau Joshi, who had won the seats four times from 1957 onwards and had been one of the Janata Party Ministers in the state government in 1977–80, was denied the ticket because of his hostility to the dominant group; he contested as an Independent and in the bargain the BJP lost the seat. In Jagdalpur (Bastar district) Dineshkumar Kashyap, the outgoing MLA, whose father Baliram Kashyap—Tribal Welfare Minister who often opposed Patwa—was denied the ticket. He contested as an Independent and the Congress-I won the seat. In Narsingarh and Manasa the renomination of the outgoing MLAs led dissidents to contest (respectively on a Shiv Sena ticket and an Independent). In both the cases they prevented the BJP from winning otherwise secure seats. Such indiscipline, though minor as compared to the norm in the Congress ranks, was unprecedented in the state BJP party.

In addition, some party activists sabotaged the party campaign, like Sakhlecha in his traditional constituency of Jawad (Mandsaur district) where he had been denied nomination once more,[19] and where the Congress could eventually win the seat. Very often, the BJP workers refused to canvass for the official candidate because they disliked him. In Chhindwara, the local party activists strongly objected to the replacement of Chanderbhan Chandhury (Public

[19] Apparently, the leaders of the dominant group also tried to prevent K. Joshi from becoming a MLA. He won for the eighth time in Bagli with a small margin of about 400 votes.

Works Minister) by an RSS-backed candidate, who eventually lost. In Narsimhapur, the replacement of Uttam Lunawat (the outgoing MLA) by Kailash Soni, the BJP district president caused a similar reaction with the same result. In Itarsi, the replacement of Sita Sharma, the outgoing MLA, by Dushyant Gaur caused similar protests. Party workers also strongly resented the choice of the party nominee in Sarangpur. In Burhanpur (Khandwa district), where Muslims account for some 53,000 out of a total population of 122,000, the BJP nominated its only Muslim candidate, Abdul Rab. In reaction, local party workers persuaded Swami Umesh Muni—a *sadhu* from the Vishva Hindu Parishad—to file his nomination as an independent candidate, and he too won.

Besides the frustrations felt by party workers the BJP suffered from its recruitment of politicians less committed to Hindu nationalism and more alien to the RSS discipline. This recruitment can be explained from two points of view.

First, the BJP grew out of the sangathanist pattern of party-building. Since the development of the BJP network relied on dedicated but obscure activists, only few charismatic leaders and even popular figures had emerged in its ranks. Moreover, the main crowd pullers of the BJP in Madhya Pradesh remained two women, Uma Bharti and Vijaya Raje Scindia in the Gwalior region. Even at the local level, the party was thus in need of better-known people. Therefore, the BJP did not hesitate in giving a ticket to ex-Congressmen or ex-Janata Dal members wherever they had a personal following.

Secondly, in areas where the BJP sangathanist network was still weak, such as in a few districts of Chhattisgarh, Vindhya Pradesh and Mahakoshal, the party often had no option other than coopting local politicians and notables with no strong allegiance to the Hindu nationalist movement. Sometimes the two factors were superimposed. For instance, Ansuya Uikey, the BJP candidate for the Lakhnadon seat (Seoni district) in 1993 was a former Minister in the Arjun Singh government. She joined the BJP in 1990. Dr Ramesh Aggarwal, who had been a member of the Jana Sangh before shifting to the Janata Dal returned to the partyfold just before the 1993 election and was nominated from Khallari (Raipur district). Another former Janata Dal man, Chandramani Tripathi was given the ticket in the Mangawan constituency (Rewa district). Tarun Chatterji, a Congress-I MLA in 1980 left his party in 1987, became a Janata Dal MLA in 1990, and contested on the BJP ticket in Raipur in 1993. Bisen Yadav, who had contested on a Shiv Sena ticket in 1990 joined the BJP in 1993 and was nominated from Durg.

The new recruits did not show the same discipline and commitment to the party as old timers with an RSS background did. Most of those who were elected in 1990 left the BJP as soon as they were denied tickets and contested as independents candidates. Bhanwar Singh Porte, a tribal leader who had served as a cabinet minister in the Arjun Singh government, quit the Congress-I on the eve of the 1990 elections to join the BJP, which rewarded him with the rank of the Minister of State. When he was denied a ticket in 1993 he resigned, and decided to contest as an Independent from Bilaspur.

A somewhat similar case occurred in Vindhya Pradesh. Though Lokendra Singh, the scion of Panna royal family, was not really a new recruit as he had been elected as an MLA in 1977 and had become an MP in 1989. He resigned from the BJP because he disapproved of the turn taken by the Ayodhya movement and because the state government had not paid enough attention to his constituency.[20] Soon after, he joined the Congress-I and contested from Panna in 1993. These defections illustrate the risk of aggregating notables or members from the princely families who have no strong ideological commitments.

The nomination of candidates alien to the RSS or even to the BJP up to the last minute often antagonized old party workers or the local RSS cadres. For instance, in Pandhurna (Chhindwara district), the BJP candidate, M. Khawse, who had been elected as an Independent in 1985 and had joined the party in 1990, faced the opposition of the RSS. That was one of the reasons why he lost.

These instances reveal for the BJP the difficulties of expanding its base and, at the same time, maintaining unity in its ranks. The rise of indiscipline was one of the reasons for the BJP's setback at the time of the state election of 1993 when its number of seats fell from 219 to 117. The spread of these dissensions prepared the ground for factionalism since they lent themselves to be articulated along personal and vertical lines.

[20] Interview with Lokendra Singh, 30 October 1991, Panna.

Vertical Splits and Personal Allegiances

After the 1993 elections, the BJP National Executive requested the Madhya Pradesh party unit to promote new faces—something the Congress had just done by appointing Digvijay Singh to the post of chief minister. Thakre left the state, to become National General Secretary, and Patwa also withdrew from the party leadership. However, the party president, L. Aggarwal was still close to him and the leader of the opposition Vikram Verma was one of his protégés. Verma, who had been appointed after the MLAs were paraded before the central observers one by one and their opinion was sought (something unprecedented in the BJP that testifies the profound suspicion between the two groups), admitted that he worked under Patwa's guidance.[21] In fact Patwa appeared as the head of the dominant group after the transfer of Thakre: this was the first step towards the making of a pure faction. He directed the BJP campaign in two important by-elections which took place in June 1994 after Digvijay Singh resigned from his Lok Sabha seat of Rajgarh and contested the MLA seat of Chachoda, as required by his new function. P. Khandelwal, who had won the Rajgarh seat in 1989 and had again contested it in 1991, was not given the ticket.

The BJP lost in both cases with such large margins that Sunder Singh Bhandari was asked to submit a report on these results to the BJP's national convention in June 1994. The opponents of the ruling group naturally criticized the way the party campaign had been organized. Aggarwal submitted his resignation to the BJP president, L. K. Advani.

The high command replaced Aggarwal by Laxmi Narayan Pandey, the Mandsaur MP and the BJP Chief Whip in the Lok Sabha. For the first time, the state party president had not been elected but appointed from above. Pandey, while forming the State Executive, nominated opponents to the till then dominant group and left out the prominent leaders: Kailash Sarang was dropped whereas N. P. Gupta became the member of the State Executive again. Sakhlecha became a member of a kind of think-tank of the party. After a highly polemical exchange with him in the newspapers, Patwa decided to leave for the United States for two months on 29 September, although local elections were to take

---

[21] Interview with Vikram Verma, 17 February 1994, Bhopal.

place in November. Patwa's followers even more directly sabo-taged the BJP's candidatures to prove their point that the party could not do without them.

The lack of coherence in the state leadership favoured increasing indiscipline and even factional realignments at the local level during the municipal election campaign. In many places, party workers revolted against the selection of candidates by the party chiefs in Bhopal. In Betul districts eight candidates contested as BJP rebels against the official nominees, while senior local leaders resigned from the selection committee of the party out of disgust. In Jabalpur, eleven party activists were suspended because they worked against the official candidates. In Rajnandgaon, 17 activists were expelled because they decided to contest against the official candidates. This was also the case with eleven BJP men in Gwalior, two in Biaora, five each in Katni and Rewa. In Indore, L. N. Pandey issued show cause to four party workers who wanted to contest against official candidates. In all, more than 100 party workers were expelled before the elections.[22] In addition, some party workers revolted or refused to canvass. In Durg, the BJP district president made such an unpopular selection of candidates that party workers assaulted him; he had to be taken home under police protection. As a result, the list of BJP candidates could not be submitted in time.[23]

The Congress was similarly affected by indiscipline and crude factionalism. The list of official candidates could not even be finalized because the state leaders (principally the Shukla brothers and Arjun Singh) wanted larger shares for their own men. Finally, they proved wise enough to give up the idea of choosing official candidates. The State Congress-I simply did not distribute tickets for the elections to 17 municipal corporations and 92 municipal councils. Congressmen joined in the fray but without the party label. However, after the elections, the party chiefs recognized the winners from their ranks, and it then appeared that Congress had won the majority in most of the places. In contrast to the 1993 assembly elections when the BJP had performed remarkably well in urban constituencies, winning all the seats in Bhopal, Ujjain, Indore, Jabalpur and Raipur, in 1994 it won the majority only in

[22] *National Mail*, 23 November 1994.
[23] In addition to that the town BJP president contested as an Independent (Ibid, 15 November 1994).

Bhopal and Rajnandgaon. It lost Indore to a party rebel by one seat. Two rebel candidates were also elected in Gwalior where the election resulted in a hung Corporation.

The case of Bhopal is particularly interesting since the rivalry among the state leaders dominated the local politics. The situation was very tense during the election campaign because several senior BJP workers had not been selected as official candidates. When eleven of them, nonetheless, filed their nominations the party leaders expelled them.[24] Despite these infights, the party won 46 seats out of 66 in the Bhopal Municipal Corporation, but the selection of the Mayor soon provided a bone of contention. The two main contenders for the post were Surendranath Singh, the president of the district unit of the party who was supported by Kailash Sarang, and Uma Shankar Gupta who belonged to the group that was newly established at the helm of the party. Finally, Gupta obtained the post through a secret ballot. The second criterion of factionalism, the vertical links uniting a leader to local followers (or clients), began to take shape, since Surendranath Singh paid allegiance to Patwa through Sarang.

Thus, the municipal elections showed how local party workers could align themselves with rival state leaders. A vertical relationship, generally of a clientelistic kind, between party men operating at the local level and chiefs of groups operating at the state level, gradually took shape. This trend had emerged only discreetly during the 1992–3 party elections when Patwa and Thakre, who were favourably inclined towards Aggarwal worked for the choice of district presidents, since they were to play a prominent role in the selection of the state party president. For instance, in Dewas district, Patwa and Thakre successfully supported a candidate hostile to Joshi.[25] However, this evolution really crystallized in the 1994 municipal elections when some local party workers aligned themselves with one or another of the groups contesting for power at the state level. Logically enough, the symptoms of such a change appeared first in Bhopal, the state capital, where the rivalries for the control of the state party apparatus were the fiercest.

[24] Ibid. 19 November 1994. Several workers from the adjacent district of Sehore were also suspended.

[25] *National Mail*, 12 May 1993. In many places party workers complained that the returning officers had announced the names of the district office-bearers without conducting the elections. The elections were declared null and void in 11

This element of factionalism also developed because the party's infrastructure, the team of the sangathan mantris had lost its prominent status. Not only was Thakre gone but the organizers he had appointed before leaving had been sidelined by the new ones. A new team of sangathan mantris had been formed by Thakre in 1992–3 with Krishna Morarji Moghe in Madhya Bharat, Meghraj Jain in Mahakoshal and Govind Sarang in Chhattisgarh. Govind Sarang was Kailash Sarang's younger brother and all of them were lieutenants of Thakre. L. N. Pandey, soon after he took over, cut down their powers by transforming them from organizing secretaries into divisional secretaries. Moghe, Jain and Sarang then informed the RSS headquarters in Nagpur that as pracharaks, they did not want to work any longer for the BJP and declined the alternate posts offered to them. This development amounted to a complete readjustment of the inner equilibrium of the party. For the first time, the leaders from the 'power politics' wing asserted their authority over the organizational wing. Questioning of the old sangathanist party-building pattern went hand in hand with the coming to the forefront of personalities involved in power politics.

In particular Patwa appeared more and more as the chief of his camp. Thakre was no longer in the fray and Aggarwal had also left the battle ground. As a result, he now appeared as a faction leader fighting for power within the party. He was apprehensive about the attempts by the dominant group to take over the party organization, and rightly so. Narendra Singh Tomar, the chief of the youth wing of the state BJP, the Bharatiya Janata Yuva Morcha, a close associate of Patwa, had been removed and its executive purged of the followers of the former Chief Minister in May 1995. Bipin Dixit, one of Pandey's supporters, had been appointed as his successor. One month later, the president of the Bhopal district

block units (ibid., 1 May 1993). In Bhopal, the party elections of September 1992 were even violent. Cases were registered of brandishing of swords and knives by party activists during the elections of the district party president. The group headed by K. Sarang—who was close to Patwa and Thakre—probably initiated these intimidation moves as well as the stoning of the car of a local MLA, S. Pradhan (ibid., 4 December 1992). Commenting upon these events, Pradhan declared: 'The fellow who damaged my car was under the order of a chief. We oppose each other. In any party there are rivalries. The decline of discipline is due to the access to power. We have lost [in 1993] because of that. We have lost our image of a disciplined party.' (Interview on 16 February 1994, in Bhopal.)

unit, Surendranath Singh was replaced by an old timer belonging to the ruling group. When the BJP, at that juncture, again lost two by-elections to the Congress, Patwa demanded the resignation of L. N. Pandey. The majority of the BJP MLAs from Chhattisgarh wrote to the party high command to support Patwa's demand for a change in the state leadership.

THE IMPOSSIBLE RESTORATION OF SANGATHANISM

Until recently, the relative autonomy of the state units has been one of the assets of the BJP. In contrast to what happened in the Congress, it enabled them to adapt to local circumstances and to select their own candidates at the time of elections. The BJP was also one of the few Indian parties in which, in contrast with the Congress, state leaders were duly elected by the members. However, the persistent infighting within the BJP unit of Madhya Pradesh led the party leadership to become increasingly involved in the local affairs. As BJP President, Advani not only appointed Pandey, but successively summoned Patwa, Vikram Verma and several other state leaders who had staged a twenty-four hour dharna demanding the replacement of Pandey and Bhandari.[26] As a result, Patwa and other senior leaders, such as N. K. Shejwalkar, one of the lieutenants of the Rajmata Scindia in Gwalior, who had taken part in this demonstration, had to tender an apology.

The party high command was then desperately looking for means to restore the sangathanist arrangement. It decided to send Thakre back to Bhopal in August 1995. However, the tensions were so acute that, for the first time, the party elections which were due soon after could not be organized. Thakre succeeded in silencing the Patwa group (to which he had been close for years) and tried hard to evolve a compromise. He made a point that Pandey's leadership should not be challenged by anyone and ensured that the latter would give adequate representation to both groups in the State Executive nominated in January 1996. While Pyarelal Khandelwal made Sakhlecha and N. P. Gupta join as members of the State Executive, Narendra Singh Tomar became

---

[26] The banner displayed by this protest movement read: 'Bhandari vapas jao' (Bhandari go back). (*National Mail*, 8 June 1995.) I am most grateful to N. Rajan for this information and for many other pieces of advice.

one of its secretaries. The team of sangathan mantris was also rehabilitated with Krishna Murari Moghe becoming one of the general secretaries.

The 1996 Elections

During the 1996 election campaign, the party succeeded in showing a facade of unity after each group was allotted its share of tickets. Thakre's election tour was more extensive than it was in 1991 and 1989. It appeared as if he had become the party's sole spokesman: the BJP organizer had obviously to be more active on the public scene to hide and defuse divisions. The promotion of Thakre as a rallying point-figure was even clearer in 1997 when the RSS decided to celebrate his 75th birthday in a most unprecedented way. A trust called Amrit Mahotsava Samiti was set up, with Patwa as its treasurer, who was given the task of collecting Rs 5 crores for the foundation of hospitals, schools in the tribal areas, etc. More than 2,000 RSS and BJP workers took part in this function.[27] The RSS probably took Thakre's birthday as an opportunity to project him as a strong contender for the post of the BJP president, since Advani's term was almost getting over; besides they wanted to restore his authority as a veteran sangathanist. Thakre tried to revive the old sangathanist strategy at the local level too by establishing 2,500 shakti kendras (power centres) at the polling booth level to manage the electioneering through party workers. Each centre had five or six polling booths under it.

However, the 1996 elections also suggested that Thakre tried to solve the internal tensions by favouring the emergence of a new generation of party workers. Senior leaders were shifted to the national scene to make room for the younger ones. Kailash Joshi had already been appointed at the helm of the BJP Kisan Morcha. Similarly, the Lok Sabha seemed to be a good place to send those who were at loggerheads with one another in the state. P. Khandelwal was nominated from Rajgarh—where he lost—and V. K. Sakhlecha was given a party ticket for the first time since 1980. He was nominated from Satna, Arjun Singh's constituency, where he lost, but where he also showed that he could still be of some use to the BJP by contributing to the defeat of the Congress leader. One year

---

[27] *National Mail*, 26 August 1997.

later, the party fielded Patwa from Chhindwara to contest a by-election against Kamal Nath, and he won. Being a Member of Parliament, the former Chief Minister then began to spend more time in Delhi and consequently lost some interest in the state affairs. But he lost the seat to Kamal Nath in 1998.

Factionalism, in this way, was somehow contained within the BJP, whereas it became acute in the Congress. In fact, the BJP's share of valid votes was slightly smaller than what it had gained in 1991 (41.32 per cent as against 42), but in most of the constituencies it won this time, i.e. 27 out of 40 (as against 12 in 1991); partly because it benefited from the divisions of its chief rival.

The Congress was weaker and more divided in Madhya Pradesh than in any other state. The Congress-T, led by Arjun Singh, polled 4.7 per cent of the valid votes. Though it won only one seat in Sidhi, it 'prevented' the Congress from winning two others in Satna and Raigarh. And the three seats lost by the Congress-I 'because of the Congress-T' do not tell the whole story. One has also to take into account the impact of this schism on the party workers since several activists followed Arjun Singh. In addition to the Congress-T (epi)phenomenon, several hawala-tainted leaders came from the Madhya Pradesh Congress: Madhav Rao Scindia, Kamal Nath, Arvind Netam and V. C. Shukla were among the most important ones with their ministerial status in Narasimha Rao's government. Scindia decided to contest as an Independent and was expelled from the party. He then formed the Madhya Pradesh Vikas Congress and won easily from Gwalior and helped the BJP—which had withdrawn its candidate in his favour by not canvassing in the neighbouring constituencies. More importantly perhaps, three ministers of Digvijay Singh, Balendu Shukla, Mahendra Singh Kalukheda and Ramnivas Rawat, openly campaigned for Scindia, along with six other MLAs. Kamal Nath and Arvind Netam admitted that they were not in a position to contest and withdrew in favour of their wives; they virtually did not canvass out of 'their' constituencies. V.C. Shukla imposed a candidate of his choice and remained also confined to 'his' constituency of Raipur.[28]

---

[28] Digvijay Singh, the Chief Minister of Madhya Pradesh, regretted that the Congress high command did not give tickets to the 'hawalawalas'. (See his interview in *Times of India*, 11 June 1996.)

In addition to intense infightings, the Congress suffered from the rise of the BSP in the constituencies bordering Uttar Pradesh and even in Chhattisgarh. The BSP won two seats, including one against Arjun Singh in Satna. Its candidates were the runner-ups in four other constituencies. The BSP increased its share of valid votes from 3.54 per cent in 1991 to 8.18 in 1996, which enabled it to emerge as a third force. Almost everywhere, it reduced the Congress support among the scheduled castes. (see Table 9.1.)

TABLE 9.1: Performance of the BJP and Congress Candidates in 1996 where the Congress-T, BSP or Others Mattered

(percentage-wise)

Constituency	BJP	Congress-I	Congress-T	BSP	Other
Morena (SC)	42.58	14.59	3.04	33.21	–
Bhind	39.21	10.07	2.13	36.08	
Gwalior	–	5.65	–	22.31	MPVC 66.33
Guna	49.78	25.89	0.6	14.71	–
Sagar (SC)	52.25	20.63	4.48	14.28	–
Khajuraho	45.27	25.12	–	9.2	–
Damoh	50.89	22.67	4.23	12.47	–
Satna	24.91	13.33	19.53	28.37	–
Rewa	24.81	17.13	–	26.91	Savarna Party 13.43
Sidhi (ST)	25.11	17.20	26.40	11.12	–
Raigarh (ST)	42.25	40.76	5.82	–	–
Bilaspur (SC)	41.96	35.49	3.66	10.07	–
Sarangarh (SC)	20.57	39.88	1.47	33.79	–
Bastar (ST)	21.86	28.51			Ind. 32.15

Source: State Election Commission, *Lok Sabha General Elections—1996*, Bhopal, 1996.

Thakre's efforts for restoring the sangathanist party-building pattern were far from being totally successful. In late November 1996, 230 BJP members, including 27 MPs, 95 MLAs and 45 district presidents were gathered together for a three-day training camp during which they were asked not to leave the premises of the party headquarters, even for a short while. Here, K. Sudarshan, the RSS Saha Sarkaryavahak, warned them that if they did not display a greater sense of discipline and unity, his organization might withdraw its support to the party. Soon after, Thakre announced in Bhopal that the BJP would observe the year 1997 as the 'organization year'. He denounced the personal ambitions which damaged the party and said, in the pure sangathanist vein, that the BJP's aim was to form a party unit in all the gram panchayats.[29] However, under the garb of re-organizing the party, Thakre eliminated certain opponents to Patwa, such as Bipin Dixit, the leader of the state Bharatiya Janata Yuva Morcha that was also purged of all the supporters of Uma Bharti, except Deepak Joshi, (the son of Kailash Joshi). The return of Thakre thus enabled Patwa to relaunch his offensive.

To Live with Factionalism

Patwa's comfortable victory over Kamal Nath in the February 1997 by-election, the constituency the Congress had never lost since 1952, not even in 1977, strengthened his position within the Madhya Pradesh BJP. After having effusively celebrated the event, he let it know that 'given a chance he would like to remain in the state', and not in the Lok Sabha.[30] Indeed, he appeared as being the main contender for the party elections which were due in late 1997, after a gap of four years. In May, Meghraj Jain, a sangathan mantri close to Thakre was appointed as 'organizational poll incharge'. In the following month, a tight programme for the polls was announced, according to which the elections of the district committees and the state representatives was to be held before 10 October and of the state president by 31 October. This schedule could not be respected because of intense infighting. Bhopal district was again the scene of violent clashes between local cadres paying allegiance to different state leaders. The local party elections were postponed by a week after a group of angry BJP workers snatched away the papers of the returning officer and even hurled a crude bomb on the party state headquarters. Incidents occurred also in other districts, such as Gwalior and Guna where, in addition to the party workers paying allegiange to Patwa and Pandey, a third group, dominated by the Rajmata Scindia—though known to be close to Patwa—could be discerned. By late October, the elections

[29] *National Mail*, 22 January 1997.
[30] *National Mail*, 23 Febuary 1997.

had been completed for only 42 district committees out of 63, and Meghraj Jain had to acknowledge that the candidates had been unanimously elected in only half of them.[31] The state leaders had to admit that elections could not be held in several districts.

The 1997 organizational elections consummated the failure of Thakre's attempt at reestablishing the sangathanist pattern, not only because the factional alignments went one step more downward, but also because local leaders increasingly distrusted his team organizers. They repeatedly asked the high command to intervene in the affairs of the party unit. The Pandey group complained to the BJP headquarters that the returning officers favoured the Patwa group. Uma Bharti even sought Meghraj Jain's removal and the appointment of central observers after elections were organized in 'her' district of Tikamgarh in her absence. She publicly arraigned Thakre—whose effigy had been burned just then by the followers of Pandey in Raipur. He was definitely not perceived by this group as a father-like figure heading the organization with impartiality, but as one of the leaders of Patwa's faction. His efforts to reach a unanimity on the name of the candidate for the post of the state BJP president failed in late October when several leaders simply did not come to the conciliation meeting he had convened in Bhopal. L. K. Advani, therefore, summoned Patwa, Joshi, Vikram Verma and Babulal Gaur to Delhi five days before the election of the state party president—BJP MLAs from both groups came separately, one to complain to the party high command about the partisan attitude of Thakre, the other to counter their move. Eventually, Nand Kumar Sai, a tribal leader was elected as state party president. Even though he was known to be close to Patwa, he was a consensus candidate. The restoration of sangathanism had failed but the party had not broken down: it has now to learn how to live with groupism and factionalism.

CONCLUSION

In the 1990s, the Madhya Pradesh unit of the BJP had experienced groupism, even factionalism and a brutal decline of party discipline. Such an evolution had much to do with accession to power: leaders started to fight for offices and activists for tickets after the

[31] *Stasteman* (Delhi), 31 October 1997.

Janata Party took over in 1977 and especially after the BJP won the 1990 elections. Indian politics is replete with similar examples. However, one of the main assets of the BJP was its sangathanist party-building pattern and the sense of unity inherited from the RSS. The erosion of its organizational ability—which the RSS leaders stigmatize as a process of 'congressization'—could only affect the party's prospects.

The evolution of the Madhya Pradesh unit of the BJP must, however, be seen in a wider perspective. In many ways, it foreshadowed developments we are now familiar with. In 1995, the party elections were more vigourously contested than ever, not only in problematic state units such as that of Bihar, but also in Delhi where, for the first time, the state unit president was not unanimously elected. Kedar Nath Sahni, a veteran leader, faced the opposition of an obscure dissident, who polled 26 votes out of 97. At the same time, in Gujarat, Shankarsinh Vaghela led a revolt of 46 MLAs against the Chief Minister, Keshabhai Patel. In this case, the two major factors of factionalism were fulfilled: the move was initiated by a single man and the division largely stemmed from quarrels over the distribution of spoils (42 state-government undertakings whose profit had been reserved to his followers by Patel). The Gujarat events show the development of personality-based politics in contrast to the sangathanist pattern. Narendra Modi, the state organizing secretary was helpless and, in fact, obliged to resign because Vaghela rejected him. The latter then formed a separate party which enabled the secessionist leader to become the Chief Minister.

In contrast with the situation prevailing in Gujarat, the Madhya Pradesh unit of the BJP has not experienced any breakaway. In a sense, it bears testimony of the resilience of the party structure: it merely suffered from groupism before experiencing factionalism, and the sangathanist team will have to live with it. This process seems to be inevitable also because the expansion of the party is bound to attract new comers not familiar with the RSS sense of discipline. This is typical of a growth crisis, which may only become critical if the party forms the government again in late 1998—till then the hunger for power may help the BJP to remain united.

10

The Ethics of Hindutva and the Spirit of Capitalism

THOMAS BLOM HANSEN

The form of imperialism that we see in the contemporary world is the culmination of man's unrestrained lust. This tendency gives birth to the desire to occupy other countries by force...unfulfilled desires lead to restless minds.*

INTRODUCTION

The slogans of 'economic nationalism' and Swadeshi have increasingly been raised by various branches of the Sangh Parivar in the last five years in reaction to the policies of liberalization implemented by the Indian government since 1991. The most conspicuous manifestation of this new front opened by the Hindu nationalist movement was the protracted campaign run in 1994–5 by the RSS-outfit, *Swadeshi Jagaran Manch*, against the American power-giant Enron's contract with the government of Maharashtra regarding the construction of a large power plant south of Bombay. Much against the will of strong forces within the RSS, the Shiv Sena/BJP government finally signed an agreement with Enron including a few minor concessions to the demands raised by the agitations (see below). The Enron-case made it amply clear that the Sangh Parivar was deeply divided on the issue of economic policies with strong forces in BJP favouring liberalization against more conservative and ideologically purist forces in the RSS and VHP viewing foreign investments as a Trojan horse of hedonistic 'consumerism' in India.

* M. S. Golwalkar, speech in Kanpur, 22 December 1972.

Although the rhetoric of Swadeshi has been raised and redirected against the spectre of globalization, i.e. the claims of a systematic 'plunder' of the Indian consumers by multinational capital that are widespread in leftist as well as rightist circles, the notion of Swadeshi has been appropriated and given a rather specific set of connotations in its usages within the Hindu nationalist movement since the 1960s. I will in the following trace some of the continuities and changes in these usages, and in the latter part of the article illustrate some of the dilemmas and contradictions facing the Hindu nationalist movement on the issue of economic strategies with examples of specific policies and disagreements emerging in the context of Maharashtra in the last few years.

CULTURE VERSUS DESIRE: HINDU NATIONALIST NOTIONS OF A 'BHARATIYA' CAPITALISM

In the very first policy statement of the Jana Sangh in 1951 it was stated that 'the spirit of Swadeshi' should be revived in order to avoid 'reckless imitation, unnecessary dependence on foreign capital and to create in us a tendency for restraint and avoidance of conspicuous consumption'.[1] In its original form Swadeshi emerged among the Bengali *bhadralok* around the turn of the century and was articulated in the campaign against the partition of Bengal from 1905 onwards as a specific strategy of economic boycott and symbolic rejection of everything British. Later, Gandhi gave the notion a slightly more generalized meaning of 'indigenization' and Swadeshi was now linked to materialized nationalist practices of dress and fabrication of *khadi* cloth,[2] to notions of an agrarian, community-based self-governance but also to broader emancipatory notions of finding an inner truth, i.e. the intrinsic non-dependent sources of self-constitution to be found in nations as well as individuals.

The chief ideologue of contemporary Hindu nationalism M. S. Golwalkar did in a similar vein only pay scant attention to the specificities of economic practices. To him economic life and production belonged to the profane sphere of human life where

---

[1] Quoted from the pamphlet *BJP Economic Resolutions*, Bharatiya Janata Party Publications, New Delhi, 1995, p. 1.

[2] Tarlo, Emma, *Dress Matters* (London: Hurst and Co., 1996).

basic (animal-like) needs for survival, housing and reproduction were provided. According to Golwalkar, this sphere had to be firmly controlled by higher and more spiritual goals of life, if humans were not to fall back on their 'animal desires and instincts', i.e. to replicate the 'demonic ways' which characterized the 'materialism of the West'.[3]

The economic policies of the Jana Sangh in the 1950s and 1960s seemed, however, to be determined mainly by a broader, if far from consistent, opposition to the planning regime of the central government and by the more immediate interests of the groups of traders and petty industrialists of North India which provided a crucial financial and political backbone in the party.[4] In 1965 a programme entitled 'Integral Humanism' written by Jana Sangh's general secretary Deendayal Upadhyaya was adopted by the party as its official doctrine. 'Integral Humanism' did not depart radically from Golwalkar's organicist thought, but supplemented it by appropriating significant elements of the Gandhian discourse, and articulated these in a version of Hindu nationalism which aimed at downplaying the communal image of the Jana Sangh in favour of a softer, spiritual, non-aggressive image stressing equality, 'Indianization' and social harmony. This creation of a new discourse, suited specifically to the dominant trends of the political field in India at the time reflected an attempt to adjust the party to the changed conditions after the political upheavals in the mid-1960s. Jana Sangh emerged from the 1967 General Election as a fast growing party in north India with a considerable following also beyond the urban middle classes and petty traders. 'Integral Humanism' served as the ideological foundation for a broader populist mobilization strategy, not only for Jana Sangh but also for the BJP in the first half of the 1980s. One of the most significant changes in relation to Golwalkar's writings was the consistent use of the term Bharatiya, which Richard Fox aptly has translated as 'Hindian', i.e. a mixture of 'Hindu' and 'Indian'.[5] The use of the

[3] Golwalkar, M. S., *Integral Man: Bharatiya Concept,* in Devendra Swarup (ed.), *Integral Humanism* (Delhi: Deeandayal Research Institute, 1992), pp 63–9.

[4] Graham, B. D., *Hindu Nationalism and Indian Politics* (Cambridge: Cambridge University Press, 1990), pp 158–95.

[5] Fox, Richard G., 'Hindu Nationalism in the Making; or the Rise of the 'Hindian'', *American Ethnological Society*, Monograph Series, No. 2, Washington, pp 63–81.

term *Bharatiya* also signified an adaptation to the political realities of official secularism and a realization that the stigmatization of the RSS and Hindu Mahasabha since the late 1940s had made explicit references to 'Hindu' illegitimate outside the religious field.

One of the more interesting features of this new programme was that it explicitly addressed the organization of the economy and the state. Echoing Vivekananda, Deendayal Upadhyaya suggested that the central cohesive factor of social life anywhere in the world was *Dharma*, which in Upadhyaya's usage was a metaphor for culture and nation and for all that which sustains life, an omnipresent 'spirit' which enables men and nature to live, and so on. The nation is 'a permanent Truth'—an organic unity of territory—will, Dharma and ideal.[6] Every nation has a soul, argued Upadhyaya, an innate nature, *Chiti*, which is like a personality—invisible, but of great intensity. Integral Humanism seemed to imply that none of the elements of this Chiti or Dharma could be clearly defined or even distinguished. It seemed to be the point in 'Integralism' to avoid definitions and precision, positing everything as always-already connected and integrated. Analytical enquiries, according to Deendayal, were parts of the Western malaise.

But the basic truth is that the individual and society are one and indivisible. In a cultured state of affairs the individual will think of society even while thinking of himself (...) Complete identification of the individual with society is itself a state of complete development for the individual. The individual is the medium and measure of the completeness of society.[7]

Drafted as a political programme, 'Integral Humanism' also contained slightly more concrete visions around two themes, morality in politics, and Swadeshi and small-scale industrialization, all Gandhian in their general thematic, but distinctly Hindu nationalist in the characteristic style of 'integralism', that is, revolving around the same basic themes of harmony, primacy of cultural-national values, discipline, etc. According to Deendayal, the paramount concern in India should be to develop an indigenous economic model, which put the human being at the centre stage,

---

[6] Deendayal in Raje, Sudhakar (ed.), *Pandit Deendayal Upadhyaya. A profile* (Delhi: Deendayal Research Institute).
[7] Deendayal in *Manthan*, 1991, pp 34–5.

and which differed sharply in this respect, from both capitalism and communism:

> The centralisation of power, economic and political, is implied in both. Both, therefore, result in dehumanisation of man. We want neither capitalism nor socialism. We aim at progress and happiness of 'Man', the Integral Man.[8]

Swadeshi and decentralization should be considered the cornerstones in an economic development which should be firmly embedded in a cultural ethos in order not to give rise to hedonism and selfishness. Similarly, foreign capital and technology should only be accepted as long as they were under firm national control, argued Deendayal. Machines should not be object of technical fetishism (as they supposedly were in the West), but should fit the conditions of the country favouring a village-based strategy of industrialization, with an emphasis on labour-intensive production. This would, in turn, reduce urbanization and all the evils of modernity flowing from big cities, Deendayal argued.

It is striking that Deendayal only operated with two societal levels, the individual and the nation, assigning primacy to the latter. The corporate life of the nation, one must assume, was to be organized by the true nationalists, the RSS. It is also noteworthy, that the most fundamental aspect of economy, ownership, was assigned a subordinate and imprecise definition just as any concrete vision of the organization of socio-economic life seemed to be lacking.

In spite of the overlaps between Gandhian and Hindu nationalist ideology, 'Integral Humanism' was mainly Gandhian at an idiomatic level by using concepts such as Swadeshi and *Sarvodhya* (welfare for all) and promoting notions of decentralization and small-scale industries. The more radical dimensions of Gandhian thought were subsumed within a framework which assigned undisputed subservience of individuals and groups to the nation as a corporate whole. Richard Fox has aptly characterized this entire operation as an 'ideological hijacking' and an 'ideological transplant' designed to appropriate the legitimacy of the Gandhian idiom in Indian politics.[9]

Although most of the political forces behind the JP-movement and later the Janata Party in 1977 supported such vaguely Gandhian

[8] Ibid., p. 58.
[9] Fox, Richard, G., op. cit. pp 69–70.

economic ideas, precious little was ever transformed into practical policies during the tumultuous years of the Janata interlude. The plan allocations for the small-scale sector were expanded somewhat and a few new programmes aiming at the strengthening of the cottage industries were launched, none of them having any significant effects in the overall distribution of investment or employment in the industrial sector.[10] Clearly, economic policies were areas of rather low priority and interest to the apex leadership of both Jana Sangh and RSS, who preferred to carve out a distinct profile on larger and more symbolic issues connected with national identity and cohesion.

THE CHALLENGE OF LIBERALIZATION

In sharp contradiction to the vaguely Gandhian economic thinking of the opposition, introduction of advanced technology in the industry, the public administration and the media and an incipient liberalization of the economy making import of technology, technical co-operation and joint-ventures with foreign firms easier, were all high-profile themes of the Rajiv Gandhi administration in the 1980s. But the much publicized dismantling of the 'License Raj' was gradually played down in the face of resistance from parts of the large-scale sector, the public sector and agrarian groups for whom the protection against international competition as well as internal liberalization was essential for continued viability and profitability. The impact of the liberalization policies were limited to the expanding consumer goods sector which, aided by numerous joint ventures with Japanese and Western firms, turned a host of new products out in the market. Cars, electronic gadgets, computers and a range of modern household items soon flooded the market, spread to provincial cities and villages and created a virtual 'consumer goods-revolution' in the latter part of the 1980s. The urban middle classes, now more than one hundred million people, reaped most of the benefits of the liberalization and modernization programmes and began to envisage their entry into the brave new world of computers, electronics and Western consumption patterns and taste. This assertive and self-confident urban middle class discarded socialist rhetoric and Gandhian temperance and wanted

[10] Rudolph, L. and S. H. Rudolph, *In Pursuit of Lakhsmi* (Hyderabad: Orient Longman, 1987), p. 228.

India to fall in tune with global trends as fast as possible. The improved access to jobs and consumption, tax-relaxation and increased access to private ownership of stocks, made the urban middle classes feel that they had joined the global modernization optimism and were joining of the modern world on increasingly equal terms and along increasingly similar cultural patterns of consumption.

It was not least the rapid growth in TV-sets, radios, video-equipment, new magazines, foreign films and introduction of international satellite and cable TV which created this middle class euphoria.[11] The growing media'ization of the public realm affected mainly the urban areas but TV-sets and videos were spreading rapidly among affluent sections of the rural population as well.[12]

These developments familiarized the urban middle classes with electronic equipment, automobile-technology and information technology of a decisively higher technical standard and better durability than the products hitherto available from the domestic consumer goods industry. The designs and user-friendliness of the new products manufactured in India on a joint venture basis thus exposed the poor quality and technological backwardness of many consumer products from the licensed industry in the country. In the automobile sector the difference between the modern Maruti car and the traditional Ambassador or Premier cars reflected a technological gap of three decades. The liberalization policies in the 1980s thus generated a certain 'foreign technology fetishism', i.e. an obsession with stereotyped symbols of modernity: Japanese efficiency, American ingenuity, German solidity, French sophistication, Italian taste, as these qualities were symbolically embedded in commodities. Commercial advertising underlined the nationality of the foreign technology behind the particular product and as elsewhere in the global economy, commodification and styles of consumption became intimately linked to imaginings of the hierarchical order of cultures and nations on scales of wealth and technological sophistication.

[11] Singhal and Rogers, *India's Information Revolution* (Delhi: Sage Publications, 1989).

[12] During a recent fieldwork in relative backward regions of Maharashtra I found that in villages of 3,000 to 5,000 people, the number of TV-sets varied from 30 to 125. Most of these sets had been purchased after 1988–9.

The 'foreign technology fetishism' which highlighted the technological backwardness of Indian industry also generated a feeling of displacement of the Indian nation, especially vis-à-vis economically successful Asian countries. The success of China and the East Asian economies attracted considerable attention among educated groups in India and played a major part in the subsequent liberalization of the Indian economy since 1991.[13] This exposure to modern technology and global media flows further depleted the credentials of the Congress party. However, a more coherent policy of economic liberalization was not implemented until the Government of India in 1991, in the face of a rapidly growing foreign debt and an acute deterioration of the Reserve Bank deposits in 1991, caused by the rising costs of oil after the Gulf-war, conceded to implement a comprehensive liberalization and reform package negotiated with the International Monetary Fund.[14]

In the latter half of the 1980s, BJP's resolutions on economic policies and criticism of the policies of Congress became organized

[13] In interviews with middle-class and lower middle-class families in Maharashtra between 1991–4, a certain reading of the precarious position of India seemed to emerge again and again: squeezed in between an oil-rich and militarily well-equipped Arab/Muslim world on one side, and a still more dynamic economic zone in East and South-East Asia attracting foreign capital and know-how, on the other side. The collapse of the Soviet Union, rendering India without a militarily powerful ally and protector, only reinforced this perceived dilemma of the position of India in the emerging post Cold War order. Another striking feature emerging from this reading of the world was the feeling of deceit by the political leadership. A common argument went: 'While so many other countries in the world prosper, India lags behind and is even forced to ask foreign companies to upgrade even basic elements in the technical and organizational infrastructure of Indian industrial production. Betting on socialism, planning and friendly relations with the Communist bloc has been a major historical miscalculation executed by a corrupt and incompetent political leadership. In the meantime the global development has overtaken and bypassed India.'

[14] For various aspects of the financial and fiscal squeezes which compelled the Government of India to implement rather far-reaching reforms, see Jalan, Bimal (ed.), *India's Economy* (Delhi: Viking, 1992) pp 141–251. For a recent evaluation of the impact of the economic reforms, see Vaidyanathan, A., *The Indian Economy. Crisis, Response and Prospects*, Tracts for the Times/7 (Hyderabad: Orient Longman, 1995). For a more critical assessment of the social interests and assumptions behind the liberalization-policy, see Bagchi, A. K., 'Globalising India: The Fantasy and the Reality', *Social Scientist*, vol. 22, nos 87–8, July–August 1994, pp 18–27.

around three main themes: firstly, that official policies were irresponsible and careless as they both allowed the foreign debt to grow and handed out tax exemptions and tax cuts to various groups. Secondly, that agriculture and the small-scale industry was neglected. The BJP had already from the mid-1980s taken over the demand for 'remunerative prices' which peasant movements effectively had propagated in various parts of the country.[15] Thirdly, that the government were 'selling out' to multinationals by relaxing the FERA regulations and letting its policies be 'under the tutelage of the World Bank' as a resolution stated as early as in 1986.[16] However, in 1990, during the short-lived reign of the National Front government supported by the BJP, the party abandoned this criticism and conceded that in view of global changes it was 'imperative to look for a new paradigm', and asserted that 'the BJP has always been in favour of debureaucratization of the industrial sector...and the party welcomes de-licensing and removal of red-tapism'. But in keeping with its overall commitments the party urged the government to protect indigenous capital against foreign competition.[17]

After the new economic policy including liberalization, deregulation and privatization of the public sector was proclaimed by the Congress government in 1991, the RSS embarked on a campaign for a Swadeshi approach to economic development. The RSS published a much discussed pamphlet listing the brand names of 326 consumer products manufactured by multinationals and mentioned an Indian produced alternative to each product. The pamphlet called for a popular movement against multinationals, and called upon its members and supporters to divert their consumption-pattern away from the products of 'exploitative multinational companies' and towards Indian produced goods. The consumerism induced by foreign companies erodes and undermines the cultural ethos of India and it weakens the economic

---

[15] See for instance the resolution on agriculture adopted at the National Executive Meeting in Agra, 8–10 April 1988.

[16] Resolution on Economic Policies at the National Executive Meeting Chandigarh, 3–5 January 1986. The entry of multinationals was also mentioned as 'alarming' in the economic policy resolution the following year at the National Executive Meeting at Vijaywada, 2–4 January 1987.

[17] National Executive resolution on New Industrial Policy (NIP), in Madras, 21–3 July 1990.

foundations of the Indian economy, it was argued. In a central passage the pamphlet stated:

Every morning we begin the job of cleansing our body with the help of products manufactured by these filthy companies which have a history of exploiting poor countries of the world.[18]

At the surface, Swadeshi reflected a call for national capitalism and a type of call for nationalist consumption-patterns that had several precedents in modern Indian history. The critique of multinational investments and the notion of *Swalambhan* (self-reliance) were borrowed from the leftist and Gandhian discourses. The RSS-chief Deoras compared multinationals to the East India Company and claimed that Swadeshi was but the natural continuation of the nationalist pre-Independence struggle and called upon 'patriots to shun everything foreign and prize everything Swadeshi'.[19] At a deeper level the pamphlet sought to allude to de-purification of culture and values brought about by 'modern consumerism' by employing the metaphors of purity and pollution. The pamphlet thus reflected the more general ambivalence vis-à-vis capitalist modernity within the Sangh Parivar as well as the desire and belief in the RSS's ability to control (capitalist) modernity—here equated with economic globalization—by mobilizing and regenerating the national culture.

The Swadeshi-campaign of the RSS brought the BJP in a somewhat awkward position. The party had initially welcomed the economic reform plans of the Congress-government, a move which had caused disgruntlement among older RSS leaders who publicly alleged that some sort of tacit understanding between the Congress and BJP had been reached on the economic front. In the RSS bi-weekly *Organiser*, a series of articles hammered on the Congress government as 'bonded to the World Bank';[20] 'MNCs as imperialist designs, subjugating and enslaving the developing countries'.[21] At the same time, there were fears in the BJP that the Congress would now make inroads and create sympathy in the erstwhile

[18] *Swadeshi Andolan: Struggle for Economic Freedom*, Sahitya Samagama, Bangalore, 1992.
[19] Interview, *Organiser*, 26 January 1992.
[20] *Organiser*, 8 March 1992.
[21] Ibid., 15 March 1992.

backbone of the Sangh Parivar constituency, the small trader and the small industrialist:

> The Congress took away our economic platform, and is now taking away our political base (...) as the economy opens up it will be exceedingly difficult to keep the middle class away from Congress.[22]

The BJP modified the pro-liberalization line of the party in the face of what was termed the 'RSS-corrective', that is, the pressure from the RSS to adopt a more Swadeshi-oriented line.[23] Three months later, the party issued a revised Economic Policy statement, which sought to combine a pro-liberalization line in internal national affairs with a strongly protectionist posture vis-à-vis the world market. The policy statement was an outcome of protracted debates in the party-leadership and the concrete shape of the programme was obviously determined by concessions granted to the 'cultural purists' in the RSS, BMS[24] and ABVP, and by the compulsions of political opposition to the Congress programme of liberalization. However, the experience of a certain 'displacement of nationhood' in the wake of the gradual opening of the Indian economy and cultural sphere to foreign commodities and cultural products also played a part. The new economic policy was

[22] Jay Dubashi in *Organiser*, 15 March 1992.

[23] In an interview in February 1992, Advani said that it was Congress which in its liberalization-programme had taken over the BJP's line, and that the party welcomed that. According to Advani, multinationals should play a role only in high-technology sectors. For the BJP, Advani said, the 'RSS-corrective' to the party programme of 1991 was 'in a way necessary'. *Sunday*, 16–22 February 1992.

[24] Activists from the *Bharatiya Mazdoor Sangh* (BMS) were the driving forces in the launching of the Sangh Parivar's front-organization designed *Swadeshi Jagaran Manch* (Swadeshi Renaissance Organisation) to fight for economic nationalism. An indication of the direction, and quality of this economic 'philosophy' may be found in a book by M. G. Bokhare (1993): *Hindu Economics*, Swadeshi Jagaran Manch, New Delhi, Janaki Prakashan, hailed in the foreword by BMS-chief D. B. Thengadi as 'a landmark of economic thinking in our country'. The author, a former Vice Chancellor of Nagpur University, claims to derive an economic philosophy and an economic system from the *Vedas*. The result is a rather substandard collection of fragments of common sense semidigested economic theory and ancient philosophy that ends up in a set of equally incredible recommendations for a new state ruled by a strong president of moral character with heavy limitations on freedom of the press, an authoritarian judiciary, etc.— a vision that according to the author is inspired by figures like Kautilya, Milton Friedman and Golwalkar (sic!)

justified by referring to the marginalization of India in the global context: 'India is today at the bottom of the international pile (...) an abject basket case that has to beg regularly for alms from International agencies that treat it with disdain'. Likewise, the increasing gap in technology, productive power and standard of living between India and many Asian countries served as background for the quest for a new model. The answer to the new challenges were to be found neither in the world market nor in unbridled capitalist growth but in developing an 'Indian Model'; in 'self-confidence and capability in consonance with our cultural mores and ethos', and in a 'Swadeshi of a self-confident, hard-working modern nation that can deal with the world on terms of equality', as the programme read.

A remarkable contradiction ran through the entire document. On the one hand, it expressed a desire to achieve national strength as fast as possible through strong, high-technological capitalist growth, while it, on the other hand, was woven around an equally powerful desire to control and check the consequences of such a development within a vision that elevated 'cultural harmony' to be the main component of the economic strategy. This obviously contradictory project was throughout the policy-document articulated as series of attacks on the regulative policies of the Congress in all fields, followed by suggestions which mainly recommended a slightly trimmed version of these same policies. The clearest example was probably in the section on industrial policies, where it is suggested to deregulate and dismantle the 'License Raj'. Immediately after it is suggested to protect and subsidise small-scale and village industries in numerous ways, to devise detailed regulations of the allocation and financing of investments in the large-scale sector, and to limit imports and the influx of foreign capital to high-technology sectors. Reasserting the classical RSS-credo of the mobilization of 'national will', 'national pride', 'character of individuals', as the true sources of economic development,[25] it was admitted that

Many suggestions and solutions may seem contradictory in isolation(!) It is therefore the spirit and the vision that underline them and inform them which

[25] This viewpoint was reasserted by the main author behind the programme, Jay Dubashi, previously one of the strongest spokesmen of liberalization, who stressed that cultural-national pride was the crucial pre-requisite for economic and social development in any country. (Interview, 12 December 1992, New Delhi).

gives relevance and purposefulness to the totality of the policy (…) The BJP is proud of the patriotic dedication and daring of the people who are enamoured of the structural adjustments in alien clutches and cosmetic changes on borrowed plumage.[26]

This new economic policy-statement enabled the BJP to make the critique—however inconsistent—of official economic policies into a new political front. The BJP launched attacks on the Congress government for being mere puppets of the IMF, to sell out to foreign capital, to increase debt and dependency, 'to open the Indian economic womb to the West' and to lead the country to further poverty, unemployment and global marginalization. The BJP-leadership launched agitations against cuts in fertiliser subsidies, agitations for a 'Debt Free India', agitations against import of wheat and other issues.[27]

The launching of the new economic strategy of the BJP and the Sangh Parivar revealed a new recasting of the older antinomy between culture and politics as strategic fields of operation within the Hindu nationalist movement. On one hand, there was the older generations of RSS-pracharaks, highly critical towards liberalization and the prospect of India getting further entangled in global currents of trade, investment and cultural products. These concerns were shared by pracharaks and activists of the BMS who in the labour field were taking the side of employees in public sector undertakings facing an insecure future or even privatization. The outlook of the BMS were largely coloured by its guiding ideas of employment first, productivity second. The organization, and its support bases had developed a certain interest in retaining status quo at the labour-market, and thus occasionally found itself in conflict with the BJP-governments in for instance Uttar Pradesh

See also Dubashi's article in *BJP Today*, 1992, no. 21, 15 November ('Liberalisation, yes! Globalisation, No!'), where he argues in line with the RSS-argument that foreigners only come to India to make money, not to develop the country.

[26] *Humanistic Approach to Economic Development (A Swadeshi Alternmative)*. Bharatiya Janata Party, New Delhi, 1992).

[27] Throughout August–November, while entire Ayodhya drama was escalating, the BJP concentrated on economic issues in its attacks on the government. The party fortnightly *BJP Today*, nos 15–22, August–November 1992, carried most of the resolutions, statements and political commentaries from the BJP leaders on these issues in the period.

and Madhya Pradesh, seeking to reform and trim certain grossly underperforming public undertakings.[28]

On the other hand, there was a growing section of especially BJP leaders and activists—many of them involved in private enterprises—who welcomed the break with decades of semi-planned economy, and who regarded liberalization and integration in the world market as a viable course. This tendency flourished among the BJP workers who in the course of their work in state governments or local level functions as brokers or business men had come close to the everyday technicalities involved in the institutional and extra-institutional governance of the economy. They dissociated themselves from the Swadeshi-programme and regarded the official reform-policies as half-hearted and far from comprehensive and radical enough.[29] Party leaders such as L. K. Advani tried to defend a moderate version of Swadeshi as the right of the country to decide its own policies, and carefully kept a distance to some of the more radical proponents of Swadeshi in the party and in the RSS.[30]

In 1993–4, opposition against the so-called 'Dunkel Draft' outlining reforms of GATT and its subsequent transformation into the World Trade Organisation (WTO) figured prominently on the agenda of the BJP and other branches of the Sangh Parivar. On this issue, the Hindu nationalist critique of what was envisaged to become a massive competition from foreign firms in many branches converged in several ways with the critique and agitations levelled by leftist parties concerned with job-security and national sovereignty, by farmers movements opposed to the entry of North

---

[28] See reports in *Sunday*, 16–22 February 1992.

[29] An interesting critique of the Swadeshi-alternative, also critical towards the lapses and pitfalls of 'Manmohanomics' was written by the BJP secretary of Pune, Pradeep Rawat and appeared in 1992 in the Bombay based RSS-weekly, *Vivek*. Rawat dismissed the *Swadeshi* vision as naive, utopian and as bereft of any deeper understanding of the logics of the market and the larger dynamics of the national as well as global economy. *Swadeshi* may, according to Rawat, at best be tantamount to a continuation and minor revision of the regulationist regime of the Nehruvian model. (*Economic Challenges and the Swadeshi Alternative*, note prepared by Pradeep Rawat, n.d.).

[30] At the National council meeting in Bangalore in June 1993, Advani quoted a Japanese professor at length for recommending that every developing nation instead of adopting Western blueprints should 'work out their own unique paths consistent with their own unique civilizations and cultures'.

American agro-business in India, and by certain sections of Indian industry asking the Indian government to retain some protection of the domestic market.[31] In a language resembling that of leftist organizations, the General Council of the RSS (Akhil Bharatiya Pratinidhi Sabha) warned that the World bank and the WTO 'only were instruments to capture the resources and markets of the third world and hand them over to the super powers'.[32]

There is little doubt that BJP's strong line on protection of domestic markets and indigenous capital has attracted considerable support from various branches of industry. Such information is notoriously difficult to get access to and verify, however, but apart from its policies the main attraction of BJP, seen from the point of view of industry and commerce, is today its sheer size and influence in many states. It is well known that many industrial houses and even small industrialists often support a number of different political parties in order to optimize their room of manoeuvre and goodwill in the state-apparatus, to ease clearance of projects and to remain on friendly terms with all major players in the political field. It would, in view of this, be somewhat hazardous to conclude that BJP merely is the instrument or the representative of the small-scale sector, or domestically oriented capital, while Congress represents 'big capital', as the reasoning often goes in leftist circles and in Indian journalism. The BJP obviously tries to combine a strong nationalist line with a strong social conservatism and a preference for a national *Bharatiya* capitalism which not unlike the Japanese example thrives on 'patriotic consumption', and an industrial sector fully owned and operated by Indians.[33]

---

[31] See Lakha, Salim, *The Bharatiya Janata Party and Globalisation of the Indian Economy*, in J. Mcquire, P. Reeves, and H. Brasted (eds), *The Politics of Violence* (Delhi: Sage Publications, 1996), pp 278–9 for an overview over some of the issues, e.g. patent-rights and intellectual properties, raised in connection with the debate on the Dunkel Draft in India.

[32] *Times of India*, 18 March 1994.

[33] In a recent interview the convenor of the Economic Policy Cell in BJP, Jay Dubashi, said: '*Swadeshi* is not a businessman's ideology. It is a view of a political party…we are not a chamber of commerce.… See, businessmen do not have an ideology. When they are small and want technology they may say 'Swadeshi is junk' but when he grows so big that foreign companies may come and grab him, then he turns *Swadeshi*' (Interview in New Delhi, 13 November 1996).

KAR SEVAKS VERSUS CAR SEVAKS

As the constituencies of the BJP has grown, it is no longer self-evident that the RSS will remain the main and primary reference-point and constituency for the party. A large number of activists and MLAs with only 'skin-deep' commitments to—or no knowledge of—the entire 'spirit of the *Sangha*' as old RSS-men prefer to call it, have been induced into the party. Generally, they belong to the pragmatic wing of the BJP-legislators and activists and are more committed to the game of winning power, of patronage and of reaping the considerable financial benefits which a certain position in politics allows for. These 'newcomers', often business-men, also generally have few apprehensions vis-à-vis the economic reforms and are also in this field anathema to the 'purist' advocates of discipline and Swadeshi. This is in many ways indicative of a conflict between two visions of politics and modernity—one a pragmatic, pro-capitalist outlook committed to an often philistine middle-class vision of a 'clean society', to the good life with consumer durables and modern living; the other being the austere, ideologically pure, more socially conscientious outlook, uncomfortable with what it sees as the brutality, fragmentation and hedonism of the modern world. These two tendencies—*car sevaks* versus *kar sevaks*—were for a long time united by a joint communalism and a joint commitment to assert a common Hindu consciousness. As the symbolic issues of religion and nation became less prominent items on the party's agenda and more 'profane' policy-issues have come to the fore, this long-standing difference has been rearticulated.

The BJP's problem was, and remains, as other political parties in India the formulation of a credible political programme which both appeals to the urban educated middle classes and private entrepreneurs and their desire for a higher material standard of living; while, at the same time, accommodating the demands from poorer groups and agricultural interests for continued subsidisation of basic foodstuff, electricity, etc. A special problem the BJP faced, and still faces in a competitive political field, is to make such a programme acceptable to the vernacular intellectuals in the RSS, and to the provincial middle classes they try to rally around a call for Swadeshi that is, to draft a credible programme for the creation of a strong, sovereign, national modernity in a situation of intensified globalization. In 1995, the RSS-Sarsanghchalak Rajendra

Singh went on a trip to the West (none of the former Sarsanghachalak ever went abroad) and returned disillusioned with the stagnation in India, the 'lack of work culture' and the rampant corruption:

Why is this country lagging behind, this India which was once hailed as the Golden Bird before foreign invaders discovered her (...) Beggars, that is what we have been reduced to, because we are going with begging bowls before the affluent nations and multinationals.[34]

The contradictory stand taken on the issue of foreign investments produced several widely debated incidents in India in 1995. The BJP-government in Delhi decided to close down a Kentucky Fried Chicken outlet in Delhi on the (somewhat flimsy) ground that flies had been recovered inside the kitchen premises of the restaurant(!). This rather selective hygienic zeal on part of the BJP administration, which previously led to the closure of Muslim owned abattoirs in Delhi, obviously employed, if only by implication, notions of impurity and amorality of 'foreign' as well as Muslim food habits. The resistance against allowing foreign companies to supply food to the Indian market is obviously fuelled by a certain construction of the 'foreign' as an alien substance to be kept out of the kitchen, the heart of the Hindu family. As Jay Dubashi angrily remarked:

I eat in my house, I don't want a foreigner to come and prepare food in my house—it is as simple as that...see, there is in this country a general prejudice against foreign companies, and against foreigners as such because of the way we have been ruled by foreigners for 1,000 years. Anytime you try to tap this sentiment you find there is a tremendous response (...) Jesse Helms once said 'I hate foreigners'—and I don't mind saying the same. Why should we give reasons—it is our house (...) Is America great because of Coke, potato chips or Pepsi? No! The country is great because of the cars, computers and machines they produce. We should do the same.'[35]

Another dimension of the Sangh Parivar positioning vis-à-vis the West was displayed in conjunction with the Enron-affair in Maharashtra: the virtuous and pure Hindu nation—by nature tolerant and open—can only earn (self)respect by displaying strength and determination. According to the convenor of the RSS-outfit Swadeshi Jagaran Manch, S. Gurumurthy, the fears of a waning

[34] R. Singh in *Telepraph*, 4 May 1995.
[35] Dubashi, 13 November 1996.

credibility of India in the international market of reluctant inves-
tors are merely the 'nightmares of cowards':

The US President Clinton banned nuclear tests. The next day France decided
to have one and within a week China actually exploded its 43rd bomb. In his
heart, Clinton will respect these countries. Nobody respects the weak. If a
third rate deceptive company like Enron is shown its place, it will give the
message that India will not allow itself to be raped (...) I will give one more
example. Deng massacred 2,900 people at the Tienanmen Square in China. The
entire world press wrote off China saying nobody would invest even one
dollar thereafter. But the MNCs went and invested billions of dollars, several
times more than they did before the incident.[36]

The BJP does, however, not take any clear stand against foreign
investments. It is, on the contrary, widely recognized that foreign
companies are indispensable to meet the enormous expectations
that is generated at a still faster pace and within still larger groups
in the Indian society.[37] The party programme from 1996 reiterates
that 'BJP welcomes foreign investment... which supplies technology and know-how' whereas multinationals producing 'consumer
non-durables' will be kept out of the market. The manifesto also
asserted that

Swadeshi is a pre-requisite for meeting the challenge of globalisation; of
preserving our identity without compromising our sovereignty and self
respect. *We reject unbridled consumerism and believe in adherence to sustainable
consumption and growth.*[38]

What remains is a peculiar double-discourse consisting of one layer
of self-depreciation 'We are reduced to beggars'. 'We lack work
culture', and another layer of tough self-assertion 'India will not
allow itself to be raped', ' the West needs India'. This discourse
which obviously caters for the urban middle classes and upcoming

[36] Interview with S. Gurumurthy, *Economic Times*, 22 August 1995.
[37] As a young high-ranking BJP organizer stated candidly in a recent interview:
'I know that we cannot stop consumerism. Everybody wants a good job, a nice
house, a car, a beautiful wife. What scares me is pressure this puts on us now that
we are in government. Thinking about that we may come to power this is what
scares me most: the enormous expectations, the pressure for education, infrastructure and a good life. We have more poor people, more illiterates, more illness, etc.
concentrated in our country than any other place in the world. Somehow we have
to solve this. But how? Sometimes I am really afraid when I think of.' (Interview,
A. Bhatkalkar, BJP-organizer, Bombay, 13 November 1995).
[38] *Bharatiya Janata Party*, Election manifesto, 1996, p. 18. (My italics, T. B. H.)

social strata anxious not to loose self-respect in the maelstroms of modern urban culture while they, at the same time, are painfully aware of their own peripherality in the global economic circuits.[39]

The notion of Swadeshi displays, in the field of economics, the more fundamental ambiguities vis-à-vis capitalist modernity inherent in the Sangh Parivar's overall quest for a strong state and its pronounced distaste for the constant rehearsal of social splits and contradictions in the sphere of democratic politics as well as in the sphere of competitive capitalism. The Sangh Parivar's mixing of a Swadeshi rhetoric thundering against 'consumerism' and its quest for a strong societal discipline and unitary state, seems, in other words, to be informed by a paradoxical yearning back to the heyday of the Nehruvian state (minus socialism). A state which rested on a solid societal hegemony and was able to assert itself in an international context while protecting the national economy and national culture of India because it was held together by a single party, and not constantly weakened by compromises and the incoherence of policies marking competitive democratic politics, or weakened by the anarchy of the market. The theme of national strength and pride remains paramount as in the statement by the BJP leader Murli Manohar Joshi regarding the competitive aspects of BJP's economic vision: ' Swadeshi should make the country so strong politically and economically that its voice is heard with respect in the international community.'[40]

IN THE MAHARASHTRIAN MAZE

In Maharashtra the BJP has in the past few years ruled the state in alliance with Shiv Sena—a party which represents a rather straightforward entrepreneurial vision of Indian capitalism. This has forced the BJP to enter into a number of compromises on vital policy-areas.

During the election campaign prior to the Vidhan Sabha election in the state in March 1995, BJP had made critique of the State

[39] I have argued that Hindu nationalism among many things is driven by a quest for recognition in the world and as a compensatory strategy dealing with a sense of peripherality and 'lack' in Hansen, Thomas Blom, 'Globalisation and Nationalist Imaginations', *Economic and Political Weekly*, vol. XXXI, 9 March 1996a, pp 603–15.

[40] *Times of India*, 2 June 1997.

government's alleged 'sell-out' to multinationals, such as the large American power company Enron, a major issue. The attitude to foreign investments soon proved to be a major bone of contention between the two alliance partners.

The RSS had earlier set up a nation-wide organization Swadeshi Jagaran Manch (SJM) to promote the notion of Swadeshi and economic nationalism. It soon became a prominent force in the anti-Enron campaign, along with mobilization of local protests organized by the BJP-leaders followed by physical confrontations on the construction site. Officially, the bone of contention was the conditions surrounding Enron's twenty-year contract with the local electricity board,[41] but underneath were attempts to prove the credibility of election promises and the RSS' wish to substantiate its commitment to Swadeshi. One of the most vocal critics of Enron, the BJP Deputy Chief Minister of Maharashtra, Gopinath Munde, who had promised to 'throw the Enron project in the Arabian Sea', headed the review committee which in August 1995 submitted a report (heavily inspired by a parallel report from Swadeshi Jagaran Manch) which recommended the subsequent scrapping of the project. The Shiv Sena leadership clearly did not feel comfortable with this result, and renegotiations commenced after the Enron executives had commenced informal negotiations with Thackeray, who once again affirmed his status as a force of his own—outside and above the cabinet, perceiving himself as a one-man 'moral force'—equivalent to the function of the RSS vis-à-vis BJP. Pressed by Shiv Sena, BJP finally agreed to resume the negotiations with Enron which in January 1996 resulted in a final approval of a redrafted project.

In spite of this high-profile ideological gesture, the pragmatic wings of the BJP-leadership and its equally pragmatic and less ideologically principled partners in the Shiv Sena, now had to concede that expansion of power production remained a *sine qua non* in the continued development of the city and the state. The political calculus also went that stable power supply in Bombay in the long run could prove more vital to the political credentials of the BJP than ideological gestures vis-à-vis foreign companies. Nevertheless, the BJP leaders in Maharashtra depicted the renegotiation as a victory: 'Now, every multinational which wants to set

---

[41] For a review of the contentious points regarding loans, pricing, costs, etc., see *India Today*, 31 July and *Economic Times*, 14 August 1995.

up a project in India checks with us. They know that if the deal is not above board we will scrutinise it, and if necessary, scrap it'.[42]

The Swadeshi Jagaran Manch (SJM) has not given up, however. Although the organization has been publicly humiliated by the BJP's signing of the revised agreement, thereby exposing the internal disagreements within the Sangh Parivar, the organization still strives to halt the construction activities at the site selected for the plant, and it tries to expose what it considers fraud and bribes in connection with the entire deal. The Mumbai-convenor of the SJM was emphatic on this point:

The state-government has vested interests in this—also Gopinath Mundhe (Dep. Chief Minister and BJP-leader, TBH), I would say. Not his own personal gains maybe, but there are some state interests at stake here. (...) It cannot be the technology, nor the spin off effects. We have all the technology here— we need work for our people. Why should we let ourselves be steamrolled by all this talk about hi-tech.[43]

The SJM has now started to focus more on general issues of consumerism, management and foreign advertising, and the organization was actively involved in the agitations against the international beauty contest in Bangalore in November 1996, and the Michael Jackson show in Mumbai in October 1996, sponsored and attended by the Shiv Sena leadership. 'Why should our government subsidise a pop-singer, even a perverted type?' the SJM convenor asked. In line with other Sangh Parivar outfits, the SJM argues against consumerism and argues that only a stronger and more dedicated leadership in India can prevent India from repeating all the follies of the West and the excesses of the East, a leadership which only the RSS can offer, the SJM argues.[44]

The strategy of the Shiv Sena/BJP cabinet on industrial policies and urban development seems to display a continuation of the economic policy favouring middle-sized and also large-scale industrial units. In line with Congress' earlier administration in the state, the Shiv Sena/BJP also seeks to boost privatization and private investments in infrastructural projects of various kinds—roads, irrigation, bridges, etc. The 'Industry Trade and Commerce Policy for Maharashtra' which the government announced in early 1996,

[42] Pramod Mahajan, BJP leader in Maharashtra, in *Outlook*, 18 October 1995.
[43] G. Mahajan, *Swadeshi Jagaran Manch*, Mumbai, 28 November 1996.
[44] Mahajan, SJM-convenor, Mumbai, 28 November 1996.

is in many ways a direct continuation of earlier policies, while Shiv Sena's unmistakable enthusiasm for grand gestures and large projects also emerges clearly from the document. In the 'Mission statement' the document says, 'It is necessary to change the mind-set of people in Maharashtra so that they are not content merely with employment but imbibe the culture of entrepreneurship.' The plan then declares that eight areas in larger provincial cities in the state will be developed as 'industrial townships' with deputed high-ranking administrative officers being at the service of inves-tors in each location, which will be equipped with what is called 'social infrastructure such as air-links, industrial housing, colleges, hospitals, Institutes of Technical Training, clubs, resorts and commercial complexes'.[45] In the colourful material produced by the Ministry of Industry and Commerce in Maharashtra, where the state is marketed as the most modern and investor friendly state in India, Mumbai is portrayed as a modern metropolis full of highways and high-rise buildings, and the state as open and 'ripe with opportunities'.[46] Chief Minister Manohar Joshi has declared that the government was also eager to make selected industrial 'five-star facilities' for large and sophisticated firms where one government officer would be resident and would be given all the necessary discretionary powers to solve the problems of industry on the spot. The government is also designing a 'red-card system', where all complaints from industrialists concerning clearance of projects 'can send a "red card" directly to me, and the concerned officers will be pulled up immediately'.[47]

Though merely declarations, the tenor of these plans indicates a clear commitment to a new kind of capitalist growth, with the state in the role as actively supporting and facilitating industrial investments. The vision of the new industrial parks clearly revolve around upper-middle class attractions of 'clubs, resorts, and five star', while labour, housing, and facilities for employees are not

[45] 'Industry, Trade and Commerce Policy for Maharashtra, 1995', Ministry of Industry, Trade and Commerce, Government of Maharashtra, Mumbai, 1995.

[46] In the material SICOM promotes the port facilities along the coast, the new industrial parks, etc. and in a special pamphlet accompanying the 'promotion-packet' a number of Indian industrialists and Non-resident Indians heading large international companies praise the state for its economic climate and friendliness to NRIs.

[47] Manohar Joshi, in *Economic Times*, 11 March 1996.

even mentioned in the plan. The labour issue is 'a very sensitive one' Joshi admits, but the Shiv Sena seems to rely heavily on its expanding control with unions in Maharashtra, where *Bharatiya Kamgar Sena* represents the largest conglomerate of unions in the state, known for its friendliness to employers, and its hard-hitting style at the shopfloor.

In spite of apprehensions concerning the degree of foreign investments, there is little doubt that the leading parts of the BJP fully endorse the strategies that will strengthen and boost entrepreneurship and industry. During the election campaign in 1996, Vajpayee stated in a much-quoted speech before industrialists in Bombay, that the BJP was neither against liberalization nor against multinationals. The party only wanted to see Indian multinationals investing abroad and in India instead of foreign companies investing in India, Vajpayee argued. Pramod Mahajan, the BJP chief of Maharashtra who has been a target of sustained criticism from purist forces in the RSS and accused of 'five-star culture' and lack of commitment to Swadeshi, argues that the BJP's policy is a 'normal' protectionist stance:

All countries, be it America and its protectionist policy against Japanese cars, or Japan and its protection of its rice, safeguard their interests. I am not against global trade, but I am first an Indian, and then a global citizen.[48]

Mahajan also argued that once in power in a state like Maharashtra, one has to adapt to the realities of power there and not at any cost maintain an austere lifestyle as the RSS-pracharaks used to do: 'After we came to power in Maharashtra, people who are worth billions came to me as party-chief in the state—I cannot ask them to stand in a queue. (...) Yesterday we did not have a car. Five or ten years from now we may have helicopters and a jet for our leaders. What is wrong in that?.'[49]

CONCLUSION

In its manifesto for the 1996 General Election, the BJP tried to distance itself from any copying of the East Asian export-led industrialization strategy. In contradiction to many of the stated objectives of the policies in Maharashtra bearing the imprint of the

[48] Mahajan, in *Asian Age*, 18 November 1995.
[49] Ibid.

Shiv Sena business enthusiasm, the BJPs official economic policy claims to be 'employment-oriented' promoting employment in all sectors, at the village level and in cottage industries, promoting labour-intensive housing schemes, and boosting more employment schemes for the rural unemployed. In the manifesto, the BJP also stresses the need to protect, redeploy and reeducate public sector employees.[50] But the election programme cannot conceal the evermore obvious discrepancies between the real-politik of industrial development in western India promoted by pragmatic leaders like Mahajan, and the strong forces within the Sangh Parivar committed to Swadeshi and an austere and 'pro-poor' profile of the party, led by stalwarts as Thengadi of the BMS, Murli Manohar Joshi of the BJP, and several of the apex leaders of the RSS.

These discrepancies are likely to persist because they not merely indicate a generational gap, but also reflect very different horizons of experience and imagining: a dynamic and intensely materialistic life in the bustling industrial centres of western India versus a less fluid social world in the plains of central and northern India, where the economic development has not yet subverted parameters of status, caste and public assertion to the extent it has happened in the western parts of the country.

---

[50] *Election Manifesto*, 1996.

AFTERWORD

The BJP at the Centre:
A Central and Centrist Party?

CHRISTOPHE JAFFRELOT

Only a New BJP can shoulder the responsibilities of the new era that is opening up for both India and our own Party. The New BJP will be guided not by the issues of yesterday, but by the agenda of tomorrow. The New BJP will be fully alive to the changing world scenario and enable itself and India to face the challenges, and also to seize the opportunities, maturing in the womb of the 21st century. The New BJP will not only be the party in Governance, but the natural party of Governance.

Inaugural Address by Shri L. K. Advani, President, Bharatiya Janata Party,
National Executive Meeting, New Delhi, 11–12 April 1998
(New Delhi: BJP, 1998, p. 12)

For the first time, a Bharatiya Janata Party (BJP) leader, A. B. Vajpayee, was appointed prime minister of India in 1998 and remained in office for more than merely a few weeks—in contrast to the 1996 short-lived Vajpayee government. As mentioned in the introduction of this book, the so-called 'second' Vajpayee government relied on a coalition of national and regional parties, the National Democratic Alliance (NDA). The compulsions of coalition politics obliged the BJP to give up the idea of implementing its election manifesto and to evolve a National Agenda for Governance with its allies instead. After 6 months, with some of this agenda's items being implemented, the BJP prided itself of several 'Achievements and Initiatives'. It referred first to the nuclear tests, which had been conducted in May 1998.[1] It also

[1] *Achievements and Initiatives, BJP-led Government's First Six Months (March 19 to September 18, 1998)* (New Delhi: Bharatiya Janata Party, 1998), p. 1.

highlighted Home Minister L. K. Advani's 'special joint action plan' to 'counter terrorism in Jammu and Kashmir' and its repressive attitude against illegal (mainly Bangladeshi) immigration. On the domestic scene, however, the main achievement of the Vajpayee government was probably the manner in which it settled the two decades-old Cauvery disputes on water-sharing between Tamil Nadu, Karnataka, Kerala, and Pondicherry.

In spite of these 'Achievements and Initiatives', the BJP lost heavily in the assembly elections which were organized during the fall of 1998 in three of its oldest strongholds, Madhya Pradesh, Rajasthan, and Delhi. The sudden—and ephemeral, as we were to see later—increase in inflation was partly responsible for this setback. The Vajpayee government was also weakened by constant tensions within the coalition. Jayalalitha, the leader of the All-India Anna Dravida Munnetra Kazhagam (AIADMK)—an indispensable partner with its 27 MPs in the Lok Sabha—adopted a problematic attitude since she insisted on the dismissal of the Dravida Munnetra Kazhagam (DMK) in Madras, a demand Vajpayee did not agree with. Eventually, she withdrew her support in April 1999, most probably because Vajpayee also refused to intervene 'to prevent government lawyers from pressing corruption cases against her in the courts'.[2] At that time, the Congress seemed to be in a position to improve its tally during the 13th General Elections, which were organized in September–October 1999.

Now, the BJP has overcome some of its handicaps, so much so that Vajpayee has been the first prime minister to win two elections in a row since Indira Gandhi in 1971. This success has often been explained by the 'Kargil war', which opposed India and Pakistan in Kashmir during the summer of 1999, but the post-election survey made by the Centre for the Study of Developing Societies (CSDS) showed that this issue affected the votes of only 15 per cent of the respondents.[3] Does the fact that Kargil alone did not explain

---

[2] Jenkins, R., 'Appearances and Reality in Indian Politics. Making Sense of the 1999 General Election', *Government and Opposition*, vol. 35, no. 1, 2000, p. 53.

[3] The architects of the survey, Yogendra Yadav, Oliver Heath, and Anindya Saha came to the conclusion that 'the BJP made a net gain out of the conflict', but that was a small gain since 'of the 15 per cent who said that Kargil influenced their vote 56 per cent voted for the BJP-led alliance and 25 per cent for the Congress (I) and its allies', Yadav, Yogendra, Oliver Heath, and Anindya Saha, 'Issues and the Verdict', *Frontline*, 26 November 1999, p. 46).

the BJP's electoral consolidation mean that the party is on its way to establish itself as the epicentral force of the Indian political system on its own? Correlatively, can we consider that the BJP is in a position to occupy that space because it has turned its back on Hindu nationalism to embrace a more liberal approach of politics? Is there anything like 'a New BJP', to use Advani's phrase. To what extent has the BJP changed its ideology and agenda? In other words, we shall ask ourselves in the following pages whether the BJP, being in office at the centre, has started to occupy the centre of the Indian political system, as a central and centrist force.

TOWARDS A DOMINANT PARTY?

In a recent book, Partha Ghosh considered that 'The emergence of the BJP as a dominant party raises the issue whether a dominant party is necessarily a national party.'[4] But one may wonder in the first place whether the BJP fulfils the criteria of a dominant party. It appeared as the winner at the 1999 elections, especially because it was the only party continuously improving its tally in terms of seats. But with 183 seats, it was almost 90 seats short of a majority and its share of valid votes has declined from 25.6 per cent to 23.7 per cent between 1998 and 1999. This is largely due to the fact that it contested only 339 seats, as against 389 (50 more) in 1998. In fact, the proportion of the BJP candidates who won in 1999 was larger than in 1998, 53.9 per cent as against 46.8 per cent. But the Congress won 2.7 percentage points more (28.5 per cent as against 25.8 per cent) even though it contested 20 seats less (457 as against 477), and if the Sharad Pawar group had not left the party it would have probably deprived the BJP–Shiv Sena coalition of many seats in Maharashtra. In fact, Pawar's National Congress Party (NCP)—which has been recognized as a national party by the Election Commission—enabled the BJP–Shiv Sena alliance to win in 20 constituencies whose seats would have gone to the Congress, had this breakaway faction remained within this party or supported its candidates.

These ambivalent figures notwithstanding, during the meeting of the BJP's apex decision-making body, the National Executive,

[4] Ghosh, P., *BJP and the Evolution of Hindu Nationalism: From Periphery to Centre* (Delhi: Manohar, 1999), p. 368.

that followed the elections, the party leaders emphasized that the BJP had significantly expanded its base in geographical and social terms since it now had Members of Parliament (MPs) from 18 states and one Union Territory (Andaman and Nicobar Islands), 25 Scheduled Caste (SC) MPs, 21 Scheduled Tribe (ST) MPs, and 15 woman MPs. But to what extent has the party been able to reach beyond its traditional stronghold of the Hindi belt and beyond the 'twice-born' this time?

Becoming an All-India Party

Kushabhau Thakre—who succeeded Advani as party president in 1998—emphatically stressed after the 13th General Elections that the BJP was now an all-India party because some of its candidates had been returned 'From Andamans to Kashmir, from Gujarat to Assam'.[5] It is true that the BJP has now reached beyond the Hindi belt in a big way since the party MPs returned from this large region represent only 61 per cent of its parliamentary group of the party in the Lok Sabha, as against 74 per cent in 1996. The BJP has also registered impressive performances in states were it was a nonentity so far, like Goa (where it won both seats with 51.5 per cent of the valid votes) and Assam (where it won 2 seats with 29.6 per cent of the valid votes).[6] It has also won 2 seats with 31.5 per cent of the valid votes in Jammu and Kashmir.[7] However, these are not large states. In fact, the only important state beyond the Hindi belt where the BJP has really consolidated its position is Gujarat where it has won 20 seats (out of 26) with 52.5 per cent of the valid votes. But Gujarat has been a stronghold of the BJP for almost 10 years as we shall see below in greater details.

Interestingly, in all the other non-Hindi belt states, either the BJP remains a marginal player (like in Kerala where it won less

[5] Meeting of the Bharatiya Janata Party National Executive, New Delhi, 3–4 November 1999. Opening remarks by Shri Kushabhau Thakre, President, Bharatiya Janata Party, p. 2.

[6] On Assam, see Srikanth, 'Communalising Assam: AGP's Loss is BJP's Gain', *Economic and Political Weekly*, 4 December 1999, pp 3412–14.

[7] On the electoral impact of the National Conference, see Chowdhary, R., 'BJP's Alliance with National Conference', *Economic and Political Weekly*, 27 November 1999, pp 3342–3.

TABLE 11.1: The Share of the Hindi Belt MPs
in the BJP Parliamentary Group in the Lok Sabha

Year	1 Hindi Belt MPs of the BJP	2 Total BJP MPs	(Col. 1/Col.2) Ratio 1/2 (per cent)
1991	87	120	72.5
1996	119	161	73.9
1998	122	184*	66.3
1999	112	183	61

* Including bye-elections

than 8 per cent of the valid votes)[8] or it depends on a regional party: the Telugu Desam Party (TDP) in Andhra Pradesh, the Janata Dal (United) [JD (U)] in Karnataka, the Shiv Sena in Maharashtra, the Biju Janata Dal (BJD) in Orissa, the Dravida Munnetra Kazhagam (DMK) and other smaller parties in Tamil Nadu, the Trinamool Congress in West Bengal, and the Shiromani Akali Dal (Badal) [SAD (Badal)] in Punjab. Even in the Hindi belt the BJP felt the need of having seat adjustments with local partners like the JD(U) in Bihar, the Indian National Lok Dal (INLD) in Haryana and the Himachal Vikas Congress (HVC) in Himachal Pradesh. As mentioned in the introduction of this book, the strategy of the BJP is clearly to expand through alliances with regional—or regionalist—parties. This strategy was first initiated in the mid-1980s when the party made a deal with the Shiv Sena in Maharashtra. It subsequently refused to have similar alliances in other states, like Madhya Pradesh, where the Shiv Sena was trying to take roots.

[8] Although the BJP remains a minor force in Kerala, the RSS is taking roots in the state, so much so that the CPI(M) government issued in 1999 an ordinance, which was primarily aim at this movement. The ordinance makes it mandatory for organizations 'imparting training to their cadres on methods of attacks in martial arts to obtain a licence from the state government'. The BJP general secretary, P. Mukundan replied promptly, as if he was an RSS spokesman, that: 'All the 5000 units of the Rashtriya Swayamsevak Sangh in Kerala will continue with the drill. Let the police arrest our boys. We will fill the jails in the state.... We have 40,000 to 50,000 boys attending the drills every day. All of them are prepared to go to jail' (Jose, D., 'RSS to defy Kerala Govt.'s curbs physical training', Rediff. on the net, 2 January 2000). Even if these figures are inflated they reflect the growing attractiveness of the RSS in Kerala. On the increasing number of violent clahses between RSS men and communist activists, see Joseph, A. V. 'Resurgence of Politics of Violence', *Economic and Political Weekly*, 18 December 1999, pp 3574–5).

TABLE 11.2: The BJP Performances in the 1999 Election, State-wise

State	Total Number of Seats	Seats Won by the BJP				Share of the Valid Votes			
		1991	1996	1998*	1999	1991	1996	1998	1999
1	2	3	4	5	6	7	8	9	10
Andhra Pradesh	42	1	0	4	7	9.6	5.6	18.3	9.1
Assam	14	2	1	1	2	9.6	15.9	24.5	29.6
Bihar	54	5	18	20	23	16.0	20.5	24	23.3
Gujarat	26	20	16	19	20	50.4	48.5	48.4	52.5
Haryana	10	0	4	1	5	10.2	19.7	18.9	28.5
Himachal Pradesh	4	2	0	3	3	42.8	39.6	51.4	46.2
Jammu and Kashmir	6	0	1	2	2	0	19.0	28.6	31.5
Karnataka	27	4	6	13	7	28.8	24.9	26.9	26.9
Kerala	20	0	0	0	0	4.6	5.6	8	7.9
Madhya Pradesh	40	12	27	30	29	41.9	41.3	45.7	46.6
Maharashtra	48	5	18	4	13	20.2	21.8	22.5	21.9
Orissa	21	0	0	7	9	9.5	13.4	21.2	24.6
Punjab	13	0	0	3	1	17	6.5	11.7	9.2
Rajasthan	25	12	12	5	16	40.9	42.4	41.7	46.9
Tamil Nadu	39	0	0	3	4	2.9	2.9	6.8	7.1
Uttar Pradesh	85	51	52	57	29	32.8	33.4	36.5	27.6
West Bengal	42	0	0	1	2	11.7	6.9	10.2	11.1

(Cont.)

1	2	3	4	5	6	7	8	9	10
Andaman & Nicobar Islands	1	0	0	0	1	4.9	24.3	35.5	52.7
Arunachal Pradesh	2	0	0	0	0	6.1	17.4	21.8	16.3
Chandigarh	1	0	1	1	0	28.8	39.1	42.4	45.1
Dadar & Nagar Haveli	1	0	0	1	0	35.4	42.4	53.7	20.8
Daman & Diu	1	1	0	1	0	31.9	40.5	42	43.1
Delhi	7	5	5	6	7	40.2	49.6	50.7	51.8
Goa	2	0	0	0	2	15.6	13.8	30	51.5
Manipur	2	0	0	0	1	8.1	5.2	12.6	34.7
Meghalaya	2	0	0	0	0	6.8	9.1	9	9.4
Tripura	2	0	0	0	0	3.0	6.5	8.2	25.3
TOTAL	537	120	161	184	183	20.1	20.3	25.6	23.7

* Including bye-elections

Source: G. V. L. Narasimha Rao and K. Balakrishna, *Indian Elections: The Nineties*, Delhi, Har-Anand, 1999, and *Frontline*, 5 Nov. 1999, pp. 122–3.

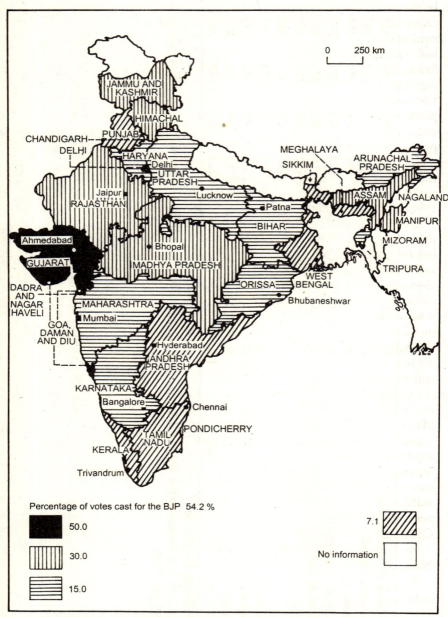

Votes Won by the BJP in the 1999 Lok Sabha Elections (State-wise)

In the mid-1990s, this strategy was implemented more systematically with regional parties which had no affinity with Hindu nationalism, like the Shiromani Akali Dal (even though the Akalis had already made coalitions with the Jana Sangh in Punjab), the Samta Party in Bihar, and the Lok Shakti Party in Karnataka, two regional parties whose leaders had some socialist background. For most of the partners of the BJP, making an alliance with this party was the best means for strengthening their position in their state, independently of any ideological commitment. Such a pragmatic approach enabled the BJP to improve its positions in regions where its position was that of a new comer. In Haryana, the BJP's share of valid votes jumped from 18.9 per cent in 1998 to 28.5 per cent in 1999. In Orissa, it rose from 13.4 per cent in 1996 to 21.2 per cent in 1998 and 24.6 per cent in 1999.

During the 13th General Elections, the BJP won more seats than its allies in Maharashtra, Punjab, Bihar, and Karnataka (in the last two states, its allies, the Janata Dal (United), the Samta Party, and the Janata Dal (S), the former Lok Shakti Party, contested elections on a common symbol, the arrow). However, this state of things was largely due to the unpopularity of the BJP's allies, which were at the helm of the government in these states—except in Bihar. The BJP would have fared better had it not made any alliance with the JD (U) in Karnataka, a state where it lost heavily during the assembly elections with only 20.7 per cent of the votes and 44 seats (as against 40.8 per cent of the votes and 132 seats to the Congress). The same line of reasoning apply to the SAD (Badal) in Punjab[9] and the Shiv Sena in Maharashtra. In Karnataka and Maharashtra the BJP won more MP seats than in 1998 but registered limited setbacks in terms of valid votes. In the latter state, state assembly elections did not enable the BJP to win more than 56 seats, with 14.5 per cent of the valid votes, becoming the fourth party in Maharashtra behind the Congress (27.2 per cent and 75 seats), the NCP (22.6 per cent and 58 seats), and the Shiv Sena (17.3 per cent and 69 seats). The post-election alliance between the Congress and the NCP formed the government in the state.

In Andhra Pradesh, Orissa, Haryana, West Bengal, and Tamil Nadu, the BJP is still a dominated partner for its local allies. In

[9] See Verma, P. S., 'Akali–BJP Debacle in Punjab: Wages of Non-Performance and Fragmentation', *Economic and Political Weekly*, 11 December 1999, pp 3519–31.

these states, it is very doubtful that the party could have won more than a handful of seats had it not made any alliance. While it registered a remarkable performance in Orissa (with almost one-fourth of the valid votes, more than its national average), it remained a junior ally to the Biju Janata Dal (BJD) and this position was reconfirmed during the assembly elections of 2000 when the BJP won 38 seats with 18 per cent of the votes as against 68 seats and 29.2 per cent of the votes of the BJD. In Haryana, also, while the BJP has made progress in the Lok Sabha elections because of its seat adjustment with the INLD, it remains its junior partner, as evident from the assembly elections results where the BJP won only 6 seats with less than 9 per cent of the votes, whereas the INLD won 47 seats with 29.5 per cent of the votes. The situation is even less favourable to the BJP in the south and in West Bengal. It could only win 9.1 per cent of the valid votes in Andhra Pradesh, 7.1 per cent in Tamil Nadu, and 11.1 per cent in West Bengal during the general elections. Its decline was especially sharp in Andhra Pradesh, but it was largely due to its seat adjustment with the TDP, which got the lion's share. The same scenario unfolded itself during the state assembly elections, where the BJP polled only 3.7 per cent of the valid votes and won 12 MLA seats (as against 44 per cent of the votes and 180 seats to the TDP and 40.6 per cent of the votes and 91 seats to the Congress).

In Tamil Nadu, the party has not been able to win more than 7.1 per cent of the valid votes in the 1999 Lok Sabha elections but it is more than twice the share it got in 1996 (2.9 per cent). This progress may not be only due to the support of the regional parties. In fact, Tamil Nadu has become gradually affected by a more surcharged communal atmosphere, largely because of the aggressively anti-Muslim strategy of the Hindu Munnani, the militant wing of the Rashtriya Swayamsevak Sangh (RSS), and the activities of Islamic groups. The tensions culminated in January 1997 in the assassination of the president of the All India Jehad Committee, Palani Baba. In November 1997, 18 Muslims died in a communal riot in Coimbatore, a place where a bomb attack aiming at L. K. Advani killed 50 people in February 1998. The tensions have never been as sharp as in Uttar Pradesh or in Gujarat in the early 1990s, but the BJP tends to benefit from a certain polarization of the electorate along religious lines. Its efforts to shun its north

Indian image may also bear fruits.[10] While the weakness of the party in Tamil Nadu needs to be qualified, it is still one of its black holes, and it would have not won any seat without the support of local partners.

The BJP, therefore, is not yet an all-India party like the Congress, whose strength is more evenly distributed, and it may not rapidly be able to improve its performance in such a way that it does not remain in the position of a dominated partner in Andhra Pradesh, Orissa, West Bengal, and Tamil Nadu. Even then, the BJP has already benefited a great deal from these regional alliances and the party will certainly try to continue its association with them. However such a deepening of its coalition strategy implies that certain conditions should be fulfilled. First, the BJP must stick to its moderate line, keeping its distance with the Hindutva rhetoric because most of its regional allies do not have any affinities with Hindu nationalism, all the more so as some of them epitomize anti-north Indian regionalist cultures (the Dravidian culture, for instance) and receive the support of Muslim voters (like the TDP in Andhra Pradesh). Second, the BJP must be generous with its regional allies—for instance, in terms of seat adjustment and share of ministerial portfolios in coalition governments. Third, the BJP's allies must continue to consider that their main enemy in their state is the Congress, the CPI(M), or any other regional force, and not the BJP—in other words, they must underestimate the capacity of the BJP to 'swallow' them, to use the terminology of the party president, Kushabhau Thakre.[11] The BJD may be the first victim of such a process, given the weak leadership of Naveen Patnaik. Sections of the Shiv Sena may meet the same fate if Bal Thackeray's successor is not in a position to keep the party united. Fourth, the BJP leaders must persuade the regional chiefs of the party in the states where they are in the position of junior partners to remain so and make the needed concessions in terms of seat adjustments and power sharing.

---

[10] The state BJP unit tried to assume Tamil colour by organizing the meeting of the National Executive of the party under the aegis of Thiruvalluvar (a Tamil saint) and Bharathiar (a nationalist poet in Tamil). See Nambath, S., 'State BJP's Unit Bid to Assume Tamil Colour', *The Hindu*, 21 December 1999.

[11] Interview with K. Thakre, Bhopal.

Till now, this set of conditions has been fulfilled without any real difficulty. First, the moderate line of the BJP is likely to prevail and A. B. Vajpayee to remain the icon of the BJP so long as the party needs allies. Second, the BJP has not been very generous with its partners at the time of forming the government in 1999, since they got only 32.85 per cent of the ministerial portfolios whereas they represent 40.32 per cent of the NDA MPs (in 1998 it was the other way around) but it made some concessions in terms of seat adjustments.[12] Usually the BJP contested more Lok Sabha seats and let more assembly seats to its regional allies and the coalition's candidate for chief ministership often came from the ranks of the BJP's regional partner. Third, the partners of the BJP may continue to underestimate the risk of being 'consumed' by this party, in comparison with the necessity to cope with their more traditional enemies such as the Congress. Fourth, the BJP leaders have succeeded in persuading the local party chiefs to keep a low profile and nominate a smaller number of candidates than they thought they were entitled to. In Andhra Pradesh and Karnataka the local BJP leaders did not give up their claims very willingly but they were not adamant either.[13]

To sum up, the BJP has taken roots in new territories but its most substantial gains have been accomplished in those states where it had made alliances with regional parties. It is still depending on them in many states, so much so that for the moment, the BJP is not yet a full-fledged 'all India party'. The social expansion of the BJP needs to be qualified too.

[12] During the most recent assembly elections, these concessions were substantial in Andhra Pradesh where the BJP contested only 24 seats but much less significant in Karnataka where it contested 149 seats and in Maharashtra where it conceded 161 seats to the Shiv Sena—in both states the party staked its claims to the chief ministership or resorted to the formula 'larger party to head government'. In February 2000 the BJP and the BJD reached an agreement before the Orissa assembly elections which left 84 seats to the latter and 63 to the former, Naveen Patnaik being projected as the alliance's chief minister in waiting.

[13] So far as Andhra Pradesh is concerned, it seems that the BJP's Vice President V. Naidu—who, hails from this state—was instrumental in convincing the local party leaders to 'fight the election jointly with the TDP' (Cited in *The Hindu*, 12 August 1999).

Beyond the Twice Born, How Far?

Yogendra Yadav, Sanjay Kumar, and Oliver Heath have suggested that the 1999 election marked the emergence of a 'new BJP's social bloc',[14] that included the traditional upper-caste supporters of the party but reached beyond this elite. Basing their argument on the CSDS election survey, they point out that 'the BJP and its allies secured the support of 60 per cent of upper caste Hindus and 52 per cent of the dominant Hindu peasant castes (which are not classified as Other Backward Classes) such as Jats, Marathas, Patidars, Reddys, and Kammas'.[15] The National Democratic Alliance, therefore, represents a cross–section of the Indian urban as well as rural elite. This social basis can be identified through the criterion of caste, but there is an element of class in it: 'The decline of the Congress-I and the rise of the BJP to power created the possibility of a new kind of cleavage-based politics, one that draws on the overlap of cleavages based on caste and class.'[16] The authors of these lines have built an index mixing caste-based and class-based criteria which show that 'the BJP draws as much as 69 per cent of its votes from the 45 per cent voters [representing the upper strata of Indian society according to these criteria]'.[17] What is new is the BJP's capacity to reach beyond the upper-caste urban elite, to incorporate lower-caste people experiencing some social mobility in India's countryside.

Yet, the 'BJP's new social bloc' has its own limitations. First, the party does not attract such a large number of voters from the dominant castes: the BJP and its allies received 52 per cent of their votes but the BJP alone, 30 per cent only, less than the Congress (31 per cent). Second, the most important groups for measuring the social expansion of the BJP are probably those situated below the dominant castes, the Other Backward Classes (OBCs) and the Dalits, the most numerous social categories. Now, in 1999, the BJP could only attract 16 per cent of the Scheduled Caste (SC) voters, according to the CSDS exit poll, 21 per cent of the upper OBCs, and 19 per cent of the lower OBCs;

[14] Yadav, Y., S. Kumar, and O. Heath, 'The BJP's New Social Bloc', *Frontline*, 19 November 1999, pp 31–40.
[15] Ibid., p. 33.
[16] Ibid., p. 40.
[17] Ibid., p. 39.

the BJP and its allies got one-fifth of the OBC vote, as against 35 per cent to the Congress and its allies.

The social bloc of the BJP, therefore, remains dominated by elite groups. This specific feature is evident from the CSDS surveys in the Hindi belt: in Uttar Pradesh, the BJP got 77 per cent of the Brahmin vote and 74 per cent of the Rajput vote, as against 11 per cent of the Yadav vote and 29 per cent of the votes from other OBC castes. In Rajasthan, the BJP received between 62 per cent and 98 per cent of the votes of different upper castes as against 12 per cent of the Gujar vote (the Gujars being the largest OBC caste). In Bihar, the BJP–JD (U) coalition won between 86 and 92 per cent of the upper castes' votes but only 79 per cent of the votes of the Kurmis and Koeris, two important OBC castes. Unfortunately, the CSDS poll does not distinguish the BJP electorate from the JD (U) voters. This is one of the reasons why it is useful to look at indicators other than opinion polls, such as the social profile of the elected representatives since they reflect the social base of the party. The other reason is that we can use this indicator to analyse the *evolution* of the social profile of the BJP over the last 10 years.

Using the CSDS data, Oliver Heath examined the evolution of the social profile of the BJP voters. But his analysis suffers from two weaknesses. First, it does not distinguish the BJP from its allies. He shows that the share of the upper castes among the voters of the BJP and its allies has declined from 52 to 42 per cent between 1991 and 1998 whereas that of the OBCs has increased from 34 to 38 per cent, that of the SC voters from 8 to 11 per cent, and that of the Scheduled Tribes (STs) from 5 to 7 per cent.[18] However the CSDS data for 1999 demonstrate, as we have just seen, that a large part of the OBC voters of the NDA are in fact not supporting the BJP but its allies. Secondly, Oliver Heath's figures bracket together the 'twice borns' and the dominant castes under the label 'Hindu Upper' whereas these two social categories often have contrasted social status. For instance, the Jats cannot be easily classified along with the upper castes—the National Commission for Backward Classes even considered that Jats of Rajasthan should be considered as OBCs.

---

[18] Heath, O., 'Anatomy of BJP's Rise to Power: Social, Regional and Political Expansion in the 1990s', *Economic and Political Weekly*, 21 August 1999, p. 2513.

It is therefore not redundant with opinion polls to look at the social profile of the BJP MPs since it enables us to suggest a more refined analysis, party-wise as well as caste-wise. We shall focus here on the Hindi belt—the Hindu nationalist traditional stronghold—where the BJP gets a majority of its seats.[19] By and large, the evolution emphasized by Oliver Heath can be also found among the party MPs since the last five elections have shown a steady erosion of the share of the upper castes among the BJP MPs of the Hindi belt, from more than 53 per cent, in 1989 to 43.8 per cent in 1998 and 39.1 per cent in 1999 (see Tables 11.3, 11.4, 11.5, 11.6, and 11.7). Those who benefit from this trend are less the OBCs than the dominant castes (mainly the Jats), whose share went up from 1.6 to 6.4 per cent between 1989 and 1999, and the Dalit candidates. The following tables show that the social profile of the BJP MPs returned in the Hindi belt is more elitist than that of the Janata Dal (and the local parties born from its breakaway factions), and even than that of the Congress-I, except in 1999. So far as the coalition of the BJP and the JD(U) in Bihar is concerned, Table 11.7 suggests that the latter is more OBC-oriented than the former.

In 1999, the state where the BJP appears to be more open to the OBCs is Madhya Pradesh. In this province, a large number of the outgoing MPs refused to contest, either because they were ageing (like Rajmata Scindia, Baburao Paranjpe, and Sartaj Singh) or because of some difference with the party leaders (like in the case of S. C. Verma, the outgoing MP of Bhopal), and the party seized this opportunity for fielding a larger number of OBC candidates. This is probably the main explanation for the attractiveness of the party for the low castes. In contrast with the situation prevailing in other states of the Hindi belt, here, the percentage of upper castes and OBCs voting for the BJP is almost the same: while 56 per cent of the upper castes voted for the BJP, 53 per cent of the upper OBCs and 49 per cent of the lower OBCs did the same according to the CSDS exit poll. These figures suggest that when the party pragmatically field candidates from the lower castes, such a strategy generates rich dividends—this is what Advani was aiming at before the 1998 elections, when he was still

---

[19] The states under consideration here are Uttar Pradesh, Bihar, Madhya Pradesh, Rajasthan, Haryana, Himachal Pradesh, and Delhi.

TABLE 11.3: Caste and Community of the Hindi Belt MPs in the
9th Lok Sabha (1989), (party-wise)

Castes and Communities	BJP		Congress-I		JD	
Upper Castes	34	(53.13)	13	(37)	34	(31.78)
Brahmin	13	(20.31)	6	(17.14)	8	(7.48)
Bhumihar			1	(2.86)	2	(1.87)
Rajput	11	(17.19)	3	(8.57)	19	(17.76)
Bania/Jain	5	(7.81)	2	(5.71)	1	(0.93)
Kayasth	2	(3.13)			3	(2.80)
Khattri	2	(3.13)	1	(2.86)		
Sindhi	1	(1.56)				
Tyagi					1	(0.93)
Intermediary Castes	1	(1.56)	3	(9)	14	(13.08)
Jat			1	(2.86)	14	(13.08)
Maratha	1	(1.56)	1	(2.86)		
Bishnoi			1	(2.86)		
Other Backward Classes	10	(15.62)	2	(5.71)	29	(27.10)
Yadav	1	(1.56)			17	(15.89)
Kurmi	4	(6.25)	2	(5.71)	5	(4.67)
Lodhi	2	(3.13)			1	(0.93)
Kacchi	1	(1.56)			1	(0.93)
Gujar	1	(1.56)				
Koeri	1	(1.56)			3	(2.8)
Mali					1	(0.93)
Panwar					1	(0.93)
Scheduled Castes	11	(17.2)	7	(19.6)	20	(18.7)
Scheduled Tribes	6	(7.8)	7	(19.6)	2	(1.87)
Christian			1	(2.86)		
Muslim	1	(1.56)	2	(5.71)	8	(7.48)
Sikh	1	(1.56)				
TOTAL	64	(100)	35	(100)	107	(100)

Note: Percentages are given in parenthesis.

Source: Field work.

TABLE 11.4: Caste and Community of the Hindi Belt MPs in the
10th Lok Sabha (1991), (party-wise)

Castes and Communities	BJP		Congress-I		JD	
Upper Castes	46	(52.27)	18	(30)	9	(16.98)
Brahmin	23	(26.13)	7	(11.67)	1	(1.89)
Bhumihar			2	(3.33)	1	(1.89)
Rajput	17	(19.31)	4	(6.67)	7	(13.21)
Bania/Jain	2	(2.27)	2	(3.33)		
Kayasth	1	(1.13)	2	(3.33)		
Khattri	1	(1.13)	1	(1.67)		
Sindhi	1	(1.13)				
Intermediary Castes	4	(4.54)	10	16.67	1	(1.89)
Jat	3	(3.4)	9	(15)	1	(1.89)
Maratha	1	(1.13)	1	(1.67)		
Bishnoi						
Other Backward Classes	13	(14.77)	8	(13.33)	21	(39.62)
Yadav			1	(1.67)	12	(22.64)
Kurmi	8	(9.01)	3	(5)	5	(9.43)
Lodhi	2	(2.27)				
Kacchi	1	(1.13)				
Gujar			3	(5)		
Koeri	1	(1.13)			3	(5.66)
Panwar			1	(1.67)	1	(1.89)
Other	1	(1.13)				
Scheduled Castes	16	(18.18)	10	(16.7)	13	(24.53)
Scheduled Tribes	5	(5.68)	11	(18.3)		
Christian					1	(1.89)
Muslim			3	(5)	7	(13.21)
Sadhu	2	(2.27)				
Sikh	1	(1.13)				
Unidentified	1	(1.13)			1	(1.89)
TOTAL	88	(100)	60	(100)	53	(100)

Note: Percentages are given in parenthesis.

TABLE 11.5: Caste and Community of the Hindi Belt MPs in the
11th Lok Sabha (1996), (party-wise)

Castes and Communities	BJP		Congress-I		SP–JD	
Upper Castes	56	(46.28)	11	(32.35)	6	(14.29)
Brahmin	25	(20.66)	6	(17.6)	2	(4.76)
Bhumihar	2	(1.65)				
Rajput	19	(15.70)	2	(5.88)	3	(7.14)
Bania/Jain	6	(4.96)	2	(5.88)		
Other			1	(2.9)		
Kayasth	3	(2.48)			1	(2.38)
Khattri	1	(0.83)				
Intermediary Castes	6	(4.96)	6	(17.65)		
Jat	5	(4.13)	6	(17.65)		
Maratha	1	(0.83)				
Bishnoi						
Other Backward Classes	21	(17.4)	3	(8.8)	23	(54.76)
Yadav	2	(1.65)			14	(33.33)
Kurmi	8	(6.61)			2	(4.76)
Lodhi	4	(3.31)				
Kacchi	1	(0.8)			1	(2.38)
Gujar			2	5.88		
Koeri	1	(0.83)			2	(4.76)
Mali					1	(2.38)
Panwar			1	(2.9)		
Teli	1	(0.83)				
Jaiswal	1	(0.83)				
Kirar	1	(0.83)				
Kewat					1	(2.38)
Bania (Bihari)	1	(0.83)				
Torak					1	(2.38)
Other	1	(0.83)			1	(2.38)
Scheduled Castes	26	(21.5)	5	(14.7)	6	14.29
Scheduled Tribes	9	(7.4)	6	(17.6)		
Christian					1	(2.38)
Muslim			2	(5.88)	6	(14.29)
Sikh	1	(0.83)				
Unidentified	2	(1.65)	1	(2.94)		
TOTAL	121	(100)	34	(100)	42	(100)

Note: Percentages are given in parenthesis.

TABLE 11.6: Caste and Community of the Hindi Belt MPs in the 12th Lok Sabha (1998), (party-wise)

Castes and Communities	BJP		Congress-I		SP–JD–RJD	
Upper Castes	53	(43.8)	10	(26.3)	8	(16.67)
Brahmin	24	(19.83)	3	(8)		
Bhumihar	2	(1.65)	1	(2.63)		
Rajput	17	(14.05)	1	(2.63)	8	(16.67)
Bania/Jain	4	(3.31)	3	(8)		
Kayasth	3	(2.48)	1	(2.63)		
Khatri	2	(1.65)				
Other	1	(0.8)	1	(2.63)		
Intermediary Castes	8	(6.61)	9	(23.7)		
Jat	7	(5.79)	5	(13.16)		
Maratha	1	(0.83	1	(2.63)		
Bishnoi			3	(7.9)		
Other Backward Classes	25	(20.7)	3	(7.9)	23	(47.92)
Yadav	2	(1.65)	1	(2.63)	12	(25)
Kurmi	12	(9.92)			4	(8.33)
Lodhi	3	(2.48)				
Gujar			1	(2.63)		
Koeri			1	(2.63)	3	(6.25)
Teli	2	(1.65)				
Jaiswal	1	(0.83)				
Kirar	1	(0.83)				
Kewat					1	(2.08)
Bania (Bihari)	2	(1.65)			1	(2.08)
Bijoy					1	(2.08)
Dhanuk					1	(2.08)
Other	2	(1.65)	1	(2.63)		
Scheduled Castes	21	(17.4)	5	(13.2)	9	(18.75)
Scheduled Tribes	9	(7.4)	9	(23.7)		
Christian					1	(2.08)
Muslim	1	(0.83)	2	(5.26)	7	(14.58)
Sikh	1	(0.83)				
Unidentified	3	(2.48)				
TOTAL	121	(100)	38	(100)	48	(100)

Note: Percentages are given in parenthesis.

TABLE 11.7: Caste and Community of the Hindi Belt MPs in the
13th Lok Sabha (1999), (party-wise)

Castes and Communities	BJP		Congress-I		JD(U)		RJD–SP	
Upper Castes	43	(39.1)	14	(41.2)	4	(26.7)	3	(9.09)
Brahmin	18	(16.4)	6	(17.6)				
Bhumihar	3	(2.7)	2	(5.9)	2	(13.3)		
Rajput	13	(11.8)	3	(8.8)	2	(13.3)	2	(6.06)
Bania/Jain	4	(3.6)	2	(5.9)				
Kayasth	2	(1.8)						
Khatri	3	(2.7)					1	(3.03)
Sindhi			1	(2.9)				
Intermediary Castes	7	(6.4)	5	(14.7)				
Jat	6	(5.5)	3	(8.8)				
Maratha			1	(2.9)				
Bishnoi	1	(0.9)	1	(2.9)				
Other Backward Classes	20	(18.2)	4	(11.8)	8	(53.3)	13	(39.39)
Yadav	4	(3.6)			5	(33.3)	6	(18.18)
Kurmi	7	(6.4)	1	(2.9)	1	(6.7)	2	(6.06)
Lodhi	2	(1.8)						
Gujar			1	(2.9)				
Koeri					1	(6.7)	1	(3.03)
Teli	1	(0.9)						
Mali							1	(3.03)
Jaiswal	1	(0.9)	1	(2.9)			1	(3.03)
Kirar	1	(0.9)						
Kewat					1	(6.7)		
Other	4	(3.6)	1	(2.9)			2	(6.06)
Scheduled Caste	22	(20)	1	(2.9)	1	(13.3)	6	(18.18)
Scheduled Tribes	11	(10)	5	(14.7)				
Christian			1	(2.9)	1	(5.88)		
Muslim	1	(0.9)	2	(5.9)			4	(12.12)
Sadhu	2	(1.8)						
Unidentified	4	(3.6)	2	(5.9)			7	(21.21)
TOTAL	110	(100)	35	(100)	15	(100)	33	(100)

Note: Percentages are given in parenthesis.

TABLE 11.8: Caste and Community of the Congress-I and BJP
Candidates to the 13th General Elections in Madhya Pradesh

Castes and Communities	Congress-I		BJP	
Upper Castes	16	(40)	13	(32.5)
Brahmin	8	(20)	6	(15)
Rajput	4	(10)	4	(10)
Bania/Jain	3	(7.5)	3	(7.5)
Kayasth	1	(2.5)		
Intermediary Castes	1	(2.5)		
Maratha	1	(2.5)		
Other Backward Classes	6	(15)	12 .	(30)
Gujar			1	(2.5)
Lodhi	1	(2.5)	2	(5)
Kurmi			4	(10)
Teli	1	(2.5)	2	(5)
Kirar			1	(2.5)
Yadav			1	(2.5)
Other	4	(10)	1	(2.5)
Scheduled Castes	6	(15)	6	(15)
Scheduled Tribes	9	(22.5)	9	(22.5)
Muslim	1	(2.5)		
Sikh	1	(2.5)		
TOTAL	40	(100)	40	(100)

Note: Percentages are given in parenthesis.

the president of the BJP. According to him the party's 'list of candidates should fairly reflect the social composition of Indian society'.[20]

Indeed, the BJP leaders apparently have decided to woo more OBC voters by changing their approach to the reservation issue. After the Mandal affair, the party was very reluctant vis-à-vis the implementation of job quotas in favour of the OBCs, as noticed

[20] *Presidential Address and Resolution Adopted at the National Executive Meeting, Bhubaneshwar: December 19, 20 & 21, 1997* (New Delhi: Bharatiya Janata Party), p. 12.

in the introduction of this volume. But it changed its strategy gradually. One could read in the 1999 election manifesto of the NDA:

If required, the Constitution will be amended to maintain the system of reservation.... We are committed to extending the SC/ST reservation for another 10 years. Reservation percentages, above 50 per cent, as followed by certain states, shall be sanctified through necessary legislation measures.[21]

These electoral promises were in tune with the National Agenda that the BJP had negotiated in 1998 with its regional allies[22]—in fact the latter were probably responsible for their insertion in the agenda and then in the NDA manifesto, but the BJP readily obliged them. Vajpayee himself, while campaigning in Rajasthan where the Jats were asking for their inclusion in the OBC category, promised them that his government would accede to their demand if voted to power and even declared that it 'would implement the reservation policy in right earnest'.[23]

However, the BJP may face some difficulty in reconciling this strategy of expansion among the OBCs with its 'new social bloc' made up of middle class people or upwardly mobile elements who may not be prepared to share their freshly acquired privileged position with the OBCs. This contradiction may be especially acute with respect to the reservation issue since most of the upper caste urban middle class is hostile to the expansion of the quotas and the inclusion of more castes in the OBC list which, in some instances, already serves to jeopardize their hegemony. Certainly the anti-Mandal feeling has somehow receded in the background since the economic liberalization has offered new opportunities to the upper caste urban middle class in the private sector which appears more attractive than the public sector. It is also true that Vajpayee tried to keep everybody happy in October 1999 when he enlarged the list of the OBCs *but* not to the extent that the

[21] National Democratic Alliance, *For a Proud, Prosperous India: An Agenda. Election Manifesto, Lok Sabha Election, 1999* (New Delhi: Printed and published by the Bharatiya Janata Party, for and on behalf of the National Democratic Alliance, 1999), p. 8.

[22] The National Agenda for Governance reads: 'We will provide legal protection to existing percentages of reservation in educational institutions at the state level'.

[23] *The Hindu*, 25 August 1999.

National Commission for Backward Classes had recommended.[24]
Furthermore, the address by the President of India to the Parliament which outlined the Vajpayee government's agenda at the beginning of the first session of the 13th Lok Sabha, diluted the NDA promises regarding reservations since it committed the ruling coalition to removing the 50 per cent cap on reservation only in states where it had existed beyond this figure *before* the 1992 Supreme Court judgement reasserting that quotas should not represent more than half of the posts. Now, before 1992, reservation in excess of 50 per cent existed only in the south, where the BJP tries to woo the very large OBC constituency. It did not exist at the centre and in the north where the party is anxious not to antagonize its upper caste supporters.

In spite of all that, the BJP's efforts at attracting the OBCs may not be so easy to implement because the party can not please everybody forever. For instance, how can it satisfy the Jats of Rajasthan without partly alienating its Rajput base? The situation in Uttar Pradesh suggests that the BJP may be, in fact, following a self-contradictory strategy. In this state, the promotion of the OBCs in the party apparatus, epitomized by the appointment of Kalyan Singh as chief minister in 1991 and again 1997, led to the crystallization of an upper caste lobby comprising K. Mishra (a Brahmin who was one of the most influential ministers), L. Tandon (a Khattri who was also a member of Kalyan Singh's government), and Rajnath Singh (a Rajput who was the chief of the BJP state unit). Kalyan Singh had tried to consolidate his OBC base by appointing an ever larger number of low caste ministers. In 1999, 31.8 per cent of the members of his government came from the low castes (as against 21 per cent in his 1991 cabinet).[25] The new upper caste lobby resented the way the OBC were gaining power and used the

---

[24] The National Commission for Backward Classes recommended the inclusion of 350 odd new castes in the category of the OBCs, but Vajpayee selected 116 castes including the Jats among them, even though the National Commission for Backward Classes Act (1993), in its Section 9(2), made it clear that the 'advice of the Commission shall ordinarily be binding on the central government'. However, the Vajpayee government added 68 new castes to the central list of OBCs as recommended by the National Commission in March 2000—as if it had to do this under pressure but had tried to operate discreetly (*The Hindu*, 17 March 2000).

[25] Jaffrelot, C., and J. Zerinini-Brotel, 'La montée des basses castes dans la politique nord-indienne', *Pouvoirs*, no. 90, 1999, p. 85.

party setback in the 1999 Lok Sabha elections for having the chief minister removed.

Kalyan Singh was requested to resign by the party high command in November 1999. He agreed and was replaced by a Bania, Ram Prakash Gupta, but replied that he was victimized by a Brahminical machination whose architect was no one else than Prime Minister Vajpayee. He criticized the way the latter had suspended the construction of a Ram temple at Ayodhya only to please the BJP allies. In December 1999, the BJP Parliamentary Board expelled Kalyan Singh for six years. Realizing that he may not be able to mobilize many supporters by returning to the Ayodhya issue that was still on the agenda of the Vishwa Hindu Parishad (VHP)—an RSS offshoot explicitly hostile to him—Kalyan Singh tried to project himself as an OBC leader. He therefore attacked Vajpayee for not including a single person from this category in the Constitution review panel formed in February 2000: 'Backward castes constitute more than 50 per cent of the country's populace and any attempt to alter the Constitution without having a representative from this section of the society smacks of a sectarian approach.'[26]

It remains to be seen whether Kalyan Singh—who has launched a new party, the Rashtriya Kranti Dal (Party of National Revolution)—can articulate the grievances of the OBCs. A handful of his loyalists, who were all expelled from the BJP, rallied around him (including state working committee member Ram Kumar Singh and the Mayor of Aligarh, A. Varshney), but his first meeting in Etah—where he pointed out that 'backward and weaker sections of society have no place in these organizations [RSS and BJP]' attracted rather large crowds.[27] In order to broaden its base among the OBCs, Ram Prakash Gupta's government, in March 2000 met the demand of the Jats of Uttar Pradesh regarding their inclusion in Schedule 1 of the OBCs under Section 13 of the UP Public Services (Reservation of Scheduled Castes, Scheduled Tribes and Other Backward Classes) Act, 1994. But in August 2000 K. Mishra was elected president of the UP BJP in replacement of a Kurmi, Om Prakash Singh, who had taken over from Rajnath Singh when the latter had become a minister in Vajpayee's government few months before.

[26] Cited in *The Hindu*, 28 February 2000.
[27] *Times of India*, 25 January 2000.

The attacks on Kalyan Singh and the replacement of Om Prakash Singh are revealing of the limited integration of the OBCs within the BJP apparatus. Kalyan Singh, after all, was the victim of the upper caste lobby. This lack of integration is also evident from the small number of OBC leaders among the party officers. The BJP National Executive which was formed in 1998 comprised about 55 per cent upper caste members. Not more than 10 per cent of its members were OBCs and Dalits.

Some tensions may develop within the BJP between the upper caste leaders and the OBCs, especially if the reservation issue becomes prominent again. On the one hand, the minister of state for personnel, Vasundhara Raje, not only reasserted that the government was not in favour of affirmative action in the private sector but also that it was considering the option of introducing income criteria for reservations and the constitution of an expert committee to review the creamy layers among the OBCs.[28] On the other hand, BJP OBC leaders have strongly advocated quotas for their 'community'. In December 1999, four OBC Union Ministers, Bandaru Dattariya, Uma Bharti, Santosh Gangwar, and Kashiram Rana conveyed their view to Vajpayee and Advani that there should be 27 per cent reservations for the OBCs within the 33 per cent quota for women in Parliament and State assemblies. Dattariya added that 'the question of full-fledged reservations for BCs could be raised at a later date'.[29] The BJP may have to reconcile these two different viewpoints.

Thus, the BJP's expansion in geographical as well as social terms needs to be qualified. The party has to make further inroads in the south and in the east and needs to attract the lower caste voters in larger numbers to become a really 'all-India party'. However the party may be viewed as the new epicentre of Indian politics because of its capacity in making alliances, which enables it to play a pivotal role in the ruling coalition at the centre. This is the key element of a larger power-oriented agenda, which explains the ideological moderation of the party.

[28] *The Hindu*, 17 March 2000.
[29] Ibid., 25 December 1999. At the state level, the BJP Backward Classes cell of Madhya Pradesh has demanded to the state government that the percentage of reservation for the OBCs should be enhanced (*Central Chronicle*, 14 March 2000). This move was supported by the party leaders since it aimed at embarrassing the Congress chief minister, Digivijay Singh, but they may have to face the same kind of demand.

THE COMPULSIONS OF COALITION POLITICS AND THE IDEOLOGICAL MODERATION OF THE BJP

In his description of Arun Jaitley, one of the rising stars of the BJP, Swapan Dasgupta claimed that he represented the new, liberal face of the BJP.[30] One may indeed conclude from the party's official discourse that it has forsaken its Hindutva identity. L. K. Advani considers, for instance, that a new, moderate phase in the career of the BJP began in 1996, when Vajpayee could not form a coalition government: 'though we were the largest party, we failed to form a government. It was felt that on an ideological basis we couldn't go further. So we embarked on the course of alliance-based coalitions...'.[31] Advani explicitly establishes a relation between the way the BJP has diluted its Hindu nationalist ideology and the making of alliances. Both phenomena culminated in 1998 in the formation of the National Democratic Alliance—a coalition using the same name as the one the BJP and Charan Singh's Bharatiya Lok Dal (BLD) had shaped in 1984. The BJP and its alliance partners evolved a 'National Agenda for Government' in March 1998 and Vajpayee formed his government on this basis.[32] Mainstays of the Sangh Parivar's programme—the Ram temple to be built at Ayodhya, the abolition of Article 370 of the Constitution, and the establishment of a uniform civil code—were not included in this agenda because the BJP allies—the Shiv Sena excepted—did not appreciate their Hindu nationalist connotations. At that time, Advani, who was still party president, started to evoke the need for a new BJP that would be a party of governance, not based on any precise ideology:

...a large area of governance has little to do with ideology—any ideology—except the overriding principle of national interests. Indeed, good governance in most spheres of national life becomes possible only when it is de-ideologized and de-politicized. Thus, if any issue, in spite of its inherent validity, acquires a strongly ideological character—in fact, so strong and ideological character

---

[30] He wrote: 'As the BJP moves from the fringes to becoming a liberal, right-wing party, the Sangh Parivar will look to him as a winning face of the next century' (*India Today*, 1 November 1999).

[31] Interview of L. K. Advani in *Outlook*, 25 October 1999, p. 38.

[32] For the full text, see *Organiser*, Varsha Pradipada Special, 29 March 1998, pp 27–30.

as to make coalition governance, and hence stable governance difficult—it is only proper to leave it out. This is precisely what we have done in the National Agenda.[33]

The BJP leaders have adhered to this line of conduct in the late 1990s. As a result, in 1999, the election manifesto of the National Democratic Alliance (NDA) promised 'a moratorium on contentious issues',[34] a phrase which referred to the construction of the Ram temple in Ayodhya, the abolition of Article 370 of the Constitution, and the imposition of a uniform civil code. The NDA also committed itself to 'genuine secularism'.[35]

Similarly, its manifesto distanced itself from the former plank of 'Swadeshi', that is economic nationalism: 'Swadeshi is not reinventing the wheel. It means that we will facilitate the domestic industry to gain enough muscles to compete with the multinationals in the local and global markets. We want domestic companies to flourish and acquire a Trans National status. At the same time the country cannot do without FDI [Foreign Direct Investments] because besides capital stocks it brings with it technology, new markets practices and most importantly employment. Our target is to achieve at least $ 10 billion per year which will commensurate with our growth objectives.'[36]

Interestingly, the same figure appeared in the manifesto of the Congress, which had been accused by the BJP of selling India to multinationals when Manmohan Singh was finance minister. The rather liberal overtone of the NDA manifesto was not due to the BJP's allies but to its own policy.[37] In early 1999, the Swadeshi Jagaran Manch, an RSS offshoot had organized a

---

[33] 'Inaugural Addresses by Shri L. K. Advani', op. cit., p. 7.

[34] *For a Proud, Prosperous India*, op. cit., p. 1.

[35] 'We will truly and genuinely uphold and practise the concept of secularism consistent with the Indian tradition of "Sarva panth samadaro" (equal respect for all faiths) and on the basis of equality of life' (Ibid., p. 3).

[36] *For a Proud, Prosperous India*, op. cit., p. 4.

[37] It reflects an evolution within the party which is well illustrated by some of the articles available on the party's website. In 2000 one can still read there a 1996 article by Tarun Das, the Director General of the Confederation of Indian Industry (CII), that there is a strong plea for liberalization, as evident from its last sentence: 'India must continue its open door policy and actively and strongly promote foreign investment' (Das, T.) 'MNCs: India's Strategy Needs Rethinking', http://www.bjp.org/major/swadeshi-4.html).

Swadeshi Mela (Fair) in order to promote the notion of 'self-reliance'.[38] Vajpayee had inaugurated it by saying: 'We are all part of the same family. It's good that you have come up with ideas but if I can't execute them, I'll say sorry '.[39] After ten months in office, he was obviously realizing that economic nationalism was not his first choice any more. Gradually, the BJP accepted his views. The party's National Executive passed in November 1999 a resolution welcoming 'financial and fiscal reforms and greater foreign investment into areas which need high capital investment'. In order to show its determination, the Vajpayee government introduced the Insurance Regulatory and Development Authority (IRDA) Bill as early as the first session of the 13th Lok Sabha in December 1999. This bill provided for the entry of private Indian and foreign companies into the insurance business, ending the monopoly of the public sector Life Insurance Corporation (LIC) and General Insurance Corporation (GIC). Even though the foreign equity was capped at 26 per cent, this bill obviously contradicted the Swadeshi credo. In February 2000, the government enhanced ceilings on foreign direct investment by 23 to 100 per cent in 8 sectors, including drugs and pharmaceuticals, mining, and the film industry. The commerce minister, Murasoli Maran then declared: 'We want to create an Indian fever [for foreign investors] just as there was a Chinese fever not too long ago'.[40] An agreement to remove import controls on consumer goods was also signed with the United States. The Swadeshi credo remained unaffected in few sectors only, notably, the media.[41]

The BJP leaders have justified their new discourse and policies by using big words. Advani said that there was no place for an

[38] Sreedathan, G., 'Swadeshi is the Mantra', *Organiser*, 7 February 1999, pp 10–11.

[39] Cited in *India Today*, 8 February 1999, p. 33.

[40] Cited in *The Hindu*, 3 February 2000. Similarly, in January 2000 Vajpayee's government began the process of public disinvestment from Indian Airlines in whose case it was decided to off-load 51 per cent equity. Before that the public sector equity of Gas Authority of India had been sold to foreign companies.

[41] In February 2000 the information and broadcasting minister, Arun Jaitley declared that entry to the foreign media could not take place. He argued that: 'We have quite an independent and free media which is doing its job well. So is Doordarshan, the national television channel' (Cited in *The Hindu*, 2 February 2000).

ideological party in India today and that an 'effective state'[42] was the main aim of the party. In 1999, he delivered a speech before the Federation of Indian Chambers of Commerce and Industry in which he announced that the government had decided to initiate 'far reaching reforms in the administration, judiciary, and the internal security' to evolve an 'effective state'.[43] The other key words in L. K. Advani's discourse after the formation of the NDA government was, as noticed above, 'good governance', *Suraj*.[44] 'Commitment to Good Governance' was one of the headlines of the NDA's election manifesto. And the BJP President, Kushabhau Thakre, in his opening remarks during the National Executive meeting of the party that followed the 1999 elections repeatedly mentioned, 'good governance' as its chief objective.[45] Besides, he pointed out:

We have to constantly bear in mind that we are a responsible ruling party, alive to the interests of all sections of our society, irrespective of their caste religion, gender or language.[46]

Such a discourse is naturally intended to present the BJP as a law and order-oriented party and to dispel its communal image. In the same vein, the NDA has published a brochure entitled 'Charter of Commitments and Our Achievements', where it is mentioned that 'ninety-eight saw the lowest incidence of communal violence in the last 10 years.[47] By making such claims the BJP projects itself as the main architect of communal harmony

[42] He deliberately preferred this expression to 'strong state' because the latter, according to him, 'may be construed to have some undemocratic connotations' (Cited in *The Hindu*, 21 November 1999).

[43] Ibid.

[44] In an interview to *Outlook* which took place during the 1999 election campaign, Advani underlined that 'what India needs most now is a dose of effective governance sans ideology (*Outlook*, 30 August 1999, p. 15).

[45] He said: 'We have to convince the people that mere sloganeering cannot deliver good governance' and 'the party and the government can together, through their joint effort, provide good governance. If we fail in this endeavour, then we will have only ourselves to blame' (Meeting of the Bharatiya Janata Party National Executive, New Delhi, 3–4 November 1999. Opening remarks by Shri Kushabhau Thakre, President, Bharatiya Janata Party, p. 4).

[46] Ibid., p. 3.

[47] National Democratic Alliance, *Charter of Commitments and Our Achievements* (New Delhi: Printed and published by Bharatiya Janata Party, for and on behalf of the National Democratic Alliance [no date], p. 15).

even though, according to the official figures furnished to the Lok Sabha there were 626 riots (in which 207 died and 2065 were injured) in 1998, as against 725 riots (in which 264 died and 2503 were injured) in 1997 and 728 (in which 209 died and 2057 were injured) in 1996.[48]

Another element in this dilution of the BJP's ideological discourse lay in its effort to channelize its nationalism *only* against foreign enemies. 'Patriotism' was the key word of the address that Vajpayee delivered on 15 August 1999 for celebrating the 52nd anniversary of India's independence.[49] He was naturally cashing in on the success of the Indian army in the so-called 'Kargil war'. This 'victory' was prominent in the BJP's 1999 election campaign. The first paragraphs of the NDA election manifesto emphatically referred to it, the coalition reiterating there its commitments to preserve 'the honour and territorial integrity of [the] motherland'.[50] Launching the BJP's campaign in Uttar Pradesh in Lucknow, Vajpayee declared in the same vein:

History has been written by jawans, which will continue to inspire the coming generation. The nation demonstrated its unity in the hour of national crises. This unity has to be maintained.[51]

The main slogan of the BJP presented Vajpayee as ' the leader you can trust. In war. In peace'. Another advertisement said: 'As a friend, he can travel far to shake a hand [that of Nawaz Sharif in Lahore in February 1999]. When betrayed, he can crush it with a Kargil.'[52]

The BJP therefore is attempting to project itself as a liberal, patriotic party striving for good governance for all. But is it really transforming itself in such a big way? Baldev Raj Nayar considers that the BJP is following a 'centrist tendency'; according to him there is 'a unilinear direction in change in party strategy

---

[48] Engineer, A. Ali, 'Communalism and Communal Violence in 1999', *Secular Perspective*, 1 January 2000 and *Muslim India*, no. 196, April 1999, p. 161.

[49] Among other things, he said: 'The patriotism that coursed through the veins of Indians should be made a permanent feature of our lives', *Prime Minister's Red Fort Address: August 15, 1999* (New Delhi: BJP, 1999), p. 8.

[50] *For a Proud, Prosperous India*, op. cit., p. 1.

[51] *The Hindu*, 19 August 1999.

[52] *Hindustan Times*, 15 August 1999.

towards moderation and coalition building'.[53] I would suggest that the moderation of the BJP is largely *due to* the compulsions of coalition building, except for the economic policy where the BJP itself remains deeply divided on the issue—a section of the party putting Swadeshi into question openly.

The party had certainly begun to adopt a more moderate approach of politics after the demolition of the Babri Masjid in 1992 and its setback in the 1993 state elections in Uttar Pradesh, Madhya Pradesh, and Himachal Pradesh, when it appeared that the north Indian voters disapproved of the violent implications of Hindutva politics. But it was only after the BJP became part of the ruling coalition in 1998 that it agreed to downplay its Hindu nationalism: it obliterated the 'contentious issues' for the first time in the National Agenda, the common platform of the NDA that was finalized in March 1998.

The moderation of the BJP does not follow a linear trend but represents merely a phase reflecting its capacity to alternate moderation and extremism. The Jana Sangh and then the BJP have always oscillated between ethno-religious mobilization and a more moderate approach of politics according to three parameters: the Hindu feeling of vulnerability; the attitude of the other political forces; and the attitudes of the party cadres as well as of the RSS, with which the party cadres often display strong affinities.

Hindu feelings of vulnerability played a crucial role in the crystallization of the Hindu nationalist movement in the 1920s, as a reaction to the Khilafat movement.[54] Sangh Parivar ideologues themselves refer today to this period for justifying the continuous need for a strong organization of Hindus. After the Vajpayee government released 'jihadists' who had been active in Kashmir in order to meet the demand of the hijackers who threatened to kill the passengers of an Indian Airlines aircraft in December 1999, Rajendra Singh declared that 'The

---

[53] Nayar, Baldev Raj, 'The Limits of Economic Nationalism: Economic Policy Reforms under the BJP-led Government', paper presented at the conference on 'India and the Politics of Developing Countries: Essays in Honour of Myron Weiner', 24–6 September 1999, Kellogg Institute for International Studies, University of Notre Dame.

[54] For a more detailed analysis, see Jaffrelot, C., *The Hindu Nationalist Movement and Indian Politics* (New Delhi: Penguin India, 1999), ch. 1.

hijacking has highlighted the cowardice in Hindu society'[55] and substantiated his 'analysis' by quoting Gandhi's comment about the Kohat riot (1924): 'The Muslim, as a rule is a bully, and the Hindu, as a rule is a coward'. The *Organiser* seized this opportunity to arraign the Indian 'soft state' in the same, historical perspective: 'Pakistan's terrorism against India is simply a repeat of the Moplah Rebellion [1921]—and a hundred others....'[56] Obviously, the Khilafat movement still haunts the psyche of the Hindu nationalists.[57]

Similar feelings were reactivated in the 1980s by the conversions of Meenakshipuram and the so-called 'pampering' of the Muslims by the Congress government in the Shah Bano case. The Sangh Parivar cashed in on such feelings, claiming that the Hindus were secondary citizens in their own country. The popularity of the Ayodhya movement largely resulted from the need that was felt in some sectors of the majority community for a Hindu backlash. However, the demolition of the Babri Masjid and the communal riots due to the Ramjanmabhoomi movement enabled the militants 'to teach the Muslims a lesson' and to 'say with pride, we are Hindus!' (to cite one of the most popular slogans of the late 1980s—early 1990s. *Garv se kaho, hum Hindu hain!*). In this context, the implementation of any strategy of aggressive ethno-religious mobilization is made more unlikely because it can hardly exploit some Hindu feeling of vulnerability—even if it is still there, in a latent state.

The attitude of the other political parties is even more directly conducive to moderation. Certainly, the BJP is not any more prevented from indulging in communal propaganda by

[55] He explained that 'Even in the aircraft, eight or 10 young men could have stood together and tried to capture the hijackers by creating a frenzy. But they failed to rise, despite the murder of a co-passenger, because of the fear of death' (Cited in *Outlook*, 17 January 2000, p. 44).

[56] Rajaram, N. S., 'Wages of a "Soft State"', 16 January 2000, p. 11.

[57] In fact, the Sangh Parivar often adopts an even larger historical perspective to justify its claim that Muslims are posing a threat to the Hindus. Their views on demographic trends are a case in point. The *Organiser*, for instance, published a graph showing that the share of the Muslim population increased from 7 per cent of the total in 1526 to 24 per cent in 1947. The author underlined that the Muslim population had shown a growth of 313 per cent during the British period, as against 98 per cent for the Hindus. (Krishna, D., 'Anglo-Muslim Alliance', *Organiser*, 26 December 1999, p. 9).

political forces which would be in a position to maintain secularism as the only legitimate discourse like the Congress under Nehru and Indira Gandhi.[58] But it has tried to become more acceptable to other political parties anyway. In the 1980s this endeavour culminated in the inclusion of the BJP in the coalition supporting V. P. Singh government after the 1989 election. The BJP was again rather isolated in the early 1990s because of its involvement in the Ayodhya movement, but it had become too strong to be ignored and, realizing the growing unpopularity of its militant Hindutva as well as its need of allies, it downplayed this political repertoire. It is not regarded as an 'untouchable' party any more. On the contrary, it is one of the most coveted allies, provided it gives up its most extreme claims. Samta Party leader, George Fernandes, a former socialist had accepted to collaborate with the BJP in 1995, even though he had been highly critical of its 'communal' or even 'fascist' agenda so far. More recently, one of the significant episodes of the 1999 election campaign was the rallying of a faction of the Janata Dal—comprising former socialist leaders like Sharad Yadav, the party president—around the NDA. The new acceptability of a moderate BJP by new political parties such as the Samta Party and the JD (U), whose leaders chose to forget some of their secular, leftist leanings for the sake of getting access to power, could only lead the Hindu nationalist party, the BJP, to put the so-called contentious issues on the backburner.

Therefore, the political context dictates its terms in such a manner that the BJP has to put its Hindutva identity into parenthesis because it can only govern in a coalition and its partners are not prepared to endorse a militant Hindu programme—especially those who have Muslim supporters like the TDP.[59] Advani reasserted in 1999 that the BJP was soft-pedalling on the 'contentious issues' because of its partners: 'There is no question of giving them up but whenever a coalition is formed on the basis of an agreed common programme it becomes the sole guide for governance.'[60]

[58] I have addressed the issue of the 'communalization' of the Congress in the last part of my book *The Hindu Nationalist Movement*, op. cit.

[59] After the election, Naidu stressed that his party 'got the minority vote' and showed that he was anxious to keep it (*The Hindu*, 11 October 1999).

[60] *The Hindu*, 20 September 1999.

One of the party's general secretaries, Govindacharya, even said that the issues of the Ram temple, Article 370, and uniform civil code were very much part of the BJP agenda,[61] obliging Vajpayee to contradict him publicly during the election campaign.

The attitude of the RSS—the last variable of our 'model'—traditionally set guidelines for the BJP's strategy. Party leaders convincingly argue that Nagpur does not decide for them but admit that representatives of the Sangh Parivar meet to establish the priority issues under the aegis of RSS men. In December 1998, the members of the RSS Executive Committee (the Akhil Bharatiya Karyakari Mandal) had a meeting with 'workers in the central teams of our like-minded organizations'—including the BJP—to use the phrase designating the Sangh Parivar in the terminology of H. V. Seshadri (the RSS general secretary).[62] Another regular occasion of the same kind takes place every year when the RSS chief meets the BJP MPs for an interactive working session. This exercise is usually organized at the time of Guru Dakshina, another indication of the RSS's desire of being recognized as the 'Raj Guru' of the BJP. Senior RSS leaders, H. V. Seshadri and K. S. Sudarshan the joint general secretary of the organization were in the front row at the swearing-in ceremony of Vajpayee government in 1999 and they gave their blessings to the newly-appointed ministers (who sought such a gesture from them). Kalyan Singh, the former chief minister of Uttar Pradesh protested against the interference of the RSS with the BJP's work and when he resigned he sent copies of his letter to Rajendra Singh (the RSS chief) and to K. S. Sudarshan. While the BJP retains some autonomy, the RSS exerts a clear influence over its policies.

Now, the RSS has not given up the contentious issues. During its 1999 annual convention, the Jammu and Kashmir National Front International, an organization which entertains strong links with the RSS, demanded the abrogation of Article 370 of the

---

[61] *Hindustan Times*, 24 August 1999.

[62] In his annual report to the Akhil Bharatiya Pratinidhi Sabha, Seshadri added that 'Prior to the all-Bharat meet, meetings were organised on similar lines in all the provinces and their thoughts and suggestions passed on to the centre where they were all processed and the final draft prepared for deliberations at Nagpur' (*Organiser*, 4 April 1999, p. 10). Such a procedure gives a clear indication of the imbrication of the components of the Sangh Parivar and their vertical integration.

Constitution which, according to the resolution it passed on the subject 'breeds the microbes of subversion. It keeps alive the unwholesome legacy of two-nation theory. It suffocates the very idea of India and fogs the very vision of great social and cultural crucible from Kashmir to Kanyakumari'.[63] The Prant Pracharak of the RSS who took part in the convention stressed 'the need of final war with Pakistan' and expressed his hope that 'India will recover a large chunk of area, which she has lost due to weak rulers'.[64]

The RSS and the VHP have not given up the Ayodhya issue either. The VHP is pursuing its programme regarding the construction of a Ram temple in Ayodhya.[65] One of its related bodies, the Ram Janmabhoomi Nyas, is supervising the cutting of stones and the carving of the 212 pillars for building the temple. Four workshops are involved in this work in Sirohi (Rajasthan) and half of the pillar are ready—the whole thing should be completed in 2 or 3 years.[66] In January 2000, Ashok Singhal, the VHP working president declared that Hindu saints would build the Ram temple at Ayodhya 'once the chiselling of stones is over'.[67] At the same time, the general secretary of the VHP's young wing, the Bajrang Dal (BD), Harish Bhai Bhatt announced that the construction of the Ram temple would take place within two years at 'lightening speed just as the masjid demolition took place' because the VHP and the Bajrang Dal did not need any 'sanction, approval, permission or help' of the centre.[68] (In early 2000, the growing

---

[63] *Organiser*, 21 November 1999, p. 5.

[64] Ibid.

[65] Incidentally, the VHP website is dedicated 'to the Martyrs of Ayodhya and their Parents' (http:/www.vhp.org./dedication.htm).

[66] *Hindustan Times*, 26 August 1999.

[67] *Organiser*, 30 January 2000.

[68] Cited in *The Hindu*, 30 January 2000. He announced that this project would be discussed in the following month during the convention of the Bajrang Dal at Bhopal. However the growing militancy of the Bajrang Dal led Digvijay Singh, the chief minister of Madhya Pradesh, to ban this convention in order to avoid any communal disturbances. The Bajrang Dal proved to be adamant and simply declared that the convention would be reduced to a one-day event. When activists tried to reach Bhopal, the state government had them arrested. Two thousand of them were put behind bars but others succeeded in hoisting a saffron flag on the convention ground before the police's *lathi* charge. Interestingly, BJP workers, after demonstrating before the Vidhan Sabha, submitted a memorandum to the governor to protest against the arrest of Bajrang Dal activists as a mark of solidarity

militancy of the VHP and the BD also found expression in their hostility to the film 'Water' that the Canada-based filmmaker Deepa Mehta was shooting in Varanasi.)[69]

The RSS itself reaffirmed its interest in Ayodhya during the 1999 election campaign. In September, its supreme chief, Rajendra Singh, emphasized that Muslims, whose rulers had allegedly 'destroyed 3000 temples', should hand over the sites of Varanasi, Mathura, and Ayodhya where mosques had been built on so-called Hindu sacred places.[70]

Yet, the RSS is not putting any apparent pressure on the BJP for the government to make any move regarding the Jammu and Kashmir issue and Ayodhya. The RSS has apparently resigned itself to the BJP's new line of conduct. Insiders maintain that the BJP has become too big for the RSS.[71] According to them, the party has emancipated itself from its mother organization. Certainly, its growth has occurred on a par with the induction of new people without any RSS background, including former Janata Dal Finance Minister Yashwant Sinha, ex-Congressmen like K. C. Pant, film actors like Shatrugna Sinha. However, those who are in command still have an RSS background. Besides members of the old guard like Kushabhau Thakre, the second line of

---

(*Central Chronicle*, 18 February 2000) and the state BJP working president Vikram Verma defended the Bajrang Dal against Digvijay Singh's accusations, saying that it was 'a prestigious and trusted socio-cultural organisation...' (Cited in *Central Chronicle*, 1 February 2000).

[69] The film showed the sad condition of a Hindu widow in the 1930s. The VHP and the BD—whose leaders had already taken exception of Mehta's previous film, 'Fire', because it showed a lesbian's life—objected that 'Water' denigrated Hinduism and the morality of the Hindus (the script mentioned an illicit relationship between a Brahmin woman and an untouchable man and describe sexual abuses to a Hindu widow). Sangh Parivar activists—under the leadership of the local BJP MLA—ransacked the set erected on the bank of the Ganga in Varanasi in January 2000. The BJP state government then asked Mehta to suspend the shooting, even though she had got the permission from the Union Ministry of Information and Broadcasting. Govindacharya publicly praised this decision. VHP leaders went further. A. Singhal declared that the script outraged the 'ancient Indian culture and traditions' and smacked of 'a conspiracy by the votaries of western culture to tarnish the image of widowhood in India' (Cited in *The Hindu*, 5 February 2000). He threatened 'more violent protests' if Mehta tried to shoot the film elsewhere in India.

[70] *India Today*, 27 September 1999.

[71] Interview with Vijay Jolly, vice-president of BJYM, Paris, 12 June 1999.

leadership, with men like K. N. Govindacharya or N. Modi, is made up of former RSS *pracharaks*. Far from severing its links with the RSS, the BJP as an organization still depends on it for door to door canvassing at the time of elections. The BJP is as much a mass party cashing in on Vajpayee's charisma as a cadre-based party relying on RSS activists. At the state level, the Sangathan Mantris are still largely in command[72] and these former *pracharaks*, who have been seconded to the BJP by the RSS, remain close to the mother organization—so much so that *swayamsevak*s may canvass under their order during election campaigns.

The main reason why the RSS does not put pressure on the BJP and accepts the compulsion of coalition politics is not primarily related to the loosening of the links between the two but has more to do with (1) the benefit the RSS derives from the BJP being in power and (2) the fact that the party's policies, especially at the state level, are not as moderate as one may judge on the basis of the discourse of all-India leaders like Vajpayee.

The ruling party offers political protection to the activities of the Sangh Parivar and enables it to exert new forms of influence. One of the first decisions Vajpayee made after he formed his government in March 1998 consisted of appointing six new governors, including five BJP members. Among them, S. S. Bhandari, Bhai Mahavir, and Suraj Bhan were *swayamsevak*s from whom the RSS could expect benevolent gestures. The Bangalore meeting of the Akhil Bharatiya Pratinidhi Sabha, in April 1998—the first meeting of the highest policy-making body of the RSS after Vajpayee became prime minister—was very revealing in that respect. Journalists could attend the session and observe the new assertiveness of the RSS leaders, which one of them, Sudarshan justified in the following terms: 'With a government in power that is not inimical to us, we shall be able to work better.'[73] The way the organization could benefit from the BJP being in office is especially obvious at the state level. This is evident from the situation prevailing in Uttar Pradesh for instance. On 25 July 1998,

---

[72] This is very much evident from the case of Madhya Pradesh where the Congress can only long for such an infrastructure (Interviews at the chief minister's office in October 1999).

[73] Cited in *Frontline*, 24 April 1998, p. 117.

Rajendra Singh formally met top bureaucrats in Lucknow and lectured them on 'nationalism and honesty'. This meeting was organized by the state minister for higher education, Narendra Kumar Singh Gaur, a former RSS *pracharak*. Among the 60-odd officers were the Chief Secretary and the Director General of Police.[74] Such an opportunity to reach the state administration would not have been possible had the BJP not been in office. A few months before, in March 1998, an order from the minister for basic education had been issued to all public schools to make the recitation of *Saraswati Vandana* and *Vande Mataram* compulsory, in place of *Saare Jahan Accha*.[75] Schools have also been directed, especially in rural areas, to involve the RSS *pracharak*s in *naitik shiksha* (moral education).[76] The RSS probably values more than anything else this new influence in the field of education where it can reshape the mind of India, something it is already attempting to do in its *shakha*s.

At the centre also, the education policy of the minister for human resources and development, M. M. Joshi, was much appreciated by the RSS.[77] While Joshi's attempt at institutionalizing the recitation of *Saraswati Vandana* at schools failed in 1998, immediately after the 1999 election he appointed personalities who had been close to the Sangh Parivar as heads of the directive body of the Indian Council of Historical Research (ICHR) and the Indian Council of Social Science Research (ICSSR), respectively B. R. Grover and M. L. Sondhi. B. R. Grover who retired from Jamia Millia Islamia as a Reader and who had become a member of the ICHR in 1998, was one of the historians who provided the Sangh Parivar with the archaeological 'evidence' that the Babri Masjid had been built over a Ram temple in Ayodhya. More specifically, he was a member of the panel of historians constituted by the VHP at the suggestion of Chandra Shekhar in 1990–1 to establish that the site of the Babri Masjid was the birthplace of Ram where a temple had been dedicated to this sacred figure. Sondhi, a former

[74] *Hindustan Times*, 27 July 1998.
[75] Noorani, A. G., 'How Secular is Vande Mataram?, *Frontline*, 15 January 1999, p. 92.
[76] Setalvad, T., 'Sabrang Alert no. 1', South Asia Citizens Web Dispatch, http://www.mnet.fr/aiindex.
[77] Cited in Bhaumik, S. N., 'Murli's Mission', *India Today*, 6 December 1999, p. 23.

Indian Foreign Service (IFS) officer, who had joined politics, had won a Lok Sabha seat in Delhi on a Jana Sangh ticket in 1967. After his electoral defeat in 1971 he had made a career in academia and had become professor of international relations at Jawaharlal Nehru University.

Besides, M. M. Joshi has appointed Krishna Gopal Rastogi, a former RSS *pracharak*, to the search committee for faculty appointment in the National Council for Educational Research and Training (NCERT). Rastogi, a retired NCERT professor from Delhi, is not so much known for his academic achievements as for an autobiographical account of the Partition in which he narrates how he shot dead a Muslim woman in 1947 to save her from a mob of Hindus on the rampage. The book has been dedicated to the RSS and its foreword has been written by K. S. Sudarshan.[78] As a member of the Programme Advisory Committee, Rastogi may well be in a position to influence the design of a new curriculum.[79]

The apprehensions that were aroused by the placement in key positions of RSS fellow travellers began to materialize in February 2000 when the ICHR 'suspended' two volumes of its series called 'Towards Freedom' edited by Sumit Sarkar and K. N. Panikkar who were known for being highly critical of the Sangh

---

[78] For more details, see *Asian Age*, 25 October 1999.

[79] Already, there has been much protest in the Lok Sabha when it turned out that the teaching of Marxism had been dropped from the Class XII political science curriculum in English. The Central Board of Secondary Education said that this omission was the printer's mistake but this episode exacerbated apprehensions among the left-oriented intellectuals (*Frontline*, 26 November 1999, p. 89). One of them, Romila Thapar, echoed these feelings in a press interview: 'School teachers I've been in touch with, those teaching history, are very concerned about what to teach the children. Because if they teach from the textbooks we have written, the kids will be penalised in the exam' (Interview in *Outlook*, 6 December 1999, p. 11). While school teachers worry, however, very few get mobilized: '...What you have at the moment is small groups of people getting together and holding discussions. But by and large there is increasingly a feeling that they don't want to express themselves in the media because who wants to get into a situation of confrontation with the government? And this feeling will increase. ...It's a case of if government policy changes we go along with it because we will get bigger and better jobs if we do. ...a majority will, for good or bad reasons, come to terms with the changes and the few who will be resisting it will be constantly pointed at and described as anti-national and a demonology of sorts will be built around them. (Ibid.)

Parivar.[80] M. M. Joshi virtually justified the withdrawal of the two books by arguing that history books always need to be updated by including new data.[81]

In addition to the education system, the media are also a priority target for the BJP leaders. The BJP has always felt some uneasiness with the reform introduced by the Janata Dal government in 1990 under the Prasar Bharati Act and implemented in 1997 by the Janata Dal Minister for Information and Broadcasting Jaipal Reddy. He appointed S. S. Gill as the executive in charge and independent part-time members who were now responsible for running the public TV Channel Doordarshan and All India Radio. The BJP criticized the new autonomy that was granted to these public media, probably because of the personality of the appointees. In 1998 the I & B minister in Vajpayee's government, Mrs Sushma Swaraj managed to get S. S. Gill to quit his post. Soon after his appointment as the new I & B minister, Arun Jaitley decided to remove two of the part-time members who were known for their secularism and leftist leanings, Romila Thapar and Rajendra Yadav. The choice of these two eminent figures was rather arbitrary since, while the Prasar Bharati Act provided that the part-time members were to retire on a one-third basis every two years, they had all been appointed for 6 years in 1997. In fact, with the removal of Professor Thapar and R. Yadav, the 15-member Board of Prasar Bharati has been reduced to three (another part-time member had already resigned) and it has no chairman and no full-time chief executive. Jaipal Reddy protested in Parliament that the BJP was trying to 'emasculate' this institution and to 'saffronise' the media.[82]

---

[80] Immediately, over 30 academics, including Irfan Habib, R. S. Sharma, and Ravinder Kumar—all former chairmen of the ICHR—denounced the 'grossest form of censorship' and a 'plan to spread a distorted and fictitious history of the national movement' (*The Hindu*, 17 February 2000). S. Gopal, the general editor of the 'Towards Freedom' project, protested also that the ICHR intervention amounted to 'an infringement of the academic rights and freedom of the authors...' (Ibid., 22 February 2000). According to K. N. Panikkar, the withdrawal of the two volumes was intended to prevent the exposure of the 'collaborative role' of the Hindu Mahasabha with the British during the colonial period (Cited in Ibid., 25 February 2000).

[81] Ibid., 19 February 2000.

[82] *The Hindu*, 25 November, 1999.

Last but not least, the RSS also appreciates the defence policy of Vajpayee's government. In May 1998, the Sangh Parivar organizations rejoiced more than any other group after the nuclear test of Pokharan. In his report before the Akhil Bharatiya Pratinidhi Sabha in March 1999, H. V. Seshadri highlighted the achievement of Vajpayee's government in the field of security issues:

The series of 5 nuclear blasts at Pokharan on May 11th and 13th of last year, carried out on the strength of entirely indigenous input by way of materials and also of sheer scientific and technological excellence placing Bharat at the top of nuclear world on par with any of the giants in that field, the absolute secrecy maintained all through until it was broadcast on the TV by our Prime Minister, the political grit and courage displayed by the central leadership in taking that historic decision in the light of our national security requirements, and the way it has acted as a great moral booster not only to our army but to all our patriotic countrymen—all this has proved to be the one greatest moment of all–round national jubilation and celebration during the Golden Jubilee Year of our independence.[83]

Seshadri also congratulated, implicitly, L. K. Advani, the home minister, for his policy in Jammu and Kashmir in the warmest terms: 'The achievement in the field of internal national security by way of liquidating and nabbing of thousand odd saboteurs and insurgents in Kashmir has been unequalled to this day.'[84] The RSS was not disappointed either by the measures the 'third' Vajpayee government took in this domain. In August 1999, the 27-member National Security Advisory Board, that had been appointed by the prime minister, spelled out a 'nuclear doctrine' that was not formally endorsed by Vajpayee but made public by his National Security Adviser, Brajesh Mishra. This doctrine pointed out that India would develop a credible minimum nuclear deterrent by weaponizing a triad of aircraft, mobile land-based missiles, and sea-based assets. Simultaneously with its nuclear policy, Vajpayee's government decided to speed up the missile

[83] *Organiser*, 4 April 1999, p. 12. The RSS has always favoured the development of nuclear weapons. In the early 1990s—Rajendra Singh himself a nuclear physicist—declared that: 'The day Pakistan comes to know that we also have a nuclear bomb, there would be an end to the possibility of a Pakistan nuclear bomb being dropped here' (Singh, R., *Ever-Vigilant We Have To Be* (New Delhi: Suruchi Prakashan, n.d.), p. 9).

[84] Ibid.

programme by developing Agni II and to strengthen the army on the front of conventional forces. About 20 Agni ballistic missiles with a range of more than 2000 kilometers should be manufactured by 2001 and the kilometers range of the Prithvi missile should be upgraded from 150 kilometers to 350 kilometers.

In February 2000, the share of the defence expenditures increased by 28 per cent in the union budget. The allocation for paramilitary forces—including the Border Security Forces—increased by about 16 per cent.

The RSS may thus resign itself for good reasons to the dilution of the BJP's ideology—regarding the Swadeshi issue, for instance—because of the compulsions of coalition politics. This strategy enables the party to be in office and, therefore, to protect the activities of the RSS and to promote some of its ideas. Furthermore, the RSS cannot really suspect the BJP of forgetting about its ideology because of some of its policies in the state where it is not depending on coalition partners in its government, that is Gujarat.

GUJARAT, A LABORATORY FOR HINDU NATIONALISM

The case of Gujarat needs to be examined separately because this is the only place where the BJP rules with the benefit of an absolute majority. In fact, the state has become the most unassailable stronghold of Hindu nationalism. The electoral performance of the BJP over the last 15 years are not matched by any other party state unit and Gujarat has been the focus of a massive attempt at developing its *shakha* network by the RSS. The then joint general secretary, K. S. Sudarshan, explained that in less than 2 years the organization had established its presence in 1780 mandals (clusters of 8 to 10 villages) whereas the total number of such mandals was already 7037 in 1998;[85] hence the unprecedented *Sankalp Shibir* (training camp) that it organized in January 2000 in Ahmedabad with the presence of about 26,000 *swayamsevaks*.[86]

---

[85] This figure was published in an RSS brochure in 1998. See Barthval Harischandra, *Rashtriya Swayamsevak Sangh: Ek Parichay* (New Delhi: Suruchi Prakashan, 1998), p. 16.

[86] *Organiser*, 16 January 2000, p. 5.

TABLE 11.9: The BJP's Electoral Performances in the
Gujarat State Assembly

	1985	1990	1995	1998
%	14.9	26.69	42.5	44.33
Seats	11	67	122	117

Source: P. Patel, 'Sectarian Mobilisation, Factionalism and Voting in Gujarat', *Economic and Political Weekly*, 21 August 1999, pp 2423–33.

With the return to power, in 1998, of Keshubhai Patel (who had been dislodged from chief ministership by a BJP dissident, Shankarsinh Waghela, as Ghanshyam Shah has shown in this volume), the Sangh Parivar had a staunch RSS follower at the helm. All the conditions were fulfilled for projecting Gujarat as a laboratory of Hindu nationalism. Its policies have been an indication of what the BJP's agenda can be when it is not working under the constraints of coalition politics. The state home minister, Haren Pandeya himself admits that 'Good governance is no doubt our priority but it is equally necessary to see that the finer points of the ideology are also implemented.'[87] The attitude of Pandeya, an RSS man himself, vis-à-vis other offshoots of the Sangh Parivar such as the VHP, exemplifies this line of conduct.

Even before the BJP came to power at the centre in 1998, the VHP had displayed its militancy in Gujarat. On 25 December 1997 it organized anti-Christian rallies in different districts of south Guajrat.[88] Six months later, the Hindu Jagaran Manch (HJM), whose leaders have links with offshoots of the RSS even though it is not formally recognized as being part of the Sangh Parivar, distributed pamphlets vilifying the Christian community in Dangs, a tribal-dominated district (out of 144,091 inhabitants, 135,376 were tribals in 1991):

Conversion activity by Christian Priest is the most dangerous burning problem at present in Dangs district. Innocent and illiterate tribals are converted through cheating, alluring by offering temptations, and other deceiving activities, under the pretext of services, these devils are taking advantage of tribal society and exploit them...Hindus, awake and struggle,

[87] Cited in Joshi, R., 'Test Flights of the Hindutva Dream', *Outlook*, 31 January 2000, p. 26.
[88] Its youth wing, the Bajrang Dal, also burnt copies of the New Testament that had been distributed in a school of Rajkot.

continuous [sic] with these robbers who snatch away your right by telling lies and teach these people a lesson.[89]

Soon after, a series of attacks on churches took place in the district: about 10 churches and prayer halls were brunt or damaged. The HJM organized an anti-Christian rally on Christmas Day in 1998. Anti-Christian slogans, such as *Hindu jago, Christi bhago* (Hindu awake, Christians flee) or *Gali gali me shor hai, padri sab chor hai,* (there is a thief in the lane, all Christian priests are thieves), were raised throughout the procession route.[90] Sixteen churches were burnt and 8 were damaged in the following days.

The National Commission for Minorities submitted to President K. R. Narayanan a report on these attacks where the Sangh Parivar-sponsored reconversions of tribals were held responsible for atrocities committed on Christians. It also blamed the state BJP government for its 'inept handling of the situation'.[91] The state machinery was indeed guilty of mismanagement. Officials contributed to create an atmosphere of distrust vis-à-vis the Christian minority[92] and did not try to check the Hindu nationalist propaganda. As a result, the scenario of December 1998 unfolded itself once again in December 1999[93] when the VHP and the HJM jointly inaugurated a Ram temple in a Christian-dominated tribal

[89] Cited in Chenoy, K. M. (ed.), *Violence in Gujarat: Test Case for a Larger Fundamentalist Agenda* (New Delhi and Bangalore: National Alliance of Women, 1990), p. 43.

[90] Cited in ibid., p. 7.

[91] Cited in *Statesman*, 3 February 1999, p. 8.

[92] In response to a suggestion, by one of K. Patel's ministers, Mangubhai Patel, the in-charge District Superintendent of Police of Dangs issued a confidential circular. This text directed that 'facts regarding Christian priests and Christian religion' should be collected because 'presently the Christian priests are carrying out proselytisation activities in full force. This has come to the notice of the Honourable Minister, and the leaders of this religion are making police complaints on the basis of false representations and exaggerated charges' (Cited in Chenoy, K. M. (ed.), *Violence in Gujarat*, op. cit., p. 6.)

[93] For instance, the Hindu Jagaran Manch had pamphlets circulated which recalled those of the previous year: 'Christian Missionaries are engaged in the activity of converting simple and innocent Vanvasis using varieties of cheating and misleading propaganda in Vanvasi areas of Bharat. The converted people are not only isolated from Hindu society. It is their daily activity to insult Hindu gods and goddesses in terribly abusive language. ...It is the evil intention of these missionaries thus to turn the whole Vanvasi area of Bharat into another Nagaland and Mizoram. ...They collect huge amount of money from foreign countries, by

village in Surat district. To begin with, the state government had forbidden the ceremony that was intended to take place on Christmas day. But the VHP and the HJM leaders were so adamant that Patel's government freed the leaders they had jailed, allowed the organization of non-Christian gatherings on Christmas day, and approved of the laying of the foundation stone of the Ram temple provided it did not take place on Christmas day. It occured on the 22nd of December, in the presence of the local BJP MLA and the BJP district president while the Christian population, fearing communal riots, had fled.

The Muslim minority was not spared either. In July 1998, 50 Muslim families had to flee their home in Randhikpur (Dohad district) under pressures from VHP and Bajrang Dal activists in retaliation against two Muslim boys eloping with two Hindu girls. The month before, riots had taken place at Bardoli in June 1998. 'Before, during and after the riots, a number of RSS, VHP and Bajrang Dal leaders made provocative speeches against the Muslims' and the local newspapers echoed and amplified them.[94] One of the pamphlets they distributed in Bardoli division claimed that 'Every year about five lakhs of Hindu girls are allured, trapped, raped and married by Muslim rogues and children are given birth by them. They are enslaved and sold to Arab countries' or that 'Muslims are destroying Hindu Community by slaughter houses, slaughtering cows and making Hindu girls elope. Crime, drugs, terrorism are Muslims' empire.'[95] Gujarat was one of the states, which was badly affected by communal violence in the late 1990s. In July 1999, a Hindu Muslim riot took place in Ahmedabad; 8 persons were killed, mainly Muslims.[96] The chain of events leading to the riot began with the celebration of the Indian cricket team's victory over Pakistan in a World Cup match, which was observed with deliberate ostentation in Muslim areas, and ended up with the teasing of a mentally disabled Muslim boy by a group of young

---

spreading such utter lies and using these amounts they are implementing vigorously their plan to intensify conversion activities…' (Leaflet reproduced on the South Asia Citizens Web Dispatch, http://www.mnet.fr/aiindex, 3 December 1999).

[94] Shah, G., 'Hate Propaganda in Gujarat Press and Bardoli Riots', *Economic and Political Weekly*, 15 August 1998, p. 2218.

[95] Cited in Chenoy, K. M. (ed.), *Violence in Gujarat*, op. cit. pp 53–4.

[96] Cited in *Frontline*, 24 September 1999, p. 87.

Hindus, something other Muslim boys tried to stop; twelve days of rioting followed this incident. In September 1999, violence erupted in Surat when the Ganesh immersion processionists were prevented by the police from passing by a mosque. They protested and pressed their case so vehemently that the police opened fire, killing seven persons and injuring 20 others. In March 2000, a Muslim was killed in Ahmedabad during a riot that was due to the way 'some self-styled volunteers of the VHP' tried to 'check' on the minorities slaughtering cows on the festival of Bakr-id.[97]

Patel's government was placed in a grip of a dilemma by the militancy of the VHP and other offshoots of the Sangh Parivar. On the one hand, the chief minister and many of his ministers shared their views but on the other hand they were anxious to maintain law and order and not further alienate western investors. The government succeeded in forcing a number of concessions from the VHP and the HJM. In December 1999, for instance, it had the 'shilanyas' programme advanced to 22 December. But it went back on its word by allowing offshoots of the Sangh Parivar to lay the foundation stone of the temple. More importantly, 10 days later it made a major concession to the RSS by lifting the ban on participation by government employees in the activities of this organization.

In 1986, the Congress-I central government had revised the list of the associations whose membership was incompatible with state service and prohibited civil servants to take part in the activities of 32 organizations including the RSS, the VHP, the ABVP, the Jama'at-e-Islami, the Students Islamic Movement, Jama'at-ul-Ulema-e-Hind, etc. In June 1999, Keshubhai Patel wrote to the central government to seek advice on the decision to remove the RSS from this list. The centre replied the following months that the Unlawful Activity Prevention Tribunal had considered the RSS as a lawful organization in 1993. Hence the Gujarat government's decision six months later, at a time when the RSS was preparing its three-day *Sankalp Shibir* (training camp) in Ahmedabad—a city in which the number of *shakha*s has doubled from 150 to 305 between 1998 and 1999.[98]

---

[97] *The Hindu*, 17 March 2000.

[98] In rural Gujarat also the RSS has recorded dramatic progress with 1750 mandals of 10 to 12 villages covering 18,000 village (these figures were given by M. Deobhankar, the RSS *Prant Pracharak Pramukh* in *The Hindu*, 7 January 2000).

Opposition leaders objected to the decision of the Gujarat government to legalize the participation of bureaucrats and custodians of the law—policemen—in RSS meetings. The former might have a partisan role as retuning officers at the time of elections and the latter were likely to adopt a biased attitude during communal riots. Congress MLAs protested vehemently in the assembly and the streets. Vajpayee publicly defended the Gujarat government order by arguing that the RSS was 'a cultural and social organization'[99] and replied to President Narayanan that, while he had no intention to lift the ban on the central government employees on joining the RSS, there were constitutional difficulties in asking the Gujarat government to reconsider its decision.[100] Opposition parties insisted that the issue be discussed in the Lok Sabha under a substantive motion (according to Rule 184) so that MPs could vote to make clear their stand, but the government were not prepared to take such a 'risk'.

This controversy, in a way, replicated the 'dual membership' controversy in 1978–80, when ex-Jana Sanghi leaders of the Janata Party were accused of paying allegiance more to the RSS than to the party on whose ticket they had been elected. But, it did not end the same way. In 1979–80, the former Jana Sanghis had given a top priority to their allegiance to the RSS and severed their links with their allies of the Janata Party. Twenty years later, possibly enriched by this experience, they have been responsive to pressures from their allies and the RSS made things easier for them. Among the BJP's partners, the DMK turned out to be one of the most embarrassed. Its chief, Karunanidhi, wrote to Vajpayee that if civil servants were allowed to take part in cultural or social associations affiliated to political parties, that would destroy the administrative machinery. Immediately, the BJP's spokesperson, J. P. Mathur replied that this issue would 'not be allowed to create a rift in the National Democratic Alliance'.[101] It seems that Vajpayee, then, persuaded the RSS leaders to provide a way out. On 6 March 2000, Rajendra Singh made a statement where he

[99] Ibid., 6 February 2000.
[100] Ibid., 20 February 2000.
[101] Cited in *The Hindu*, 12 February 2000. A majority of the Jammu and Kashmir MLAs, including those of the National Conference, ally of the BJP at the centre passed a resolution urging the central government to have the Gujarat order revoked. Ibid., 3 March 2000).

said that the RSS appreciated the Gujarat government's decision, but emphasized that 'the RSS had not sought the withdrawal of the circular prohibiting Government employees from participating in its activities, because RSS work has never been dependent on any government's attitude, positive or negative, towards it'.[102] The following day, the BJP high command asked Patel to rescind the order, which was done immediately. This episode reflects the RSS eagerness not to provoke the fall of the coalition government because of some radical policies likely to alienate the BJP's partners.

Gujarat is also a 'model state' from the RSS point of view because of its education policy. In all states where the BJP had an absolute majority in the 1990s, textbooks were 'rewritten'.[103] Gujarat is no exception. The Gujarat State Board of School Textbooks published a Standard IX Social Studies book in which Muslims, Christians, and Parsis were presented as 'foreigners' and which stated that 'in most of the states the Hindus are a minority and the Muslims, Christians and Sikhs are in a majority'—a good example of the exploitation of the Hindu feeling of vulnerability. In a Standard VIII Social Studies Book, one also finds a very derogatory description of the Christian priests: 'The accumulation of power and wealth in the priests resulted in a perversion of the religion. Some of the priests became pleasure-loving and badly behaved.'[104]

The policies of Gujarat have found some echo outside the state.[105] The 'Christian issue' was taken up by the VHP and

---

[102] Cited in ibid., 6 March 2000.

[103] A. A. Engineer mentions a textbook prescribed for B. A. in Maharashtra where one can read that 'wherever the Islamic hordes went, they not only conquered the countries, but killed millions of people and plundered their homes and places of worship and, above, all their art works... Islam teaches only atrocities' (*The Hindu*, 16 November 1999). For more details see the special issue of *Seminar*, no. 400, December 1992.

[104] Das, R., 'In Gujarat's Textbooks, Minorities are Foreigners', *Hindustan Times*, 25 July 1999.

[105] Uttar Pradesh tried to emulate the Gujarati pattern under the chief ministership of Ram Prakash Gupta. He said, for instance, that his government would not take any action against state government officials participating in the activities of the RSS. The UP government had also passed a controversial bill in the Vidhan Sabha, the UP Regulation of Public Religious Buildings and Places Bill, 2000, which empowered the state government to frame laws to regulate the use

the RSS, for instance, in such a way that one can see a division of labour at work, with the BJP maintaining a moderate line at the centre and the rest of the Sangh Parivar still involved in Hindu militant activism.

THE HINDU NATIONALIST DIVISION OF LABOUR

While anti-Christian militancy was primarily in evidence in Gujarat, the issue was taken up by the Sangh Parivar in many other places. In September 1999, the Punjab Christian Movement (PCM) alleged that there had been 28 cases of attacks on religious places and disruptions of religious functions of Christians in Punjab since 1997.[106] However the places which were affected the most were Madhya Pradesh, Orissa, and Gujarat. In Madhya Pradesh, four nuns were raped in September 1998 in the tribal district of Jhabua. In Orissa, one Australian missionary, Graham Staines, was burnt to death with his two sons in his car in January 1999. Nine months later in September, a Roman Catholic priest, a native from Tamil Nadu, was killed in a remote tribal village of Mayurbhanj district.[107] So far, the only Commission of Inquiry whose report has been made available concerns the Staines murder. This one man commission headed by Justice D. P. Wadhwa, a serving judge of the Supreme Court was appointed by the Vajpayee government on 29 January 1999. It presented its report on 21 June. The prime accused who masterminded the crime was identified as being Dara Singh who, in August 1999 had also allegedly burnt to death a Muslim shopkeeper, Sheikh Rehman, in another village of Mayurbhanj district, after having chopped off his hands. Justice Wadhwa wrote:

Dara Singh understood the psyche of the tribals. He played on their emotions and provoked their ire saying that Christian missionaries were destroying Hindu religion.... Staines was killed by these fanatics and with him his two

---

and construction of public buildings and places for religious purposes. The All India Muslim Forum immediately saw in the Bill a device to disallow construction of mosques and madrasas on the excuse of fighting Islamicist or Pakistani influences in UP. But the governor, Suraj Bhan—a former BJP MP—referred the Bill to President Narayanan for his assent.

[106] *The Hindu*, 21 September 1999.
[107] *Frontline*, 24 September 1999, p. 110.

children also perished.... There is no evidence that any authority or Organization was behind these gruesome killings.[108]

While some local commentators had pointed out that Dara Singh had links with the Sangh Parivar, the Wadhwa report implicitly gave the RSS-combine a clean chit.[109] Yet, when Dara Singh was arrested in late January 2000, a BJP MP, Dilip Singh Judeo, who was involved in the reconversion activities of the Vanavasi Kalyan Ashram in Jashpur (Madhya Pradesh),[110] offered him legal assistance. He was directed to withdraw this offer by K. Thakre but the RSS had already taken up the Christian issue. In the *Organiser*, the RSS mouthpiece, M. V. Kamath, one of the regular columnists, wrote that the Constitution allows proselytizing activities provided it does not affect public order, morality, and health:

> If conversions or attempts at conversion lead to public disorder, the Government has a duty to sternly deal with guilty Missionaries. If Government does not step in on liberal pretences, then violence can be predicted by insulted citizens. It is time that Christian Missionaries understand that India—and Hinduism—cannot be taken for granted. There is a limit to tolerance. The calculated assaults on Hindu territory have to be put down. Christian barbarism needs to be exposed for what it is: pure barbarism.[111]

Another contributor to the *Organiser*, Shyam Khosla, advocated the need for reviewing Article 25(1) of the Constitution guaranteeing 'the right freely to profess, practise and propagate religion' because 'the right to propagate might be misused by certain elements to indulge in large-scale conversions and then to demand another partition of the country have unfortunately been proved right'.[112] Similarly, the then general secretary of the RSS

[108] Cited in Raina, J. 'Wadhwa Absolves Sangh Parivar' *Hindustan Times*, 6 August, 1999.

[109] It is probably the reason why the relevant portions of the Wadhwa report are available on the VHP website (http://www.vhp.org/wadhwa.htm).

[110] See my article, 'Militant Hindus and the Conversion Issue (1855–1990): From Shuddhi to Dharm Parivartan. The Politization and the Diffusion of an "Invention of Tradition"' in Assayag, J. (ed.), *The Resources of History: Tradition and Nation in South Asia* (Pondicherry: Ecole Française d'Extrême Orient, 1999), pp 127–152).

[111] Kamath, M. V. 'Christianity and Missionary Work in India', *Organiser*, 7 November 1999, p. 18.

[112] Khosla, S., 'Need to Review Article 25(1)', *Organiser*, 4 April 1999, p. 7.

himself, H. V. Seshadri, gave an interview to the *Organiser* in which he put a stress on the legitimate dimension of the anti-Christian Hindu reaction:

The charge about attack on the so-called religious freedom of 'minorities' is like rubbing salt into the already wounded Hindu psyche. The entire Hindu people know for their sorrow that it is in fact their religious freedom which is being systematically subverted by the Christian Missionaries who are funded enormously by the Christian countries abroad.[113]

The Sangh Parivar leaders argue that the Hindu society is vulnerable and contrast this powerlessness with the strength of the missionaries who benefit from the financial support of outsiders and convert assiduously. Hindu nationalists even claimed that the missionaries were aiming at transforming India into a Christian nation.[114] They reproduce the same discourse as the one they used about the Muslims, but it is remarkable that it could be spelled out vis-à-vis the much smaller Christian community whose population declined from 2.6 per cent in 1971 to 2.44 per cent in 1981 and 2.32 per cent in 1991.

The anti-Christian campaign of the Sangh Parivar reached its acme during the Pope's visit in November 1999. One of its offshoots, the Sanskriti Raksha Manch (SRM), organized a *Jagran Yatra* between Goa and Delhi that was 'aimed at creating an awareness among the people about the church's atrocities against Hindu, particularly during inquisitions in Goa'. Demonstration were also planned for focusing 'attention on the use of fraudulent means in coverting tribals in various parts of the country'.[115]

Leaders of the SRM asked the Pope to 'express regrets for the atrocities on Hindus during the Portuguese rule in Goa'.[116] The VHP general secretary, Acharya Giriraj Kishore, made the same demand and declared that it also wanted the Pope to withdraw all foreign missionaries from India because they indulged in conversions through allurements and because 'extremist groups in the

[113] Seshadri, H. V., 'Another Christian Conspiracy Unfolds', *Organiser*, 19 September 1999, p. 5.

[114] Sadananda Kakade, the international joint general secretary of the VHP argued that the 'conversion target' of the Christian missionaries was 10 crores people (*The Hindu*, 4 November 1999).

[115] Khosla, S., 'An Acrimonious Visit: Anti-Hindu Forces Must Take the Blame', *Organiser*, 7 November 1999, p. 22.

[116] Ibid., p. 23.

North-East are being financially supported and encouraged by the Church'.[117] The VHP also asked for a law banning conversions.[118]

Thus while the BJP leaders more or less maintained their moderate line, the RSS and VHP leaders adopted by and large the same attitude vis-à-vis the Christians as the one they had developed vis-à-vis the Muslims. For this reason, the atrocities in Gujarat and Orissa cannot be regarded as purely local developments. There was probably no centralized master plan against the Christians, initially, but local activists certainly felt more secure after the VHP leaders endorsed their mischiefs. They even felt protected by the state machinery, first in states like Gujarat and then at an all-India level since the home minister, L. K. Advani, by and large, downplayed anti-Christian activities.

But how can we explain that the Christians were more victimized than the Muslims? Probably because they might have appeared as offering a soft target. Attacking the Muslims was more difficult after the BJP had taken over because the party was now largely responsible for the law and order situation. This accountability factor had no such inhibiting impact so far as the Christians were concerned since they were in such a small number that they could not create large-scale public disorder. The Sangh Parivar could show that it was true to its Hindu nationalism without tarnishing the image of the BJP or embarrassing it.

To sum up, the BJP has certainly embraced a more moderate approach of politics for several reasons pertaining to (1) the state of the public opinion—while the Hindus' psyche is 'wounded', they have recovered their self-esteem during the Ayodhya movement and they have shown that they felt more concerned by economic issues and public order than by ethno-religious mobilizations; (2) the compulsions of coalition politics, given the willingness of regional and other parties to cooperate with the BJP, provided it toned down its Hindu militancy; and (3) the attitude of the RSS, which approves of the moderation of the BJP so long as it enables the party to be in office for implementing the educational and security policies of the RSS's liking and for covering up anti-minority schemes like in Gujarat. In order words,

[117] Cited in *The Hindu*, 6 November, 1999.
[118] *The Hindu*, 4 November, 1999.

moderation at the centre is agreeable to the RSS so long as it permits extremists to have their ways somehow.

CONCLUSION

In what sense does the BJP occupy the centre of the Indian political system? Electorally, it has reached a plateau and cannot claim to be a full-fledged national party because of its persisting weaknesses in the south and in the east as well as among the lower castes. However, it does play a central role, as the pivotal force of the ruling coalition thanks to its mastery at making alliances. Ideologically, Vajpayee, who is in a stronger position than during its previous mandates, is probably willing to have the BJP returned to its first 'centrist' incarnation—that of the early 1980s, based on a moderate approach of politics. The political context—the advent of coalition politics—and the attitude of the RSS have contributed to this process. The new line is also well in tune with the expansion of the party beyond the Hindi belt and beyond the twice-borns, a two-fold evolution which implies some ideological dilution. One may, therefore, conclude that the BJP is on its way to becoming the dominant party of India in the form of a catch-all party with (non-communal) nationalist and (economically) liberal leanings.

This scenario can only unfold itself if the BJP meets important challenges. To be a centrist catch-all party it needs to accommodate people coming from all kinds of social background especially from the lower castes, and give them due respect and responsibilities. If the party makes such a decision and therefore further acknowledges the role of lower castes in the Indian polity its ideology will be inevitably diluted (what kind of Hindu Rashtra would emerge from a collection of castes?) and the upper caste leaders who are still at the helm may not resign themselves to this new power equation. In Uttar Pradesh, the eviction of Kalyan Singh party reflected their reluctance towards such an evolution. The election of a Scheduled Caste leader from Andhra Pradesh, Bangaru Laxman, as party president in August 2000 was a clear indication of the party's eagerness to woo the Dalits but it came also as a reconfirmation of its reluctance towards any mandalization process vis-à-vis the OBCs.

Secondly, for establishing itself as a pan-Indian party, the BJP needs to consolidate its positions in states where it is still weak.

In that perspective it must first gain more strength as the pivotal force of a large coalition. Now, the compulsions of coalition politics are not easy to meet, given the fact that the RSS leaders do not approve of it, except as a means for being in office. The RSS resigns itself to the BJP's moderation so long as it helps the movement to promote some of its priorities and does not hamper local extremist deeds. The anti-Christian activities and/ or discourse of several components of the Sangh Parivar suggests that there is a real division of labour at work. Now, the RSS may become more militant under the leadership of K. S. Sudarshan who took over from Rajendra Singh in March 2000—officially because Singh was ageing. Sudarshan, 69, is the first RSS *sarsanghchalak* who was born in south India. He is known for his strong attachment to the mainstays of Hindu nationalism such as the Swadeshi plank. In an interview he gave in February 2000, he said: 'Swadeshi is not being raised in the right manner. There is a conflict between the US lobby in the Government and swadeshi. That is the real struggle.'[119]

Thirdly the moderation of the BJP itself is certainly not irreversible. Policies of the Gujarat government show that its agenda can be more radical when it does not depend on coalition partners. The BJP may be experiencing a new phase of moderation as it did in the past. Not so long ago, between 1980 and 1988, when Vajpayee was president of the BJP it adopted a similar line of conduct. At that time, its slogans where 'Positive secularism' and 'Gandhian socialism'. The existence of inner tensions within the BJP was exemplified by the drafting of the 'Chennai Declaration'. Prepared by the party high command, this text was called that way because it was submitted first to the BJP's National Executive in December 1999 at Chennai. In 1998, at the Bangalore National Executive, Vajpayee had obtained from the BJP a guarantee that it should not interfere in the decisions of the government. The Chennai declaration went one step further since it was intended to show the world—and in particular the BJP's allies—that the party had given up the contentious issues and was making a transition to a more centrist party of governance. However, the key sentence—which suggested that the BJP had no agenda other than the common programme of the NDA—had to be diluted

[119] *India Today*, 21 February 2000, p. 23.

because 'hardliners'—such as Union Minister Sunderlal Patwa, objected that the party should not give up its identity.[120] Similarly, the statement that the BJP's ideology was 'flexible' also had to be rephrased: in the ultimate version the party's policies, not ideology, are supposed to be flexible.

[120] The key sentence, 'Each and every activist of the party must fully understand that the BJP has no agenda other than the common agenda of the NDA', was rephrased: 'The BJP expressed confidence that every BJP worker understands that our agenda for governance is the national agenda for good governance'—but the BJP's programme, so far as non-governance issues are concerned, remains its own.

Index

Gupta, Ram Prasad 338, 362n
Gupta, Uma Shankar 282
Gurumurthy, S. 307, 308n

Habib, Irfan 354n
Hansen, Thomas Blom 1, 10, 12,
121, 132n, 146n, 291, 309
Hari, R. 207n, 208, 221, 222n
Haryana Vikas Party 19
BJP's alliance with 2, 7–8, 14,
69, 227
Hasan, Mushirul 89n, 96n
Hasan, Zoya 74n
Hawala case 2
Hazare, Anna 155, 156
Heath, Oliver 316n, 327, 328, 329
Hedgewar, K. B. 24, 27, 213n, 254
Hegde, Ramakrishna 19, 172, 176,
177, 184, 193, 198n, 201
Himachal Vikar Congress (HVC)
319
Hindi belt, BJP in 18, 68, 328–9
caste and community of
members of parliament of
9th Lok Sabha 330
10th Lok Sabha 331
11th Lok Sabha 332
12th Lok Sabha 333
13th Lok Sabha 334
'Hindu consciousness' 206, 221, 306
Hindu–Christian acrimony, in
Kerala 206
Hindu consolidation, in Kerala
212–18
'Hindu culture' 24
'Hindu Dharma Raksha Samiti'
246
Hindu Jagaran Manch (HJM)
101n, 357–60
Hindu Mahasabha 122, 123, 127, 294
Hindu Maha Mandalam, Kerala
206, 208
Hindu Milan Mandir (HMM),
Gujarat 251–2

Hindu Munnani (Front), Kerala
209, 214, 215, 216, 218, 219,
226, 324
Hindu–Muslim(s), relations/
tensions 100, 214, 247
In Uttar Pradesh 89, 92
'Hindu nation' 76, 148, 202
Hindu nationalism 23, 30, 119,
243, 293, 317, 325, 345
in Gujarat 356–63
in Karnakata 189
in Kerala and, limits of 202–27
in Rajasthan 101, 102, 104,
107–8, 109, 120
and ergionalization of politics
8–11
and pluralist politics 225–7
Hindu nationalist(s) 222, 224, 227,
346
in Kerala 208, 214, 218, 220
dilemma 30–3
division of labour 363–7
ideology 23, 52, 69
movement 5, 6, 10, 11, 13, 22,
60, 102, 107, 111, 118, 217,
247, 291, 292, 303, 345
'Hindu Rashtra' 10, 23, 74, 245,
252
'Hindu Sangathan' 29
Hinduism 105, 230, 265
process of 'fundamentalizing' in
Rajasthan 119
Hindutva 1, 2, 6, 10, 82, 86, 98,
100, 129, 136, 202, 228, 244,
248, 257, 347
BJP's philosophy of 70n
BJP and politics of, in
Maharashtra 121–62
and castes 250–7
to consensual politics 72
and ethics of, and spirit of
capitalism 291–314
in Gujarat 243–66
ideology 20–2, 251